ENGAGED PURE LAND BUDDHISM
Challenges Facing Jōdo Shinshū in the
Contemporary World

ENGAGED PURE LAND BUDDHISM

CHALLENGES FACING JŌDO SHINSHŪ IN THE CONTEMPORARY WORLD

STUDIES IN HONOR OF PROFESSOR ALFRED BLOOM

Edited by

Kenneth K. Tanaka
and
Eisho Nasu

WisdomOcean Publications
Berkeley, California

Copyright © 1998 WisdomOcean Publications
All rights reserved

Printed in the United States of America

Library of Congress Cataloging-in-Publication Data

Engaged Pure Land Buddhism: challenges facing Jōdo Shinshū in the contemporary world / edited by Kenneth K. Tanaka and Eisho Nasu

ISBN 0-9658062-1-9

1. Pure Land Buddhism - Social aspects - Japan - United States - Doctrines - History. I. Tanaka, Kenneth K. II. Nasu, Eisho.

Library of Congress Catalogue Card Number: 98-60200

The Photo on cover and calligraphy in the frontispiece are courtesy of Rev. Senkei Kazuyoshi Sasaki

Cover design by Legacy Media, Inc.

To Professor Alfred Bloom,
our colleague and mentor

Hōzō
by
Dr. Alfred Bloom

Contents

Acknowledgment x
Editors' Introduction xi

PART ONE: SOCIAL ENGAGEMENT

Shin Buddhism in the West: The Question of Authenticity
    Taitetsu Unno 3

An Essay on Socially Engaged Buddhism
    Paul O. Ingram 27

Jōdo Shinshū's Mission to History: A Christian
Challenge to Shin Buddhist Social Ethics
    James Fredericks 48

Shin Buddhist Social Thought in Modern Japan
    Mark T. Unno 67

Concern for Others in Pure Land Soteriological and
Ethical Considerations: A Case of *Jōgyō daihi* in
Jōdo Shinshū Buddhism
    Kenneth K. Tanaka 88

PART TWO: EXPRESSIONS IN HISTORY

A Brief History of Pure Land Buddhism in Early Japan
    James C. Dobbins 113

Hōnen and the *Tale of the Heike*
    Maya M. Hara 166

Pure Land Belief and Popular Practice:
The *Odori Nembutsu* of Ippen Shōnin
    James H. Foard 189

Ordination Ceremony of the Honganji Priests in
Premodern Japanese Society
Eisho Nasu 201

Glorious Gathas: Americanization and Japanization in
Honganji Hymns
George J. Tanabe, Jr. 221

PART THREE: CONSTRUCTIVE ENGAGEMENT OF THE TEACHINGS AND PRACTICE

The Visions of Vaidehī: Transformative Symbolism in a
Visualization Practice
Richard K. Payne 241

Existentializing and Radicalizing Shinran's Vision by
Repositioning It at the Center of Mahayana Tradition
Gregory G. Gibbs 267

The Essence of Shinran's Teaching: Understanding to Praxis
Shigeki J. Sugiyama 285

A Bibliographical Summary of Studies on Myōkōnin:
Retrospect and Prospects
Zenshō Asaeda 316

Healing Laughter: A Shin Dharmology of Māra
Roger Corless 329

An Abridged Curriculum Vitae of
Dr. Alfred Bloom 343

Contributors 357

Acknowledgment

We are deeply grateful to those listed below for their generous financial assistance, without which this project would not have become a reality:

Rev. Gyodo Kono Memorial Scholarship Fund

North American Branch of the International Association of Shin Buddhist Studies

Buddha Dharma Kyokai, U.S.A.

Editors' Introduction

Shinran's characteristics of concern, commitment, and compassion are all qualities that must be realized in all of us in the search for truth and meaning if there is to be any resolution or advancement of our contemporary problems.[1]
—Alfred Bloom—

Shortly after arriving in Berkeley in 1986 to assume the position of Dean and Head Professor at the Institute of Buddhist Studies, Dr. Bloom was in a motor scooter accident and taken to a hospital. We rushed to the hospital, where we found Dr. Bloom lying alone in bed in an emergency recovery room, mumbling incoherently, a possible sign of delirium from the accident. Approaching his bed cautiously, we could hear to our surprise and relief, that he was actually chanting to himself! He was conscious and chanting the *Jūseige*, verses from the *Larger Pure Land Sutra* whose primary message is that of Amida Buddha's compassionate vow to liberate all beings. Still unaware of our presence, Dr. Bloom continue to chant quietly but at one point repeated one of the lines several times. That line was "i shū kai hō zō," which means, "Opening the storehouse of Dharma for all sentient beings." (As it turns out, Dr. Bloom's calligraphy shown in this volume is of two characters from this line: "hō zō.") Fortunately, the injuries proved relatively minor, and he was able to leave the hospital in a few days. But that one sutra line we heard at the hospital, "i shū kai hō zō," came to symbolize the spirit of inclusivity, openness, and engagement that defined Dr. Bloom's administrative, scholastic, and teaching style during his eight-year tenure at the Institute of Buddhist Studies.

It is this spirit of engagement that has informed the topic and title of this volume, *Engaged Pure Land Buddhism*. In the West, the term "engaged Buddhism" is attributed to Thich Nhat Hanh, a noted

INTRODUCTION

Vietnamese monk whose 1963 book was published under that title. The original French term "engagé," meaning politically outspoken or involved, was in common usage in French Indochina before World War II. In recent years, "engaged Buddhism" has gained wider usage among progressive groups such as the Buddhist Peace Fellowship, particularly in its B.A.S.E. (Buddhist Alliance for Social Engagement) program, and the International Network of Engaged Buddhists. The Naropa Institute in Colorado has instituted an M.A. degree program in Engaged Buddhism. And in recent years, more books have been published bearing "engaged Buddhism" in their titles.[2]

It is important, however, to acknowledge that "engaged Buddhism" does not denote a new or unique school of Buddhism but describes Buddhism in its intrinsic nature. Thich Nhat Hanh clarifies this point when he explains, "Engaged Buddhism is just Buddhism. If you practice Buddhism in your family, in society, it is engaged Buddhism."[3] "Engagement" is an integral, not a separate or an added, dimension of the Buddhist tradition. We are, therefore, using "engagement" to refer to a more heightened and active level of both lay and monastic involvement in a full range of activities: interpreting the tradition, reaching out to others, and working socially and environmentally to reduce suffering in the world. These "engaged" activities are natural outcome of any viable religious tradition that continues to adapt and grow in changing times and locations.

In part, this engagement involves the reconciling of two spheres: the world-transcending (Skt. *lokottara*; Jpn. *shusse*) and the worldly (*laukika; se*). This division parallels other dualities: the ultimate and the relative, the religious and the secular, the self and society, and the individual and others. We may add to these the well-known Buddhist distinction between nirvana and *saṃsāra* (the cycle of births and deaths).[4] Within this context, engagement generally involves the return from the former to the latter; this is represented by Shakyamuni Buddha who after realizing enlightenment for himself devoted forty-five years of his life to teaching others, and in the classical Bodhisattva ideal of realizing enlightenment for oneself (*svārtha; ji-ri*) in order to benefit others (*parārtha; ri-ta*). In Jōdo Shinshū parlance, this is referred to as "to realize *shinjin* and to guide others to *shinjin*" (*jishin kyōninshin*).

For this book, we chose to focus on "engaged Pure Land Buddhism" for two reasons. First and foremost, this topic has remained an enduring interest and, in our view, a passion of Dr. Bloom throughout his career. No doubt his passion was sustained by his high regard for Shinran (1173–1263), the founder of the Jōdo Shinshū (also known as Shinshū or Shin) school,[5] whose life exemplified a way to bridge the divide between the ultimate and the world. In Dr. Bloom's view, a genuine religious tradition should not only focus on meeting the spiritual needs of the individual but should spiritually and ethically uplift society as well. In fact, this sentiment was recently articulated by the eminent spiritual leader of the Hompa Hongwanji,[6] Rev. Ohtani Kōshin, Monshu, who declared, "Today, as the destruction of the global environment continues and the nature of our family life comes under critical review, we realize that a religion that stops at only solving one's own pain and anxiety can no longer be called authentic."[7] Alfred Bloom would clearly be in total agreement.

Our second reason for selecting this volume's topic stems from our wish to dispel the prevailing popular image of Pure Land Buddhism as the most other-worldly stream within Buddhism, a religion which has already been labeled "pessimistic" and "passive" by certain Western critics. The Sukhāvatī Pure Land conjures up images of a fantastical paradise accessible only after death. Within this soteriological scheme, Pure Land followers appear bent on forsaking this world in favor of the next. These perceptions are, to be sure, not wholly false when we examine the entire panorama of Pure Land Buddhist development in Asia. More importantly, there is no need to be apologetic for this "other-worldly" promises, as Pure Land tradition has offered comfort and hope to millions of Buddhists in dealing with the existential human fear of death and the uncertainty of an afterlife.

However, this limited set of images represents only a partial picture of the Pure Land tradition, which also contains an abundance of elements that can be characterized as this-worldly. The *Contemplation Sutra*, for example, speaks of a transformative realization not in the Pure Land after death but here in the present life: ". . . your mind becomes a buddha; your mind is a buddha; and the wisdom of the buddhas—true, universal, and ocean-like—arises from this mind."[8] This emphasis on the present life is expressed in Shinran's thought. Unlike his predecessors in the Pure Land lineage, he argued that the state of non-retrogression (*avaivartika; futaiten*) took place not in the Pure Land but in the present life. Through a spiritual transformation known as *shinjin* (faith; true entrusting; true and real mind) in this very life, one gains assurance of not backsliding to lower spiritual levels and also of realizing Buddhahood immediately after death.

Despite Shinran's this-worldly orientation, the conservatism of later Jōdo Shinshū institutions particularly during the Tokugawa period (1600–1867) led to a retrenchment in their engagement with the world. This rather passive posture of the institutions was supported by the prevailing ideology of "the King's law, Buddha's law" (*ōbō buppō*) and "the two truths of the ultimate and the mundane" (*shinzoku nitai*) which advocated a strict separation between the political and secular arenas. In so doing, Pure Land institutions generally turned inward and rarely challenged the political establishment, a far cry from the open criticism once expressed by Shinran, who protested in his major writing *Kyōgyōshinshō*, "The emperor and his ministers, acting against the dharma and violating human rectitude, became enraged and embittered."[9]

To be fair, at that time virtually all Buddhist institutions in East Asia were under strict political control, a situation that cannot be fully understood or appreciated by those of us in modern democratic states who take religious freedom as our constitutional right. Furthermore, we witness this freedom being exercised within a growing religious diversity. Hence, within this contemporary context, we can grasp the opportunity to revive Shinran's original inspiration, moving toward a greater engagement with society and secular concerns. Borrowing

INTRODUCTION

an image from John Hick, the Pure Land Buddhists have been walking down a long valley, separated and hidden from others who have walked down their respective valleys; today, due to global communication and immigration patterns, these religious "tribes" have come onto the same plain in full sight of each other.[10] We now share the same space and are compelled to live together within a religiously pluralistic environment. Within this religious climate, Pure Land Buddhists will be encouraged, and even pressured, to engage more actively with other Buddhists as well as members of other faiths in order to address social issues. It is these factors that make up the backdrop for the fifteen essays collected in this volume.

The essays in Part One, "Social Engagement," explore Jōdo Shinshū's engagement of social and ethical issues from institutional and doctrinal perspectives. In the opening essay, Taitetsu Unno describes some of the historical and doctrinal reasons for the limited societal involvement exhibited by Shin organizations in the United States, and proposes what he calls the "'higher path' to authenticity" as an approach by which Shin Buddhism can evolve into a fully engaged religious institution in the West. Paul Ingram, an active participant in Buddhist Christian dialogues, calls into question many of the standard Christian criticisms of Buddhist ethical weakness, while presenting numerous examples of Buddhist social and ethical engagement based on its interrelated worldview and Bodhisattva ideal. James Fredericks suggests, from a Christian theologian's perspective, aspects of Jōdo Shinshū teachings that can be constructively developed in working toward a more dynamic social engagement. Mark Unno's essay introduces us to a number of socially active individuals in modern Japan, most notably Suekawa Hiroshi, who were all influenced by Shin Buddhist thought. Concluding this section is Kenneth Tanaka's attempt to retrieve and amplify a classical Jōdo Shinshū doctrine as a rallying point for greater involvement with others.

Professor Bloom regards his own academic approach as "historical" and has often acknowledged the influence of his teacher, Dr.

INTRODUCTION

Kenkō Futaba, a noted Shinshū historian. History has provided Dr. Bloom with ample evidence to convince him that, despite its stereotypical other-worldly image, Pure Land Buddhism has interacted actively and creatively with society from its earliest phase in Japanese Buddhist development. Among the five essays in Part Two, "Expressions in History," James Dobbins' article reveals an active presence of Pure Land practices within older schools of Buddhism before Hōnen and Shinran's time, thus providing a valuable sketch of a phase of Japanese Pure Land Buddhism has been less well-known in the West. Maya Hara reveals the degree of influence Pure Land thought and practices had on one of the greatest Japanese classics, *The Tale of the Heike* (*Heike monogatari*) and the culture that it reflected. James Foard discusses the intriguing role played by Ippen, a medieval itinerant Pure Land monk, who not only popularized the teaching through folk dancing but also utilized folk expressions as a resource in reconciling doctrinal dilemmas that affected the Pure Land elite. Eisho Nasu's article introduces us to an ordination practice that was influenced by the prevailing hierarchical social conditions, even while struggling to remain faithful to Shinran's egalitarian core values. In George Tanabe's article, we examine a collection of *gāthas* (hymns) composed by a Caucasian Buddhist teacher, and their subsequent influence within the changing needs of a Hawaiian Pure Land institution from the 1920s to the present day.

As previously defined, "engagement" also refers to the enterprise of constructively reinterpreting Jōdo Shinshū in accord with the current cultural and linguistic environment. Dr. Bloom has, again, worked tirelessly in this area, making the teachings accessible to the general English-speaking public, while at the same time maintaining utmost respect for the careful balance between tradition (*dentō*) and personal realization (*koshō*). This commitment is reflected in Part Three, "Constructive Engagement of the Teachings and Practice." Richard Payne's psychological interpretation of the Pure Land visualization practice reveals a process of spiritual transformation that appeals to a growing segment of contemporary audience who are

INTRODUCTION

attracted to Buddhism on account of its affinity to Jungian and other psychotherapeutic approaches. Gregory Gibbs' essay challenges the traditional characterization of *shinjin* and nembutsu, maintaining that Shinran's original understanding of those terms automatically fosters support for human rights and social involvement. Shigeki Sugiyama's article proposes new ways of conceiving and expressing Shinran's primary teachings from *shinjin* to good-and-evil and to *jinen-hōni* that are consistent with his original meaning as found in the writings. Senshō Asaeda offers a glimpse into modern Japanese studies on Myōkōnins, spiritually realized Jōdo Shinshū Buddhists whose biographies and testimonies are strong proof of the effectiveness of the tradition in engaging the spiritual needs of ordinary people. The book ends with Roger Corless' effort to create a richer interpretive framework; in proposing what he calls "Shin Dharmology," Corless integrates the insights of academic studies taught in universities with the doctrine of Shin teachings preached in temples.

It is our hope that the essays collected for this volume will build on a lifelong contribution made by Dr. Bloom to realize a Pure Land tradition that is true to its original inspiration, one of spiritual and social engagement.

NOTES

1. Alfred Bloom, "Shinran and Modern Culture: A Philosophy for Existence," in *Shinran wo meguru mō hitotsu no bunkaron*, Futaba Kenkō, ed. (Kyoto: Nagata Bunshodo, 1997), 69.

2. See Christopher S. Queen and Sallie B. King, eds. *Engaged Buddhism: Buddhist Liberation Movements in Asia* (Albany. N.Y., New York: State Univ. of New York Press, 1996), 34. Other titles include, Sulak Sivaraksa, *Socially Engaged Buddhism* (Bangkok: Thai Inter-Religious Commission for Development, 1988) and Fred Eppsteiner ed. *The Path of Compassion: Writings on Socially Engaged Buddhism* (Berkeley: Parallax Press, 1988). An excellent resource on the subject is Kenneth K. Kraft, *Inner Piece, World Peace: Essays on Buddhism*

INTRODUCTION

and Nonviolence (Albany, N.Y.: State Univ. of New York Press, 1992).

3. Kraft, *Inner Peace, World Peace*, 18.

4. Contemporary Buddhist teachers have explained this relationship with an effective image of the intersecting vertical (the ultimate) and the horizontal (the worldly) lines, and suggesting that each dwell at the point of that intersection.

5. Today, this is the largest school within the Pure Land branch in Japan.

6. One of the ten branches of Jōdo Shinshū school to which most of the Shin temples in North America belong.

7. *Wheel of Dharma.* (The monthly publication of the Buddhist Churches of America) vol. 15, no. 1 (New Year issue, 1998), 1 (Japanese section).

8. Ryukoku University Translation Center, trans. *The Sūtra of Contemplation on the Buddha of Immeasurable Life* (Kyoto: Ryukoku University, 1984), 51.

9. Dennis Hirota et al, trans. *The Collected Works of Shinran* (Kyoto: Jōdo Shinshū Hongwanji-ha, 1997), 289.

10. John Hick, *God Has Many Names* (Philadelphia: The Westminister Press, 1980), 41.

PART ONE
Social Engagement

Shin Buddhism in the West: The Question of Authenticity

Taitetsu UNNO

I

As the Shin Buddhist organizations in America—the Honpa Hongwanji Mission of Hawaii (HHM) and the Buddhist Churches of America (BCA)[1]—mark a century of existence in this country, reflections on their past and present become critical for their future. Among those who have seriously considered this matter, one of the leading voices has been Alfred Bloom. As a long-standing lay member of Shin Buddhism, scholar of religious studies, and finally an ordained Shin minister, Bloom brings considerable knowledge and experience to the question of the future of Shin Buddhism in the West. While space does not permit a complete summation of his views, we will outline some of his basic ideas and submit them for consideration by all concerned people.

In concluding his keynote speech at the Seventh Biennial Conference of the International Association of Shin Buddhist Studies, held at the Buddhist Study Center, Honolulu, in 1995, Bloom expressed his hopes for the future:

> The challenge for Shin Buddhist Studies, it seems to me, is clear. We are entering a world stage. Shin Buddhism has taken root in many contexts and is no longer to be understood as simply a Japanese religion. It is a world religion with the potentiality to bring insight and wisdom to a suffering humanity. Shin Buddhist Studies, hence, has the obligation to open its storehouse of knowledge and wisdom for all people,

transcending national and cultural boundaries and responding
to the yearnings of humanity for meaning and fulfillment.[2]

His hopes, however, are tempered by a critique—the need for a radical change in direction—contained in an earlier lecture given in the Harvard Buddhist Studies Forum.[3] Bloom correctly identifies the historical changes that now require Shin Buddhism to undergo transformation from an ethnic religion to an open, universal faith:

> Shin Buddhism became an ethnic tradition, despite the fact that as a Buddhist tradition its teaching has a universal character. While the ethnic character was important in providing a rallying point for the community under the stress of discrimination, segregation, and distrust from the dominant society, it has now become a problem (of) how to transcend its ethnic character to become a universal religious faith. There is search for a way to appeal to all people, while at the same time, not abandoning the ethnic and cultural heritage of their parents, particularly of the first generation immigrants who sacrificed so much to establish the teaching in America.[4]

Bloom goes a step further in a talk he gave at a research meeting of Shin Buddhist ministers in Hawaii in 1997. After a century of existence, Shin Buddhist institutions remain basically the same because their leadership, both ministers and lay, have not undertaken any effort for change. One of the reasons for this is that Shin Buddhism has not been able to retain thinking lay people and progressive ministers who might spearhead the transformation. In his words:

> Shin Buddhism is a universal faith, but in America, for historical and social reasons, it has been obstructed by an ethnic character and emphasis that defeats Buddhism. While the ethnic connection was important in the past, the mobility and integration of Japanese-Americans in American society has reduced the significance of this ethnic background. Those Japanese-Americans who have become successful in American

society have for the most part not used their skills and understanding of society for the benefit of the temple. The temples function largely today as they have for 50 or 100 years ago.[5]

In the same paper Bloom outlines two forms of crises facing both BCA and HHM: institutional and doctrinal. He is careful to locate the institutional crisis within the larger framework of the contemporary religious scene—the decline of traditional Christian churches, including loss of membership, income, and clergy and the rise of evangelical and fundamentalist sects. However, the problem facing the Buddhist Church is severe, because of its small membership, the lack of a financial base, shortage of ministers, and the obvious fact that it is an alien tradition in the Christian West. The critical issue, however, is that the crisis is not being directly confronted.

Underlying the institutional problematic which is intertwined with the doctrinal is a distinction that Bloom points out between a member who is *monto* and who is *shinja*, a distinction originally made by Kakue Miyaji. The latter, *shinja*, is a Shin Buddhist because of a personal appreciation of the teaching, involving a faith commitment; and the former, *monto*, is a member in name only by virtue of family connections with the temple which may have begun many generations ago. Since membership in HHM and BCA has been based on the *monto*-system, which once may have been viable in Japan, it contributes to the decline of membership, especially with the dispersal of the family unit in American society and the high percentage of outmarriages among Japanese Americans which is said to be approximately sixty percent.

Compounding the problems arising from the *monto*-system is that the lay leaders of HHM and BCA are not necessarily chosen because of their Buddhist faith; rather, they are selected because of their prominence and influence in the Japanese American community.[6]

This is not uncommon in American religion which has intimate connections with ethnicity. "Religion often supports ethnicity by providing the institutional setting for the maintenance of tradition, but at the same time ethnic identity can also supersede religion as the source of individual and group identity, particularly in a highly secularized culture."[7] The insufficient efforts to transmit the teaching, the lack of religious education, especially for the laity, and the paucity of *shinja*-members are inseparable from the doctrinal crises facing Shin Buddhism in America.

Even though a temple run under the old *monto*-system is impractical in American society where individuality is cherished, the Shin ministers from Japan brought up in this system have felt that their primary responsibility is not transmitting the nembutsu teaching but caring for the *monto*, maintaining harmony within the temple, supporting the family unit through funerary and memorial rites, and focusing on various activities—annual services, Bon festivals, and other communal events. Unfortunately, it seems that even American-born ministerial aspirants sent to Japan to complete their formal training are influenced by the old system, making it difficult to transform the temple from a social center to a truly religious institution. The onus of the *monto*-system continues to hinder both ministers and lay members, even if they are so inclined, to engage in any meaningful educational and religious activity.

More critical than the institutional crisis is the doctrinal. Bloom identifies five basic problems. First, the recourse to traditions other than Shin to explain its basic teaching, the most prominent being Zen, especially that of D.T. Suzuki, and psychology or psychotherapy, particularly that of C.G. Jung. When they replace traditional Shin teachings, Bloom claims that they tend "to render Shin a more emotional or sentimental expression of Buddhism focused only on our personal evils and limitations and the interior life. There is a bent toward blaming the victim."[8]

Second, the neglect of Shinran's critical perspective on society and institutional religion. This neglected aspect of Shinran's thought was the basis for the *ikkō-ikki* uprisings in the Tokugawa period, when peasants, traders, and merchants, often under temple leadership, rebelled against oppressive regimes. This neglect comes partially from the overemphasis on the personal dimension of Shin faith at the expense of its historical contributions in medieval Japan, as well as its role in the modernization of Japan. Galen Amstutz's recent work, *Interpreting Amida*, gives a detailed critique of this neglected aspect of Shin Buddhism.[9]

Third, the anti-intellectual trend, compounded by the same tendency in the wider American society, which hinders inquiry and devalues the intellectual framework. According to Bloom, "It is a rule of thumb from my own experience in both Christianity and Buddhism that efforts to disarm followers of their rational ability by devaluing the intellect is a sign of authoritarian religion. A follower is deprived of the ability to question." [10]

Fourth, the lack of a core of intellectual members to lead in the discussion of doctrinal issues confronted by Shin Buddhism in the West. The Japanese American community has produced a high percentage of professional people, yet very few are found within Shin organizations. As Bloom states, "Everyone need not be a scholar, but the sangha must develop its intellectual resources in order to participate in the religious dialogue in society."[11]

Fifth, the otherworldly and inner-directed orientation of Shin faith obstructs the development of social ethic. Bloom cites Hee-Sung Keel's *Understanding Shinran: A Dialogical Approach,* a work that is sympathetic yet critical of this weakness in Shin Buddhism.

Bloom concludes his remarks by suggesting the major task that awaits Shin Buddhists as follows:

> Shinran's thought is of high spiritual calibre and can offer an understanding of life and reality that can be meaningful to modern people. Our problem is not the teaching but, in the commercial context, our delivery system. It requires us to upgrade the education of our members and those who are going to be ministers by providing them with information and insight concerning current trends in contemporary thought and how Shin Buddhism may relate to them. The vitality of

our sangha in the future depends on establishing mutual discourse, dialogue with the surrounding culture, local and worldwide.[12]

The criticisms directed to the current state of HHM and BCA are valid, and I generally agree with Bloom, but the source of the problems may have deeper roots, that is, in the Shin doctrinal system, known as *Shinshū-gaku*, especially the dominant tendency in the Nishi Hongwanji.

During the Tokugawa period (1600-1868), the government adopted Confucianism as a major force in society, virtually displacing Buddhism as a social force. Since Buddhism could pose a potential threat to Tokugawa rule, they utilized all kinds of strategies, such as temple registration (the basis of the *monto*-system), and encouraged sectarian scholarships by awarding prizes and favors to weaken institutional Buddhism. Thus was born Shinshū-gaku, a scholastic interpretation of Shinran's teaching, turning inward and deflecting any criticism of the government. In its place was secured Confucian ideology which was ideally suited for a hierarchical feudalistic order. Among the several branches of Shinshū-gaku within the Nishi Hongwanji, one of the more conservative branches became dominant, and Shin doctrine became rigidly ideological. As a consequence, Shin has become irrelevant to the needs of contemporary people in Japan and even more so to the Japanese Americans.

Since the orthodox Shin teaching has stressed the working of absolute Other-power exclusively, any exploration of the individual to attain such an awareness has been rejected as a self-power deviation. The label of heterodoxy (*ianjin*) has been used to cut off any meaningful discussion of the personal quest. Hee-Sung Keel goes a step further and claims that Shinran's interpretation of faith itself is "too abstract to be a concrete psychological experience for ordinary men and women and for it to be meaningful in their lives."[13] Since this is the case—absolutism on the one hand, and abstraction on the other—it is only natural that some Shin ministers utilize resources easily available to them to explain the teaching, whether it be Zen or psychology or any other humanistic approach. This recourse to alternative works is understandable at this stage of history, since very few works in English relate Shin teachings to everyday life.

Bloom also notes the *dōbō-dōgyō* (fellow seeker, fellow practicer) ideal with its social and political implications, as well as Shinran's critical perspective on society. This is one area that awaits development, especially in relation to our world today with all its complexities. The mainstream Shinshū-gaku, however, does not show interest, let alone attempt to develop this aspect of Shinran's thought. While Bloom mentions some contemporary movements within Hongwanji that engage in social criticisms centered on the Yasukuni Shrine, *burakumin* discrimination, no-war constitution, and so on, they are marginal movements limited only to a small segment of Shin faithfuls. The fatal shortcoming of this lack of critical spirit was demonstrated clearly in the wartime complicity of the Hongwanji during the Pacific War.[14] Since no fundamental change seems to be occurring in mainstream academic Shinshū-gaku, the students who graduate from Shin seminaries and universities are unprepared to deal seriously with social and ethical issues.

The stress on absolute Other-power, the exclusive emphasis on faith, the discouragement of any questioning, the appeal to human feelings and so on all contribute to the anti-intellectualism contained in traditional Shin discourse. Shin Buddhism today has become an authoritarian religion, rejecting all forms of independent thinking and questioning. This is not to deny that some individual teachers within the Hongwanji have criticized this very method and have encouraged a more religious and existential engagement with the teaching.

In sum, the criticisms that Bloom makes about Shin Buddhism in the U.S. are found as a basic pattern within traditional Shinshū-gaku, and only a radical change coming from its innermost depth, based on Shinran's thought, can bring about any real positive change. That neither HHM or BCA is even considering such a possibility is at the core of the doctrinal crisis.

II

The problems that face the BCA were objectively described by an outsider, the journalist Jorge Aquino, in a lengthy article entitled "Dharma Bummed: The Buddhist Churches of America's Struggle to Keep the Faith," carried in the January 1996 issue of *SF Weekly*, an alternative newspaper published in San Francisco.[15] Its main point not only corroborates Bloom's critique of the ethnic Buddhist Church but describes how the church is regressing rather than progressing. The article states that "Conservative ministers have recently gained the upper hand in BCA politics, responding to the crisis with a sweeping reorganization—slashing departments and transferring personnel in a bid to make the organization more sectarian. They have elected a bishop with strong ties to the BCA's mother temple in Kyoto, Japan, which has reciprocated with increased pledges of financial support."[16]

The author notes the gradual loss of membership, due to the assimilation of the third-generation Japanese Americans, dispersal of members to suburbia, and other factors. But the primary cause goes much deeper into some of the doctrinal issues that have been discussed in the previous section:

> Perhaps the most visceral reason for the exodus is the spiritual lassitude that has seized the limbs of the church—a failure of the ministry to invigorate the basic religious ideas of Jodo Shinshu by connecting them directly and personally to the passions and pains of the ordinary temple-goer.[17]

This lack of focus on relating the teaching of Jōdo Shinshū to everyday life is compounded by the turn towards Japan, evident in several recent phenomena: the BCA ministerial leadership whose primary language seems to have reverted to Japanese, the adherence to traditional rituals without clarifying their spiritual basis, the strengthening of ties with the mother temple in Kyoto to garner greater financial support. Aquino puts the problem squarely, when he writes, "If the aim is to recover the lost *Sansei* generation with its postmodern sensibility, its cultural perks, and its aspirations for a more authentic spiritual experience the sectarian turn toward Japan seems counterintuitive."[18] Since the ties with Japan are historically determined with deep ethnic roots, they should not be lightly regarded. But it is important to fashion this relationship properly, so that it becomes a strength, rather than a weakness, for the future of Shin Buddhism. Before simply castigating the Buddhist Church as ethnic, it may be helpful to review the history of American religions.

When we study the evolution of religion in America, the first obvious fact is that it reflects the immigrant nature of our society.[19] The intimate connection between ethnicity and religion is obvious everywhere you look. In our area of Western Massachusetts, for example, there are various kinds of ethnic churches: Greek Orthodox Church, Lithuanian Catholic Church, German Lutheran Church, Hispanic Catholic Church, African Methodist Episcopal Church, Amherst Korean Church, Russian Baptist Church, and so on. All this attests to the famous statement ascribed to Martin Luther King, Jr.: "The most segregated hour in America is 11 A.M. on Sunday mornings."

Even the churches which we consider mainline today originated as ethnic churches. A local newspaper, *Daily Hampshire Gazette,*[20] reported the merger of four local Lutheran Churches, during which one of the pastors stated, "A great deal of Lutheran history is ethnic, the history of immigrant communities." He explained that the merger was occurring among churches that belonged to the Lutheran Church of America, mainly composed of German Americans, the American Lutheran Church, made up predominantly of immigrants from Scandinavia, the Association of Evangelical Lutheran Churches which had a mixed ethnic representation, and its parent body the Missouri Synod.

Likewise, the *Springfield Union News*[21] reported the extensive restoration for the centennial in the year 2004 of the Immaculate Conception Church, founded in 1904 by Polish immigrants. Ninety-five percent of the parishioners are still of Polish descent. Polish masses are held during the week at 6:30 a.m. and twice on Sunday. The pastor, the Rev. Adrian Benoit, stated that "The Polish language is still used very, very much in our parish." The inscriptions on the stained-glass windows and the walls are all in Polish. Even the Polish national symbol, the eagle, is enshrined.

According to another report, the city of Springfield, Massachusetts, has at least ten distinct ethnic groups which use their respective languages even after almost a century of existence. Thus, the Immaculate Conception Church in Indian Orchard uses Polish, Our Lady of Fatima in Ludlow uses Portuguese, St. Rose DeLima in Chicopee uses French, and so on. The same news article mentions that in the city of Los Angeles, Sunday masses are celebrated in 42 different languages. The *Springfield Union News* [22] also reports the merger of two ethnic congregations, one Italian and one French; their churches have existed for almost 70 years, separated by only a few buildings. Due to the shortage of priests, however, the congregations have decided to combine into one church.

In brief, the experience in the new world was "traumatic to at least some degree for virtually all immigrants—an uprooting from one's hometown, kinfolk, the familiar round of existence. It engendered loneliness, a sense of loss, fear of the new and unknown."[23] Thus, people naturally turned to religion for comfort and guidance. The article also cites the famous study by H. Richard Niebuhr, *The Social Sources of Denominations*, that shows the origin of religious pluralism among European immigrants as rooted in European nationalism.

In this religious landscape the ethnic Buddhist temples—Japanese, Chinese, Korean, Vietnamese, Cambodian, and others—are simply following precedent. In the case of BCA and HHM with their history of a hundred years, however, unlike the European immigrant churches and the more recent Asian Buddhist ethnic groups, isolation from the mainstream was compounded by the racism directed against Asians since the late 19th century. The legal and social discrimination—said to number approximately 600 local, state, and

Federal laws against Asians—culminated in the mass evacuation of 120,000 Japanese Americans, two-thirds of whom were American citizens by birth, during World War II. Incarcerated behind barbed wire fences in ten concentration camps and countless Department of Justice detention centers in the U.S., they were virtual prisoners-of-war. Buddhist ministers and other community leaders were arrested by the FBI and jailed without due process of law, temples were closed and often looted, family units broken up, and membership dispersed. It was during this time in the camps that the original name, Buddhist Mission of North America, was changed to the Buddhist Churches of America. In fact, to be Buddhist was regarded as unpatriotic, and many young people became Christians because the adoption of Christianity was the hallmark of becoming more American.[24]

The ethnic history of American religion escapes the notice of outside observers, such as Takamaro Shigaraki, professor of Shin Buddhism and later president of Ryukoku University, who wrote an otherwise perceptive analysis of the current state of HHM and BCA.[25] Shigaraki visited and spoke at many temples during his one-year sabbatical in the United States. Noting the exclusive Japanese American membership in Shin temples, especially on the West Coast, he made a number of valid criticisms, but he failed to appreciate the ethnic character of American religions. But this ignorance is also reflected in the exclusion of Shin Buddhism in works on American Buddhism,[26] including the negative comments about ethnic Buddhism not contributing anything to the development of "American Buddhism." This, of course, depends solely on the definition of what constitutes American Buddhism, but the attitude reflects what is called the visible-invisible syndrome in minority ethnic studies. That is, Asian Buddhists are most "visible" of any Buddhist groups, but they really don't count, they are "invisible."[27]

Having situated the Buddhist Church within the ethnic landscape of American religions, however, does not mean that the ethnic Buddhist Church should remain as such, if it is to be historically meaningful. After all, the universal implication of the Buddha Dharma is evident in the successful transplantation that it has accomplished in diverse cultural spheres outside the land of its origin over a period of 2,500 years. How did Buddhism transcend the linguistic, cultural, and ethnic boundaries and spread throughout the Asian continent? It did so by affirming its deep spiritual roots but at the same time acculturating itself to indigenous cultures. The Buddha Dharma did not remain static; it confronted new challenges and struggled to respond appropriately. Shin Buddhism in America must also be grounded in its deep spirituality and cherish its proud tradition, but at the same time it must look beyond itself and interact with the wider society. This is imperative if Shin Buddhism is not only to survive but to make a contribution to enriching American religious life.

The Buddhist Churches located in areas of large Japanese American population, such as Southern California, may choose to remain ethnically oriented for the time being, but eventually they, too, will have to open their doors to seekers of all ethnic backgrounds. The Buddhist Church without such a population is compelled now to open its doors to all people, or else face extinction in the very near future. This is being taken up as a serious agenda by the New York Buddhist Church, founded in 1937 by the Rev. Hozen Seki and located in a prime area in Manhattan. Beginning in early 1998, members have begun a series of symposia to discuss the future of the Buddhist Church, centered around two basic poles. First, the ethnic Japanese roots will be cherished and maintained, but at the same time the Sangha will welcome into its fold anyone interested, regardless of race, color, class or ethnicity. In order to proceed with this forward movement the Sangha faces a challenge that is not only institutional but also doctrinal, a fact that will question some basic assumptions in Shinshū-gaku.

Before discussing the doctrinal challenges, let us address the issue of maintaining authenticity of Shin Buddhism in a new land. They can choose to move in one of two directions: transmit the traditional practices, teachings, and rituals from Japan as they are to America, or establish authentic Shin Buddhism rooted in American soil, responding to spiritual, ethical and social needs of the people. To paint a clearer picture of what is involved in this question of authenticity, we will reflect on the evolution of Japanese gardens in the American landscape.

III

Even though generally unnoticed, almost every botanical garden or arboretum in the U.S. must have a Japanese garden, and the wealthy who can afford it have their own private Japanese gardens. The proliferation of these gardens has lead David Slawson, a well-known landscape designer and author of *Secret Teaching in the Art of Japanese Gardens*, to question their authenticity.[28] In trying to answer this question, he proposes to consider two kinds of authenticity; what he calls the the lower path of authenticity and the higher path of authenticity. We will take a brief excursion into the question of authenticity in Japanese gardens, since it may reveal interesting insights into what might constitute an authentic Shin Buddhism in the West.

According to David Slawson, the first "lower path" to authenticity

> follows a literal, precedent-driven interpretation of the tradition . . . . Here, creativity is rigidly constrained by external norms which favor the status quo. The primary recourse is to precedent (for the designer, existing types of stereotypes) rather than to universal principles and the intrinsic nature of the situation.[29]

As an example of this lower path, Slawson cites the City of Miami's *San-An-Ai* Garden. Created in the 1960s by a wealthy Japanese businessman, he donated all the material necessary for a Japanese garden; he sent 500 orchid trees, a 300-year-old lantern, an eight-ton, eight-foot high granite statue of Hotei, the smiling god of posterity. He also shipped a 15-foot stone pagoda, six more stone lanterns, three bridges, a teahouse, and an arbor. He also sent over an landscape architect, six carpenters, and three gardeners. This garden is "authentic" in one sense, reproducing the past, but it might be described as a Disneyland approach to Japanese gardens.

In contrast is the second, "higher path" to authenticity which follows the basic ideals of Japanese garden design that responds to the reality of the American landscape. According to Slawson, it

> follows a metaphorical, principle- and situation-driven interpretation of the tradition. Here, the authority comes from within—from the desires and culture of those who will use the garden, from the site and surroundings, and from locally available materials . . . . When the designer is attuned to the situation, intuition may, and often does, lead to a breaking with precedent. Such attainment is enhanced by a deepening knowledge of the tradition.[30]

Authenticity in this second sense is born from the sensitivity to the needs of the local people, new site, and available material. This may break with some time-honored traditions, but it cannot emerge without a deep knowledge and appreciation of the basics of Japanese garden design. The artist who "firmly roots himself in the traditions . . . is not afraid to take a new step, but the reason he is stepping out of the tradition is because he knows it so well. His inspiration to step out comes from that tradition." Slawson thus proposes to proceed by following what he calls the Accord Triangle, that is, creating a Japanese garden based on three components: 1) response to client's needs and hopes, 2) response to topography, prevailing climate, solar orientation, etc., and 3) response to locally available material, rocks, plants, soil, etc. The focus is on the American context in which the Japanese garden will be seen not as an exotic import but as a natural outgrowth of the landscape.

Slawson shows how gardens evolved in Japan by following the higher path of authenticity. It meant breaking with the past and creating new garden models. Just to cite two examples, the famous dry landscape garden of Daisen-in in Daitokuji monastery was a revolutionary design; and the tea gardens which recreated the deep nature ambiance of a rustic cottage were unprecedented. Both broke with tradition to follow the calling of the higher path. One must be willing to shatter, or at least modify, existing precedents:

> It would appear that the literal mind has difficulty grasping the situational nature of design discourse and is not open to the metaphorical leap of creativity that such understanding engenders. The tendency then is to gravitate toward time-worn cliché, and to perceive rigidity and longevity as guarantees of faithfulness to the tradition, when in fact they may be signs that the art form is in a period of decline and stagnation.[31]

The general characteristics of these two kinds of authenticity may be applicable to the transmission of Shin Buddhism from Japan to the West. Do we want to transmit the tradition of Jōdo Shinshū, developed over a period of 700 years in Japan, just as it is? This means importing the sectarian doctrine, Shinshū-gaku, the mastery of arcane subjects verging on scholasticism; Hongwanji rules and regulations woven from Japanese precedents; material accouterments—the multicolored robes, the gilded sanctuary (*naijin*), ritual implements; and the elaborate ritual chanting, even if this is sometimes powerful and moving. This would be following the lower path of authenticity, some of which might be retained if placed in proper context. But such a direct importation of Shin Buddhism cannot grow, because it is not born from the American soil and disregards the contextual realities.

The "higher path," while rooted in the great Shin tradition, responds creatively to the American landscape, answers to the needs of all people, and relies on the resources in our culture—material, social, and intellectual—for its self-articulation. This inevitably involves a maturing process, beyond any systematic planning, but should include the following: a new vocabulary in English to express the time-honored teachings of nembutsu; systematizing Shin doctrine within the larger framework of Mahayana Buddhism; an imaginative recreation of rituals, including chanting in English and securing a place for quiet sitting; and developing the ethical and social implications of Shin teachings. The formal structure will be a natural outgrowth of these changes: training and ordination of clergy in this country without going to Japan, ritual implements and vestments befitting our cultural tastes, an egalitarian ministerial body manifesting the nembutsu.

An authentic Shin Buddhism, born on the American soil, will inherit the basic principles of Mahayana Buddhism and the Japanese tradition, but at the same time it will respond to the needs of contemporary America. This, needless to say, will require tremendous effort and dedication, for the doctrinal transformation necessary will involve the meeting of Asian and Western values cultivated respectively over thousands of years of history. The focus is not on whether one is desirable or even superior to the other but on an intercultural dynamics that may produce a more sensible, meaningful understanding of self and the world than anything offered today. It may, for example, contribute to answering one of the major crises facing American society as summed up by Robert Bellah and his colleagues in their collaborative venture, *Habits of the Heart:*

> The question is whether individualism in which the self has become the main form of reality can really be sustained. What is at issue is not simply whether self-contained individuals might withdraw from the public sphere to pursue private ends, but whether such individuals are capable of sustaining either a public or private life. If this is the danger, perhaps only the civic and biblical forms of individualism—forms that see the individual in relation to a larger whole, a community and a tradition—are capable of sustaining genuine individuality and nurturing both public and private life.[32]

The problem addressed here is the excessive individualism that destroys the fabric of American life at the expense of the public good.

This is also a challenge for Buddhism which stresses individual awakening on the one hand and advocates the interdependent nature of all life on the other. This tension exists in the bodhisattva ideal between ascent, the quest for supreme enlightenment, and descent, the compassionate action on behalf of suffering beings.[33] An authentic Shin Buddhism will have to grapple with this question, among others, and suggest ways in which the two poles can be integrated.

IV

The contrast between traditional Asian and current Western values can be described in multiple ways, but a revealing example is recounted in the Buddhist quarterly *Tricycle* by Victor Sogen Hori. He talks about an interesting experience he had attending a Chinese Ch'an retreat.[34] At the conclusion of the retreat participants shared their thoughts with each other which led to two different reactions. While the ethnic Chinese felt an overwhelming sense of shame and repentance vis-à-vis their families, the Caucasian Buddhists felt that they had gained a measure of self-confidence. According to Hori,

> The white Americans spoke uniformly of how the long hours of meditation had helped them get in touch with themselves, given them strength and sanity to cope with the pressures of society, and assisted them in the process of self-realization.

But the reaction of a Chinese woman was quite different:

> The week of meditation had made her realize how selfish she usually was; she wanted, right then and there, to bow down in apology before her family; she wanted to perform some act of deep repentance.[35]

In brief, the meditation session for the latter was an opportunity for self-examination but for the former it was a moment for self-realization. This contrast is related to what an American Zen monk once observed while in Japan: in the West the predominant form of Buddhism is "psychotherapeutic," while in Japan it is "faith" Buddhism. The aim of the latter is succinctly stated by Hori,

> Buddhist practice is conceived as breaking habits of selfishness in order to become open, responsible, and compassionate with others; meditation is personal reconditioning designed ultimately to dissolve attachment and de-realize the self.[36]

The de-realized self is located in the nexus of interdependence and interconnectedness of life. Such an awareness of self is not limited to Buddhism, for it is also emerging in the West. Among recent writers, a new sense of self is articulated by Kenneth Gergen:

> As the self as a serious reality is laid to rest and the self is constructed and reconstructed in multiple contexts, one enters finally the stage of the *relational self*. One's sense of individual autonomy gives way to a reality of immersed interdependence, in which it is relationship that constitutes the self.[37]

Hayao Kawai contrasts the individuality in the modern West and the selfhood (which he calls "eachness") in Buddhism in his revealing book, *Buddhism and the Art of Psychotherapy*. He sums up the difference as follows:

> The premise of modern individuality is to establish the ego first. In the young adult state, ego will be the existence which is independent of others and equipped with initiative and integration. Reaching adulthood means that you have established your own identity. Ego which is established in such a manner will develop one's individuality.... Human beings in Buddhism, as so well clarified by Hua-yen thought, exist in relationship. When taken out of relationship, a person loses "self-nature" and thus ceases to exist.... Accordingly, if one

tries to respect one's own eachness, one has to be aware of others before contemplating her/his own independence.[38]

While human beings are characterized by self-centeredness the world over, how this is dealt with varies among different cultures and peoples. In the Asian tradition the self ideally undergoes some form of self-discipline and self-cultivation, so that a person reaches maturity, becomes less self-centered and realizes the interdependency with all life. From the reality of this interdependence and interconnectedness emerges the mature self. Since one's existence is made possible by virtue of all others, this naturally awakens a feeling of shame and repentance for any egocentric thought or behavior. In turn, this awareness deepens a sense of gratitude to all of existence.

The classic formulation of interdependence and interconnectedness in Buddhism is found in the system of Hua-yen thought which works with an entirely different assumption about the self. First, Hua-yen interdependence is based on an organismic worldview in which relationships take priority over individual beings. The nexus of interrelationships—social, political, philosophical, and natural—is elemental to the enduring Asian worldview, regardless of cultural, religious, and ethnic differences. Second, interdependence is not a given but must be achieved as a new sense of self and reality through the optimum functioning of mind and body. And third, this inevitably involves a religious path consisting of spiritual discipline, mental training, and bodily integration; hence, the preponderance of the Way (*tao*), requiring some form of personal transformation in the Asian tradition.[39]

In Shin Buddhism we find a practical, lived expression of the Hua-yen universe in which the relational self is realized through living the nembutsu. In the saying of namu-amida-butsu, *namu* is the isolated self which is lost, directionless and confused. But within the boundless compassion of Immeasurable Light and Life that is *amida-butsu*, one finds oneself, gains a sense of unique individuality interrelated and interconnected with all life. This is the fundamental experience of *shinjin*, living the nembutsu. In the words of the myokonin Ichitaro: "*Shinjin* means that you're able to truly relate to another being. Not only human beings but with plants and animals. Even those things that cannot speak, you're able to hear their feelings. Namu-amida-butsu."[40]

The balanced self-understanding which avoids the extremes of excessive individualism is a challenge for contemporary people. It is a real challenge because of the simple fact that everyday English language goes against the idea of interdependence. We notice, for example, the preponderance of self-reflexive words in our vocabulary which supports the delusional "I" as the center of life. The *Random House Dictionary of the English Language* lists approximately 1,100 compounds using self, beginning with "self-abhorrence" and ending with "self-wrought." Moreover, the active and passive voices also focus on the "self," whether it suggests controlling one's destiny in the active voice or the primacy of outside forces impacting the self found in the passive voice. What we need is a "middle" voice that is not centered on either the self or the other but on the integration of the two.

Shin Buddhism in America began as an ethnic religion due to historical necessity but now its existence is at a crossroads—either die a slow death, or be reborn on American soil, constantly growing new shoots. If the Shin teachings can make even a small contribution towards fulfilling the goal of balancing "genuine individuality and nurturing both public and private life," then Shin Buddhism will truly become a part of the American landscape.

NOTES

1. HHM has about 30 temples; it celebrated its centennial in 1989, and BCA with 60 temples will observe its centennial in 1999. Both belong to the Honpa Hongwanji or Nishi Hongwanji branch of Jōdo Shinshū. In addition to HHM and BCA there are other Pure Land traditions in the U.S—Jōdoshu, Otani or Higashi Hongwanji, and Pure

Land practices from Vietnam, China, Korea, and so on.

2. Alfred Bloom, "Shin Buddhism Advances in the Post-Modern Horizon," *New Horizons in Shin Buddhism*, Conference Papers and Abstracts (August 21–23, 1995), 18.

3. Alfred Bloom, "The Best Kept Secret of Buddhism: The Contextual Situation of Shin Buddhism in America" (Unpublished paper delivered at the Harvard Buddhist Studies Forum, April 6, 1996).

4. Ibid., 4

5. Alfred Bloom, "Shin Buddhism: The Contemporary Situation," (Unpublished manuscript, dated November, 1997), 2.

6. This was the major criticism made by Takamaro Shigaraki in his article, "*Amerika ni okeru shinshu kyodan*" [The Shin Church in America], *Shinshūgaku* 61 (February 1985): 1-21.

7. *The Encyclopedia of American Religious History*, vol. 1 (New York: Facts-on-File, Inc. 1996), 220.

8. Bloom, "Shin Buddhism: The Contemporary Situation," 7.

9. Galen Amstutz, *Interpreting Amida: History and Orientalism in the Study of Pure Land Buddhism* (Albany, N.Y.: State University of New York Press, 1997). This heavily annotated work shedding light on the Western neglect of Pure Land Buddhism should be a required reading for Shin Buddhist ministers and lay people, even if one may disagree with some of the viewpoints expressed.

10. Bloom, "Shin Buddhism: The Contemporary Situation," 9.

11. Ibid., 10.

12. Ibid., 16.

13. Quoted by Bloom, Ibid., 15.

14. See, for example, Minor L. Rogers and Ann T. Rogers, *Rennyo: The Second Founder of Shin Buddhism* (Berkeley: Asian Humanities Press, 1991), Chapter 7 "Nishi Hongwanji: Guardian of the State."

15. *SF Weekly*, vol. 14, no. 47, page 11–19. The major portion of the article is devoted to analyzing the sexual harassment case that was brought by a female minister against a male minister. The BCA resolved the matter by recourse to legal strategies rather than utilizing the wisdom and compassion available in the Buddha Dharma.

16. Ibid., 12.

17. Ibid., 16.

18. Ibid., 19.

19. For a comprehensive overview, see *Encyclopedia of the American Religious Experience*, vol. 3, eds. Charles H. Lippy and Peter W. Williams (New York: Harper and Row, 1988), 1477-1491. See also Catherine Albanese, *America Religions and Religion* (Belmont, Calif.: Wadsworth Publishing Co., 1991).

20. January 8, 1988 issue.

21. October 11, 1997 issue.

22. February 12, 1998 issue.

23. *Encyclopedia of the American Religious Experience*, 1479.

24. Bloom, "The Best Kept Secret of Buddhism," 7.

25. Sigaraki, "The Shin Church in America," 1–21.

26. See Rick Fields, *How the Swans Came to the Lake* (Boulder, Colo.: Shambala, 1981); John Snelling, *The Buddhist Handbook* (London: Century, 1989); Don Morreal, editor, *Buddhist America: Centers, Retreats, Practices* (Santa Fe, N.M.: John Muir Publications, 1988); and although the focus is on Europe, see also Stephen Batchelor, *The Awakening of the West: The Encounter of Buddhism and Western Culture* (Berkeley, Calif.: Parallax Press, 1994).

27. It is interesting to note that Jan Nattier's objective description of different forms of Buddhism is entitled, "Visible and Invisible," in *Tricycle: The Buddhist Review* (Fall 1995): 42–49. The three types are what she calls import Buddhism, export Buddhism, and baggage Buddhism. The first two are primarily white, middle and upper

middle class; the third is the Buddhism of Asian immigrants. The photo illustrating "baggage Buddhism," shows a Japanese American child, seated on a suitcase and awaiting incarceration in an internment camp during World War II.

28. David Slawson, *Secret Teaching in the Art of Japanese Gardens* (New York: Kodansha International, 1987). Slawson trained under the well-known landscape architect, Nakane Kinsaku, who designed the Japanese garden at the Boston Museum of Fine Arts. Slawson himself has built Japanese gardens at Carleton College, Garden Center of Greater Cleveland, Smith College, etc. The Japanese Garden for Reflection and Contemplation at Smith College uses rock formations to depict important events in the life of Buddha.

29. David Slawson, unpubished manuscript, "Authenticity in Japanese Garden Design," 2.

30. Ibid., 2.

31. Ibid., 4.

32. Robert N. Bellah, Richard Madsen, William M. Sullivan, Ann Swidler, and Steven M. Tipton, *Habits of the Heart: Individualism and Commitment in American Life* (New York: Harper and Row, 1985), 143.

33. For a brief discussion of ascent and descent, see Gadjin M. Nagao, *Madhyamika and Yogacara* (Albany, N.Y. : State University of New York Press, 1991), Chapter 14.

34 . Victor Sogen Hori, "Sweet-and-sour Buddhism," *Tricycle: The Buddhist Review* (Fall 1994): 48-52.

35. Ibid., 48.

36. Ibid., 49.

37. Kenneth Gergen, *The Saturated Self* (New York: Basic Books, 1991), 147.

38. Hayao Kawai, *Buddhism and the Art of Psychotherapy* (College Station: Texas A and M University Press, 1996), 108.

39. See my article, "Hua-yen Vision of Interdependence: A Cross-cultural Perspective," *Kegon-gaku Ronshū* [Essays on Hua-yen Buddhism], *Festschrift in Honor of Kamata Shigeo* (Tokyo: Daizō shuppan, 1997), 91-108.

40. Tetsuo Unno, *Jodoshinshu Buddhism* (San Francisco: Heian International, 1980), 114.

An Essay on Socially Engaged Buddhism

Paul O. Ingram

As a Christian historian of religions engaged in dialogue with Buddhists, I am often annoyed by uncritical caricatures some Christian scholars too regularly foist upon Buddhist tradition. In more charitable moments, I think such caricatures are unintentional, their purposes usually benign. Most Christians engaged in dialogue with Buddhists have no explicit evangelical agenda. Yet caricatures persist in scholarly Christian discourse about Buddhist tradition. Since these occur in the work of Christians who admire Buddhist tradition and seek to learn from it, they are all the more distorting and disturbing—at least to me.

One caricature that still haunts Christian encounter with Buddhist faith and practice like a Chinese hungry ghost is the assumption that Buddhist tradition as a whole is socially unengaged and therefore in need of serious reformation through dialogue with Christian tradition. Important Buddhist teachers and philosophers have also bought into this caricature. For example, Masao Abe, in relation to justice issues, writes:

> But some Buddhist thinkers, including myself, are aware that Buddhism must develop itself through confrontation with Christianity. It may not be related to the most fundamental point. But with such problems as that of justice and the understanding of history in regard to justice, I think Buddhists must learn from Christianity, because the idea of justice is very weak and unclear in Buddhism.[1]

An influential example of this caricature of Buddhist tradition is also at work in the theology of Abe's main Christian dialogical partner, John Cobb. In comparing the ethical and social implications of Buddhist and Christian "universalism," Cobb notes that despite many striking parallels, Buddhist and Christian teachings make different universal claims. According to Buddhist teaching, Gautama is one of many embodiments of Buddha-nature, so that the once-and-for-all uniqueness of the historical Jesus is not asserted about the historical Buddha.[2] The claim that the Buddha-nature is in all things and events—a Mahayana not a Theravada teaching, be it noted—and that the enlightenment attained by Gautama is the proper goal of all sentient beings is not the same as Christian claims about the resurrection. That is, the "structure of Buddhist existence" is not the same as the "structure of Christian existence."[3]

This implies for Cobb that Buddhist practice and experience have broken the "dominance of the self" or the "I" because all boundaries and distinctions between self and other are ontologically canceled at the moment of enlightenment. In so doing, Buddhist experience frees persons from anxiety and egoistic self-concern. Thereby, buddhists are able to achieve a unique openness to the structures of reality. Christian tradition, however, heightens self-transcendence by objectifying one's self as separate from other selves. Thus Christians are taught that individual selves can and should assume responsibility for what they do and for what they are. Consequently, Cobb thinks there is fuller ethical and social consciousness in Christian experience than in Buddhist experience.[4]

For this reason, in Cobb's opinion, the Christian notion of *agape* is different from the Buddhist notion of *karuṇā*. In Mahayana tradition especially, when non-attachment is attained, the Bodhisattva is thereby filled with compassionate empathy for the suffering of all unenlightened sentient beings. But even though this is a "beautiful idea," Cobb thinks the Christian notion of *agape* is ethically more sensitive to issues of social justice. *Agape,* he writes, centers on awareness of selves involved with, yet ontologically independent of other selves. It also implies ontological separation between human selves and the self of God. Since selves in separation from God are in a state of sin, no self can become virtuous through living an ethically good life. However a morally good life might be conceived, sinful selves do not establish it in relation to other selves or to God by any form of moral behavior or social activism. Since salvation is a gift of God's graceful *agape,* moral and social behavior is "Christian" only if it expresses gratitude for what God's loving grace has bestowed on the self. That is, Christians have moral and social obligations to be performed as expressions of gratitude: performing moral and social obligations do not make one "good," since all selves, even selves graced by God, remain in a state of sin.

Consequently, *agape* seems to Cobb to be less "defused" than *karuṇā* and therefore ethically and socially more relevant to the life experiences of selves existing separately, yet interactively, in the world. It is, therefore, his judgment that *agape* has historically provided norms of ethical and social organization that are more fully developed in Christian tradition than in Buddhist tradition.[5]

In fairness, it must be emphasized that Cobb's point is not that actual Buddhists are less moral or less loving than actual Christians. His point is that as Christian faith can be theologically transformed by appropriating Buddhist denials of substance categories in reference to the self, so Buddhist tradition can be ethically transformed by appropriating Christian notions of transcendence and thereby deepen its tradition of social activism.[6]

While at first glance there seems to be much in the formative Theravada and Mahayana lineages of Buddhism that supports this caricature, I shall argue that what Buddhists now call "social engagement," while conceived differently than Christian ethical-social teaching, has always been at the heart of Buddhist teaching, practice, and experience. That is, ethics and social engagement have played as important a role in Buddhist teaching and practice as ethics and social activism have played in Christian teaching and practice. Indeed, Buddhist "awakening" is never an unethical event that withdraws an awakened one from engagement with the needs of society at large. The same is true for the practice of Christian faith: salvation is never an unethical or socially unengaged event.

Since what Buddhists mean by "social engagement" is interconnected with Buddhist traditions of ethics, it seem prudent to analyze three "obstacles" in Western philosophical ethical reflection that George Dreyfus thinks hinder Western appreciation of the role of ethics in Buddhist thought and experience.[7] I shall argue that these same obstacles also distort much Christian—and Buddhist— understanding and appreciation of the role played by social engagement in Buddhist tradition as a whole. This will be followed by a summary description of traditions of engaged Buddhist practice in their Theravada and Mahayana lineages. But first, some preliminary observations.

ON THE MEANING OF "ENGAGED BUDDHISM"

"Engaged Buddhism" is a relatively recent term that describes Buddhist social activism. Winston King notes that it was first used by the Vietnamese Zen monk, Thich Nhat Hanh in 1963 in a book he wrote entitled *Engaged Buddhism*.[8] As defined in another book Thich Nhat Hanh wrote during the Vietnam War entitled *Lotus in a Sea of Fire,* the focus of "engaged Buddhism" is the creation of a nonaligned, nonbelligerent Buddhist antiwar coalition which he described as "an enemy of neither combatant."[9] In subsequent works he wrote that Buddhist tradition has always been "socially engaged."[10]

Because of the growing popularity of Thich Nhat Hanh's thought, both Buddhists and non-Buddhists, especially in Europe and the United States, picked up this term as a designation and description of something that had not occurred before in Buddhist history. So the first question to be addressed is why this should be the case. Is there anything new in "engaged Buddhism" that has not been characteristic of previous Buddhist history? I shall argue that while the term "engaged Buddhism" is new, it points to traditions of ethical

AN ESSAY ON SOCIALLY ENGAGED BUDDHISM

discipline and social activism that have always been central to Buddhist thought and practice. What is new about "engaged Buddhism" is what this term means in its present contemporary context.[11] To see this, it is necessary to engage in a critique of traditional Western assumptions about ethics that predominate in Western philosophy and currently govern most Christian ethical and social thought.

THREE WESTERN OBSTACLES

As Dreyfus notes, even when Western interpreters notice that Buddhist meditational practices are relevant to ethical self-discipline and social engagement, they incorrectly tend to view social activism as something quite external to the Buddhist experience of awakening. Thus, most Christians interpret śīla (morality) mainly as a set of injunctions to avoid certain kinds of conduct, such as the five precepts emphasized in Theravada tradition or the ten virtues emphasized in Tibetan tradition, that help Buddhists gradually withdraw from the world into a private experience of an enlightenment that detaches individuals from social and worldly care. Three assumptions seem to guide this view.

First, most contemporary Western ethical theories assert that ethics is primarily about rules and injunctions, and less concerned with the development of good character. This assumption is particularly common to utilitarian theories, which emphasize choosing the right course of action for the sake of the greatest happiness for the greatest number. Notions of injunctions and rightness are also emphasized in deontological theories. Deontology, associated with Kant, holds that the goodness of moral life does not consist in the development of human qualities such as good character, but consists in the ability to act according to universal moral laws. Thus, to be moral is to decide to act upon certain agreed rules of action—the maxims which conform to these universal moral laws.

Second, most contemporary Western ethical theory asserts the duality of reason and emotion, along with the privileging of reason. This dualism is also strongly characteristic in Kantian traditions of ethical theory. To perhaps oversimplify, we cannot help what we feel, but only what we do. So no one can be said to have a duty to feel certain emotions or to act from certain emotions. Ethics must be understood as a system of obligations. Since emotions cannot be made objects of obligations, they are without ethical relevance. Neither their presence nor their absence can reflect on a person's morality, since they are outside the scope of personal responsibility. Seen from this point of view, ethics becomes the exploration of the rationality of limited decisions reached through weighing the advantages or disadvantages of alternatives, all in isolation from human emotional experiences and human participation in religious or cultural traditions.

Third, most contemporary ethical theory asserts a duality between external agency and internal attitudes. Here again, the Kantian tradition is representative of the widely shared Western view that ethics become a matter of thinking clearly, and then proceeding to outward dealings with other human beings. But the attitudes we have or the emotions we experience in these dealings are ethically irrelevant. To be moral does not mean to possess good human qualities, as in most traditional cultures and in Buddhist tradition, but to choose the right course of action.

This essay's thesis is that since the aim of Buddhist ethics is to become virtuous, not merely to adhere to objective moral rules arrived at rationally, Western virtue ethics approaches—those that originate in Platonic and Aristotelian philosophy—rather than utilitarian or deontological approaches might provide Christians a more useful hermeneutical bridge from which to dialogically encounter Buddhist traditions of social engagement. Accordingly, as a "thought experiment," I shall employ a virtue ethics approach as a heuristic device through which to examine and interpret the ethical sources of traditional Buddhist activism, now referred to as "Buddhist social engagement."

AN ESSAY ON SOCIALLY ENGAGED BUDDHISM

THE BROAD HISTORICAL CONTEXT: THERAVADA AND MAHAYANA TRADITIONS

The earliest Pali traditions of Buddhist ethics clearly pay attention to achieving virtue.[12] Ethics is about the "good life," meaning a life oriented towards a good end through "social engagement." That is, in common with, but not identical to, Greek traditions of virtue ethics, the *telos* (orientation) of Buddhist ethics and social engagement is *eudaimonia,* or happiness and well-being, in which "the good" is a whole made up of interlocking and interrelated parts, forms of activity, both internal and external, in accordance with the practice of certain virtues.[13] This is so because Buddhist moral life and social engagement, like everything else in Buddhist tradition, is grounded in the teaching of *pratītya-samutpāda,* or "dependent co-origination."[14]

This is clearly the emphasis of the Pali Canon. Yet on the surface, the majority of passages in the Pali texts seem to present the meaning of Buddhist practice as escape from the world and its social involvements. Certainly, these texts say very little about the world's renewal or changing society's social structures. World renewal and social change seem left to the impersonally operating cyclic forces of *saṃsāra* flowing according to the Law of Karma. Thus, the truly Buddhist method of interrelating with the world and society is to form an order of monks—a society within a larger society, but yet apart from this larger society, in hope of attaining enlightened freedom (*nibbāna*) from all worldly attachments.[15]

But this picture, while a large part of the Pali texts, is not the whole picture. Theravada literature presents a much broader conception of Buddhist goals and practices that is not often acknowledged either by non-Buddhists or non-Theravada Buddhists. In fact, Pali literature describes three goals of Buddhist practice, all of which are said to be "good."[16] On the lowest level is the practice of ethical precepts such as the five precepts in order to achieve a more positive future rebirth. This is the traditional goal of Theravada Buddhist laypersons, and is considered by the Pali texts to be limited and provisional, its purpose being to move the mind away from attachment to worldly concerns.

On the highest level is the goal of arhathood, the state of a person liberated from the causes of suffering through the practice of morality (*śīla*), wisdom (*paññā*), and insight (*jhāna*). One achieving this state has attained the perfection of knowledge and compassion. It is the attainment of a certain level of moral excellence that posits certain social goals to Buddhists that are constitutive of them. Furthermore, these goals all share common fundamental virtues that constitute the "good life": a life of compassionate, yet detached, social activism in which human beings are first and foremost concerned with the well-being and flourishing of all sentient beings and who express this compassionate concern within the rough-and-tumble of social, political, and economic existence.[17]

Consequently, monks and laity are ethically and socially interdependent in their Buddhist practice; each needs the other and must serve the other in the creation of an ideal community called the *saṃgha*. Monks need food and shelter and depend on the laity for their efforts to achieve nibbanic freedom from society; but monks are expected to teach the *dhamma* to laypersons, work to relieve their suffering, and to model the virtues of Buddhist practice, even though laypersons must remain in the secular world.

Thus the practice of virtues for monks—the third intermediate level—entails wise and compassionate engagement with the world, while yet remaining detached from the world—which I interpret to mean "being in the world, but not of the world."

However, the traditions of Buddhist social engagement did not end with the Theravada tradition. During the two-thousand or more years that the Buddhist Way spread to China, Tibet, Korea, and Japan, an extensive body of Mahayana ethical and social teachings evolved that produced ideals that continue to undergird Buddhist social engagement today. The key to this expansion is specifically Mahayana interpretations of the doctrine of "dependent co-origination" (*pratītya-samutpāda*) as this teaching interrelates with the Bodhisattva concept, along with the resulting importance given to the significance of Buddhist laypersons.

To state the matter perhaps too simply, the bodhisattva, "one whose being is enlightenment," a "Buddha-in-the-making," became every person's ideal in Mahayana teaching about achieving the good life in-community. Here, the usual Theravada ideal of the secluded monk, "wandering alone in the forest like an elephant" until he achieves awakened detachment that allows him to be engaged with the world while not being of the world, was replaced by a different ideal: the Buddhist monk or layperson who through endless deeds of wisdom and compassion though numerous cycles of rebirth strove for Buddhahood by vowing to help all sentient beings attain enlightenment.

My favorite Mahayana text that describes the good life as compassionate wisdom in social engagement with all sentient beings-in-community is Śāntideva's *Bodhicaryāvatāra* (Entering the Path of Enlightenment):

> May I too, through whatever good I have accomplished by doing all this, become one who works for the complete alleviation of the sufferings of all beings.
>
> May I be medicine for the sick; may I also be their physician and attend them until their disease no longer recurs. With showers of food and water, may I eliminate hunger and thirst, and during the intermediate periods of great famine between eons, may I be food and drink.
>
> And may I be an inexhaustible storehouse for the poor, and may I always be first in being ready to serve them in various ways.
>
> So that all beings may achieve their aims, may I sacrifice, without regret, the bodies, as well as the pleasures I have had, and the merit of all the good that I have accomplished and will accomplish in the past, present, and future.

> Nirvana means to renounce everything. My mind is set on nirvana, so because I am to renounce everything, it is best to give it to others.[18]

Another example of the Mahayana ideal of social engagement grounded in the teaching of dependent co-origination is portrayed in the *Vimalakīrti-sūtra* (The Discourse of the Layman Vimalakīrti). In this text, one of the most popular in Mahayana literature, Vimalakīrti is described by Gautama the Buddha as a sort of "super-bodhisattva" who even surpasses the Buddha's own disciples in wisdom and virtue. He is fully enlightened as a lay bodhisattva thoroughly involved in the rough-and-tumble of society, whose compassionate wisdom exceeds that of cloistered monks and nuns; he is fully enlightened and fully socially engaged. As the sutra describes him:

> At that time there lived in the city of Vaisali a certain Licchavi, Vimalakīrti by name . . . . He wore the white clothes of a layman, yet lived impeccably like a religious devotee. He lived at home, but remained aloof from the realm of desire . . . . He had a son, a wife, and female attendants, yet always maintained continence . . . . He seemed to eat and drink, yet always took nourishment from meditation. He made his appearance in the fields of sports and casinos, yet his aim was always to mature those people who were attached to games and gambling.[19]

In business, in government affairs, equally at home with teachers, warriors, politicians, and ordinary folk, all without spiritual and moral ethical compromise, Vimalakīrti models the highest ideal, for laypersons and ordained monks and nuns, of Buddhist ethical virtue (*śīla*) expressed through compassionate social engagement with all sentient beings. Understanding this assertion requires a brief description of how Mahayana tradition expanded the meaning of *śīla* in terms of its interpretation of dependent co-origination and the bodhisattva ideal.

As in Theravada thought, roughly speaking, there are three levels of śīla in Mahayana teaching and practice. In many ways, these levels are similar to Theravada understanding, but their meanings are stretched beyond their Theravada origins. The first level of Mahayana śīla focuses on moral injunctions, the keeping of moral precepts and rules to ward off immoral faults and actions. These "faults," as discussed in detail in the Vinaya literature, fall into two categories: (1) "natural faults" and (2) "conventional faults." "Natural faults" are actions that are karmically negative and directly harm others and the person who does them regardless of who they are, such as killing or lying. Anyone engaging in such acts is not virtuous and generates negative karma.

"Conventional faults" are incurred by disobeying conventional moral injunctions. For example, for lay Buddhists, it is not non-virtuous to eat after noon. For monks and nuns, however, eating after noon constitutes a moral fault because of the conventional rules that apply to their lives when they accepted ordination. Among these two types of fault, natural faults are more important. Thus for all Buddhists, "morality" is defined as the resolution to abstain from harming others.

The second meaning of śīla in Mahayana tradition is more ethically inclusive. Here, śīla entails the whole range of virtuous practices in which a person engages after making a commitment to achieve enlightenment for the sake of all sentient beings. Anyone making this commitment is a bodhisattva; for such persons, bodhisattva practices like patience, giving, contemplation, and meditation are forms of śīla. But this form of practice is beyond moral injunctions. That is, for the bodhisattva, śīla is not keeping the precepts in a legalistic, shop-ethical way: the practice of śīla is living the good life in accordance with the practices of virtues. Thus it is not enough for a bodhisattva to merely refrain from specific acts of violence; the bodhisattva must become nonviolent through the practice of nonviolence.

Finally, the third level of Mahayana conceptions of śīla goes beyond the domain of moral injunctions and relates directly to the life of the bodhisattva as modeled by Vimalakīrti. At this level, *śīla* is identical with "social engagement." The bodhisattva, working for the sake of all sentient beings, is compassionately focused on service to others: nursing the sick, leading the blind, helping the oppressed, providing food and clothing for the poor. This level of Mahayana *śīla* is interesting for two reasons: (1) it dispels the misconception that Buddhist faith and practice promotes self-involvement, and (2) it clearly demonstrates the importance of service to all beings in Buddhist tradition.

The third level of Mahayana *śīla* practice is also more evident in Mahayana tradition than the second level. Though intended for bodhisattvas, the ethics of collecting virtues can be extended to other Buddhist practices. This is not so with the ethics of helping others. Although similar practices are indeed recommended in Theravada tradition, these are subordinate to attaining enlightenment for oneself. Here, Mahayana tradition differs: helping others is a goal of practice in and of itself since in an interdependent universe, no one is fully enlightened until all are fully enlightened. Likewise, as the suffering of one person diminishes all persons, so the enlightenment of any Buddha engenders wise compassionate benefit for all suffering sentient beings. No one is fully liberated from suffering unless all beings are liberated; no one is fully enlightened unless all beings are enlightened. We are all interdependently together in this universe.

Consequently, at this third level, Mahayana tradition emphasizes that the bodhisattva's compassion is aimed at helping others—not merely to develop concern for others, but to actively help others. The bodhisattva's "wisdom"—knowledge that reality is so interdependent that there is no separation between self and others—engenders compassionate social engagement that aims to relieve all sentient beings from suffering within the structures of social, political, and economic existence.

Concrete examples of this ideal mark the social and political histories of both Theravada and Mahayana traditions. For example,

AN ESSAY ON SOCIALLY ENGAGED BUDDHISM

Aśoka Maurya's conversion to Buddhism in the third century B.C.E. began the spread of Buddhism as a state religion across South Asia and the creation of Buddhist-centered civilizations. This "Aśokan ideal"[20] became a justification for political activism everywhere in Asia, and continues today in South Asia, where criticism of government leaders in Śri Lanka, Thailand, and Burma is still "significantly most effective," when "they are charged with being un-Buddhist." Donald Swearer notes how in contemporary times the Venerable Buddhadasa continues the Aśokan ideal in the model community he established in northern Thailand where he carries on his "harmonious, noncompetitive" Buddha-dharma that emphasizes interdependence, restraint, and generosity.[21] Buddhadasa's lay disciple, Sulak Sivaraksa at one time exiled by the Thai government because of his political activism against that government's exploitation of its people, continues to struggle for social, political, and economic justice.

The "Aśokan ideal" is also exemplified by the history of Mahayana tradition. In China, Korea, and Japan, Buddhist social and political engagement brought the Dharma out of the monastery and into society and statecraft. One need only read the histories of Chinese Buddhist social engagement during the T'ang and Sung Dynasties;[22] the social roles of Buddhist institutions in Korea to relieve the suffering of the poor and those oppressed by authoritarian governmental policies;[23] or the political and social activism on behalf of the politically and economically exploited by the "Kamakura" schools of "reform" Buddhism—Zen, Jōdo Shū, Jōdo Shinshū, and Nichiren Shū—in Japan from the thirteenth to the fifteenth centuries to see the Aśokan ideal at work in Buddhist history.[24]

In the late sixties, it was Buddhist political activism led by the monk Tri Quang that brought down the oppressive government of Diem Ngo Dinh in spite of American support,[25] a tradition of nonviolent social engagement continued by Thich Nhat Hanh. So too is the Aśokan ideal at work in the contemporary Won Buddhist movement, founded by the Korean monk Sot'aesan (1891–1943), whose members and leaders continue the founder's struggle for world peace not only through interreligious dialogue, but through social engagement with the political, social, and economic forces that engender worldwide violence.[26]

In an interdependent universe, then, what is the key virtue of Buddhist ethical practice that grounds distinctively Buddhist social engagement? It can only be the first of the five precepts, nonviolence. The most persuasive recent Western discussion of contemporary Buddhist socially engaged nonviolence is a collection of eight essays edited by Kenneth Kraft entitled *Inner Peace, World Peace: Essays on Buddhism and Non-Violence*.[27] Kraft's essay notes that because individual greed, hatred, and delusion are the central human problems from which all need deliverance, "social work entails inner work."[28] That is, social reform pursued merely from a socio-ideological or an economic-ideological point of view will at best provide only temporary solutions to social and economic issues, and at worst perpetuate the very ills social reform aims to cure. This is the fundamental principle of every form of distinctively Buddhist social engagement. The inner motivations of reformers must always be kept under close scrutiny—by reformers and by those they seek to reform. Or stated more positively, distinctively Buddhist social engagement assumes a "virtue ethics" orientation. In the processes of ethical self-discipline, one *becomes* virtuous and exercises virtue in social engagement within the rough-and-tumble of political and economic existence in the hard struggle for community.

There is, of course, great diversity of Buddhist opinion about the meaning and application of this principle. Thich Nhat Hanh is sometimes understood to have a quietist view of Buddhist social engagement. One's mind must become nonviolent in social engagement for world peace. Consequently, he stresses that meditative practice is as necessary for Buddhist social engagement as social engagement is for meditative practice.[29]

Robert Thurman thinks the Dalai Lama's philosophy of nonviolence is the operating principle of Tibetan Buddhist notions of the ideal social order. The Dalai Lama prays for the Chinese who invaded and still occupy Tibet because even violent oppressors must be objects of compassion. He never ceases to point out that because the world is filled with violence, it is perfectly arranged to promote humanity's compassionate development. Indeed, he constantly teaches that in an interdependent world of suffering beings, toward whom is there not ample opportunity to exercise compassionate social engagement?[30]

Finally, Sulak Sivaraksa is, by Western standards, the most "activist" of the examples of Buddhist social engagement I have noted, mostly because of his social and political activities in Thailand—at considerable personal risk—and because his views are explicitly political in nature. He writes: "The Buddhist approach to peace demands self-awareness and social awareness in equal measure."[31] Accordingly, while meditation loosens the hold of personal and social prejudice, the Five Precepts—not to kill, not to steal, to speak the truth, to abstain from illicit sexuality, to avoid intoxicants—must be interpreted in realistic and flexible terms. For example, non-killing should mean seeking remedies in situations in which some persons live in rich abundance while others live in poverty. Speaking the truth refers equally to personal truthfulness and refraining from clinging (*tanhā*) to ideologies in the mistaken notion that they are identical with unchanging truths. Avoiding intoxicants means engaging the social and economic conditions that make the drug trade profitable. He also believes that some sort of world government is congenial with Buddhist principles.

SOME CONCLUDING OBSERVATIONS

Often, as I have participated in dialogical discussions between Buddhists and Christians on such topics as the environment, justice, poverty, or violence, it is easier for me to identify a distinctively "Buddhist" position than a distinctively "Christian" position. Of course, the problem may be strictly my own. But I often have difficulty identifying what makes a particular form of social activism "Christian" and not something else, say, Jewish or Islamic or Buddhist. Buddhists seem as compassionate and as loving as Christians; Buddhists are as concerned about justice, economic exploitation, and environmental degradation as Christians; Buddhists seem as concerned with world peace as Christians. Agapic love of one's neighbors can be and often is affirmed by Buddhists; compassion for all suffering beings is recognized and even celebrated by many Christians.

I suspect my difficulty originates in the way in which Christian ethicists talk about social issues. Much of this talk seems to view Buddhist ethical theory and social engagement through the filter of Western utilitarian or deontological thought, rather than through Western virtue approaches. Furthermore, "Christian ethics" often seems to me more a matter of duty rather than of virtue, since the stress of much Christian discourse and social activism is on performing obligations consistent with the gift of God's love to humanity created by the events surrounding the historical Jesus.[32] Thus, from a Protestant perspective, at least, Christian ethics and social activism do not demand that persons become virtuous. Nor is meditation or contemplative prayer a required ingredient of ethical behavior or social activism.

The upshot seems something like this: sinful human beings in a sinful world can never become virtuous. But illumined by God's grace, sinful persons can recognize this existential context for making ethical and social choices and behave morally in social activism as an act of gratitude for what God has accomplished for humanity through the life, death, and resurrection of the historical Jesus. *But one need not be a Christian or experience Christian faith to live according to the same moral obligations guiding Christian social activism.* There seems to be little that distinguishes Christian ethics and social activism from non-Christian ethics and social activism, so that what "makes" a moral choice or participation in social activism particularly "Christian," and not something else, often escapes me.

AN ESSAY ON SOCIALLY ENGAGED BUDDHISM

I usually do not experience the same difficulty understanding what "makes" traditions of ethics and social engagement "Buddhist." Buddhist traditions of social engagement are bound to a specific worldview—"dependent co-origination." Christian traditions of ethics and social activism are not worldview specific. That is, the core of Buddhist ethics and social engagement is a strong sense of the intimate, organic interrelatedness of all sentient beings—a worldview upon which everything "Buddhist" depends. Accordingly, Buddhists are led from rigid absolutist distinctions that cut individuals off from creative social relationships in community to an openness that is fully aware of the dynamic interrelatedness of all things and events at every moment of space-time. Furthermore, awareness of interdependency does not blur awareness of differences of personal, social, and historical distinctions and identities; it enables compassion to flow more freely in creative interaction with others through recognizing that while others are different, they remain tightly bound together in the universal web of dependent interrelationships that constitute the whole of reality.

Accordingly, my concluding observations are these: (1) Buddhist traditions of ethics and social activism are not less fully evolved than these traditions are in Christian experience; they are merely different. Nor are Buddhist traditions of ethics and social engagement more fully evolved than they are in Christian faith and experience; they are merely different. (2) The question of which tradition is more ethically and socially engaged is neither important nor, finally, interesting. Therefore, it should not be a focus of Buddhist-Christian dialogue. (3) Buddhists and Christians share the same world and the same problems all religious human beings share: the necessity of being socially engaged with the forces that endanger the human community along with all life on this planet. Poverty, political oppression, racism, and ecological degradation of the environment are so serious in their present scope that religious differences are insignificant. From the perspective of the needs of persons for liberation from poverty, political oppression, and violence; from the perspective of the current ecological crisis that endangers all sentient beings on Planet Earth, Buddhists and Christians need to share in each other's visions in our collective human struggle "for the common good"[33] of all beings, not just human beings. For all sentient beings are interdependently related, not just "Christian" or "Buddhist" human beings.

NOTES

1. Masao Abe and John B. Cobb. Jr., "Buddhist-Christian Dialogue: Past, Present, Future," *Buddhist Christian Studies* 1 (1981): 24.

2. John B. Cobb, Jr., *Christ in a Pluralistic Age* (Philadelphia: Westminster Press, 1975), 206.

3. For Cobb's definition of "structure of existence," see John B. Cobb, Jr., *The Structure of Christian Existence* (Philadelphia: Westminster Press. 1972), 16–17.

4. Cobb, *Christ in a Pluralistic Age,* 208–209.

5. Ibid., 215–218. Abe also agrees with Cobb's assessment. See his conversation with Cobb in "Buddhist-Christian Dialogue: Past, Present, Future," 13–29.

6. See my fuller critique of Cobb's dialogue with Buddhism in "To John Cobb: Questions to Gladden the Atman in an Age of Pluralism," JAAR 45, no. 2 Supplement (June 1977): L753–788.

7. George Dreyfus. "Meditation as Ethical Activity," *Journal of Buddhist Ethics* 2 (1995): 31 34, [Online]. Available FTP: ftp.cac.psu.edu Directory: JBE2/1995 File: dreyfus.text.

8. Winston L. King, "Engaged Buddhism: Past, Present, Future," *The Eastern Buddhist*, n.s. 27 (Autumn 1994): 14.

9. Thich Nhat Hanh, *Lotus in a Sea of Fire* (London: SCM Press, 1961).

10. See Thich Nhat Hanh, B*eing Peace* (Berkeley: Parallax Press, 1988);

idem, *The Heart of Understanding: Commentaries on the Prajñāpāramitā Sūtra* (Berkeley: Parallax Press, 1988).

11. This conclusion is argued rather well by King, "Engaged Buddhism: Past, Present, Future," 14–29. I will not repeat his arguments.

12. Charles S. Prebish, "Text and Tradition in the Study of Buddhist Ethics," *Pacific World* 9 (1993): 49–68.

13. See Phra Rajavaramuni, "Foundations of Buddhist Social Ethics," *Ethics. Wealth, and Salvation: A Study of Buddhist Social Ethics*, Russell F. Sizemore and Donald K. Swearer, eds. (Columbia, S.C.: University of South Carolina Press, 1992), 29–40.

14. See, for example, Damien Keown, "Are There Human Rights in Buddhism," *Journal of Buddhist Ethics* 2 (1995): 3–27, [Online]. Available FTP: ftp.cac.psu.edu Directory: JBE\21995 File: Keown.text See Dreyfus for a friendly critique of Keown's specific application of virtue ethics to Buddhist ethics, especially the Western notion of "human rights."

15. See Winston L. King, *In Hope of Nibbāna* (La Salle, Ill.: Open Court. 1964). 203.

16. Rajavararnuni, "Foundations of Buddhist Ethics," 46–53.

17. Frank E. Reynolds, "Ethics and Wealth in Theravada Buddhism," in *Ethics, Wealth, and Salvation: A Study of Buddhism Social Ethics*, 50–76. See also David Little's response to Reynolds in "Ethical Analysis and Wealth in Theravada Buddhism: A Response to Frank Reynolds," *Ethics, Wealth, and Salvation*, 77–86.

18. John S. Strong, ed., *The Experience of Buddhism: Sources and Interpretations* (Belmont, Calif.: Wadsworth Publishing Company, 1995), 162–163.

19. Robert R. Thurman, trans. *The Holy Teachings of Vimalakīrti* (University Park, Pa.: Pennsylvania State University, Press, 1976), 20, cited in King, "Engaged Buddhism: Past, Present, Future," 17.

20. Ibid., 22–23. Also see Harold D. Lasswell and Harlan Cleveland, eds., *The Ethics of Power* (New York: Harper and Row, 1992), 53.

21. Donald K. Swearer, *Buddhism and Society in South East Asia* (Chambersburg, Pa.: Anima Books. 1980), 59–69. Also see Swearer, ed., *Me and Mine: Selected Essays of Bhikkhu Buddhadasa* (Albany, N.Y.: State University of New York Press, 1989), chapters 10–12 and Sulak Sivaraksa, *A Socially Engaged Buddhism* (Bangkok: The Interreligious Commission for Development, 1988).

22. See Kenneth K. S. Ch'en, *Buddhism in China: A Historical Survey* (Princeton. N.J.: Princeton University Press. 1979), chapter 16.

23. Henrich Dumoulin and John C. Maraldo, eds., *Buddhism in the Modern World* (New York: Collier Macmillan, 1976), chapter 16.

24. Dumoulin and Maraldo, eds., *Buddhism in the Modern World*, chapter 17.

25. The best description of Vietnamese Buddhist social engagement prior to the end of the Vietnam War is still Jerrold Schecter's *The New Fact of Buddha* (Tokyo: John Weatherhill, 1967), chapters 8–11.

26. See Bonkin Kirn, "The Irwon Symbol and its Ecumenical Significance," *Buddhist-Christian Studies* 14 (1994): 73–87.

27. Kenneth Kraft, ed., *Inner Peace, World Peace: Essays on Buddhism and Non-Violence* (Albany N.Y.: State University of New York Press, 1992).

28. Ibid., 12.

29. Ibid.

30. His Holiness Tenzin Gyatso, *Kindness, Clarity, and Insight* (Ithaca. N.Y.: Snow Lion Publications. 1984), 56–64; idem, *The Way to Freedom* (San Francisco: Harper San Francisco: 1994), 58–64.

31. Cited in King, "Engaged Buddhism: Past, Present, Future," 24.

32. However, contemporary Catholic ethical theory, rooted in the theology of Thomas Aquinas, whose ethical thought was in turn grounded in Aristotle's ethics, has engendered Catholic understanding of and deep appreciation for Buddhist social engagement. For an excellent discussion of the differences between Protestant and Roman Catholic ethics, see James M. Gustafson,

Protestant and Roman Catholic Ethics: Prospects for Rapprochement (Chicago: The University of Chicago Press, 1978). Also see Etienne Gilson, *The Christian Philosophy of St. Thomas Aquinas* (New York: Random House, 1956), 251–356.

33. Herrnan Daly and John B. Cobb, Jr., *For the Common Good* (Boston: Beacon Press, 1994).

Jōdo Shinshū's Mission to History: A Christian Challenge to Shin Buddhist Social Ethics

James FREDERICKS

In recent years, the encounter between Buddhism and Christianity has reached a level of creativity and maturity which is auspicious, involving not only scholars, but monastics and laity as well. Perhaps most noteworthy of all is the motivation which lies behind these dialogues. Whereas in times past, Christians were interested in learning more about Buddhists in order to convert or to contrast Buddhism with Christianity for apologetic reasons, increasingly Christians and Buddhists are coming together for dialogue in the hope of deepening their own religious understanding. In this regard, following John Cobb's suggestion,[1] we might say that the great promise of Buddhist-Christian dialogue today is the mutual transformation of these traditions through their creative encounter. If this be the case, then dialogue partners must not be too hasty in affirming the similarities which unite their traditions. The point of dialogue is not to discover the truth of one's own tradition in the tradition of another. This would be to domesticate the religious truth by finding in the other simply "more of the same" (to use David Tracy's phrase). Rather, the great promise of interreligious dialogue today is to discover a religious truth in the other that is not like the truth of one's own tradition and to be enriched by this truth.

The reflections which follow presume that Buddhism is for Christianity both a challenge and an opportunity for its transformation—and, of course, the reverse is also to be hoped, *viz.* that the contemporary encounter with Christianity might be for Buddhism the occasion of its enrichment as well. Since the issue to be addressed in this paper is Jōdo Shinshū and its potential for

JŌDO SHINSHŪ'S MISSION TO HISTORY

providing an innately Buddhist basis for social activism, the focus will tend to remain on the challenge Christianity poses to Buddhism. Nevertheless, the problems that will be raised are part of a wider, bilateral conversation in which Christians receive as well as give.

THE NEED TO REVISE TRADITIONS

Among Christians, there is increasing concern for the relative adequacy of their religious symbols and doctrines, especially in relation to the impact these symbols and doctrines have on the activity of Christians in the world. Take, for instance, developments in Latin America. Christian theologians, such as Gustavo Gutierrez, Juan L. Segundo and Leonardo Boff, have been successful in raising fundamental questions in regard to the ideological function of Christianity as a religious legitimation of unjust social structures and the necessity of relating orthodoxy with orthopraxis.[2] A similar theological concern for the contemporary adequacy of symbols can be noted among North American theologians as well. To offer one example, in his little book, *Theology for a Nuclear Age*,[3] Gordon Kaufman argues that, in an age which holds for itself the power to bring history to a nuclear end, the traditional Christian notion of a providential God, sovereign over history and shepherding his creation until the completion of his plan, is seriously inadequate. In a nuclear age, it is the creature that has the power to bring an end to history. Kaufman's conclusion is worth noting. Religious symbols and doctrines, however honored by tradition, which do not lead believers to take greater responsibility for the "fate of the earth" need to be revised, or perhaps even abandoned altogether.

Religious symbols and doctrines are almost never neutral in their ethical import. They either lead us to take more responsibility and act more compassionately or they numb us to the needs of the world. This is as true of Buddhism as it is of Christianity. Buddhist formulations of the Dharma either hurt or help. To use a more traditionally Buddhist way of making the same point, the Dharma can be preached either skillfully or unskillfully. For this reason, Buddhists, like Christians, must criticize the adequacy of their symbols and doctrines in order to remain true to the Buddhist vision of unbounded compassion for all the peoples of the world.

With some notable exceptions, Buddhists have generally manifested a weak sense of the social dimension of ethics.[4] It has preferred on the whole to focus its ethical criticisms on the activity of individuals as opposed to calling into question the adequacy of social structures. The reasons for this state of affairs have been must discussed. Among others, I would single out the following three doctrinal factors.

First, from its earliest development, Buddhist doctrinal formulations of the Dharma have preferred a language more psychological in character than social or political. Despite later Buddhism's enormous achievements in metaphysics, early Buddhism may be described as a kind of empirical psychology of suffering.[5] This point can be seen especially in the second and third of the Four Noble Truths and the generally psychological approach taken by the Abhidharma scholastics. The Second Noble Truth identifies the origin of sorrow in craving based on a false view of the self. As the origin of sorrow lies in the psychology of craving, the Third Noble Truth locates the deliverance from sorrow in the elimination of this psychology. The Abhidharma scholastics develop the psychology of craving found in the Sutra Pitaka with their attempts to deconstruct the false view of the self by analyzing this illusion into various configurations of more basic components (*skandhas*).[6] The pervasive thrust of early Buddhist doctrine is focused on the afflictions of the individual and not the remaking of social structures. Early Buddhism's "psychology" of false views, of course, does not preclude an appreciation of the social or institutional dimensions of *duḥkha* (pain; suffering). The psychological approach has, however, bequeathed to Buddhism a general preference for the individual instead of the social.

Second, there is the Buddhist understanding of justice. In monotheistic religions like Judaism, Christianity and Islam, rooted as they are in the prophetic affirmation of a creator God who judges heaven and earth and who commands the wealthy and established to care for the poor, the helpless and the foreigner, justice is not only an eschatological hope, but a moral imperative in the present. In Buddhist tradition, justice has generally been imagined in the form of a karmic retribution. The Buddhist theory of causality (karma), rightly or wrongly, has functioned psychologically to help one to cope with present suffering. Karma also functions somewhat like a theodicy in the monotheistic religions in that it provides a religious framework for legitimating the ultimate justice or rightness of the universe despite the evident injustice of actual social conditions. Karma may be slow, but in the long run it is just. Present suffering is merited from infinite lives past. The effect of this doctrine has been similar to that of the Buddhist psychology of suffering. Karmic theories of justice have not required Buddhism to call the morality of social structures into question. Admittedly, this doctrine is stronger in Buddhist traditions formed by the Pali Canon than the Mahayana scriptures. At the same time, partially as a result of the ethics implicit in this doctrine, Mahayama Buddhism as well has demonstrated a remarkable willingness to adapt to diverse sociopolitical systems without seeing the need to confront those systems.[7] As with the early Buddhist psychology of suffering, the doctrine of karma does not preclude an appreciation of the social or institutional dimensions of duḥkha. Ken Jones, for example, has written persuasively about the dangers of using this doctrine as the basis for what he calls a socially unengaged Buddhist "quietism."[8]

Third, there is the early Buddhist doctrine of the "non-self" (anātman). There has been some recent discussion regarding the ability of Buddhism to embrace the notion of inalienable human rights in light of this doctrine.[9] The question of whether the notion of human rights is appropriate to the Buddhist worldview must be left in abeyance. For the present, let me note that Buddhism, in keeping with its psychology of suffering, locates the roots of the violence and the inhumanity of social relations in the individual's construction of false views of the self. Thus, the *anātman* doctrine has an important function in establishing the Buddhist view of the relationship between the individual and society and the ethical implications which accompany this relationship. The world of suffering (*saṃsāra*) is an illusion which arises along with the false view of the self. Salvation is a matter of "extinguishing" (nirvana) the passions and cravings of the substantial self. Like the psychology of evil discussed above, the import of this view of salvation has been to focus the religious ingenuity of Buddhist practitioners on the liberation of the individual and away from an investigation of the political, social and economic dimension of that liberation.[10]

Buddhists, it should go without saying, are ethical—and not in merely a conventional way or in a way that irremediably excludes the social dimension of ethical commitment. More to the point for Christians interested in learning from Buddhism, when Buddhists do engage in social activism, their ethical motivation does not come from sources external to their Buddhist heritage. As an example of a thoroughly Buddhist movement for social change in Asia, the Sarvodaya Shramadana movement in Sri Lanka and its founder, A.T. Ariyaratne, come easily to mind.[11] In the historical development of the Buddhist tradition, however, ethical interest has tended by and large to be centered on the activities of individuals instead of the transformation of social structures.[12]

Simply to contrast Buddhism's general preference for the individual as opposed to the social and political dimensions of salvation with Christianity's allegedly more socially oriented views would be very misleading. Before making any such self-assured comparisons between Buddhism and Christianity, it is worth remembering that activist movements within Christianity such as the "theology of liberation" and the "social Gospel," along with the numerous social encyclicals of the Roman Catholic popes, are rather recent developments in the history of Christianity.[13] There are, however, good reasons why one would expect Christianity to have a greater affinity for the social, political and economic dimension of ethics. These reasons have to do with Christian doctrine, but are also related to the fact that Christianity's history is very different than that of Buddhism. The doctrinal factors contributing to Christianity's appreciation of the social dimension of religious ethics can be traced to Christianity's roots in the ethical monotheism of the Jewish people.

First, Christianity is the heir to the Jewish heritage of covenant theology. The notion of "people" (*kâhâl*) has been more central a category for the Jews than the individual. Thus the roots of the Christian *ekklêsia* can be traced proximately to the Jewish *synagôgê* and more distantly to the Jewish experience of being the "people of God" (*k^ehal yahweh*). In keeping with this legacy, Christians generally imagine salvation in terms of the experience of community, the *communio sanctorum*. Furthermore, this "communion of the saints" is not confined to a wholly transcendent heaven beyond this world, but spans this world and the next. For this reason, community has a sacramental meaning for many Christians. Here, "sacramental" means that the Christian's encounter with God is mediated by the communal life of the church. Not surprisingly, Christianity has two basic metaphors for salvation. One is individual: the resurrection of the body. The other is social: the Kingdom of God.

Second, Christianity is heir to the Jewish prophetic tradition. The Hebrew scriptures present the conflict between the prophet and the king, in which prophetic proclamation ruptures the universality and harmony of the sacred cosmos. Concretely, the prophet calls into question the religious legitimacy of the monarch's political authority by appealing to the Word of God, which transcends and judges all social and political structures. The book of the Prophet Amos is very influential in this regard. Amos condemns the Hebrew king and the wealthy class by proclaiming God's desire for justice, not elaborate religious ceremonies (Amos 5:21-24). For the Hebrew prophets, virtue is measured not by cultic purity, but by the social standard of meting out justice for those who cannot compete economically, "the poor, the widow and the stranger in your land" (Zech. 7:10; Is. 1:17; Ps. 146:9). Social harmony (sacred cosmos symbolized in divine kingship and religiously legitimated social structures) is not decisive for religious truth. Society is brought under the judgment of the Word of God.[14]

Third, Christianity has been shaped decisively by Jewish eschatological expectation. The communal and social dimension of salvation for Christianity is implied by the image of the Kingdom of God. This image also is related to Christianity's eschatological understanding of history. Thus, for Christians, historical existence has been radically transformed by the religious experience of hope. The religiously charged meaning of eschatological hope leads Christians to a heightened awareness that human beings create economic and political structures within history, that nothing created can be ultimate and finally that those who create are responsible before God for what they have created.[15] Commenting on social meaning of Christianity's view of salvation, activist Daniel Berrigan S.J. remarked in an interview that his faith requires him to be dissatisfied with any society that is not yet the Kingdom of God.

Christianity's awareness of the social dimensions of religious ethics is also related to external, historical factors with which Christianity has had to contend. In a way that is not true of Buddhism to the same extent, Christianity has had to respond to the European Enlightenment, its critical historiography and the hermeneutics of suspicion which have grown out of it. Arguably, it has been this factor, more so than the doctrinal factors, which has acted as the catalyst in Christianity's relatively recent interest in social justice. Enlightenment social theory has been critical of religious legitimations of social structures. Since 1789, social reform movements in Europe have been decidedly secularist and disestablishmentarian. At the height of the industrial revolution, Karl Marx underscored the role played by religious institutions as ideologies supportive of oppressive social structures. For the most part, Christian institutions have reacted with hostility to Marxism. However, in a movement involving Christian theologians and pastoral workers beginning in Latin America and then spreading worldwide, Marxist hermeneutics have been

JŌDO SHINSHŪ'S MISSION TO HISTORY

integrated with Christian eschatology in the hope of working out a "theology of liberation" with decidedly social, political and economic ramifications.[16]

The foregoing account was not intended to end the discussion of Buddhism's potential for generating its own religious understanding of social ethics. Rather, it should serve as the starting point for further discussion. The reflections that follow suggest that dialogue between Jōdo Shinshū and Christianity may be helpful in leading Buddhists to look again at their own tradition with this in mind.

JŌDO SHINSHŪ AND THE SOCIAL DIMENSION

The work of not a few commentators would suggest that Jōdo Shinshū is an unlikely candidate for leading Buddhism to a deeper appreciation of social ethics. For instance, Shinran's doctrine of faith as total reliance on "Other-power" (*tariki*) seemingly presents us with a very pessimistic religious anthropology leading to antinomianism and the loss of any motivation for ethical behavior. If a human being is helplessly steeped in sin and ascetic practices are unavailing, indeed, if sin is inevitable and salvation is completely unmerited, then ethical striving as well must be consigned to the realm of faithless "self-power" (*jiriki*). This situation is exacerbated by Shinran's own idealization of the evil person as favored by Amida for salvation and the ensuing controversy over "licensed evil."[17]

Similar problems have been raised from the perspective of the sociology of religion. In his now classic work, *Tokugawa Religion*, Robert Bellah associates Jōdo Shinshū with the disenchantment (Weber's term) of Japan's sacred cosmos.[18] During the Heian period, Buddhism in Japan was ensconced within a magico-religious culture where the sacred was diffused throughout the social world and permeated cultural values and everyday activities. With the modernization of Japanese culture during the Tokugawa period, the sacred was increasingly rationalized into a wholly transcendent,

55

otherworldly reality experienced by the individual as grace. An important aspect of this rationalization was the privatization of religion. Here again, Jōdo Shinshū's contribution was noteworthy. Bellah offers as an example Rennyo's distinction between "outer obedience" to civil authority and "inner obedience" to Amida.[19] In releasing the believer from "diligence" (*shōjin*), the true sign of saving faith came to be "peace of mind" (*anjin*). Prophetic outrage over injustice leading to a religiously motivated struggle for social transformation would seem to be no more than Buddhist variety of works righteousness.

These interpretations of Jōdo Shinshū, however, are misleading. Jōdo Shinshū has in fact had a liberating role in the history of Japan. For instance, in its early development, Jōdo Shinshū found itself in conflict with Shinto groups as well as with some of the established schools of Buddhism for its criticism of astrology and divination practices performed for the purpose of attaining worldly benefits. But even more important to the issue of social ethics is Shinran's vision of Jōdo Shinshū as a "religion of the ordinary sinner" (*bombu*). Herein lies one of the great contributions of Buddhism to Japanese culture. According to Shinran, the saint and the sinner, the clergy and the laity, the sovereign and the slave are equally sinful, equally helpless in their attempts to bring about their own salvation and thus equal in their need for grace. The doctrine of the *bombu* has served as a basis for a critique not only of religious meritocracy but also social hierarchy. This latter observation is borne out by noting the appeal of Jōdo Shinshū to peasants trying to establish their independence from the feudal aristocracy and the old estate system. The historical role this aspect of Jōdo Shinshū teaching has played in mounting a critique of Japanese society needs to be better appreciated.[20]

These points notwithstanding, Jōdo Shinshū shares with Buddhism more generally a neglect of the social dimension of the Dharma. What follows are some probings from a Christian perspective which are offered in the hope of stimulating conversation not only between Christians and Jōdo Shinshū believers, but perhaps even more importantly, among Jōdo Shinshū believers themselves in the hope of better identifying and articulating Jōdo Shinshū's potential for providing a foundation for genuinely Buddhist social ethics. As will become clear below, this process has already begun within Jōdo Shinshū, quite apart from any overt prompting from Christians. In the reflections that follow, perhaps Jōdo Shinshū believers will find some stimulus for the continued development of their own tradition.

SOME PROBINGS

In exploring the social implications of their own religious tradition, Jōdo Shinshū believers may wish to reflect on Christianity's need to develop a demythologizing hermeneutics. As mentioned above, one of the major legacies of the European Enlightenment for Christianity has been what Max Weber called the "disenchantment" of the medieval world. The Enlightenment's intolerance for mystifications forms the basis of modernity's critique of traditional Christian belief. Traditional Christian doctrinal statements, more than simply being wrong, are rendered meaningless with the decline of the mythological cosmos in which they were first articulated. One Christian theological response to this challenge has been to make Christian religious symbols and doctrines more intelligible and acceptable to the modern world by means of a twofold movement of demythologization and existential reinterpretation. This strategy was primarily apologetic in its intent. By reinterpreting itself, Christianity would be able to defend itself against its secular critics. The biblical exegesis of Rudolf Bultmann is the foremost example of this theological strategy.[21]

Christian thinking, however, has gone beyond Bultmann's apologetic concerns in ways that may be significant to Jōdo Shinshū. Today, many Christian theologians go beyond Bultmann in maintaining that a demythologized and existentially reinterpreted Christianity can form the basis for a religiously grounded critique of the modern world, including its social, political and economic structures. For these theologians, demythologizing hermeneutics does not lead to an accommodation of the tradition to modern society, but rather a critique of it. This group of post-Bultmannian theologians include theologians who have chosen an explicitly "revisionist" or "correlationist" theological method (such as Langdon Gilkey and David Tracy) as well as those who incorporate a Marxist or feminist hermeneutics of suspicion into their theological criticism of both traditional Christianity and society (such as Latin American liberationist theologians and North American feminist theologians).

Jōdo Shinshū scholars are familiar with the process of demythologizing their premodern texts. However, somewhat parallel to Christianity, the apologetic potential of a demythologizing hermeneutics for rendering the Jōdo Shinshū tradition more palatable to modern society has been recognized first. A fine example of an apologetic use of demythologizing hermeneutics by a Jōdo Shinshū scholar is the work of Takeuchi Yoshinori, who not incidentally was a colleague of Bultmann at Marburg for a brief period.[22]

Will Jōdo Shinshū scholars also recognize the potential of this method for mounting a religiously founded critique of society as has been the experience of their Christian colleagues? Perhaps the foundation stones for a Buddhist critique of society from the Jōdo Shinshū perspective have already been laid. In the Meiji period, for example, Kiyozawa Manshi (1863-1903) objected to the tendency in Jōdo Shinshū to think of rebirth in the Pure Land as an event after death. According to Kiyozawa, one of the major inadequacies of this view of salvation was that it rendered Jōdo Shinshū an otherworldly religion. As such, Jōdo Shinshū was incapable of mounting a criticism of State Shinto as an officially sanctioned religion.[23] In the Taishō period, there is the work of Nonomura Naotarō. In a book entitled, *A Critique of Jōdo Teaching*,[24] Nonomura wrote that "Rebirth in Amida's Pure Land in the West" is an Indian myth which Shinran chose as a verbal symbol to convey the religious truth of the transformation of the individual gripped by self-attachment. In order

JŌDO SHINSHŪ'S MISSION TO HISTORY

to recover the essence of Shinran's religious genius as well as its practical import, the mythological elements of this religious symbol need to be translated into more existentially meaningful categories. Although Nonomura's efforts in this regard were eventually rejected by the Jōdo Shinshū mainstream, perhaps his program for demythologizing Jōdo Shinshū doctrine merits a more sympathetic reading today. Nonomura's views have found at least one supporter in Futaba Kenkō, who suggests that we go beyond Nonomura's concern for the existential meaning of salvation to the individual in order to appreciate more deeply Jōdo Shinshū's "mission to history."[25] In this way, according to Futaba, the Jōdo Shinshū community might discover within its own tradition a basis for moving beyond Buddhism as "protector of the state" and take on a more critical role vis-a-vis the "ego-centered power of the state."

In addition to reflecting on Christianity's use of demythologizing hermeneutics, Jōdo Shinshū practitioners in dialogue with Christians may wish to reflect on the peculiar character of Christian eschatology. One important factor in the renewal of Christian social activism has been a recognition of the need to revise Christian understanding of the "Kingdom of God" in the preaching of Jesus of Nazareth. For much of its history, Christians have tended to think of the Kingdom of God either as an otherworldly event coming at the end of time, or more triumphantly as a reality present here and now in this world in the institutional form of the church.

New Testament exegesis in the twentieth century has restored a greater sense of this doctrine's complexity. In the preaching of Jesus, the Kingdom of God is neither a future expectation purely and simply nor a reality unambiguously present here and now. God's Kingdom is, in the words of Hans Küng, "already, but not yet." Implied, therefore, in the preaching of Jesus is a tension between a fully "realized" eschatology (the "already") and a "futurist" eschatology (the "not yet").[26] The tension between realized and futurist eschatologies is not resolved by assigning them to two different periods in the preaching of Jesus. The tension is rooted in the character of Christian eschatological hope itself. For this reason, to lose the tension by focusing either on the "already" or the "not yet" to the exclusion of the other is to lose the truth proclaimed by the symbol. Neither otherworldliness nor triumphalism are acceptable alternatives to the tension implied in the Christian practice of "waiting in joyful hope for the coming of the Kingdom of God."[27]

The restoration by the exegetes of the tensive eschatology implicit in the "Kingdom of God" doctrine has helped Christians to reflect more deeply on the religious foundations for their social ethics. Traditional Christianity's tendency to think about the Kingdom of God as an exclusively future event at the end of time has tended to promote a religious passivity and otherworldliness which is content to ignore the injustices of this world in favor of the "eternal." At the same time, an exclusively "realized" eschatology seems to have the same stultifying effect on social awareness. This is detectable in theological attempts simply to equate the institutional church with the Kingdom of God. In this case, the demand for concrete historical *praxis* for the building up of the Kingdom is obscured by a self-satisfied, triumphalist view of the church which remains oblivious to social injustices. By maintaining the tension between realized and futurist eschatologies, the Kingdom of God is experienced as both gift (the "already") and as historical mission (the "not yet"). In this way, Christian social ethics hopes to remain politically committed to concrete historical *praxis* in building up the Kingdom without thereby losing sight of its sheer gratuity and the danger of equating temporal structures (including ecclesial structures) with God's final will.

An exclusively "futurist" eschatology has figured prominently in the Jōdo Shinshū understanding of salvation with a similarly stultifying effect on its ability to mount a religious critique of social structures. Rebirth in the Pure Land (ōsō) came to be commonly understood as a soteriological event occurring after the death of the believer. According to Futaba Kenkō, this has led to three consequences: (1) the Pure Land has come to be understood as a realm that lies totally beyond history and its social vicissitudes, (2) rebirth in the Pure Land has come to be understood merely as an escape from this world of suffering, and (3) faith in the Vow of the Amida has come to be understood as the patience to endure hardship in this world until deliverance after death. Futaba calls this phenomenon the "burial of Shinran."[28]

Most important for our present inquiry are Futaba's views of why this otherworldliness is inadequate for a contemporary understanding of Jōdo Shinshū faith. In Futaba's view, when the reality of rebirth in the Pure Land is restricted to the afterlife, the this-worldly and historical meaning of Jōdo Shinshū faith is thereby obscured. By "burying Shinran" in the afterlife, the world transforming power of faith is neutralized along with the import of Shinran's teaching for social ethics. In this way, according to Futaba, the Jōdo Shinshū movement was rendered subservient to the priorities of the prevailing social order.[29]

In interreligious dialogues, Christians might pose the following question to Jōdo Shinshū practitioners. Can Jōdo Shinshū envisage a "tensive" eschatology analogous to the structure of eschatological hope Christians have in the Kingdom of God? Can rebirth in the Pure Land be simultaneously "already but not yet"? If ōsō is not simply an event that occurs after death, might gensō (the return to this world in compassion) be interpreted in terms of historical *praxis* within the world? Must ōsō and gensō be understood as temporally sequential? Can their relationship rather be understood as two aspects of one religious action? Hajime Tanabe clearly was moving in this direction in his revisionist reflections of Shinran's *Kyōgyōshinshō*.[30] In *Philosophy as Metanoetics*,[31] Tanabe argued that in order for Jōdo Shinshū's notion of faith in "Other-power" to be reconciled fully with the Mahayana Buddhist notion of nothingness (*mu*), a doctrine of mediation (*baikai*) is required. "Other-power" is present and efficacious only mediately in "self-power" even as "self-power" is thoroughly transformed by "Other-power." At the very least, more of an appreciation of their non-dualism and simultaneity may lead, as has Christian reflection on the "already but not yet" character of

Christian eschatological hope, to increased appreciation for the religious meaning of an activist ethics in this world rooted in the Jōdo Shinshū vision of Buddhism.

If Jōdo Shinshū can understand itself along lines analogous to what Christianity recognizes as "eschatologies in tension," then the doctrine of "building the Pure Land" (*shōgon jōdo*) would be a likely candidate for a revisionist interpretation. Must "building the Pure Land" be understood solely as the act of Amida Buddha even to the extent that the doctrine renders human action in the world (and thus human ethics) superfluous and meaningless? Perhaps the Christian doctrine of the Kingdom of God as both "sheer gift" and "mission to history" will illuminate this problem for Jōdo Shinshū believers. The foundations of a Jōdo Shinshū social ethics, however, will be Buddhist, not Christian. Thus Tanabe's revisionist approach to Shinran should be reexamined.

Religions live, not merely by serving as "sacred canopies"[32] for the societies in which they find themselves, but also as cultural forces which shape those societies. Buddhism is no exception to this rule. The Dharma holds within itself the potential to call into question the legitimacy of social structures and shape the historical course of societies compassionately and skillfully for the benefit of the common good. In its social ethics, I predict that Buddhism will distinguish itself from Christianity. Engaged Buddhism and activist Christianity arise from religious visions that differ significantly. These differences should not be lamented. By developing its social ethics more explicitly and practicing that social ethics skillfully, Buddhists have an opportunity to show great compassion toward their Christian neighbors. This is because Christians have much to learn from Buddhists who are socially engaged. The encounter between engaged Buddhists and politically active Christians will not leave Christianity untouched. Christians will be enriched by the opportunity to reflect on their own tradition in light of an innately Buddhist approach to social ethics. In this respect, a revised understanding of Jōdo Shinshū may have much to contribute to the conversation.

NOTES

1. John Cobb, *Beyond Dialogue: Toward the Mutual Transformation of Christianity and Buddhism* (Philadelphia: Fortress Press, 1982).

2. The "theology of liberation" has, of course, produced a substantial body of literature to date. For Gutierrez, see *The Theology of Liberation* (Maryknoll, N.Y.: Orbis, 1973). For Segundo, see *The Liberation of Theology* (Maryknoll, N.Y.: Orbis, 1976). For Boff, see *Church: Charism and Power* (New York: Crossroad, 1985).

3. Gordon Kaufman, *Theology for a Nuclear Age* (Philadelphia: Westminster, 1985).

4. One obvious exception in Japan is Nichiren Buddhism and its various offshoots. In India, an exception would be the reign of Emperor Aśoka. For a careful examination of early Buddhist literature regarding the relation between the early Samgha and Indian society, see Uma Chakravarti, *The Social Dimensions of Early Buddhism* (Delhi: Oxford University Press, 1987).

5. For an interpretation of early Buddhism as both empirical and psychological, see David Kalupahana, *Buddhist Philosophy: A Historical Analysis* (Honolulu: University of Hawai'i Press, 1976).

6. For a very detailed account of the psychological approach to Abhidharma scholasticism, see Christopher Key Chapple, "Abhidharma as Paradigm for Practice," in *Pali Buddhism*, Frank Hoffman and Deegalle Mahinda eds. (London: Curzon Press, 1996), 79–99.

7. For a discussion of this religious adaptation to culture, see Joseph M. Kitagawa, "Paradigm Shifts in Buddhism," in *On Understanding Japanese Religion* (Princeton, N.J.: Princeton University Press, 1987), 250–270.

8. Ken Jones, *The Social Face of Buddhism: An Approach to Political and Social Activism* (London: Wisdom Publications, 1989).

9. For discussions of Buddhism's response to the human rights approach to social action, see Damien Keown, "Are There 'Human Rights' in Buddhism," and Kenneth Inada, "A Buddhist Response to the Nature of Human Rights," available on-line in *The Journal of*

Buddhist Ethics, http://jbe.la.psu.edu.

10. The doctrine of the non-self, especially, has made the affirmation of inalienable human rights a difficulty for Buddhism, at least a theoretical difficulty. Commenting on these difficulties, Robert Traer writes,

> Thus Buddhists do affirm human rights as central to their understanding of the Dharma and the living out of the Buddhist precepts. Despite the conceptual difficulties of justifying human rights as central to Buddhist faith, at least some Buddhists find human rights language expressive of their religious commitment to the Three Refuges: the Buddha, the Dharma, and the Sangha.

See, Robert Traer, "Buddhist Affirmations of Human Rights," *Buddhist-Christian Studies* 8 (1988): 17.

11. The most comprehensive discussion of this movement in English is found in Robert Bobilin, *Revolution from Below: Buddhist and Christian Movements for Justice in Asia, Four Case Studies from Thailand and Sri Lanka* (Lanham, Md.: University Press of America, 1988), 21–48.

12. For another doctrinal analysis supportive of this conclusion, see Winston King, "Buddhist Self-World Theory and Buddhist Ethics," in *The Eastern Buddhist,* n.s. 22, no. 2 (Autumn 1989): 14–26. King's conclusion is that, "The Buddhist mandate is not to 'save' the world by 'reforming' it but to enable the individual 'self' to overcome it from within—for the world order is fundamentally unsaveable." (p. 26).

13. 1991 marks the one hundredth anniversary of *Rerum Novarum,* the first of a series of papal encyclicals having to do with the moral implications of social issues.

14. On the notion of prophetic oracle as a critique of sacred cosmos, see Paul Ricoeur, "Manifestation and Proclamation," *Journal of the Blaisdell Institute* 12 (Winter, 1978): 13–35.

15. On the eschatological meaning of Christian hope, see Jurgen Moltman, *The Theology of Hope* (New York: Harper and Row, 1967).

16. For a discussion of the potential of Marxist analysis for helping in

a retrieval of the biblical roots of Christian eschatological hope, see José Porfirio Miranda, *Marx and the Bible* (Maryknoll, N.Y.: Orbis, 1974).

17. For a discussion of the "licensed evil" controversy during Shinran's life, see James Dobbins, *Jōdo Shinshū* (Bloomington, Ind.: Indiana University Press, 1989), 47–62. Neither is this problem unique to Pure Land Buddhism. The charge of antinomianism was similarly leveled against Martin Luther's doctrine of grace which itself, like Shinran's teaching on *tariki*, was intended as a criticism of moribund religious doctrines, practices and institutions. On the problem of antinomianism in Luther and Shinran, see Fritz Buri, "The Concept of Grace in Paul, Shinran and Luther," *The Eastern Buddhist*, n.s. 12, no. 2 (1976): 21–42.

18. Robert Bellah, *Tokugawa Religion, the Values of Pre-Industrial Japan* (Glencoe, Ill.: Freepress, 1957).

19. He does this as part of a discussion of Jōdo Shinshū's appeal to the great Ōmi merchants such as the Matsui. See Bellah, 117–126.

20. Dobbins' work is suggestive. See Dobbins, 16, 19, and 63.

21. An English translation of Bultmann's famous programmatic essay "Neues Testament und Mythologie" is available in *Kerygma and Myth*, H.W. Bartsch ed. (New York: Haper and Row, 1961), 1–44.

22. Takeuchi Yoshinori's demythologizing approach to Buddhism in general is readily apparent in his *The Heart of Buddhism* (New York: Crossroad, 1983) as well as in the essay, "Buddhism and Existentialism: the Dialogue between Oriental and Occidental Thought" in *Religion and Culture, Essays in Honor of Paul Tillich* (New York: Harper and Brothers, 1959), 291–318. See also his *Probleme der Versenkung im Ur-buddhismus* (Leiden: Brill, 1972). For works dealing specifically with Jōdo Shinshū thought, see his *Shinran to gendai* (Tokyo: Chūōkōronsha, 1974), and *Kyōgyōshinshō no tetsugaku* [Gendai Bukkyō meishō zenshū 6] (Tokyo: Ryūbunkan, 1965).

23. Kenko Futaba "Shinran and Human Dignity: Opening an Historical Horizon," *The Pacific World*, n.s. 4 (Fall 1988): 53. For Kiyozawa Manshi, *December Fan: the Buddhist Essays of Manshi Kiyozawa*, Nobuo Haneda, trans. (Kyoto: Higashi Honganji, 1984); *Kiyozawa bunshū* (Tokyo: Iwnami shoten, 1928 and 1935); *Selected Essays of*

Manshi Kiyozawa, Kunji Tajima and Floyd Shacklock, trans. (Kyoto: The Bukkyō to Bunka Society, 1936); and the essay "My Faith," in Haya Akegarasu, ed., *Selections from the Nippon Seishin Library* (Kitayasuda, Ishikawaken: Kōsōsha, 1936).

24. Nonomura Naotarō, *Jōdokyō hihan* (Kyoto: Chūgai shuppan, 1924). See also his *Shūkyō to rinri* (Tokyo: Heigo shuppansha, 1909).

25. Futaba, 53.

26. Hans Küng, *The Church* (New York: Sheed and Ward, 1967), 59–70. Küng's views are shared by a wide range of New Testament exegetes. See also John Donahue, S.J., "Biblical Perspective on Justice," in *The Faith That Does Justice,* John Haughey, ed. (New York: Paulist, 1977), 86–92; Norman Perrin, *The Kingdom of God in the Teaching of Jesus* (London: SCM Press, 1963), 74–78 and 81–87.

27. This phrase is taken from the Roman Catholic Mass.

28. Futaba, 51-59. Futaba tends to blame these developments on Rennyo. I will leave it to scholars far better versed in the development of Jōdo Shinshū doctrine than I to adjudicate this issue.

29. Futaba, 53.

30. Hajime Tanabe, *Philosophy as Metanoetics,* Takeuchi Yoshinori trans. (Berkeley: University of California Press, 1986), 211–220. Tanabe's approach to the Jōdo Shinshū doctrine of rebirth was seminal in the development of his ethically and socially oriented criticism of the philosophy of Kitarō Nishida. Tanabe's reading of Shinran, however, is by no means mainstream. For an evaluation critical of Tanabe's use of Shinran, see Yoshifumi Ueda, "Tanabe's Metanoetics and Shinran's Thought." For a more positive evaluation, see Taitetsu Unno, "Shin Buddhism and Metanoetics." Both of these essays have been collected in *The Religious Philosophy of Tanabe Hajime,* Taitetsu Unno and James Heisig eds. (Berkeley: Asian Humanities Press, 1990), 134–149 and 117–133 respectively.

31. Tanabe Hajime, *Philosophy as Metanoetics,* 6–9, 17–19, 152ff, passim.

32. Peter Berger, *The Sacred Canopy, Elements of a Sociological Theory of Religion* (Garden City, N.Y.: Anchor Books, 1969).

Shin Buddhist Social Thought in Modern Japan

Mark T. Unno

If the present unfolds at the juncture of the past and future, then present reflection on future possibilities must take into consideration the past. As the Confucian adage states, "Rekindle the old to know the new."[1] In commemoration of the career of Dr. Alfred Bloom, who has contributed much to our understanding of Shin Buddhism and continues to do so as both a scholar and a practitioner, it may serve us well to examine some of the past legacy of tradition as it evolved through recent history. In keeping with the theme of this volume, this essay analyzes the interaction of Shin Buddhist thought with society. Beginning with some background from the late-nineteenth to the mid-twentieth centuries, attention is brought to bear on the interaction of modern Shin thought and socialist currents. This is followed by an examination of the work of Suekawa Hiroshi, a modern Shin Buddhist who was a legal scholar and university administrator, democratic in his social and political thought but also influenced by socialist thinking. The relation between thinker, ideology, and society is particularly important for our understanding, since the significance of a thinker lies not only in his ideas but in his actions as they are manifest in society.

SHIN BUDDHIST THOUGHT FROM THE LATE-NINETEENTH TO THE MID-TWENTIETH CENTURIES

Throughout the history of Shin Buddhism, there has been a complex interrelationship between the social concerns of this world and the spiritual concerns of the next, the Pure Land. The Japanese Buddhist term *shinzoku nitai* has signified as much the sociopolitical relationship between state and religion as it has the soteriological relation between mundane and highest truths for which the compound was originally used in translation. While this relationship evolved largely within Japan from the medieval period until the modern, there was an influx of new influences beginning with the Meiji that enriched the mix of ideas and people, ideology and society.

At one end of the spectrum, there were defenders of tradition, such as Shimaji Mokurai, who were instrumental not only in protecting the interests of Honganji but also in rallying many Buddhist institutions in the face of the *haibutsu kishaku*, what he and others saw as the persecution of Buddhism carried out under the name of the separation of church and state, *seikyō bunri*.[2] At the other end, there were self-identified communist revolutionaries who rejected both traditional religious institutions and the established government.

Those who worked with the state to preserve Buddhist institutions sometimes became so closely identified with both that the language of religious faith might have been conflated with that of loyalty to the state. For others whose views were unacceptable to either state or religious institutions, Shin Buddhism provided a venue to subvert them. Hayashida Shigeo, for example, states,

> My six years in prison proved to be a great plus, if only because I discovered Shinran. Of course there are many other communists who studied Shinran in jail and came out in praise of the *nembutsu* . . . . The reason I'm writing about Buddhism is that . . . if only Shinran's spirit were properly harnessed, it could become a major force in rescuing Japan from its current [postwar] crisis.[3]

Between the conservative and the revolutionary poles, there was a wide spectrum of figures who appropriated Shin Buddhist thought to engage society from various perspectives.

There were those, for example, who focused on psychology and psychiatry as the interface between inner, individual life and external society. Kozawa Heisaku, who studied with Freud in Europe, was a founding figure of Japanese psychiatry who incorporated Pure Land thought into Japanese psychoanalysis; coming from a Shin Buddhist background, he replaced the Oedipus complex with what he called the Ajase complex, based on the story of the Indian Prince Ajatasatru who plotted against his father and mother.[4] Kishimoto Ken'ichi, another Shin Buddhist psychiatrist who was institutionally and clinically influential, taught in the School of Medicine at Nagoya University and advocated what he called Self-awakening Psychotherapy.[5] A psychotherapeutic movement that has retained its ties to Shin Buddhist temples is Naikan therapy which involves a kind of confessional introspection.[6]

Shin Buddhist thought has also influenced art and literature. Yanagi Sōetsu, a leader of the folk arts movement, or *mingei undō*, drew on the Shin Buddhist discourse of the commoner as inspiration for his art and writing.[7] Likewise, the work of such poets as Asahara Saichi and Enomoto Ei'ichi has drawn interest beyond Shin Buddhist circles.

Within the Shin Buddhist organization of Higashi Honganji, intellectuals such as Kiyozawa Manshi, Soga Ryōjin, and Kaneko Daiei introduced doctrinal innovations and worked for institutional reform; all three were at various times rejected and ostracized as well as admired and respected.[8]

During the Meiji period, the confrontations between church and state mentioned above not only led to the consolidation of institutional power but also helped to effect the liberation of *kakure nembutsu* adherents—hidden, outlawed, and persecuted nembutsu practitioners living in various parts of Japan.[9]

The foregoing represents just a sampling of the many directions taken by Shin Buddhists in modernity. As diverse as they were, the majority of these figures shared in the fact that they were influenced by Western ideas and culture. In that sense, modern Shin Buddhist thought turned out to be as much a synthesis of Japanese and Western elements as it was the renewal and reform of tradition from within. Among those who engaged social concerns most explicitly and self-consciously, there were many who drew on Marxist and socialist thought. Yamaori Tetsuo goes so far as to suggest that socialist critique provided the only vital means of examining the historical context of modern Japanese society:

> Shinran's philosophy of metanoia emerged with force onto the socio-historical stage for the first time in unison with socialist thought. The socialist critique would be virtually the only effective means of historical self-examination for the processes set into motion in the Meiji Restoration. Through its encounters with Shinran this critique opened the way for . . . the social application of a metanoic ethos.[10]

Although Yamaori may be overstating the case, it is true that many thinkers turned to Shin thought for perspectives on socio-historical concerns. The account of modern Shin Buddhist thought and its synthesis with socialism that follows is based on Yamaori's work.[11]

MODERN SHIN BUDDHIST THOUGHT AND SOCIALISM

Although by no means socialist in their orientation, such Shin Buddhists as Chikazumi Jōkan (1870–1941) and Kiyozawa Manshi (1863–1903) introduced social consciousness into their interpretations of faith in a way that departed from previous understandings. The relation between the individual's inner life, society, and Amida Buddha as transcendent reality formed a new constellation of ideas that emerged in the aftermath of the *haibutsu kishaku* and through the influences of Christianity and Western philosophy. This can be seen clearly in Kiyozawa's *Skeleton for a Philosophy of Religion* (*Shūkyō tetsugaku gaikotsu*)[12] as well as later works and more indirectly in Chikazumi whose three years in Europe had a subtle but significant effect. This new consciousness was marked by the emergence of individual autonomy over against institutional authority, a dialectic that had a well-established genealogy in the West but which in Japan had for the most part been idiosyncratic at best. Where previously individuals such as Hōnen, Ikkyū, and Hakuin had simply parted ways with dominant institutional structures or introduced reforms without wholly negating existing forms, Kiyozawa sought to displace entirely what he had come to perceive as an outdated feudal system with a revolutionary new movement, *seishinshugi* (spiritualism). While his attempts at revolutionary reform turned out to be less than successful at the institutional level, his ideas and personality continue to exert their force even today.

The influence of a Christianity dialectically informed by socialism upon Shin Buddhist thought became clear in the work of such writers as Kinoshita Naoe (1869–1937). Kinoshita became disgusted with Buddhism even as a young boy when he learned about corrupt monks and institutions in his elementary history texts. Thus, he turned to Christianity and then to socialism, but through this circuitous route he returned to Buddhism and especially to Shinran where he found what he believed was a socially conscientious Buddhist voice.

Although he publicly severed his ties with the socialist movement in 1907 with the publication of his work *Zange* (Repentance), socialism continued to influence his thinking, and in 1911 all of his works up to that point were outlawed in the wake of the *Daigyaku jiken* (Great Treason Incident) in which dozens of intellectuals were convicted and some even executed for socialist and anarchist activities. As is widely known, the Japanese government suppressed and persecuted leftist movements and intellectuals from the second decade of the twentieth century onward as they were perceived to pose a threat to its capitalistic and militaristic aims. Increasing pressure was placed on intellectuals to curtail all activities related to socialism and communism.

In 1912 Kinoshita published *Hōnen to Shinran,* in which he synthesized Christian, socialist, and Shin Buddhist ideas to paint a portrait of the two Pure Land masters as leaders of a resistance movement against the ruling class, as the voices of freedom working on behalf of the oppressed.

Another writer who became involved in socialism was Kamei Katsuichirō (1906–1966). A student in the Department of Art at Kyoto Imperial University and a new member of the communist party, he was arrested along with other communists throughout Japan in 1929 for disturbing the peace. Stricken with a liberal conscience because he lamented his privileged upbringing, he wrote that his three-and-a-half years in prison were like a vacation bestowed upon him which freed him from his guilty liberal conscience. On the one hand, reading Marx's critique of Hegel's philosophy of right (*Kritik des Hegelschen Staatsrechts*)[13] deeply influenced his turn towards Marxism; on the other hand, his preoccupation with Greek and Renaissance art shaped his aesthetic views and lent a romantic air to his socialism. He gradually moved away from Marxism after he was released from prison in 1930 with a secret agreement that he would never engage in antigovernmental activities again.

His encounter with Shin Buddhism began around 1940, and in the next four years he published two works that reflected this new influence, *Shinkō ni tsuite* (On the Question of Faith) and *Shinran*. As intellectuals found themselves caught between their search for personal integrity and the nationalist agenda of the government, Kamei also experienced the tension between his newfound faith and the political situation. For him, Shinran provided an answer, one in which the foolish being was made to see his own blind passions but was thereby saved by Amida; the need for outward action is conspicuous by its absence in his reading of Shinran. Of Amida's compassion he wrote,

> It is the continuity of Buddha-nature in the face of the discontinuity of human love. It is the eye that lovingly scrutinizes the individual human being for eternity . . . .To respond to

this eternal scrutiny is to submit to the struggles of the foolish being filled with blind passion; it is also to abide in the joy of the Dharma—the struggle of being scrutinized and the consequent experience of gratitude.[14]

While the work of such figures as Kiyozawa, Kinoshita, and Kamei contained ambiguities in thought as well as in action, we see therein not only the intersection and interaction between Shin Buddhist thought, Western ideas, and society, but individuals who committed themselves to their ideals sufficiently to endure persecution, imprisonment, and ostracism. Yet, whatever considerations they gave to questions of society and religion, their ideas were articulated largely within a framework that did not question the role of Japan within world history. This is partly attributable to their status as pioneers and partly also to the exigencies of circumstance. Before 1868, Japanese intellectuals were largely ignorant of the linear and dialectical conceptions of history that were integral to the very notion of world history as found in much of modern discourse. Thus, they were also unaware of the problems inherent in appropriating such conceptions uncritically.[15]

It is with the philosophers of the so-called Kyoto school that the question of Japan's place within world history was first addressed on a large scale. Tanabe Hajime (1885–1962) and Miki Kiyoshi (1897–1945) were two of the most prominent thinkers tied to this school who appropriated to one degree or another Shin Buddhist thought as well as socialist and Marxist-Leninist discourse. In addition, there were others who were closely affiliated, such as Tosaka Jun (1900–1945), who infused Marxist vocabulary into the current philosophical debates.

The majority of Kyoto school thinkers have been criticized by other Japanese intellectuals ever since the Pacific War of colluding with the government in its imperialistic agenda. In the West, this debate has only recently been taken up by scholars studying the philosophy of the Kyoto school, culminating in the anthology of articles,

Rude Awakenings.[16] A full treatment of the question of complicity in wartime ideology is beyond the scope of the present essay. For now, suffice it to say that a simplistic answer in favor of either condoning or condemning probably fails to take into account the complexity of the issues involved and the ambiguities of political discourse. As James Heisig states,

> There is of course no way to inoculate oneself against the criticisms of the age. And even if there were, the very thought of trimming one's thinking to such a measure offends the very spirit of philosophical inquiry and forecloses the possibility of ideas coming to birth posthumously. To allow our judgment of [Tanabe's] ideas to be dominated by the fate they met in postwar Japan is no less an error than to uproot them from their native soil [and socio-historical context].[17]

What will be sufficient for our purposes is to simply note that the question of Japan's place within world history became a problem of religious as well as political consciousness for the likes of Tanabe and Miki. Tanabe's most dramatic confession of the tension between his spiritual life and political consciousness comes at the beginning of his *Zangedō to shite no tetsugaku* (Philosophy as Metanoetics), written in 1944:

> On the one hand, I was haunted by the thought that as a student of philosophy I ought... to be addressing the government frankly with regard to its policies ... even if this should incur the displeasure of those currently in power .... On the other hand, there seemed something traitorous about expressing in time of war ideas that, while perfectly proper in time of peace might end up causing divisions and conflicts among our people that would only further expose them to their enemies ....
>
> At that moment, something astonishing happened. In the midst of my distress I let go and surrendered myself humbly to my own inability .... My penitent confession—metanoesis

(*zange*)—unexpectedly threw me back on my own interiority and away from things external.[18]

What he encountered in his own interiority was what he came to call the mediation of absolute nothingness, a term reflecting his appropriation of Amida Buddha as Other-power. So far, this movement towards interiority strongly resembles Kamei's inward turn cited earlier. But as Yamaori notes, the sense of repentance which is central to Tanabe's work is absent in Kamei; this is also not unrelated to the fact that there is a social, political, ethical, and religious movement back to the external world in Tanabe's discourse that is absent in Kamei.[19] Tanabe, drawing on a Shin Buddhism informed by socialism, eventually called for the Japanese people as a whole to repent their wartime aggression and to rebuild Japanese society based on religious principles.

Yet, as various scholars contributing to the discussion in *Rude Awakenings* suggest, it is unclear as to just how sincere, realistic, and thoroughgoing Tanabe's sociopolitical consciousness was. In the end, Tanabe himself did not take much outward action to embody his political philosophy, and his abstruse, philosophical call for repentance had little effect on either the government or the people of Japan. As Heisig states, these consequences, or lack thereof, do not by themselves invalidate Tanabe's efforts. Perhaps what we see in Tanabe is just how difficult it is to bridge the gap between the inner and the outer. Whether he took a stance to the left or the right, multiple factions criticized him for being, alternately, too conservative or not conservative enough, too Marxist or not Marxist enough.

Tanabe was a disciple of the well-known philosopher Nishida Kitarō (1870–1945), the putative founder of the Kyoto school, but Tanabe parted ways with Nishida's Zen-centered approach to philosophy and turned towards Pure Land ideas. Similarly, Miki Kiyoshi, another disciple of Nishida, also left the fold and moved towards the Pure Land thought of Shinran, with a more direct appropriation of Marxist thought than Tanabe.

Although Miki himself disavowed the Marxist label, much of his life was nevertheless framed within actions that were closely associated with Marxists, socialists, and communists. In May of 1930, while he was on the faculty of Hōsei University, Miki was arrested and taken to Toyotama Prison where he was incarcerated for six months for aiding and abetting communists. In a series of informal expositions that he wrote at the time, he explained that he was not a Marxist and in fact saw himself as basically religious. Yet, he continued to be associated with communists and Marxists throughout his career, as he found in their statements and actions views that resonated with his own critical historical sense that Japan was heading in an errant, capitalistic, and imperialistic direction. This critical view of history was heavily informed by his reading of Shinran, and his life came to a close embodying this synthesis of Shin Buddhist thought and Marxist-oriented critique; he died in Toyotama Prison leaving his final manuscript *Shinran* to be published posthumously by his friends and students.

Through his modernist eyes, Miki saw in twentieth-century Japan a significant parallel with Shinran's Kamakura period. A time of political and spiritual crisis brought out the true character of a time in which the contradictions of the material conditions of existence brought into relief the subjective heart of human existence. For Miki the Shōwa and Kamakura periods were alike moments of *mappō*, the final, degenerate age in which blind passions and evil karma ruled the day. Miki, however, did not see *mappō* ideology as an excuse to blame one's troubles on the conditions of the age: "[T]he awakening of the self within the historical moment does not lead to the rationalization of the self by conferring responsibility for one's sins on the age in which one lives."[20] According to this understanding, class oppression and imperialism were the outward material manifestations, but their scrutiny helped to reveal the true subjective reality of the self. He stated,

The historical view of the Three Ages of the Dharma was not

merely a discursive account for Shinran .... More than a merely [objective] critique, it became an opening out onto the profound grief [of the self's true existence]. The unsalvageable present overwhelms one as present actuality ....[21]

The discursive landscape of *mappō* as relative to other periods in history, then, gave way to the eternal reality of the self as one looked deeper within. There, in the depths of the self, it became apparent that karmic evil was pervasive throughout not only recorded history but eternity as the ceaseless condition of existence as such. Only in the awareness of this karmic depth could the light of absolute compassion be discerned.

> Shinran emphasized the historicity of the teachings. One might ask if such a historicism was not also a kind of relativism .... The truth, the true teaching, must be absolute .... The absolute character of the teaching became known through its eternal character .... The teaching of Other-power compassionately leads all beings bound by blind passion and evil karma, regardless of whether they live in the age of the True, Semblance, or Final Dharma .... On the one hand, this teaching is particularly suited to the final age; on the other, it applies universally to all ages .... Within myself, ... history is already manifest as the subjectivity of the *nembutsu*.[22]

As Yamamoto Hiroko suggests, Miki strove for a complex synthesis of material history and spiritual myth.[23] The question arises as to why one should act at all in the matrix of such a synthesis. Whether one sees the relative reality of discursive, material conditions as the manifestation of an eternal spiritual myth, or vice versa—eternal myth made discernable in the reality of the relative present—it seems hopeless to act within a history where all ages are fated to be evil.

Yet, paradoxically, Miki may have been moved to action precisely because of this seeming mutual negation of myth and history. Without responding to the historical present, the eternal myth remains hidden, unrealized; without awakening to the subjective depth of eternity, one cannot be moved to manifest the nembutsu in history. In going into the depths of the self, one becomes aware of one's true interconnectedness with all suffering beings, and this necessarily moves one to compassionate action.

Not everyone, however, was easily convinced by either Miki's logic or his outward actions. One of his most prominent critics was Hattori Shisō, the son of a Shin Buddhist priest turned Marxist. Hattori also saw in Shinran the forebear of modern Marxism, and he traced a socialist genealogy from the founder of Shin Buddhism through the peasant uprisings of the *ikkō ikki* to postwar Japan. For him, Miki not only failed to realize the materialist promise germinating in Shinran but ended up reducing the dialectical tension of the twofold truth (mundane/highest; social/religious) to a mere idealism.[24] For Hattori, Miki's death in Toyotama Prison was the ignominious end of a failed intellectual, not the courageous self-expression of a true Marxist.

Through his work on Shin Buddhist history, Hattori went on to influence later historians and Buddhologists, but of course, *his* dreams of Marxist revolution did not materialize.

It is beyond the scope of the present essay to judge whether Miki's synthesis of Shinran's thought and Marxism was successful or whether Hattori's critique gave the truer picture. Suffice it to say that Miki, Hattori, and the other figures examined in this section struggled with the constellation of ideology, social reality, and religious life that each confronted within and without. If a common thread can be detected, perhaps it is that their attempts to address issues of classism, imperialism, and other sociopolitical issues with philosophical discourse were simultaneously compelling and disappointing to those around them. One cannot deny the importance of the ideas that were articulated, as well as the impetus to match those ideas against the realities of life. At the same time, it is also difficult to overlook the apparent gaps between the scale of their rhetoric and the social realities that their discourses affected.

SHIN BUDDHIST THOUGHT IN MODERN JAPAN

SUEKAWA HIROSHI

Suekawa Hiroshi (1892–1977) was not a Marxist or a communist. He was a legal scholar, social activist, and Chancellor and President of Ritsumeikan University. His worldview was informed by Shin Buddhism religiously and democratic thinking socially and politically. Nevertheless, he has also been called "the leader of the leftists,"[25] and the force of socialist ideas has left an indelible mark on his thought and actions.

As professor of law at Kyoto University during the war, Suekawa was a leading member of the Society for Social Scientific Research (*Shakai kagaku kenkyūkai* [SKK]), devoted to the study of Marxism, socialism, and communism. In the very midst of mounting governmental pressure for all intellectuals to curtail activities related to socialism and communism, Suekawa published some of the results of his research in *Civil and Labor Law in Soviet Russia* (*Sovieto Roshia no minpō to rōdōhō*) and wrote his doctoral dissertation in 1931 entitled *Theory of Rights Violations* (*Kenri shingai ron*).

In 1933 the Department of Education fired Takigawa Kōshin, Suekawa's colleague in the Faculty of Law and a leading member of the SKK, and demanded that the SKK be disbanded. Protesting the violation of academic freedom, Suekawa and other members of the Faculty of Law as well as graduate students resigned their posts and left Kyoto University. This has come to be known as the Kyoto University Incident (*Kyōdai jiken*). It is worth noting that Suekawa's actions differ from those of other intellectuals at Kyoto University, such as Tanabe Hajime who decided to remain silent about his misgivings concerning the Japanese war involvement and stayed in his post at Kyoto University without speaking out until after the war.

Suekawa's specialization was in civil law with a focus on civil rights. He was also known for his general knowledge of law and was the editor of the seminal *Iwanami roppō zensho* (The Complete Iwanami Edition of the Six Classifications of Law), the first encyclopedia of Japanese law. After the war, he did not return to Kyoto University but went on to become Chancellor and President of Ritsumeikan University, an institution known for its evening degree programs for the working class and for its pacifist orientation.[26]

In 1946 labor unions were legalized in Japan for the first time, and Suekawa became the Director of the Kyoto Prefectural Labor Board (*Kyōto-fu rōdō iinkai kaichō*) of the labor union organization. Later he also became President of the Kyoto Prefectural Korea-Japan Friendship Association, serving as an advocate for Koreans in Japan. In 1948 he became a founding member of the Kyoto Freedom and Human Rights Association (*Kyōto jiyū jinken kyōkai*) and worked as both legal advocate and scholar on behalf of the Burakumin, the outcast class of Japanese society.[27]

Although Suekawa's actions and words were not as revolutionary as some of his contemporaries, it might be argued that by maintaining a democratic stance informed by socialist thinking, he was as or more effective than others who were revolutionary in thought only—armchair Marxists—, or who perished in the heat of their struggles. Certainly, he was not as ideologically Marxist as Hattori Shisō who saw in Shinran a Japanese precursor to Marx. Religiously, Suekawa remained a Shin Buddhist throughout his life while he worked for and helped to effect what he saw as socially responsible legal and sociopolitical reforms as a scholar, social activist, and administrator.

The influence of Shin Buddhism on Suekawa's understanding of society can be seen in at least three ways. First, he worked on behalf of and in unity with those who had been excluded from various rights and privileges. Second, his religious awareness was inseparable from the courage to stand by his convictions. Third, his Shin Buddhist awareness of his limitations as a human being, as a *bombu* (foolish being), contributed to a sense of character perceived by those around him as humble and magnanimous.

On the first of these points, Suekawa wrote, "Whether they were farmers or fishermen, Shinran went into their midst; he reflected on and taught about the way [of life and nembutsu] with them to the end."[28] Of course, the reflection of this thinking in Suekawa's actions is more significant than the articulation of ideas. On the one hand, one might question whether taking the path of scholarly endeavor and becoming a university administrator really represented a means of becoming one with the people. On the other, he may have been able to do more for various people: socioeconomically deprived, Korean, Burakumin and the like, precisely by taking the route that he did.

This leads to the second point, the courage to act with conviction. When, as a young man, he went to college, he did seriously question whether the intellectual pursuits that he was engaged in would lead him to his own peace of mind, to an authentic life. At eighteen, he quit college and returned to his parents' farm, thinking that, like Shinran, the best way would be to live close to the land and among the people.[29] But he decided that, in his case, this would not be the best way for him to contribute to society, and he returned to finish his studies.

For Shinran, who lived in the twelfth and thirteenth centuries, to be one with the people meant to live among the farmers and fishermen even though he had been pardoned from his exile and could return to the urban capital of Kyoto. For Suekawa, living in the urban-centered culture of twentieth-century Japan, to be one with the people meant to leave his birthplace in the countryside and live in the city and work within its social structures. This determination arose from a religious conviction about what it meant to be faithful to oneself. For this reason, he sometimes took actions that might have led to his exclusion from these structures, as when he resigned his academic post in the Kyoto University Incident.

In his role as administrator, he often found himself at difficult junctures of social, political, and personal conscience. In 1968–1969, there were student antiwar protests and demonstrations at Ritsumeikan University just as there were at other institutions in Japan, the United States, and elsewhere. During this time, the police went to Ritsumeikan to arrest the leaders of these demonstrations. At that time, Suekawa and Saeki Chihiro, a member of the Faculty of

Law, had a confrontation with the police. Saeki had been a close colleague of Suekawa ever since the Kyoto University Incident, when both had resigned their posts, and Suekawa had asked Saeki to join him at Ritsumeikan. Saeki spoke out at the time of the confrontation:

> "We will take responsibility for order within this campus.... We administrators and faculty will take care of things, so we don't need you police here. We never asked you to come, and we don't want you to come." Then the police chief said that that was not the agreement. I replied, "Who agreed to have you come? No one here made such an agreement." We ended up arguing heatedly, and I said something to the effect, "We can't stop you if you come in by force, but we didn't ask you to come, and we won't cooperate."[30]

The police did force their way into the campus, and arrests were made. The tension on campus at the time is reflected in the words of Suekawa's secretary, Ōnuma Yōko.[31] She describes the ways in which people had extreme feelings at the time and how these emotions were expressed in letters sent to Suekawa:

> Sometimes, he received letters that stated, "I'll kill you," or "You're not qualified to be an educator." Even animal carcasses arrived in the mail.
> He would read all of these letters and didn't seem to be fazed at all. He soothed my frayed nerves by saying softly, "There are people with all kinds of different ideas in the world."[32]

Suekawa conceived of human beings as both spontaneous expressions of deepest, boundless life and as the creators of their own karmic destiny, as Buddha-nature and karmic nature, as "created and creator," to use a phrase he cited frequently.[33] He saw in Shinran someone who traversed this difficult intersection of two natures, which he saw in himself as well as in others: "I think [Shinran] throughout his life grappled [with these questions]. I don't think he ever reached a point where he felt, 'I'm enlightened, I've found final spiritual repose.'"[34] In his later years, Suekawa is often said to have uttered, "Bandits in the mountains are easy to defeat, but bandits in the heart are difficult to destroy."[35]

Suekawa did not have any easy answers to questions concerning the relationship between ideology, society, and action in the life of the Shin Buddhist intellectual. At the same time, his very unease and continual questioning seemed to be fueled and sustained by a passion for socially conscientious action and spiritual compassion.

CONCLUSION

In this brief foray into modern Shin Buddhist social thought, we have gained but a glimpse into the lives and thoughts of a few individuals whose conceptions of society were influenced by Shin Buddhism. For these figures, ideas of individual autonomy, class consciousness, world history, and ethnicity were fresh challenges that tested the limits of their intellectual, moral, and religious self-understanding. In the postmodern present, further concerns present themselves to Shin Buddhists and to all who take seriously the conditions of postmodern diversity: gender, environment, information technology, and so on.

Unraveling the diverse strands of society, ideology, and action we begin to gain some critical insight into the ways in which a few modern Shin Buddhists faced the issues of their day and their own lives. This essay will have more than fulfilled its purpose if it serves as an occasion for reflecting upon the ways in which each of us weaves together the strands of our own lives. As such, it is perhaps appropriate to offer more questions than a tidy conclusion.

How is the life of the spirit informed and influenced by society in the form of research, institutional practices, and social awareness? What is the balance between ideology, society, and action in the life of the public intellectual? How does the Shin Buddhist examine these questions and offer creative responses based on the legacy of tradition and the conditions of postmodernity?

NOTES

1. Chinese:*Wen ku erh chih hsin* (Japanese: *furuki wo atatamete atarashiki wo shiru*) My translation of this passage is based on a Japanese annotated version of the *Analects* (*Rongo*, Japanese translation and annotation by Kanaya Osamu, Iwanami bunko 202-1 [Tokyo: Iwanami shoten, 1963], 32). Unless otherwise noted, all English translations are mine.

2. For a detailed study of this see James Ketelaar, *Of Heretics And Martyrs In Meiji, Japan: Buddhism And Its Persecution* (Princeton, N.J.: Princeton University Press, 1990).

3. Hayashida Shigeo, *Takumashiki Shinran* (Kyoto: Daihōrinkaku, 1950), 203.

4. Kozawa Heisaku, "Zaiaku ishiki no nishu: Ajase kompurekkusu" (originally published in 1954), and "Ajase-ō monogatari ni tsuite" (originally published in 1931), *Gendai no esupuri: Seishin bunseki Furoito ikō* 148 (1979): 166–154.

5. Kishimoto Ken'ichi, "Self-Awakening Psychotherapy," *Psychologia* 28, no. 2 (June 1985) 90–100, and *Ningen kaifuku no michi: Bukkyō to seishin igaku* (Tokyo: Yayoi shobō, 1984).

6. Yamamoto Haruo, et al., *Naikan ryōhō* (Tokyo: Igakushoin, 1972); David K. Reynolds, *The Quiet Therapies: Japanese Pathways to Personal Growth* (Honolulu: University Press of Hawaii, 1980), 46–65.

7. Yanagi Sōetsu, "The Pure Land of Beauty," trans. by Bernard Leach, *The Eastern Buddhist*, n.s. 9, no. 1 (May 1976): 18–41.

8. See, Kiyozawa Manshi, *December Fan: The Buddhist Essays of Manshi Kiyozawa*, trans. by Nobuo Haneda (Kyoto: Higashi Honganji, 1984); Tsumagari Junzō, *Shinran no daichi: Soga Ryōjin zuimon nichiroku* (Tokyo: Yayoi shobō, 1982); Hirose Takashi, ed.,

Ryōganjin: Soga Ryōjin, Kaneko Daiei shokan (Tokyo: Shunjūsha, 1982).

9. See, for example, Yonemura Ryūji, Junkyō to minshū: kakure nenbutsu kō (Kyoto: Dohōsha shuppan, 1979); Kataoka Yakichi, Tamamuro Fumio, and Oguri Junko, Kinsei no chika shinkō: kakure Kirishitan, kakure daimoku, kakure nenbutsu, (Tokyo: Hyōronsha, 1974).

10. Yamaori Tetsuo, "Shinran to kindai Nihon no shisō," Kawade jimbutsu dokuhon: Shinran (Tokyo: Kawade shuppan, 1985), 203. "Metanoia" is a translation for "zange" which is given a philosophical flavor by Yamaori.

11. Ibid., 195–209. Although I introduce my own analyses based on cited sources, I am indebted to Yamaori for the main thrust of ideas in the following section, especially as they relate to analyses of Kinoshita Naoe, Kiyozawa Manshi, Chikazumi Jōkan, Kamei Katsuichirō, and Hattori Shisō.

12. Kiyozawa Manshi, "Shukyō tetsugaku gaikotsu," in Kiyozawa Manshi zenshū 2, ed. Akegarasu Haya, Nishimura Kengyō (Kyoto: Hōzōkan, 1971).

13. G. W. F. Hegel, Critique of Hegel's 'Philosophy of Right', trans. Annette Jolin and Joseph O'Malley (New York: Cambridge University Press, 1977).

14. Yamaori, 199.

15. Of course, Western thinkers and governments also often failed to be fully self-critical in their historical agendas. Even today, nations in Europe and Asia continue to raise questions about the United States' government's self-appointed role in world affairs.

16. James W. Heisig and John C. Maraldo, Rude Awakenings: Zen, the Kyoto School, and the Question of Nationalism (Honolulu: University of Hawai'i Press, 1995).

17. James W. Heisig, "Tanabe's Logic of the Specific and the Spirit of Nationalism," in Rude Awakenings, 288.

18. Tanabe Hajime, Philosophy as Metanoetics, trans. by James Heisig

(Berkeley: University of California Press, 1986), xlix–l.

19. Yamaori, 199–200.

20. Miki Kiyoshi, "Rekishi no jikaku," in Yoshimoto Ryūmei, ed.,*Shinran*, Shisō dokuhon (Kyoto: Hōzōkan, 1987), 169. (Originally published in *Shinran*, in *Miki Kiyoshi zenshū* 16 [Tokyo: Iwanami shoten, 1949]).

21. Miki, "Rekishi no jikaku," 172.

22. Ibid., 173–175.

23. Yamamoto Hiroko, "Rekishi to chōetsu: Miki Kiyoshi no naka no Shinran," *Bukkyō bessatsu* 1:*Shinran* (1980), 206–207.

24. See especially Yamaori, 205–206.

25. Kuwabara Takeo, "Saha no chōja," in *Tsuiso: Suekawa Hiroshi,* ed. by Suekawa Hiroshi sensei tsuitō bunshū henshū iinkai (Tokyo: Yūhikaku, 1979), 247–254.

26. In 1950, a statue named *Watazumizō* was created as a statement of peace and antiwar sentiment, as a symbol of the voice of students who were drafted into the Pacific War. The statue found its home at Ritsumeikan University after other institutions refused to display the statue because of its antigovernmental connotations. It is now housed in Ritsumeikan's World Peace Museum which opened in 1992.

27. See Kimura Kyōtarō, "Buraku mondai to Suekawa Sensei," in *Tsuisō: Suekawa Hiroshi,* 283–285.

28. Suekawa Hiroshi, "Shinran Shōnin to watakushi no jinseikan," in Asada Sumio, ed., *Suekawa Hiroshi: Sono hito to jinseikan* (Kyoto: Hyakkaen, 1975), 19.

29. Ibid., 72.

30. Saeki Chihiro, "Deai 'Suekawa Sensei no koto,'" in *Suekawa Hiroshi,* 110.

31. Asada Sumio, "Nembutsusha to shite no Suekawa Sensei," in *Suekawa Hiroshi,* 78.

32. Ibid., 78.

33 Suekawa, 9–10.

34. Ibid., 19.

35. Ibid., 51.

Concern for Others in Pure Land Soteriological and Ethical Considerations: A Case of *Jōgyō daihi* in Jōdo Shinshū Buddhism[1]

Kenneth K. TANAKA

The classical Western view of Buddhism as "ahistorical," "passive," and "pessimistic" is well-known. According to Thomas Tweed, a scholar of early Buddhism in America, these very qualities[2] contributed to the failure of Buddhism to make greater inroads into American culture in the late 19th and early 20th century. Among the various Buddhist traditions, Pure Land doctrine is especially prone to this characterization on account of the otherworldly, transcendent qualities of its cardinal doctrines. Sukhāvatī Pure Land, for example, is said to exist far beyond our Sahā World, "billions of Buddha lands to the west."[3] Similar separation characterizes later views of the relationship between the spiritual and the secular realms. Rennyo (1415–1499), for example, urged his Jōdo Shinshū followers to keep their faith private: "First of all, outwardly, take the laws of the state as fundamental.... Inwardly, rely single-heartedly and steadfastly on Amida Tathāgata for [birth in the Pure Land in] the afterlife."[4]

Contemporary writers continue to subscribe to these views, especially concerning Jōdo Shinshū, which has the largest following among the Pure Land traditions in Japan today. Christian theologian John Cobb, Jr., for example, states:

> Jodoshinshu has not yet worked through the crisis of the relation of history to faith. If this crisis must be faced, then in some respects its problems are more acute even than those faced by Christianity, for its basis is still further removed from the actual course of history.[5]

JŌGYŌ DAIHI IN JŌDO SHINSHŪ BUDDHISM

Similarly, Shin'ichi Hisamatsu, a Zen scholar and practitioner, notes:

> In Shinshū, even though we may have attained *shinjin* [6] in this life, we are incapable in our present existence of performing any actions associated with the aspect of returning.[7]

In the eyes of both of these writers who sit outside the tradition, Jōdo Shinshū teaching and, by implication, its modern manifestation do not lead to an active involvement in the world. Cobb expresses this separation in classically Christian terms, "of the relation of history to faith," while Hisamatsu focuses on Jōdo Shinshū's apparent belief in one's inability in this life to help others with spiritual as well as social and economic issues.

In a rebuttal to such critiques, Jōdo Shinshū scholar Takamaro Shigaraki argued for the existence of a socially active dimension in the Jōdo Shinshū teachings, based largely on the writings of the founder, Shinran (1173–1263).[8] While I find Shigaraki's arguments convincing, the rebuttal focused on the founder's views articulated some 750 years ago, and did not address the conditions of contemporary Jōdo Shinshū institutions. Shigaraki, an outspoken critic of the Nishi-Honganji establishment,[9] would be the first to admit to the chasm that exists between the actual teachings of Shinran and the socially passive stance of contemporary institutions.

In recent years, however, we have witnessed some socially progressive initiatives within the Nishi-Honganji institution. A prime example is the antidiscrimination movement (*dōbō-undō*) which was initiated forty some years ago to eliminate discrimination against the Burakumin ("hamlet people"),[10] many of whom are Jōdo Shinshū Buddhists.[11] Secondly, Jōdo Shinshū priests and laypersons are at the forefront of a nationwide campaign to oppose what they regard as a constitutional breach of the separation of church and state. They are critical of the government's support of Yasukuni Shinto Shrine, evidenced in its public patronage by high government officials, including the prime minister.[12] Further, there has been a growing self-criticism among certain segments within both Nishi- and Higashi-

Honganji institutions for their role in the doctrinal and political affirmation of the war efforts during World War II (*senji kyōgaku*).[13]

These developments may indicate an evolution towards greater social engagement, but they are still limited to select groups. The majority of Jōdo Shinshū temples show little evidence of active involvement in these issues. As one of the "established" Kamakura period schools, the Jōdo Shinshū institutions as a whole remain, relatively speaking, socially conservative. This becomes apparent when they are compared to Risshō Kōseikai and Sōkagakkai, two of the largest schools that have attained prominence since World War II. The reluctance of most contemporary Nishi-Honganji members to become more active socially is reinforced by doctrinal explanations of the teachings. Nowhere is this seen more clearly than in the frequent citing of the following section from Chapter Four of the *Tannishō* (An Essay Lamenting Deviations): [14]

> Compassion in the Path of the Sages is to pity, sympathize with, and care for beings . . . . *Compassion in the Pure Land path lies in saying the Name, quickly attaining Buddhahood, and freely benefiting sentient beings with a heart of great love and great compassion.* In our present lives, it is hard to carry out the desire to aid others however much love and tenderness we may feel; hence such compassion always falls short of fulfillment. *Only the saying of the Name manifests the heart of great compassion (daijihi-shin) that is replete and thoroughgoing.*[15] (emphasis added)

Here we find a direct reference to a "heart of great compassion," which manifests completely only in recitation of the Name of Amida ("Namo Amida Butsu"). One is encouraged to recite the Name in this life and quickly become a Buddha in the next, wherein one is freely able to benefit others. However, recitation is carried out in the present life without any expressed or conscious concern for others. Any benefit to others is postponed until one realizes Buddhahood upon death. Therefore, in this life, the reciting of the Name is seen as the *only* way to do full justice in manifesting the mind of great compassion. The scope of one's spiritual activity is limited to oral recitation of the Name within the context of one's own realization of Buddhahood. The expression of compassion in this life is, therefore, limited to one form—recitation—and is noticeably introverted and lacking any clear sense of interconnection with others and their spiritual search.

I would here argue, as Professor Shigaraki did earlier, that this characterization is inadequate to the total body of Shinran's teachings, and go a step further in stating that it also does not agree with later Jōdo Shinshū thinkers, some of whom lived during the extremely conservative Tokugawa period (1602–1867). This essay derives its cue from modern researchers who have shown that contemporary religious understandings are often neither as original nor authentic as the respective traditions would have us believe. According to these findings, received traditions are often the product of recent interpretations. As examples of recent publications, *Curators of the Buddha* supports this argument concerning a number of traditions, and *The Rhetoric of Immediacy* and *Dōgen's Manuals of Zen Tradition* have accomplished the same for the Japanese Zen tradition. With regard to East Asian Pure Land Buddhism, *Visions of Sukhāvatī* followed a similar line of investigation, focusing on the role played by Shan-tao (613–81). My own work, focusing on another Chinese Pure Land figure, Ching-ying Hui-yüan (523–92), questioned many of our assumptions about the development of Chinese Pure Land thought.[16]

JŌGYŌ DAIHI AND ITS INTERPRETATIONS

Shinran's view of spiritual transformation in this life (known chiefly as *shinjin*) is that it automatically expresses itself in one's involvement with others. This is seen particularly in the doctrine of *jōgyō daihi* ("constantly practicing great compassion") that constitutes one of the "ten benefits in the present life" (*genshō jisshu no yaku*). These ten are found in the "Faith Chapter" of Shinran's *magnum opus,* the *Kyōgyōshinshō* (Teachings, Practice, Faith and Realization): 1) being protected and sustained by unseen powers, 2) being possessed of supreme virtues, 3) our karmic evil being transformed into good, 4) being protected and cared for by all the Buddhas, 5) being praised by all the Buddhas, 6) being constantly protected by the light of the Buddha's heart, 7) having great joy in our hearts, 8) being aware of Amida's benevolence and of responding in gratitude to his virtues, 9) constantly practicing great compassion, and 10) entering the Stage of the Truly Settled (*shojoju*).[17]

Today, the precise meaning of *jōgyō daihi* has become, in my view, noticeably vague or generally not well understood. If there is any general consensus among Shin Buddhist adherents today, this term is understood—and vaguely at that—to mean "to recite the Name" in a similar fashion as the *Tannishō* Chapter Four passage discussed above. However, since Shinran did not fully explain its meaning in the *Kyōgyōshinshō*, this common modern understanding could very well have evolved after Shinran's time, particularly in the doctrinally conservative environment resulting from the Sangōwakuran Controversy (described below) which concluded in 1806.

During the Tokugawa period, the government used the Buddhist temples as government outposts where the people's official records were kept. All members of the same family were required to belong to the same school, and priests were discouraged from suggesting any new ideas that were not already in the tradition. Within this restrictive environment, the Buddhist schools were banned from preaching the Dharma to convert new followers.

A major doctrinal argument broke out among the scholars of Nishi-Honganji at the end of the 1700s. On one side stood the professors of the Academy (the highest center of sectarian learning) in Kyoto and on the other side were the scholar-priests in the Nishi-Honganji branch temples. The Academy professors emphasized the dynamic, active dimension of *shinjin* as manifested in one's daily activities. They valued the importance of expressing spiritual understanding through thought, speech, and actions. The technical name for this is "the three karmic actions" (*sangō*) of mind, body, and speech, from which the name of the controversy is derived.

On the other hand, the scholar-priests from temples in the outlying areas argued that the serene mind (*shingyō*) of *shinjin* is central to the life of the person of *shinjin*. In their view, the privileging of three karmic actions by their opponents came dangerously close to self-power (*jiriki*) practice, which Shinran categorically rejected. The clash between the two factions can be seen as that between a more active and outward interpretation versus a more passive and inward emphasis.

While arguments about doctrine were nothing new to the Shinshū scholarly community, this dispute is notable in the degree to which the government controlled and interfered in the affairs of religious institutions. Given the conservative tenor of Tokugawa society, it is not surprising, therefore, that the government courts finally brought an end to the argument in 1806 by deciding against what it perceived as change in the established doctrine. The courts ruled in favor of the more passive definition favored by the scholar-priests, a decision based largely on one simplistic rule: Accept the old and reject the new. Chido, the head professor of the Academy at the time, not only lost the case but faced exile to a distant island. Although Chido died in prison before this verdict was handed down, it is reported that his ashes were sent to the island in his place!

This dispute and the way it was solved had a strong impact on subsequent interpretations of the teachings, for today, the passive definition of *shinjin* is dominant in the Nishi-Honganji teachings. Emphasis is on the activities of Amida Buddha over those of the human seeker, the discussions of which are generally framed in such doctrinal categories as *hottoku* ("Dharmic virtues" of Amida) and *kisō* ("the characteristics of the capacity" of seekers), respectively. With the dominance of the *hottoku* position, there is less representation of the active definition of *shinjin*, whose advocates lost out in the government decision of 1806.

SUBSEQUENT JŌDO SHINSHŪ COMMENTATORS

The passive modern understanding with regard to *jōgyō daihi* is shown in a completely different light, however, when we look at the earliest Shin writings on the subject. Zonkaku (1290–1373), in his *Rokuyōshō*, the earliest extant commentary on Shinran's *Kyōgyōshinshō*, comments:

> The ninth benefit of *jōgyō daihi* is to be understood in accord with the meaning as explained in the passage from the *Great Compassion Sutra* that is quoted in this scroll.[18]

That passage from the *Great Compassion Sutra* is quoted in Shinran's *Kyōgyōshinshō* in the section on the "Buddha's true disciple" and as part of a long section cited from Tao-ch'o's *An-le-chi*:

> The *Sutra of Great Compassion* states: What is "great compassion"? Those who continue solely in the recitation of the Name of the Buddha (nembutsu) without any interruption will thereby be born without fail in the land of happiness at the end of life. If these people *encourage each other and bring others to recite the Name*, they are all called "people who practice great compassion."[19] (emphasis added)

This sutra passage advocates a range of activity that goes beyond mere recitation solely for one's own benefit. Followers are to mutually encourage oral recitation, and succeed in *getting others to recite the Name*. A mere recitation for oneself is insufficient, for only by encouraging others would followers qualify as "people who practice great compassion." This activity, furthermore, is to be actualized in this life, *prior* to both the realization of birth in the Pure Land and realization of Buddhahood.[20]

Zonkaku, then, comments on this sutra passage and, in my view, expands its meaning even further:

> In the latter passage, the statement "Those who continue solely

..." reveals the benefit of birth [in the Pure Land] as benefit for oneself (*jiri*). The statement "If these people encourage..." reveals the benefit of the great compassion as benefiting others (*rita*)."[21]

By invoking the well-known Mahayana concept of benefiting others (Skt. *parārtha;* Jpn. *rita*), Zonkaku significantly broadens the passage's meaning. The act of encouraging others to recite the Name constitutes an activity that benefits others in distinction to that which benefits oneself.

A similar view is expressed by Kaku'on (Senpu'in, 1821–1907).[22] In his evaluation of the ten benefits mentioned earlier, Kaku'on includes the benefit of *jōgyō daihi* under the category of "the two benefits carried out by the practitioner" (*gyōja niri*). And of the two categories, he characterizes *jōgyō daihi* as benefiting others (*rita*), while the seventh and eighth benefits are seen as benefits for oneself (*jiri*). Kaku'on, therefore, clearly acknowledges *jōgyō daihi* as benefiting others as opposed to the self. Of particular interest to this discussion is the emphasis of this benefit as an attribute or activity of the seeker, not only that of Amida. Even though the source of compassion derives ultimately from Amida, Kaku'on sees this benefit as an explicit activity of the seeker, and one that is specifically directed to benefiting others.

Gizan (Gankai'in, 1824–1910) further expands Kaku'on's position:

> Next, *jōgyō daihi* is based on the *Great Compassion Sutra* quoted in the *Anrakushū* which is cited below. The *Wasan* (*Shozōmatsu,* verse #97) states, "Without any repentance and shame," which addresses the point of view of Dharmic virtue (*hottoku*) as the object of faith and of recitation. However, Rōken'in maintains that if a practitioner today were to give a Dharma talk to his wife and children it would constitute a dimension of *jōgyō daihi*. He has said that since the *Anrakushū* states, "If these people encourage each other and bring others

to recite the Name, they are all called 'people who practice great compassion,'" *the activities of propagating great compassion should not be confined exclusively to the recitation of the Name.*[23] (emphasis added)

Gizan explicitly acknowledges modes of exercising great compassion by means other than the recitation of the Name, for example, that of giving a Buddhist sermon to one's own spouse and children. While he gives no other examples, his view of exercising *jōgyō daihi* clearly includes benefiting others. I would further argue that, in the context of his commentary, Gizan went out of his way to make this point.

This broader perspective focused on human activity raises another interesting point in that Gizan expressly proposes his views in contradistinction to what he calls "Dharmic virtue" (*hottoku*), which as alluded to above refers to the point of view of the activity of Amida or the ultimate. The Dharmic virtue point of view was articulated by En'getsu (Jōman'in, 1818–1902):

The three benefits beginning with the seventh [benefit] constitute the manifestation (*sōhotsu*) of the practicer. . . . According to Jōshin'in, the benefit of *jōgyō daihi* derives from the fact that the Name is none other than the practice which is the transference of Tathāgata's great compassion, and that the recitation of the Name is none other than the practicing of Tathāgata's great compassion. The *Wasan*, "Without any repentance and shame, even though I lack any element of true mind, the virtues fill the ten directions of the universe with the Name that is transferred to us by Amida." How can this not be the practice of great compassion![24]

En'getsu's position emphasizes Dharmic virtue. Amida Tathāgata is herein given a prominent role as the ultimate source and agent of the great compassion. The *Wasan* that is quoted reinforces the greatly diminished capabilities of the practitioner (*kisō*) in contrast to the virtues of the Name that fills the universe. In contrast, Gizan's position as discussed earlier does not base itself on the perspective of Dharmic virtue but instead emphasizes the perspective of the practitioner. Gizan also makes it clear that his perspective is not informed by that of Dharmic virtue; accordingly, he does not appeal to the *Wasan* passage which En'getsu specifically cited in support of his Dharmic virtue perspective.

A representative exegete of the Ōtani or Higashi-Honganji Branch, Jinrei (Kōgatsu'in, 1749–1817) had earlier articulated a position similar to that of Gizan when he commented:

> The ninth benefit, the *jōgyō daihi* is based in the *Great Compassion Sutra* as quoted in the *Anraku-shū* passage cited below.
>
> *Jōgyō daihi* refers to the practicers of Other-power *shinjin* who constantly engage in continuous recitation of the Name and mutually encourage others [to recite the Name] in the spirit of "*to realize shinjin and lead others to shinjin*" (*jishin kyōninshin*). The one moment (*ichinen*) of *shinjin* endowed by the Other-power is none other than the "*mind to save all beings*" (*do-shujō-shin*). Consequently, when one obtains this mind of saving others, one becomes a person who constantly practices the Buddha's great compassion that is expressed as "to realize *shinjin* and guide others to *shinjin*."
>
> The eighth and the ninth benefits form a set. Being aware of Amida's benevolence and of responding in gratitude to his virtue (*chi'on hōtoku*) [the eighth benefit] constitutes the benefit to oneself expressed to the Buddha, while the [ninth benefit] of *jōgyō daihi is the benefit of converting others.*[25] (emphasis added)

Jinrei, thus, promotes an even greater active involvement of the practitioner in sharing the teachings with others. He cites a well-known Pure Land Buddhist ideal "to realize *shinjin* and guide others to *shinjin*," a phrase attributed to a T'ang period Chinese proponent of Pure Land teaching, Shan-tao. And this is also associated, if not identified, with the concept of "the mind of saving sentient beings." In effect, Jinrei regards the practitioner as embodying (*mi ni suru*) the mind of saving sentient beings which emanates from Amida. That Jinrei associated *jōgyō daihi* with the practitioner's act to reach out to or involve others is clearly evident in his usage of the term "benefit of converting others."

JŌGYŌ DAIHI AS A DIMENSION OF *HŌ'ONGYŌ*

This demonstration of the deeper meaning of *jōgyō daihi* should hardly be surprising, as it relates directly to the well-established Jōdo Shinshū teaching of *hō'ongyō*, "action of responding in gratitude to the Buddha's benevolence." *Hō'ongyō*, a term known widely and intimately by many lay followers, is defined by former professor of Ryūkoku University Fugen Daien as "the propagation of great compassion (*daihi denke*)."[26] In support of this view, Fugen cites the well-known passage from Shan-tao's commentary:

> To realize *shinjin* and to guide others to *shinjin* is among the difficult things yet even more difficult. To awaken beings everywhere to great compassion is truly to respond in gratitude to the Buddha's benevolence.[27]

It would, thus, be safe to understand *jōgyō daihi* as a central element of *hō'ongyō*, or at the very least one of its expressions.

In Jōdo Shinshū doctrinal development, theories and debates abound with regard to the range of activities that constitutes *hō'ongyō*. The Kūge doctrinal school, for example, maintained that *hō'ongyō* is expressed in the Five Contemplative Gates (*gonenmon*).[28] The Seikisen school, in contrast, focused on the Five Correct Practices (*goshō-gyō*)[29] and stressed the recitation of the Name (*shōmyō*) as the primary action (*shōgō*), with the other four as supporting actions (*jogō*).

These discussions on the scope of *hō'ongyō* have generally been articulated within the categories of the Five Contemplative Gates and the Five Correct Practices. However, Daien Fugen has raised serious questions about limiting *hō'ongyō* to these categories. He cites the contributions of past teachers and lay practitioners who built temple halls, erected statues, and lit lanterns and burned incense. These actions, he argues, should be included as *hō'ongyō* so long as they are carried out in appreciation for the Other-power without the attitude of self-power.

Fugen, then, proceeds to include within the term *hō'ongyō* all actions in both the secular and religious arenas. To support this claim, Fugen notes that both Shinran and Rennyo (1415–1499)[30] prohibited the criticism of the teachings of other Buddhists and non-Buddhists, discouraged unethical actions, and encouraged the respect of secular authority and virtues. All of these, in Fugen's view, should be subsumed under supporting actions (*jogō*). To support this opinion, Fugen cites a passage from the *Wagotōroku* and underscores a section that stresses activities that are ordinarily not regarded as religious, "Actions related to the three activities of clothing, eating, and dwelling are the supporting actions of nembutsu." These mundane activities qualify as proper *hō'ongyō*, enabling one to lead a truly religious life. Gizan articulated an enhanced scope of activities when he, as we saw earlier, cited preaching to his wife and children as a form of *jōgyō daihi* and concluded, "The activities of the propagation of great compassion should not be confined exclusively to the recitation of the Name."[31]

Jōgyō daihi as one of the expressions of *hō'ongyō* particularly strengthens the element of reaching out horizontally to others. This was amply evident in many of the commentators such as Zonkaku, Kaku'on, and Jinrei who singled out *jōgyō daihi* among the ten benefits as one that specifically benefited others. Jinrei was particularly forceful in making this point as he contrasts *jōgyō daihi* with the eighth benefit, that of being aware of Amida's benevolence and of responding in gratitude to his virtue. Jinrei sees the eighth benefit as a self-benefit expressed to the Buddha, while *jōgyō daihi* constitutes a benefit of converting others. Jinrei further amplified this distinction when he invoked the concept of *jishin kyōninshin*, "to realize *shinjin* and to guide others to *shinjin*," as one of the primary features of *jōgyō daihi*.

In conclusion, our examination of several representative premodern and modern commentators shows that *jōgyō daihi* has not always been interpreted simply as one's act of oral recitation. Starting with Zonkaku, there has existed a strong tendency to regard this benefit in a broader context as: 1) encouraging others to engage in oral recitation, 2) manifesting the benefit in actions other than oral recitation, 3) regarding these actions as benefiting others in the classical Mahayana sense, 4) stressing the practitioner's role over that of Amida Tathāgata, and 5) concentrating on the activities of the present life.

In unearthing a broader meaning to *jōgyō daihi* as we have done, we find ourselves with a more solid doctrinal grounding for encouraging and justifying Jōdo Shinshū involvement in the world. These interpretations further compel us to reevaluate the modern common understanding of *jōgyō daihi* as epitomized by the narrow reading of the *Tannishō* Chapter Four passage examined at the outset of this essay. In so doing, we became open to a more nuanced reading of that passage, inspired by another passage from the *Tannishō*, this time in Chapter Five:

> For all living beings have been my parents and brothers and sisters in the course of countless lives in the many states of existences.[32]

JŌGYŌ DAIHI AS A MODERATING FORCE IN CONTEMPORARY ETHICS

In considering the implications of the above conclusions, I believe that *jōgyō daihi* reveals a paradigm for a basis of action that is 1) more spiritually-based and 2) more self-reflective[33] than the dominant forms of ethical models found in the West. As such, *jōgyō daihi* has the potential to add fresh insights to the field of contemporary ethics.

As demonstrated above, *jōgyō daihi* is not divorced from but an integral dimension of a spiritual or soteriological transformation referred to in Jōdo Shinshū as *shinjin*. *Jōgyō daihi* is, thus, part of the paradigmatic Buddhist aim of realizing enlightenment by overcoming greed, hatred, and delusion, which are the root of one's spiritual pain (*duḥkha*) and, by extension, the suffering caused by social ills.

In this sense, *jōgyō daihi* can be seen in the context of Buddhist social and ethical actions which are regarded as inseparable from spiritual cultivation. Kenneth Kraft, for example, observes that modern Buddhist activists, especially Westerners, find a distinctive Buddhist perspective in that "social work entails inner work," and that while other religiously motivated activists share this view to some degree, it is the engaged Buddhists who apply this most consistently.[34] The same integration of spiritual cultivation and social action is also well attested to in the life and writings of Thich Nhat Hanh, whose "engaged Buddhism" emerged from applying the insights gained in monastic practice to social relief and peace work done during the Vietnam War.[35]

The above Buddhist perspective contends that, without the spiritual cultivation and transformation of the individual, society faces only temporary solutions. That is precisely the reason why ethical actions and social reforms based on socioeconomic ideologies are believed to be ultimately inadequate.[36] Influencing these ideologies are the rationally-based, Kantian-inspired ethical models known generally in the West as deontological and teleological.[37] In both instances, one's motivation for action is not necessarily rooted in the spiritual dimension.[38]

In contrast to these categories, *jōgyō daihi* is similar to another category of Western ethics, generally known as "virtue ethics."[39] While "virtue ethics" and *jōgyō daihi* are not identical, they are similar in terms of the value placed on cultivating the self and the importance of one's virtue as the basis of ethical action.[40] A practitioner in this mode of ethics is, therefore, spontaneously motivated by compassionate concern for others arising from his or her personal virtues, and, in the case of *jōgyō daihi*, by the realization of an intimate interconnectedness with others in which he does not see himself as standing separate from and superior to others.

I wish now to turn to the second of two points, the self-reflective character of *jōgyō daihi*. This character can, ironically, be discerned in the very same *Tannishō* Chapter Four passage whose narrow modern interpretation I criticized in the first half of this paper. However, my criticism was directed at the passive and self-centered interpretation of human *actions*, as I personally agree with its evaluation of human *nature*. From the latter perspective, I find this excerpt from that passage particularly resonant:

> . . . it is hard to carry out the desire to aid others however much love and tenderness we may feel; hence such compassion always falls short of fulfillment.[41]

How often do we find ourselves falling miserably short of our idealistic aspirations to help others? Time and time again in my own life, I have been struck by the truth of Shinran's penetrating insight. I can see that my character is full of noble intentions, but in the final analysis unable to deliver even one-tenth of the initial inspiration. Not only am I not capable of giving fully to others but am actually taking a great deal from others. In fact, my very livelihood hinges on the sacrifices of other living beings. To be blunt, my salary depends on the sale of thousands of barbecued chickens at the temple bazaars, a major source of income of the Buddhist temples that support our educational institution. The Dharma encourages non-taking of life, but this Dharma "teacher" must depend on that very transgression. My profession, in a sense, is a dilemma, as is my very existence if I seek to fulfill Buddhism's highest ideal, which is refraining from taking life.

I have felt a similar sense of uneasiness and guilt about the Vietnam War. Over sixty thousand Americans of my generation paid the ultimate price, and many still continue to suffer from severe physical and psychological scars. My sorrow extends to the over two million Vietnamese who died and were maimed in the conflict as a result of weaponry bought with the taxes I paid. I did what I could to oppose the war, yet my efforts are no consolation for the victims. I did not condone the war, yet I was and continue to be a citizen of the U.S., which has become the most affluent and dominant nation in the world. As a member of this nation, I am partly responsible for its actions, no matter how insignificant my influence in this society. I am even more ashamed that these remorseful thoughts do not last long. Most of the time I am too busy and involved in my day-to-day life. As the Vietnam War slips further into the shadows of our history, it fades from my memory too easily.

These personal reflections lend credence to Shinran's self-appraisal in the Postscript of the *Tannishō*:

> I know nothing of what is good or evil. For if I could know thoroughly, as is known in the mind of Amida, that an act was good, then I would know the meaning of "good." If I could know thoroughly, as Amida knows, that an act was evil, than I would know "evil." But for a foolish being full of blind passions in this fleeting world—this burning house—all matters without exception are lies and gibberish, totally without truth and sincerity. The Nembutsu alone is true and real.[42]

The point of this statement is not moral relativism or anarchism, as Shinran clearly acknowledged the importance of conventional morality and ethics.[43] Instead, Shinran felt he lacked the ability to know good and evil in the ultimate sense, from an ultimate perspective as expressed in the phrase, "known in the mind of Amida."[44]

Shinran's reticence to be adamant and absolutist regarding the question of good and evil was due not only to his evaluation of human nature but also rooted in his assumption that Amida did not participate *directly* in his ethical decision-making. This issue was elaborated by later Jōdo Shinshū commentators. For them, Amida as the ultimate truth does not manifest *directly* in human actions or deeds. The only exception is the spontaneous utterance of the Name, "Namo Amida Butsu." The Name is considered the only direct emanating action (*sōhotsu*) while other actions are carried out indirectly based on human reason (*risei*). Gizan of the Sekisen school describes this with a metaphor of a man who is under the influence of alcoholic beverage (*sake* in this case). The man begins to sing and dance. However, according to Gizan, his singing and dancing are the effects of being drunk, not the *direct* effect of the *sake*. Just as *sake* is not the direct source of this man's merry behavior, Amida is not the direct source of human ethical actions. Rather, the *realization* of *shinjin* results in compassionate and ethical actions.[45]

I have discussed at length the Jōdo Shinshū evaluation of human nature in relation to ethical considerations in order to counteract the tendency in some ethical models to place excessive faith in human capability, without placing sufficient value on the need for serious spiritual cultivation. This tendency is evident in the deontological and, perhaps to a lesser extent, in the teleological models mentioned above.

Even within progressive Christian circles, considerable credence and faith is given to human ethical judgment, based on the strength of God's participation. Professor Cobb, for example, speaks of actions that are motivated by the "promptings of the Spirit":

> For Christians the goal is to decide in accordance with the promptings of the Spirit. In this way the blind will to live finds its true fulfillment in real life.[46]

How do these promptings manifest themselves? And how does one know if these promptings are those of the Spirit/God or merely his own? Whatever the answer, the response will be ultimately be a *human* response. And given the above discussion of human nature, I find myself being extremely cautious of ethical actions that are based on divinely-sanctioned impulses. In the hands of a virtuous person within a supportive and self-reflective community as in the case of Dr. Martin Luther King, Jr., a divine prompting can unleash a powerful prophetic message. However, there is potential for immense abuse by psychologically deranged or emotionally unstable persons. Assassinations of well-known leaders from Gandhi to Yitzak Rabin have been inspired by divine impulses; the assassins are frequently members of the victims' ethnic or religious group.

In contrast, *jōgyō daihi* offers an approach that is more self-reflective, as well as tolerant of other differing positions. Some may find that it lacks the certitude of a divinely-inspired action. However, self-criticism, humility, and openness to others are crucial qualities in a world of nations and communities with widely divergent value systems. Perhaps *jōgyō daihi* can be included among other resources in the formulation of uncharted ethical considerations for healing old wounds and forging new cooperation.

NOTES

1. This essay is included in Roger Jackson and John Makransky eds., *Buddhist Theology: Critical Reflections by Contemporary Buddhist Scholars*, Critical Studies in Buddhism, no. 7. (Richmond, Surry, UK: Curzon Press, 1998). I wish to express my appreciation to the editors and Curzon Press for their permission to reprint this essay for this volume. This essay also includes one section from another essay, "*Jōgyō-daihi*: Constantly Practicing Great Compassion: Re-evaluation Based on Tokugawa Scholars for a Basis of Shin Involvement in the World," *The Pure Land*, n.s. 10–11 (December, 1994): 93–104.

2. Specifically, the late-Victorian Christian critics "agreed that Buddhism was passive and pessimistic." These features contrasted with activism and optimism. Thomas Tweed, *The American Encounter with Buddhism 1844–1912: Victorian Culture and the Limits of Descent* (Bloomington 1992 and Indianapolis: Indiana University Press), 133–56.

3. *Taishō shinshū daizōkyō,* edited by Takakusu Junjirō and Watanabe Kaigyoku (Tokyo: Taishō issaikyō kankōkai, 1924–1932), vol. 12, 270a, 346c.

4. Minor L. Rogers and Ann T. Rogers, *Rennyo: The Second Founder of Shin Buddhism* (Berkeley: Asian Humanities, 1991), 215–16.

In fairness to Rennyo (the Eighth *monshu*, or Head of the Honganji branch), his admonition should be appreciated as a survival strategy, for his fledgling religious community in an unstable, warring political environment. However, his views became mainstream even after his school subsequently evolved into one of the most dominant and established Buddhist institutions.

5. Cobb, John Jr. *Beyond Dialogue: Toward a Mutual Transformation of Christianity and Buddhism* (Philadelphia: Fortress Press, 1982), 139.

6. The term literally means "trust or faith (*shin*)" and "mind-heart (*jin*)," and refers to a spiritual transformation that is realized in this life. Having attained the state of non-retrogression, a person of *shinjin* is assured of realizing Buddhahood immediately upon death in the Pure Land.

7. Cited in Takamaro Shigaraki, "*Shinjin* and Social Action in Shinran's Teachings," trans. David Matsumoto, *The Pure Land,* n.s. 8–9 (December, 1992): 221.

"Aspect of returning" (*gensō*) refers to the phase of returning from the Pure Land to a world of *saṃāra* as an enlightened Bodhisattva, when one is freely able to carry out actions to benefit others. This is in contrast to the "aspect of going" (*ōsō*) to the Pure Land, when one is still unenlightened and thus incapable of freely and completely benefitting others. Hence, Hisamatsu is arguing that since a person of *shinjin* is still in the aspect of going, he is not able to carry out thoroughgoing actions to help others completely.

8. Shigaraki, 219–49.

9. Nishi-Honganji (officially rendered "Nishi-Hongwanji) is one of the two largest branches of Jōdo Shinshū, the other being Higashi-Honganji. They are also known as Honpa-Honganji and Ōtani, respectively. Prior to their split in 1580, they were of one school known as Honganji.

10. Buraku-min refers to an outcast segment of the Japanese population, whose ancestors in the medieval period were involved in reviled occupations such as butchering animals and working with hides. Despite their legal equality since World War II, their descendants

continue to be subjected to social discrimination, particularly in marriage. Their identity is traced through their family registries and addresses that are often identified with hamlets where the Burakumins were ghettoized.

11. Nakao Shunpaku, *Sabetsu to Shinshū* [Discrimination and Shinshū] (Kyoto: Nagata Bunshodo, 1992), 195–251.

12. Then Prime Minister Yasuhiro Nakasone, for example, paid a visit to the shrine in 1985. Hishiki Masaharu, *Jōdo Shinshū no Sensō Sekinin* [Jōdo Shinshū's War Time Responsibilities] (Tokyo: Iwanami Shoten, 1993), 15.

13. Ibid., 2–16.

14. For example, Shigaraki cites this to point out the uniqueness of compassion in Pure Land Buddhism. (See, Shigaraki, 238). Further, I personally recall this passage being invoked by those who voted against a proposed human rights statement at a 1993 National Council meeting of the Buddhist Churches of America.

15. Dennis Hirota, *Tannishō: A Primer: A Record of the words of Shinran set down in lamentation over departure from his teaching.* (Kyoto: Ryukoku University, 1982), 24.

16. Donald Lopez, ed. *Curators of the Buddha: The Study of Buddhism Under Colonialism* (Chicago: The University of Chicago Press, 1995); Bernard Faure, *The Rhetoric of Immediacy: A Cultural Critique of Chan/Zen Buddhism* (Princeton, N.J.: Princeton Univ. Press, 1991); Carl Bielefeldt, *Dōgen's Manuals of Zen Meditation* (Berkeley: University of California Press, 1988); Julian Pas, *Visions of Sukhāvatī: Shan-tao's Commentary on the Kuan Wu-Liang-Shou-Fo Ching* (Albany, N.Y.: State Univ. of New York Press, 1995); Kenneth Tanaka, *The Dawn of Chinese Pure Land Buddhist Doctrine: Ching-ying Hui-yüan's Commentary on the Visualization Sutra* (Albany, N.Y.: State University of New York Press, 1990).

17. Yoshifumi Ueda, et al eds., *The True Teaching, Practice and Realization of the Pure Land Way. A Translation of Shinran's Kyōgyōshinshō,* vol. 2 (Kyoto: Hongwanji International Center, 1983–90), 257–8.

18. Zonkaku, *Rokuyōshō,* in *Shinshū Shōgyō Zensho,* vol. 2 (Kyoto:

Ōyagi kōbundō, 1941), 298.

19. Ueda, et al., 270.

20. Departing radically from earlier Pure Land traditions, Shinran regards 1) birth in the Pure Land and 2) realizing Buddhahood as virtually a simultaneous process. One becomes a Buddha immediately upon birth in the Pure Land. Pure Land is no longer a locus of spiritual practice.

21. Zonkaku, *Rokuyōshō*, 305–306.

22. *Shinshū hyakurondaishū, ge*, in *Shinshū sōsho*, edited by Shinshū sōsho hensan sho, vol 2 (Kyoto: Kōkyō shoin, 1930), 967.

23. Ibid., 699.

24. Ibid., 696.

25. Bukkyō taikei kanseikai, ed., *Kyōgyōshinshō kōgi shūsei*, vol.6 (Kyoto: Hōzōkan, 1975), 470.

26. Fugen Daien, *Shinshū kyōgaku no hattatsu* [The Development of Shinshū Doctrine] (Kyoto: Nagata bunshodō, 1963), 296.

27. Ibid., 296.

28. The five are bowing, praise, aspiration for rebirth, visualization, and transfer of merit.

29. The five, according to traditional Jōdo Shinshū understanding, are chanting of sutras, visualization, bowing, recitation of the Name, and praise and offering.

30. The eighth *monshu* of the Honganji Branch prior to the split into Nishi and Higashi.

31. *Shinshū hyakurondaishū, ge*, 699.

32. Hirota, *Tannishō: A Primer*, 25.

33. I am using "self-reflective" to refer to an outlook that directs one's critical evaluation onto one's own assumptions, motivation, and

behavior rather than onto others'.

34. Kenneth Kraft, "Prospects of a Socially Engaged Buddhism," *Inner Peace, World Peace: Essays on Buddhism and Nonviolence*, edited by Kenneth Kraft (Albany, N.Y.: State University of New York Press, 1992), 12.

35. Ibid., 17–23.

36. One such example, though admittedly overly generalized, is the pervasive corruption among Communist Party leaders; its contribution to the disintegration of the Soviet system is now all too well-known.

37. The deontological approach understands morality primarily in terms of duty, law or obligation. The concern in this approach focuses on right versus wrong. The teleological approach sees morality as a means for realizing what lies at the end as the ultimate goal (e.g. the union with the Ultimate or a birth in a paradise) and is concerned less with the question of right but more with relationship to the goal. See Mircea Eliade, ed., *Encyclopedia of Religion*, vol. 3 (New York: MacMillan, 1987), 341a.

I would be remiss if I failed to note that Buddhist precepts contain elements of the teleological and deontological. For example, the Theravada monks' adherence to the 227 Paṭimokkha rules are motivated by their aim to reach their goal (telelogical) of enlightenment and by the fact that they are required (deontological) to follow the rules as their monastic requirement.

38. This statement requires qualification since there have been ethical thinkers who were spiritually inclined but who also subscribed to teleological or deontological approaches. My intent here is to focus on the rationally-based and spiritually-diminished nature of these models, largely rooted in the Kantian perspective on ethics.

39. Virtue ethics is often associated with the classical Greek philosophers, most notably within the Socratic-Platonic line. In both *jōgyō daihi* and virtue ethics, one's innate virtue (not one's sense of obligation or pragmatic considerations) informs and determines his or her handling of ethical issues.

40. One point of divergence can be seen in the manner in which virtue is cultivated: dialectic for Socratice and true entrusting for

Shinran. There is a need for more comparative analysis of the two approaches beyond the essay by Lee and Leong (David W. Lee and Markus Leong, "Jōdo Shinshū in Contemporary America: A Preliminary Comparative Study of Trans-ethical Responsibility and Socratic Virtue-ethics," *The Pure Land*, n.s., no. 10–11 [1994]: 288–302).

41. Hirota, *Tannishō: A Primer*, 24.

42. Ibid., 44.

43. Shinran severely reprimanded "lincensed evil" (*zōaku-muge*), when some mistaken disciples advocated that they could intentionally commit evil since the Vow of Amida Buddha was unobstructed by evil deeds. He thus admonished, "Do no take a liking to poison just because there is an antidote." The antidote refers to Amida's Vow. See Hirota, *Tannishō: A Primer*, 33–34.

44. It is important to remember that Shinran's evaluation was not forced upon him by the weight of his tradition but emerged in a context. In the course of twenty years of spiritual cultivation as a Tendai monk accompanied by intense, uncompromising introspection, Shinran arrived at his evaluation of himself as a *bonnō guzoku no bombu*, "a foolish being full of blind passions." It must, however, be pointed out that this devastating but honest self-evaluation emerged within the context of his being affirmed unconditionally by the compassionate Vow of Amida, concretely expressed in the Nembutsu, or the oral recitation of the Name.

45. Fugen, *Shinshū kyōgaku no hattatsu*, 286.

46. John Cobb, Jr., "On the Deepening of Buddhism," in *The Emptying God: A Buddhist-Jewish-Christian and Coversation*, edited by John Cobb, Jr. and Christopher Ives (Maryknoll, N.Y.: Orbis Books, 1990), 98.

PART TWO
Expressions in History

A Brief History of Pure Land Buddhism in Early Japan

James C. DOBBINS

Pure Land Buddhism has long been an active and pervasive religious tradition of Japan. Most Pure Land schools trace their lineage back to Hōnen (1133–1212), Shinran (1173–1262), or Ippen (1239–1289) and therefore posit their beginnings in the Kamakura period (1185–1333). Certainly, these three individuals are the most prominent figures in the history of Japanese Pure Land, since their teachings on the exclusive nembutsu (*senju nembutsu*), on faith (*shinjin*), and religious life in general have become doctrinal cornerstones of Japan's Pure Land believers. Nonetheless, it would be wrong to assume that Hōnen, Shinran, and Ippen conceived their ideas in a vacuum. On the contrary, they stood on the shoulders of a long tradition of Pure Land thinkers. By the time they presented their teachings to the world, Pure Land Buddhism had already passed through six hundred years of history and development in Japan. Without such a heritage, none of these three could have arrived at the religious conclusions they did, nor would there have been a populace prepared to embrace their teachings. Hence, the first step in understanding the development of Japanese Pure Land and the basis for Hōnen's, Shinran's, and Ippen's thinking is to elucidate its early history. That is what this study seeks to do.

THE PRE-HEIAN PERIOD

Pure Land Buddhism first entered Japan as one component among the extensive cultural imports absorbed from the Asian continent in the sixth, seventh, and eighth centuries. During its early years in Japan, it was hardly distinguished from the other forms of Buddhism imported alongside it. The prevailing trend was to use Pure Land elements in memorializing ancestors and in transferring religious merit to deceased relatives for their repose. Beginning in the Nara period (710–784), the basic tenets of Pure Land thought became more clearly understood, primarily by monks who studied sutras and commentaries received from the continent. At the same time, there was an increase in Pure Land's general popularity among aristocrats as well, resulting in the proliferation of Amida images and copies of Pure Land texts. From this time on, Pure Land Buddhism began to assume more identity as one path to Buddhist salvation. The study of Pure Land concepts and the expansion of Amida worship during the Nara period thus laid the groundwork for a solid Pure Land following in Heian times.

The arrival of Pure Land Buddhism into Japan probably occurred around the turn of the seventh century. There is evidence for the presence of Pure Land texts and ideas as early as the time of Shōtoku Taishi (574–622). First of all, the *Yuimagyō gisho* (T. 2186), a seventh century commentary attributed to Shōtoku, bears a quotation from a Pure Land sutra, the *Muryōjukyō* (T. 360), and in another place uses the term Pure Land (*jōdo*).[1] Second, an inscription on the Shaka image at the Hōryūji which is said to have been dedicated to the recovery of the ailing Shōtoku Taishi, contains the words, "... go up to the Pure Land and rise quickly to that sublime fulfillment" (*ōjō jōdo sōshō myōka*).[2] Third, the inscription to the so-called Tenjukoku Mandala, attributed to Shōtoku's wife at the time of his death, declares that he "... will be reborn in the heavenly kingdom of unlimited life" (*ōshō yo tenjukoku shi chū*).[3] This "kingdom" has been identified by many scholars as the Pure Land, though the issue is still open to some controversy.[4] Fourth, entries in the *Nihon shoki*—which admittedly is late, written in 720—indicate that the monk Eon, who had recently returned from years of study in China, lectured at court on the *Muryōjukyō* first in 640 and again in 652.[5] Each of these pieces of evidence has its own particular problems of authenticity, dating, and interpretation, but based on them scholars generally acknowledge the presence of Pure Land texts and terminology in Japan as early as Shōtoku Taishi's time.[6]

The mere presence of Pure Land texts and ideas in the early seventh century does not imply that Pure Land Buddhism was widespread or popular at that time. On the contrary, it did not gain much currency in either aristocratic or Buddhist circles until the Nara period itself. Textual evidence verifies that only over the course of the eighth century did Pure Land become a visible theme in Japanese Buddhism. A catalogue of Nara texts preserved at the Shōsōin reveals that the number of copies of Pure Land sutras rose steadily during this period. A tabulation of them follows:

COPIES OF PURE LAND SUTRAS[7]

Title	Early Nara	Late Nara	Total
Amidakyō (T. 366)	32	37	69
Shōsanjōdokyō (T. 367)	7	14	21
Muryōjukyō (T. 360)	12	22	34
Muryōshōjōbyōdōgakukyō (T. 361)	5	13	18
Kanmuryōjukyō (T. 365)	15	25	40
Hanjuzammaikyō (T. 418)	5	15	20

These figures reflect a uniform increase in the popularity of Pure Land sutras over the Nara period. The same catalogue also indicates a concomitant rise in the number of copies of Pure Land commentaries and treatises in circulation. The most prominent among these were:

COPIES OF PURE LAND
COMMENTARIES AND TREATISES[8]

Title and Author	Early Nara	Late Nara	Total
Muryōjukyō shūyō By Wŏn-hyo	1	6	7
Ryōkan Muryōjukyōsho By Ui-jŏk	1	5	6

Title and Author	Early Nara	Late Nara	Total
Ryōkan Muryōjukyō kōmoku Author Unknown	1	7	8
Ryōkan Muryōjukyōki By Hyŏn-il	1	3	4
Muryōjukyō jukki By Hyŏn-il	0	4	4
Ryōkangyō jishaku Author Unknown	7	3	10
Kanmuryōjukyōsho By Shan-tao	2	6	8
Shōsanjōdokyōsho By Ching-mai	11	8	19
Hanjuzammaikyō ryakki By Wŏn-hyo	1	12	13
Muryōjukyōron By Vasubandhu (?)	2	13	15
Anrakushū By Tao-ch'o	3	9	12
Saihō hōji sanmon By Shan-tao (?)	13	4	17
Ōjō raisan By Shan-tao	10	3	13

Scholars have observed that among these works, ones written by Chinese were more prominent during the first half of the Nara period, whereas those by Koreans dominated the second half.[9] Hence, the Korean tradition must be ranked alongside the Chinese in tracing the origins of Pure Land Buddhism in Japan.

The expansion of Pure Land popularity in the Nara period is also corroborated in iconographic evidence. A record of Buddhist statuary cast at the Kōfukuji, one of the foremost aristocratic temples in Nara, yields the following figures:

NUMBER OF ICONS CAST AT THE KŌFUKUJI, 707–806[10]

Buddhist Image	707–715	715–724	724–749	758–764	764–770	781–806
Shaka	1	0	0	0	0	0
Miroku	0	2	0	0	0	0
Yakushi	0	0	1	0	1	1
Kannon	0	0	1	2	0	3
Amida	0	0	0	1	2	7

These tabulations show clearly that the Pure Land images, Kannon and Amida, were the most numerous and that their popularity increased as the Nara period wore on.[11]

The popularization of the Amida cult within aristocratic society does not necessarily mean that it understood the content of Pure Land doctrine. Inscriptions and dedications associated with Nara iconography indicate that the real reason aristocrats commissioned Pure Land images was to commemorate deceased relatives. For instance, around 778 at the Kōfukuji, an Amida triad was dedicated to a Fujiwara lady as a succor to her rebirth. In 791, another Amida triad was enshrined there on the occasion of a memorial service for a deceased empress from the Fujiwara family.[12] Such services show that aristocratic veneration of Amida Buddha hardly differed from reverence for any other Buddha. All were worshipped for the benefits that they offered—in this case, efficacy in aiding the dead. One scholar believes that aristocratic sponsorship of such Buddhist functions reflects a more indigenous kind of religion, the veneration of ancestors, which antedated Buddhism's arrival in Japan.[13] Without assessing such theories or ascribing ancestor practices to Japanese origins rather than continental influences, it is at least possible to say that aristocrats patronized the Amida cult less out of a desire for their own rebirth in the Pure Land than from a sense of concern for the dead. This kind of devotion to Amida stands in contrast to the salvation oriented practices of Pure Land Buddhism which were avidly embraced by aristocratic society in the Heian period.[14]

While Nara aristocrats preoccupied themselves with such pietistic concerns, the Buddhist community began to delve into the doctrines of the Pure Land tradition. The three major Buddhist schools of the Nara period—the Hossō, the Kegon, and the Sanron—all produced monks who cultivated one interest or another in Pure Land teachings. In the Hossō there was Zenju (723-797), in the Kegon Chikyō, and in the Sanron Chikō (709-781?). All these were eminent thinkers in their own right within their respective traditions, but each in addition wrote commentaries or treatises on the Pure Land sutras as well.[15] Of these, Chikō and the Sanron school are generally recognized as exemplary of Pure Land developments in the Nara period.

Chikō's life coincided approximately with the dates of the Nara period itself. He was born in 709 and died sometime during the reign of Emperor Kōnin (r. 770-781). At the young age of nine he began religious training and over the course of his career became steeped in the Sanron teachings of the Gangōji.[16] Among the works attributed to him in the *Tōiki dentō mokuroku* (T. 2183) is a five fascicle Pure Land treatise, now lost, called the *Muryōjukyō ronshaku*.[17] Fortunately, this work was quoted extensively by later Pure Land writers, and from these sources Chikō's interpretation of Pure Land teachings can be reconstructed.

The prevailing theme of Chikō's Pure Land writings is the primacy of meditative experience. Faith and the verbal nembutsu, which became the focus of the Kamakura Pure Land movements, occupy a relatively minor role in his teachings. Chikō's view of these two is best summed up in the following passages taken from his *Ronshaku:*

> Meditative visualization refers to religious understanding, whereas faith refers to religious practice. Now, if a people first have understanding, then they can immediately give rise to practice. Among religious practices, we regard faith as the first, and because of this we cultivate a heart of faith even now. The expression "to initiate visualization" means to focus one's concentration on a single spot and to visualize with clarity the [Pure] Land. The expression "to nurture faith" means for a

number of sentient beings to hear [the name of] Amida Buddha, to have a heart of faith, to rejoice to such an extent that they have only one thought, and to achieve, one and all, rebirth in the Pure Land, and only then to extirpate wrong teachings. Moreover, will they not fully cultivate all types of good merit also?[18]

The term "exclusive and single-minded concentration" refers to the nembutsu of which there are two types. The first is the meditative nembutsu and the second is the verbal nembutsu. The meditative nembutsu also has two types: concentration on the material body of the Buddha, revealing his eighty-four thousand physical characteristics, etc., and concentration on the Buddha's body of wisdom, revealing the power of his great compassion, etc. As for the verbal nembutsu, if the mind has no power in itself, then by engaging the mouth and concentrating on the Buddha, one can cause the mind not to be distracted.[19]

Clearly, the focal point of Chikō's interpretation is meditation. For him, faith and the verbal nembutsu are expedient means for achieving the higher religious experience of meditative visualization. In that experience, true liberation and realization occur. Faith and the verbal nembutsu are preparatory stages and do not contain salvation in themselves.[20]

The Chikō Mandala,[21] a graphic representation of the Pure Land from the Nara period attributed to Chikō, is perhaps the kind of object used by him for meditation. According to legend, Chikō was inspired by a dream in which the Buddha revealed to him the splendors of the Pure Land, and upon awakening he immediately recorded his vision in the form of this mandala.[22] Such Pure Land representations were sometimes used as objects of worship or as adornments to Buddhist altars, but passages in Shan-tao's writings indicate that their central function was as objects of contemplation and meditation.[23] Such a use of the Chikō Mandala would certainly be consistent with his heavy emphasis on meditation in the *Ronshaku*.

As early as the fourteenth century, Buddhist thinkers such as Gyōnen (1240–1321) and Gyōe (d. 1395) argued that Chikō wrote his *Ronshaku* using the *Muryōjukyōubadaisha ganshōgechū* (T. 1819) by T'an-luan (476–542) as the basis of interpretation.[24] Both works were written as treatises on the *Muryōjukyō ubadaisha* (T. 1524) attributed to Vasubandhu and to that extent bear a common structure and theme. Scholars, however, have come to question the link between the two works. They point out that T'an-luan treated the verbal nembutsu as an alternative to meditative practices, available to people of limited religious ability, whereas Chikō viewed it as one stage leading toward meditative realization. This difference has prompted them to associate Chikō's interpretation more with the meditative slant found in the writings of Chia-tsai (ca. 627–649) than with T'an-luan's position.[25]

Among the influences on Chikō in formulating his view of the Pure Land teachings, the impact of Sanron thought must not be overlooked. Chikō was first and foremost an adherent of the Sanron school, in the tradition of Kumārajīva (344–413), Ch'i-tsang (549–623), and the Gangōji. A list of his writings reflects this influence and includes such titles as the *Hannyashingyō jutsugi*, the *Chūron shoki*, and the *Shogaku sanron hyōshūgi*.[26] Hence, standing behind Chikō's interpretation of Pure Land concepts were all the basic Mahāyāna axioms which hallmark Sanron teachings—i.e., that nonsubstantiality has neither arising nor creation (*kū mushō musa*), that all beings have the Buddha-nature (*shitsuu busshō*), etc.[27] With Sanron's comprehensive philosophy of Buddhism as a backdrop, Pure Land became an ancillary teaching, which could be used as a program of religious practice, but was not an independent or self-contained branch of Buddhism. As a result, Pure Land occupied a subsidiary role both in Chikō's scheme of Buddhist thought and in Nara Buddhism as a whole.

In the Nara period, one other figure, besides Chikō, had an impact on the development of the Pure Land tradition—the itinerant monk

A BRIEF HISTORY OF PURE LAND BUDDHISM IN EARLY JAPAN

Gyōgi (or Gyōki, 668–749). Though Gyōgi has been associated with Pure Land Buddhism in such semi-legendary literature as the *Nihon ryōiki*,[28] his importance lies not so much in whether he actually observed Pure Land practices as in the religious life-style he pioneered. Though nurtured in the Hossō tradition, Gyōgi chose to leave the confines of temple life and to dedicate himself to good works and proselytization among the common people. He is credited with the construction of roads, bridges, ponds, canals, and forty-nine Buddhist chapels.[29] His life as a saintly itinerant represented a religious alternative to institutional Buddhism. In his wake, a fledgling apostate tradition emerged in Japan in which religious aspirants turned their back on the Buddhism of aristocratic society and the political establishment in favor of a wandering life of poverty and altruism, foreshadowing Ippen much later. Though Gyōgi's life-style had only a tenuous connection to Pure Land in the Nara period, it ultimately exerted a tremendous influence on the tenor, content, and dissemination of Pure Land Buddhism throughout the country.

The Nara period, in summary, can be described as the root-taking stage of the Pure Land tradition in Japan. At this time, the first shoots of a full-fledged Pure Land movement began to take shape within three distinct spheres of Nara religious affairs. First, in aristocratic society laypeople became more and more enthralled with Amida worship and sponsored the construction of Amida images and the copying of Pure Land sutras. These worshippers, however, gained little comprehension of Pure Land concepts but rather adopted Pure Land ceremonies as memorials for the dead. Second, at certain large Nara temples Buddhist clergy began to delve into the teachings of Pure Land, wrote their own Pure Land treatises, and even incorporated Pure Land elements into their religious practices, but they treated Pure Land as only one concern in a much larger system of Buddhist thought and practice. Third, in society at large the rise of the itinerant monk movement, though not yet associated with Pure Land practices specifically, provided a potential vehicle for the propagation and development of Pure Land thought. These three types of religious activity existed alongside one another in Nara times, but over the course of the Heian period they gradually coalesced to form the Pure Land tradition.

THE EARLY HEIAN PERIOD

While the Nara period marked the first stage of Pure Land development in Japan, the Heian period (794–1185) witnessed the unfolding of the tradition in full. During the first half of the Heian period, the Tendai complex at Mt. Hiei, to the northeast of Kyoto, became a center of Pure Land activity, and from there Pure Land teachings spread among both laypeople and clergy. This activity reached a watershed in the time of Genshin (942–1017), one of the foremost Pure Land figures of Heian Japan, and during his generation the Pure Land emerged as a prominent religious concern in aristocratic society. After Genshin's time, Pure Land themes continued to pervade the religious affairs of the Heian period, especially as the apocalyptic sense of *mappō*, the age of decline, gripped the population. During this period, Pure Land teachings diversified and were often couched in various Buddhist frameworks, and certain doctrines gradually evolved in the direction of Kamakura Pure Land's teachings.

At the beginning of the Heian period, just as the capital of Japan shifted from Nara to Kyoto, so the focal point of the Pure Land tradition moved from the large temples at Nara to the Tendai Buddhist center at Mt. Hiei on the outskirts of Kyoto. A link had existed between Tendai and Pure Land since the time of Chih-i (538–597), the Chinese founder of the Tendai school. His work, the *Makashikan* (T. 1911), presents among the four types of Tendai meditation the *jōgyōzammai*, a meditative ritual with a statue of Amida Buddha as the center of worship and the nembutsu as the meditative chant.[30] Notwithstanding this link, Tendai practices, as they were first established in Japan by Saichō (767–822), did not include the *jōgyōzammai*, and it was not until two generations later, when Ennin (794–864) returned from China in 847, that the *jōgyōzammai* was introduced at Mt. Hiei. Ennin imported this practice from the Chu-lin Ssu at Mt. Wu-t'ai where a five-tone (*goe*) method of chanting the nembutsu flourished. Though this method is not exactly the type outlined for the *jōgyōzammai* by Chih-i in his *Makashikan*, it nonetheless came to be used for that purpose, first at Mt. Wu-t'ai and later at Mt. Hiei. After Ennin's death in 864, another nembutsu ceremony was also inaugurated, the *fudan nembutsu*, in which nembutsu practice was maintained around the clock on designated occasions at the Jōgyōzammaidō, a meditation hall established in 848 by Ennin in the Tōtō precinct of Mt. Hiei. Ennin's introduction of the *jōgyōzammai* into monastic activities at Mt. Hiei did not necessarily catapult Pure Land teachings into the religious limelight. On the contrary, esoteric Buddhism (*mikkyō*) generally commanded greater attention during Ennin's life, and only gradually in subsequent decades did Pure Land also come to the fore.[31]

After Ennin, the next major figure at Mt. Hiei to take an active interest in Pure Land was the eighteenth head priest, Ryōgen (912–985). He was pivotal in establishing a substantive link between Pure Land thought and Japanese Tendai, since he was the first Tendai priest in Japan to compose a work concerned exclusively with Pure Land teachings, his *Gokuraku jōdo kubon ōjōgi*.[32] This work focuses on the nine levels of the Pure Land presented in the *Kanmuryōjukyō* (T. 365) and attempts to elucidate the requirements for rebirth at each level. Ryōgen's discussion of rebirth at the highest level, the *jōbonjō* is the longest of the nine sections, comprising about one-fourth of the entire work.[33] From the length of this section, it is clear that Ryōgen regarded rebirth in the *jōbonjō* as the central message of Pure Land teachings.

According to the *Kubon ōjōgi*, religious practices leading to rebirth in the *jōbonjō* are predicated on the cultivation of three kinds of mind (*sanshin*): *shijōshin*, *jinshin*, and *ekōhotsuganshin*. Ryōgen interprets these to mean 1) a mind meditating on the supreme truths of Buddhism and distancing itself from the distortions of wrong views, 2) a mind seeking the profundity of enlightenment, and 3) a mind turning toward the practice of good works and vowing enlightenment for itself and benefit for all sentient beings.[34] According to this interpretation, cultivation of the three minds demands a complete routine of religious concerns, including meditative training, ethical discipline, and devotional activities. All are necessary for rebirth at the highest level of the Pure Land, and together they constitute a program of practice which adheres faithfully to the Tendai concept of religious development.[35]

Ryōgen's treatment of the forty-eight vows of Amida, found in a later section of the *Kubon ōjōgi*,[36] underscores his conviction that rigorous religious efforts are the crux of the Pure Land teachings. The following passage, which focuses on the crucial eighteenth and nineteenth vows, summarizes Ryōgen's view that religious exertion is more highly esteemed than the mere desire to be reborn in the Pure Land expressed in the chanting of the nembutsu.

> Except for people who commit the five heinous acts or who slander the true teachings, all wrongdoers, if they have the desire, will definitely be allowed to achieve rebirth [in the Pure Land]. This is the eighteenth vow. Since the good works of such persons are not very extensive, [the vow] does not state that [Amida] will appear before them along with his host, greeting them and taking them [to the Pure Land]. In the nineteenth vow, people declare their intention to achieve enlightenment and undertake all kinds of virtuous practices. Because of this, [Amida], surrounded by his great multitude, appears before them and takes them [to the Pure Land]. This is the difference between these two vows.[37]

The upshot of this distinction is that people of intense religious effort are more exalted than those who rely on the nembutsu alone. Their superiority is confirmed at the time of death when Amida appears at their deathbed and ushers them into the Pure Land. In contrast, the commonplace wrongdoer, depending merely on the nembutsu, enjoys no such welcome and in effect assumes an inferior place in the religious realm. Hence, to Ryōgen's way of thinking, the nineteenth vow, rather than the eighteenth, is the pivotal one for the person aspiring to the Pure Land, and religious exertion rather than the verbal nembutsu is the proper way of achieving it.[38]

While the prevailing theme of the *Kubon ōjōgi* is rebirth in the Pure Land, its underlying premise is that the Pure Land teachings are only a practical method for realizing the more sublime principles of Tendai thought. The importance of Tendai concepts is reflected by the works that are quoted in the *Kubon ōjōgi*. The one most frequently cited is the *Kanmuryōjubutsukyōsho* (T. 1750), a commentary that was intimately associated with the early Tendai school in China and commonly attributed to Chih-i himself, which emphasizes meditation and the cultivation of good works as the core idea of the *Kanmuryōjukyō*. In addition to other Tendai treatises, such as Chih-i's *Yuimagyō gensho* (T. 1777), *Hokke mongu* (T. 1718), and *Makashikan* (T. 1911), other frequently quoted works in the *Kubon ōjōgi* include the Pure Land commentaries of earlier Korean and Nara monks. Among these, Chikō's writings apparently made a strong impression on Ryōgen, since his *Kubon ōjōgi* consistently follows Chikō's interpretation of Amida's forty-eight vows. Conspicuously few are quotations from the so-called Pure Land patriarchs of China whom later Kamakura Buddhists cited frequently: T'an-luan (476–542), Tao-ch'o (562–565), and Shan-tao (613–681).[39] These sources show that Ryōgen's concept of the Pure Land derived primarily from a meditative tradition and that it virtually ignored the devotional Pure Land movement of China.

Overall, the impact of Ryōgen's *Kubon ōjōgi* was twofold. First, it helped to foster in Japan an abiding link between Tendai and the Pure Land teachings. This may be one reason for the ubiquitous presence of Hokke elements from Tendai in Pure Land practices during the Heian period.[40] Secondly, though the *Kubon ōjōgi* was never a popular work among laypeople, it nonetheless escalated interest in

Pure Land teachings among monks at Mt. Hiei and prompted a plethora of Pure Land works during the last half of the tenth century. In the wake of Ryōgen, there arose a host of Pure Land enthusiasts at Mt. Hiei, many of them his direct disciples.

Two of Ryōgen's contemporaries who were active in this Pure Land awakening were Senkan (918–983) and Zen'yu (909–990). They also composed Pure Land works written from a Tendai point of view. Senkan's *Jūgan hosshinki*[41] incorporates rebirth in the Pure Land into the career of a bodhisattva, a goal to which, in his view, all religious devotees should strive. According to his interpretation, rebirth in the *jōbonjō* level of the Pure Land constitutes the first stage in that career, where the bodhisattva cultivates pervasive wisdom (*mushō bōnin*) and thereupon returns to earth to work for the benefit of all sentient beings. In content, Senkan's work draws on the *Kanmuryōjubutsukyōsho* and the *Jōdo jūgiron* (T. 1961), both attributed to Chih-i and, in concept, it identifies the Pure Land as an intermediate goal in a much larger scheme of religious development.[42] Zen'yu's *Amida shinjūgi*,[43] for its part, makes a sharp distinction between the ten *nen* performed by someone reborn in the *jōbonjō* and the ten performed by one reborn in the *gebonge*, the lowest level of the Pure Land. The former are the ten virtuous states of mind, listed in Wŏn-hyo's *Ryōkan Muryōjukyō shūyō* (T. 1747),[44] which the arduous devotee cultivates. The latter are ten verbal repetitions of the nembutsu, to which the ordinary wrongdoer may resort. Despite this differentiation, Zen'yu acknowledges that wrongdoers can achieve rebirth in the Pure Land, and he even argues for the eventual salvation of incorrigibles who commit the five heinous acts and slander the Dharma. He bases his argument on the Tendai doctrine of the four teachings (*shikyō*), within which universal salvation is recognized as an ultimate principle. In structure, Zen'yu's *Amida shinjūgi* is patterned after Chih-i's *Jōdo jūgiron*, mentioned above, though the specific issues discussed in it differ.[45] These works by Senkan and Zen'yu, along with Ryōgen's *Kubon ōjōgi*, are indicative of the pervasive influence of Tendai thought in Pure Land writings of the early Heian period.

Ryōgen may have been a pivotal figure in the rise of Pure Land activity at Mt. Hiei, but surprisingly enough his biography is not included among those of his eminent disciples in the three earliest Ōjōden collections.[46] Its absence suggests that for over a century after his death, when the first three Ōjōden were composed, Ryōgen was not regarded as a prominent figure of the Pure Land movement.[47] The reason for this may lie in his political involvements at Mt. Hiei. Ryōgen was perhaps the most illustrious priest at Mt. Hiei of his generation. During his younger years he distinguished himself in scholarship and debate, and of 966 he rose to the position of head priest. Over the course of his nineteen year tenure, he devoted himself to the reconstruction of facilities destroyed in a massive fire in 966, to the solicitation of aristocratic patronage, to the development of the secluded Yokawa section of Mt. Hiei, and to the consolidation of power by his own political group of Ennin's followers against the rival faction of Enchin (814–891).[48] During Ryōgen's time, however, there began to emerge among many Pure Land followers a sense of disdain toward worldly power and prestige. In many cases, this was directed against Mt. Hiei itself, where ambitious cliques vied with each other for control and where religious excellence was often measured in aristocratic support. Disenchantment with that world prompted Senkan to leave Mt. Hiei in 962 and to pursue his own religious practices in isolation in Settsu province. Likewise, the monk Zōga (917–1003), one of Ryōgen's disciples, retaliated with outrageous behavior, and he too eventually forsook Mt. Hiei to seclude himself in the mountains of Yamato province.[49] Ryōgen, who stood at the pinnacle of the Mt. Hiei establishment, diverged at this point from this emerging trend within Pure Land circles.

Of all the Pure Land figures in the Heian period, the itinerant monk Kōya (or Kūya, 903–972) best epitomizes these apostate sentiments. Like Gyōgi of the Nara period, he rejected the religious life prescribed by the large Buddhist institutions and in its place he dedicated himself to altruistic acts, stringent religious practices, and nembutsu chanting. Little is known of Kōya's background, though some sources allege that he came from aristocratic or even imperial blood. He first became prominent in Kyoto around 938, where he gained a reputation as the "marketplace *hijiri*" (*ichi no hijiri*) or the *Amida hijiri*. He would wander through the capital aiding the poor, performing works beneficial to the community, and propagating the nembutsu. Kōya's selfless behavior eventually drew the attention of Mt. Hiei officials, and in 948 he took the Buddhist precepts and received religious instruction from the head priest Enshō (880–964). But instead of cloistering himself there for the twelve years of compulsory training, Kōya returned to his evangelistic activities in the city among the people. As his fame grew, an entourage of more than six hundred followers gathered around him, and even members of the aristocracy contributed to his religious projects, such as constructing Buddhist images and copying sutras. Kōya died in 972, according to his biographies, in a fashion typical of one about to enter the Pure Land—bathed and clothed in white, offering up fragrant incense, facing the Western Paradise, eyes closed in contemplation, and surrounded by his companions.[50]

Kōya was by no means an isolated figure of his period, but rather was representative of an entire religious undercurrent at work in Heian society. Since Gyōgi's time, religious itinerants had been active in Japan and were instrumental in disseminating rudimentary Buddhist concepts and practices among the common people. In early times these holy men were referred to as *zenji, bosatsu, ubasoku, shami,* or *jikyōsha*, but around the turn of the tenth century the terms *hijiri* and *shōnin* also came into common parlance. These types of religious activists usually emerged outside the confines of organized Buddhist institutions, but as the Heian period wore on, more and more monks at established temples patterned their life-styles after them. Generally, *hijiri* were associated with either the Hokke or the Pure Land tradition.[51] Pure Land *hijiri* were renowned for chanting the nembutsu literally tens of thousands of times a day. The nembutsu dominated not only their own personal practices but also their

A BRIEF HISTORY OF PURE LAND BUDDHISM IN EARLY JAPAN

message to the masses. Considering, however, the shamanistic orientation of the *hijiri* movement, their nembutsu no doubt differed in crucial ways from that in Tendai scholarship. Most likely, the *hijiri nembutsu* was fraught with magical and ecstatic implications, whereas the Tendai one was primarily contemplative and tranquilizing.[52] Nonetheless, Pure Land *hijiri* succeeded in familiarizing common people with the nembutsu, whether they understood its doctrinal interpretations or not.

While *hijiri* were active below among the common people, aristocratic society above also became preoccupied with Pure Land teachings. Pure Land's association with funerals and memorial services, which had been well established in Nara times, persisted in aristocratic circles during the Heian period. For example, in 930 at the funeral of Emperor Daigo (855–930), the processional route was lined on both sides with monks striking bells and chanting the nembutsu.[53] Over and above such funerary practices, aristocrats gradually became concerned about their own prospects for rebirth in the Pure Land. This concern probably stemmed from a growing consciousness of impermanence and misfortune among them. In the Nara period, the world had been viewed in positive terms, and the desire for benefits in this world (*genze riyaku*) had dominated aristocratic religion. Around 900, however, attitudes began to shift in response to changing political and economic conditions. First of all, the Fujiwara family gained a stranglehold on Heian politics through the innovation of the *sesshō kanpaku*, the office of the regent who handled all affairs and decisions of the Emperor. Fujiwara ascendancy resulted in the eclipse of other aristocratic families and in effect fostered in them a sense of pessimism over their own lot. Secondly, the economic system, based on estates (*shōen*) from which the Kyoto aristocrats drew their wealth, began its long process of deterioration around 900, and with it the living standards of its Kyoto beneficiaries, including the Fujiwara family, slowly but surely dropped.[54] The declining status and fortunes of Heian aristocrats gave them pause to reassess their fate and drove many to seek consolation in religion, particu-

129

larly in Pure Land beliefs and practices.

Concretely, Kyoto aristocrats expressed their interest in the Pure Land in a number of ways. First, there were traditional forms of patronage—the commissioning of Buddhist art, the construction of temples, and the support of Pure Land monks and their projects. From a relatively early period, the Fujiwara family—specifically, Morosuke (908–960), Kaneie (929–990), Tamemitsu (942–992), Michinaga (966–1027), and Yorimune (993–1065)—offered support of Pure Land practices, and many of them went on to become monks after retirement in order to pursue such practices.[55] Second, the Heian literati began to use Pure Land themes in their writings. The earliest known example of this is a poem by Shimada Tadaomi (828–892) entitled "A View at Evening by a Pond in the Woods."

> Flowers bright, waters turbulent,
>   there are pines filled with wind.
> Passing by, I plow the tracks of
>   Amida Buddha.
> In doing so, I contemplate his sublime
>   kingdom in the Western region.
> My voice, singing praises, harmonizes
>   at that moment with the eventide bells.[56]

Although such themes were rare in ninth century literature, they became more and more prevalent during the late tenth and early eleventh century. Third, aristocrats began to participate in religious societies, many of which stressed Pure Land practices. In 907 the Heian poet Miyoshi Kiyoyuki (847–918) wrote perhaps the first record of such a society, entitled the *Jōdoji nembutsu engi*, and may have been an active member of the society himself.[57]

Among the religious societies of the Heian period, the Kangakue is one of the most celebrated. It exemplifies the kinds of devotions that were current among aristocrats in the tenth century. This society began in 964 and continued its meetings until around 986. Its membership consisted of about twenty monks from Mt. Hiei and twenty collegians from the court academy (*daigakuryō*). They would meet twice a year, just when the seasons were changing, for a full day of religious activities. During the third and the ninth months, on the night of the fourteenth, the monks would descend from Mt. Hiei and rendezvous with the lay members of the society who had made their way up from the capital. Together they would proceed on foot to an appointed place, with the monks chanting verses from the *Lotus Sutra* and the collegians reciting poems from Po Chu-i (772–846). On the fifteenth, lectures on the *Lotus Sutra* would occupy the morning hours, while the afternoon and evening were devoted to the composition of poems based on verses from the sutras. At night nembutsu chanting began and meditation on the Pure Land would continue until the next morning. This biannual event was solemn and intense. It gave lay members, most of whom emerged from the intermediate ranks of the Heian aristocracy, an opportunity to apply literary and aesthetic sensibilities to common religious concerns and to experience firsthand the religious rigors of monks.[58]

From among the members of the Kangakue, one individual distinguished himself as the motive force behind the society and as perhaps the most illustrious lay devotee of Pure Land Buddhism in the tenth century—Yoshishige no Yasutane (d. 1002). His fervor for the Pure Land teachings is reflected in the introduction to his *Nihon ōjō gokuraku ki*.

> From my childhood days I have fixed my thoughts on Amida Buddha, and for over forty years those desires have become ever more intense. With my mouth I chant his name and with my mind I contemplate his features. Not even for a moment, whether walking or standing still or sitting or lying down, do I forget him. In both distress and defeat, I hold to him without fail.[59]

As the second son of a court scholar of Chinese divination (*onmyō*), Yasutane grew up in a thoroughly intellectual environment. Nonetheless, he lacked the wealth and comforts possessed by other Heian aristocrats and could not afford a proper residence of his own. These conditions no doubt propelled him in the direction of religion, and along with other aristocrats of similar circumstances he founded the Kangakue.[60]

In 985–986 Yasutane wrote his *Nihon ōjō gokuraku ki*, a seminal work in the history of Pure Land literature. Prior to it, all Pure Land works composed in Japan were highly abstruse and overly scholastic, circulating among priests but having little impact on the population at large. Yasutane's *Gokuraku ki* broadened popular appeal by skirting doctrinal intricacies and couching Pure Land concepts in simple, didactic biographies. He took the idea for this work from the Chinese Pure Land priest Chia-ts'ai (ca. 627–649), who incorporated a similar collection of biographies into the last fascicle of his *Jōdoron* (T. 1963). The *Gokuraku ki* focuses on Japanese men and women, both clergy and laypeople, who achieve rebirth in the Pure Land through a variety of religious practices. Altogether, it contains forty-two such rebirth stories (*ōjōden*), featuring such eminent figures as Shōtoku Taishi, Chikō, Gyōgi, Ennin, Kōya, and Senkan. Yasutane drew inspiration from the lives of these individuals, and by recording their biographies he sought to motivate others toward the Pure Land ideal. The *Gokuraku ki* enjoyed much popularity in its own time and, as the first collection of rebirth stories in Japan, it prompted a series of so-called *Ōjōden* in subsequent centuries, including the *Zoku honchō ōjōden*, the *Shūi ōjōden*, and the *Goshūi ōjōden*.[61]

In the same year that Yasutane completed his *Gokuraku ki* he made one of the momentous decisions of his life—to forsake his position as a Kyoto aristocrat and to take up the life of a monk in the secluded Yokawa area of Mt. Hiei. Yokawa, also referred to as the Ryogon'in, lay on the north side of Mt. Hiei, isolated from the main temple complex. It had been established by Ennin in 848 as a personal retreat for meditation and sutra copying but had fallen into disuse after his death. A century later Ryōgen engineered the revival of Yokawa, first by establishing a personal hermitage there in 954 and later by supervising the construction of its chapels and monasteries during his tenure as head priest. During Ryōgen's own lifetime, Yokawa gradually became a rallying point for Pure Land monks, particularly those who rejected the world of power and vanity which had engulfed much of Mt. Hiei's hierarchy. The Eshin'in built in 983 through the patronage of Fujiwara no Kaneie, later became the seat of Yokawa's Pure Land activities, especially with the guidance of Genshin.[62] Yasutane, under the clerical name Jakushin, cast his lot with these Pure Land monks in Yokawa and, in doing so, turned his back on both the Kyoto aristocracy and the Mt. Hiei establishment.

With Yasutane's withdrawal from lay society, the Kangakue soon disbanded for lack of strong leadership, but a similar religious circle called the Nijūgozammaie arose in Yokawa shortly afterwards and absorbed most of the Kangakue's activities. The new society, which began around 986, conducted its meetings at the Shuryōgon'in, the main temple in the Yokawa precinct. Originally, the group had twenty-five charter members, who all pledged religious allegiance to one another. Its meetings differed only slightly from those of the Kangakue—on the fifteenth of each month its members would assemble for a day of religious activities consisting of lectures on the *Lotus Sutra*, a presentation of personal supplications to the Buddha, nembutsu chanting throughout the night, and the recitation of the *Amida Sutra*. The Nijūgozammaie met on a monthly basis, rather than only twice a year as the Kangakue did. Furthermore, its members carried on their own private programs of nembutsu chanting and Pure Land meditation over and above these monthly meetings. Perhaps the most interesting practice of the society was its ritual for assisting dying members into the Pure Land. When members fell gravely ill, their comrades would take turns sitting with them and would chant the nembutsu to keep them ever mindful of the Pure Land. If death seemed imminent, they were moved to a chapel and all the other members were assembled. There the dying member would lie facing the western direction where an image of Amida had been enshrined, and until the moment of death all those assembled would chant the nembutsu together to assist the member in concentration on the Pure

Land.[63] Yasutane, who was not one of the original members of the Nijūgozammaie, joined the group soon after its inception, and throughout his remaining years dedicated himself fully to its activities and provided valuable insight and leadership to the society.

Of all the members of the Nijūgozammaie, Yasutane was overshadowed by only one other person—Genshin. The breadth and the depth of Genshin's influence, both during his own lifetime and for centuries afterward, distinguished him as perhaps the foremost Pure Land monk of the Heian period. Like many other illustrious figures at Mt. Hiei, he began his religious training as a boy, and under the tutelage of Ryōgen he excelled in both studies and religious practices. Genshin seemed destined to assume a position of authority at Mt. Hiei, but before he reached the age of forty he withdrew from the mainstream of Hiei politics and confined himself to Yokawa, where he spent most of the next thirty-five years of his life. There he was caught up in the flurry of Pure Land activities, and by 985 he completed his monumental work on the Pure Land, the *Ōjōyōshū* (T. 2682).[64]

As a Pure Land piece, the *Ōjōyōshū* addresses first and foremost the question of the nembutsu, using passages from Pure Land sutras, treatises, and commentaries that bear on this topic. Genshin expresses this theme in the preface to the work:

> I have gathered together here a few essential passages from sutras and treatises based on a single path, the nembutsu. They will be easy to understand when delved into and easy to practice when undertaken. Altogether, there are ten sections (to this work) and, when divided, they make up three fascicles. The ten are: 1) Abhorrence of the Tainted World, 2) Desire for the Pure Land, 3) The Basis for the Pure Land, 4) The Nembutsu Properly Practiced, 5) Methods of Enhancing the Nembutsu, 6) The Nembutsu on Special Occasions, 7) Benefits of the Nembutsu, 8) The Basis for the Nembutsu, 9) Acts Leading to Rebirth in the Pure Land, and 10) Some Interpretations through Question and Answer.[65]

A BRIEF HISTORY OF PURE LAND BUDDHISM IN EARLY JAPAN

These ten chapters of the *Ōjōyōshū* fall into three distinct sections. Chapters four, five, and six, which elucidate the nature and practice of the nembutsu, are the core of the work. The first three chapters set the context for this discussion, and chapters seven, eight, and nine provide attendant details on the nembutsu. Chapter ten is an addendum dealing with miscellaneous questions not included in the previous chapters.[66]

Chapter four, "The Nembutsu Properly Practiced," contains the heart of Genshin's interpretation of the nembutsu. In it he adopts the fivefold categorization of the nembutsu which is found in the *Muryōjukyō ubadaisha ganshōge* (T. 1524), commonly called the *Ōjōron* or the *Jōdoron* attributed to Vasubandhu. These five are 1) the nembutsu of worship (*raihai*), 2) the nembutsu expressing praises (*sandan*), 3) the nembutsu in which the desire for rebirth in the Pure Land is generated (*sagan*), 4) the nembutsu of meditative visualization (*kanzatsu*), and 5) the nembutsu of response through altruism (*ekō*). Among these, Genshin emphasizes the fourth, the meditative nembutsu. This kind of nembutsu entails a prolonged program of meditative training in which a person progresses in stages from the visualization of specific attributes (*bessōkan*) of the Amida Buddha and his Pure Land to an all-encompassing vision (*sōsōkan*) of them. For the benefit of persons unprepared for such a rigorous program, there is a third type of meditative nembutsu called simplified visualization (*zōryakukan*) which does not require as much religious exertion as the other two. At the most elementary, this is reduced to simply saying the nembutsu and reflecting on the Pure Land. In Genshin's words,

> If there are those who are not equal to visualizing the characteristics of the Buddha, then they should single-mindedly intone the nembutsu while thinking of refuge, or of salvation, or of rebirth in the Pure Land.[67]

This verbal type of nembutsu becomes accessible to even the untutored and unsophisticated follower and hence has much broader appeal than the more difficult meditative ones. The *Ōjōyōshū* treats these three kinds of meditative nembutsu as the key to rebirth in the Pure Land. The *sagan nembutsu* constitutes the ground from which this meditative nembutsu arises, and the other three forms of nembutsu act as a succor to the meditative also.[68]

Genshin's doctrinal position in the *Ōjōyōshū* resembles in some ways that of Ryōgen in the *Kubon ōjōgi*. Both regard strenuous religious undertakings as the crux of Pure Land practices, and yet each makes allowances for sentient beings who are incapable of such rigorous religious training. The two, however, differ in important ways, and it is these differences which set the *Ōjōyōshū* apart as a milestone in Pure Land history. First of all, the *Ōjōyōshū* avoids the scholastic bent found in the *Kubon ōjōgi* and thereby addresses itself to a much larger community than just the Buddhist clergy at Mt. Hiei. In form, it is not so much an academic treatise as a handbook for the practice of the nembutsu. Admittedly, some sections of the work are rather technical in nature, but others contain simple, straightforward advice relevant to monk and layperson alike. This diversity of contents gave the *Ōjōyōshū* currency within a broad spectrum of religious practitioners, and it did much to promote the nembutsu, in one form or another, as the central practice of Pure Land Buddhism.[69] Secondly, the *Ōjōyōshū* draws on a different scholarly corpus than the *Kubon ōjōgi*. Ryōgen's heavy reliance on works attributed to Chih-i, particularly the *Kanmuryōjubutsukyōshō* (T. 1750), places the *Kubon ōjōgi* squarely in the Tendai tradition. The *Ōjōyōshū*, on the other hand, quotes extensively from such sources as Tao-ch'o's *Anrakushū* (T. 1958), Shan-tao's *Kanmuryōjubutsukyōsho* (T. 1753), *Kannen Amidabutsu sōkaizammai kudokuhōmon* (T. 1959), and *Ōjō raisange* (T. 1980), and Huai-kan's *Shaku Jōdo gungiron* (T. 1960), all Pure Land classics which were virtually ignored in earlier Heian writings. These works present the Pure Land as the easy path (*igyōdō*) to salvation and the nembutsu as an easy practice (*igyō*) accessible even to the common wrongdoer. Without repudiating Tendai doctrine, the

A BRIEF HISTORY OF PURE LAND BUDDHISM IN EARLY JAPAN

Ōjōyōshū imbibes enough from these works to give it a non-Tendai flavor and to suggest Pure Land practice as a complete path to salvation in and of itself.[70]

The impact of the Ōjōyōshū on the religious history of Japan has been considerable. In Genshin's own lifetime, it was circulated widely in manuscript form, and copies of it even reached Sung China where it received ample praise at Mt. T'ien-t'ai.[71] During that period the Ōjōyōshū became a religious manual for both monks and laypeople. Lower-class aristocrats, such as Kamo no Chōmei (1153?–1216), as well as political giants, such as Fujiwara no Michinaga, embraced it as one of their favorite religious texts, and countless religious societies, beginning with the Nijūgozammaie, adopted it as a guide to nembutsu practice. The work also imprinted images of the splendors of the Pure Land and the terrors of the hells on the mind of literate society, and it inspired Pure Land themes in the popular fiction and poetry of the times.[72] Within a hundred years of Genshin's death, the first wood-block edition of the Ōjōyōshū appeared, and from that time onward it was reprinted perennially, with thirty-three editions of it issued in the Tokugawa period (1603–1867) alone.[73] Over and above its popular impact, the Ōjōyōshū stimulated new trends in Pure Land doctrine, primarily through the promotion of Tao-ch'o's and Shan-tao's teachings. Its influence on Hōnen, for example, is visible in his Ōjōyōshū ryōken, written two centuries later. In it he states:

> Genshin, by reason perforce, has defined the criterion for rebirth in the Pure Land using Shan-tao's writings on the exclusive practice [of the nembutsu] and on other practices as his guideline. Furthermore, it can be seen that he quotes Shan-tao's interpretations everywhere. Therefore, persons who would employ Genshin's [teachings] should by all means go back to Shan-tao's [also].[74]

Though Hōnen came to interpret the nembutsu in a very different way from Genshin, there is little doubt that he used Genshin's Ōjōyōshū as a starting point and through it drew inspiration from

Shan-tao's works as well.

While the *Ōjōyōshū* proves Genshin to be a pioneer of Pure Land thought, other works, such as his *Kanjin ryakuyōshū*, reveal him as a Tendai syncretist of the highest order. These two sides of Genshin are best contrasted by the prefaces to these two works. In the *Ōjōyōshū* he says:

> The teachings and practices for rebirth in the Pure Land are the eyes and the legs for those living in this tainted world during these latter days. Whether cleric or layperson, whether aristocrat or commoner, who is there that would not turn to them? Admittedly, there are no few works dealing with the esoteric and exoteric teachings of Tendai, and religious practices which result in phenomenal or transcendental attainments are manifold. Persons of exceptional wisdom and intense discipline may not regard them as difficult, but how can someone dull and stupid like myself dare attempt them? Therefore, I have assembled here a few essential passages from sutras and treatises based on a single path, the nembutsu. They will be easy to understand when delved into and easy to practice when undertaken.[75]

Here Genshin relinquishes difficult religious practices in favor of the nembutsu, but in the *Kanjin ryakuyōshū* he reverses himself and reaffirms the more strenuous path of Tendai meditation.

> Meditation is the quintessence of all the Buddhas and the heart of their teachings. Because of this, it has been taken by the Tendai school as its paradigm.... Now our age has reached a point of degeneration and people have very few beneficial qualities. In pursuing that path it is difficult for one to penetrate its profound subtleties, and in drawing on that tradition it is rare for one to plumb its foundations. What then of a dull and benighted person like myself? For such people, the will deepens with broadening, and thinking sharpens with assistance. Imperceptibly, they begin to yearn for the

A BRIEF HISTORY OF PURE LAND BUDDHISM IN EARLY JAPAN

meditative mind of the great [Tendai] master and they wish to open their wisdom eye which knows no difference between self and other. Therefore, I have copied here a few passages from the works of former masters and have named them "A Collection of Essentials for the Meditative Mind." [This work deals with] a single path, the practice of meditation.[76]

The *Kanjin ryakuyōshū*, written perhaps twenty years after the *Ōjōyōshū*, shows Genshin's unfailing dedication to mainstream Tendai thought, over and above his interest in Pure Land teachings. In contrast to the *Ōjōyōshū*, it quotes heavily from standard Tendai texts, particularly the *Makashikan*, and omits completely references to Tao-ch'o's and Shan-tao's writings.[77] Moreover, Genshin integrates Pure Land concepts into the Tendai superstructure, as is evidenced by the following passages from the *Kanjin ryakuyōshū*:

> Since the Buddha's Pure Land of bliss is also something which arises from causes, it is nonsubstantiality (*kū*), provisioned reality (*ke*), and the Middle Way (*chū*). In what sense is it nonsubstantiality? In that it arises from causes—i.e., from Amida's karmic rewards and untainted acts. There is no independent existence in what arises from causes, and what has no independent existence is nonsubstantial. In what sense is it provisional reality? In that it still arises, even without having independent existence. Hence, it is convention. In what sense is it the Middle Way? In that it does not deviate from the nature of dharmas. And they altogether belong to the Middle Way. What we should realize is that the Pure Land is the three thousand worlds found in a single instant of thought. It is absolute nonsubstantiality, the Tathāgata-garbha, and true nature, all at one and the same time. While not being these three, it is these three, and while being these three, it is not these three. The Pure Land, as it is perceived in meditation, is like this. Moreover, the body and the mind, which perform this meditation, are also thus.[78]

> Since this body of mine is Amida and Amida is this body, the tainted world is the same as the Pure Land and the Pure Land the same as this tainted world.[79]

This kind of treatment of the Pure Land demonstrates Genshin's abiding Tendai outlook, and it confirms him as a true disciple of Ryōgen.

Except for a few excursions away from Mt. Hiei, Genshin spent most of his adult life attached to one temple or another in the Yokawa section of the mountain. There he dedicated himself to studies and writing, maintained an ongoing regimen of private Pure Land practices, participated actively in the Nijūgozammaie, and cultivated religious associations with monks and laypeople of both aristocratic and lowly origins. In time Genshin rose in fame for his wisdom and religious accomplishments, and inevitably a large circle of followers gathered around him. In 1004 he received the honorary position of *gon shōsōzu*, an imperially appointed adviser on Buddhist affairs, and he thereby ascended to prominence in the Buddhist world. This kind of attention, however, did not accord with Genshin's own religious preferences. He resigned the title during the following year and retreated to the innermost recesses of Yokawa where he built himself a modest hermitage. There Genshin spent the rest of his days in seclusion from Mt. Hiei's affairs and occupied himself with religious concerns—study, writing, sutra reading, and prolonged nembutsu chanting. At the age of seventy-six, Genshin fell gravely ill, and for ten days, surrounded by his closest disciples, he lay on his right side facing the western direction, chanting the nembutsu and reciting verses from the sutras. In this repose, with his mind fixed on the Pure Land, Genshin died in 1017.[80]

In many ways the life of Genshin marks a high point in the development of Japanese Pure Land Buddhism, for he was, in a certain sense, the culmination of Pure Land trends up to that time. Since the Nara period, Pure Land had evolved along three discernible lines— an aristocratic, a scholastic, and an apostate tradition. Genshin, as a product of all three, did much to bring them together into a single movement. Through his *Ōjōyōshū*, he infused new dimensions of interest in the Pure Land among aristocrats, where funerary practices had prevailed earlier. Through his *Kanjin ryakuyōshu*, he extended the scope of Tendai scholarship on the Pure Land and integrated it more tightly into Tendai doctrine. Through his life-style of retirement and seclusion, he expressed his dissatisfaction with the religious and secular establishments and his sympathies with the apostate values of the *hijiri* movement. In these ways Genshin drew together the Pure Land trends of his own day. More important than these accomplishments, however, was Genshin's *Ōjōyōshū*, for it paved the way for the innovations of the Kamakura period. This work became a source of inspiration to generations of monks and laypeople after him, and it did more for the promotion of the nembutsu as the chief practice of Pure Land Buddhism than anything prior to it. Genshin himself, with one foot in Tendai doctrine and the other in Pure Land devotions, was a watershed figure in Pure Land history, and his *Ōjōyōshū*, provoking new interpretations through the revival of Tao-ch'o's and Shan-tao's teachings, was a revolutionary volley.

THE LATER HEIAN PERIOD

After the death of Genshin, Pure Land Buddhism began to expand in a variety of directions. The dissemination of the *Ōjōyōshū*, on the one hand, and the intensification of a sense of *mappō*, the period of decline, on the other, helped to heighten Pure Land Buddhism's overall popularity. As Pure Land spread, it began to break away from the Tendai tether to which it was bound through much of the Heian period. Tendai monks, of course, continued to embrace it and to interpret its concepts in a Tendai vein, but other forms of Buddhism also sought to adapt its ideas to their own particular doctrines. Moreover, individual monks, who became preoccupied with Pure Land interests, often separated themselves from the religious establishment and began propagating their teachings independently. All these events worked to diversify the Pure Land movement in society and to saturate Japan's religious order with Pure Land activities. As the movement approached a critical mass in the late Heian and early Kamakura periods, the teachings of Hōnen, Shinran, and Ippen emerged from this milieu as the prevailing trend in the evolution of Japanese Pure Land Buddhism and as the rallying point for a formal Pure Land school.

Among aristocrats, Pure Land patronage came to full blossom in the early eleventh century when Fujiwara no Michinaga (966–1027) became one of its avid supporters. Michinaga's period of political control is commonly regarded as the apex of Fujiwara rule and as the golden age of Heian aristocracy. In politics Michinaga was a shrewd and sometimes ruthless power broker, but in the social graces he was a true aesthete and man of letters. Despite his wealth, power, and fame, Michinaga's life was not all happiness and good fortune. He was chronically plagued with illness and underwent numerous family crises, including the estrangement of his son and the premature death of a daughter. It was perhaps these tribulations that disposed Michinaga to religion. As early as 1004 he came into contact with Genshin, and from that time he became an enthusiastic reader of the *Ōjōyōshū*. In 1019, after his retirement, Michinaga took Buddhist vows as a priest and at the same time began construction of what was perhaps the most dazzling Buddhist temple of his day, the Hōjōji. There Michinaga resided in religious retirement, all the while maintaining his political ties, until his death in 1027.[81]

Michinaga's death occurred in the Amida Hall of the Hōjōji in accordance with traditional deathbed ritual for Pure Land believers. Though it is difficult to substantiate, such deathbed practices may represent remnants of Pure Land's association with funerals, death, and ancestor worship dating back to pre-Nara times. This kind of ritual had increased in popularity during the tenth century, especially with the rise of nembutsu societies such as the Nijūgozammaie, but when used for the final rites of Michinaga, the most powerful political figure in Heian Japan, it achieved such prominence in Kyoto society that it became a common practice among aristocrats. The *Eiga monogatari*, a historical narrative of the eleventh century, describes Michinaga's deathbed scene in the following way:

> He had them open up the western vista, where folding screens had been set up, and he had them attend to the nine images of Amida Buddha.... He then thought continuously and intently on the nembutsu as his death approached. He did not desire to see any configuration other than the characteristics of the Buddha, nor to hear any sound other than the sound of the Buddhist teachings, nor did he think on anything other than the next life. With his eyes, he perceived the characteristics of the Tathāgata Amida; with his ears, he listened to the blessed nembutsu; with his mind, he contemplated the Pure Land; and with his hand, he held a string [which linked him] to the hand of the Tathāgata Amida, all while lying with his pillow to the north so he could face the western direction.[82]

Michinaga's example led countless other aristocrats to adopt the nembutsu as their last rites, and it thereby solidified Pure Land practices among aristocrats. For such deathbed rituals, Genshin's *Ōjōyōshū*—specifically, chapter six which describes such practices—became the standard handbook of format and procedure.

While Pure Land ritual spread among aristocrats, Tendai priests continued their scholastic tradition of Pure Land interpretations. One of Genshin's contemporaries, Kakuun (953–1007), presented a particularly ingenious interpretation of Pure Land doctrine which exemplified Tendai's syncretistic spirit. As a scion of one branch of the Fujiwara family, Kakuun grew up in the midst of Kyoto's high society, and throughout his life he maintained close ties with members of the aristocracy. At Mt. Hiei, he became a disciple of Ryōgen, and after making a name for himself in Buddhist debate he established himself in the Dannain, a temple in the Tōtō precinct of the mountain. Kakuun's interests were broad, encompassing not only standard Tendai doctrine and Pure Land teachings but also the Tendai esoteric tradition. As Kakuun's fame grew, disciples gathered around him, and by the turn of the eleventh century he had a following, called the *dannaryū* which rivaled even Genshin's *eshinryū*. Kakuun, who in many ways is a study in contrasts to Genshin, also received the honorary title of *gon shōsōzu*, but instead of declining it he duly held the office and went on to receive the higher appointment of *gon daisōzu*.[83]

Kakuun's works on Pure Land Buddhism[84] are all rather short, only a few pages each, so none have doctrinal points worked out in great detail. Of these, his *Nembutsu hōgo*, written primarily in verse, contains the most developed form of his Pure Land ideas. The gist of this work is that Śākyamuni, Amida, and Dainichi Buddha are all the same in essence. The basis for this identification is the concept of the eternal enlightenment (*kuon jitsujō*) of the Buddha, found in the *Lotus Sutra*. First, Śākyamuni, the central Buddha of the *Lotus Sutra*, is characterized as identical with that eternal enlightenment, despite the appearance that he achieved enlightenment at a particular time on earth at Bodh Gayā. Amida is next described as following the same example—that is, giving the appearance of the Pure Land Buddha depicted in the scriptures, while actually remaining one with the primordial enlightenment of Buddhahood. Finally, eternal enlightenment is divided into its active and passive (*nō-sho*) facets, which in turn are identified with the Dharma body (*hosshin*) and the reward body (*hōjin*) of the Buddha and subsequently with the Taizōkai and Kongōkai mandalas of esoteric Buddhism. Since these two mandalas symbolize aspects of Dainichi Buddha, he ultimately is linked to the eternal enlightenment of Buddhahood also. Hence, these three Buddhas—Śākyamuni, Amida, and Dainichi—all partake of the same source and therefore represent manifestations of the same principle.[85] The implication of Kakuun's thesis is that Tendai, Pure Land, and esoteric Buddhism are all one and the same. This kind of doctrinal synthesis echoed Ryōgen's earlier unification of Pure Land and Tendai teaching, but Kakuun carried it a step further with the inclusion of esoteric concepts as well. Though Kakuun's writings had little popular impact in Pure Land history, they made him, more than Genshin, a true heir of Ryōgen's brand of Pure Land syncretism.

During the eleventh century, not long after the death of Fujiwara no Michinaga, a new phenomenon began to sweep the Kyoto aristocracy—the belief that *mappō*, or the age of decline, had commenced. This idea was not an innovation of Heian times but rather originated in Buddhist texts from India and China. Long before the eleventh century, it influenced the Pure Land writings of Tao-ch'o in China, and found its way into numerous early works in Japan, such as the following passage from the *Nihon ryōiki*, which gives a fairly clear description of *mappō* as comprehended in the late eighth century:

> When we search the scriptures from the life of the Śākyamuni belonging to our present world cycle, we find that there are three historical periods. The first is the age of the true Dharma (*shōbō*) amounting to five hundred years. The second is the age of the imitation Dharma (*zōhō*) amounting to one thousand years. The third is the age of the decline of the Dharma (*mappō*) amounting to ten thousand years. From the time that the Buddha passed into Nirvāṇa down to our present year of 787, 1722 years have gone by. Hence, we have passed through the *shōbō* and the *zōhō* periods and have now entered the age of *mappō*. From the time that Buddhism was first transmitted to Japan down to our present year of 787, 236 years have gone by.
>
> A flower may bloom, but it does not speak. A rooster may crow, but it sheds no tears. When we look at our present world, men who practice good are as [rare as] the flowers on a hill of rocks, whereas men who commit wrongdoings are as [dense as] the grass on a fertile mountain. Not to mend one's karmic ways but to go on doing evil is like a blind man taking a walk without any concern for the tail of the tiger. To relish fame and fortune and to kill sentient beings is like a man crazed in spirit about to take hold of a poisonous snake. Evil is not something which crumbles away, whereas good is hardly visible.

> The fruits of evil come back to a person so quickly that it is like a reflecting pool. As soon as one turns to it, there they appear. Good actions are soon covered over, so they are like an echo in the valley. But if one shouts into it, surely there will be a response. The karmic retribution which we experience in the present is also like this, so how could a person not act prudently? If we pass through this present life living in vain, then though we might regret it later, we will still derive no benefit from it. As for this temporal body, who is there that may reside in it for any great length of time? And as for this transitory existence, who is there that may rely on it forever? Already we have entered the age of *mappō*. How can we dare not exert ourselves? Ah, how pitiful we are in all things! How are we to escape the destruction of our age?[86]

Here the dating for *mappō's* beginning differs considerably from the 1052 date adopted by most mid-Heian thinkers. Nonetheless, the sense of pessimism and urgency expressed in this passage accurately portrays the feelings that beset Kyoto's aristocracy in the eleventh century and which pervaded the provincial aristocracy and eventually the common people during the next century and a half. By Kamakura times, *mappō* was a concept built into the mind-set of the Japanese population.

Anxiety over *mappō* arose in tandem with a constellation of historical changes that gradually overtook Japan during the second half of the Heian period. In the eleventh and twelfth centuries Japan fell prey to a series of natural disasters—fires, cyclones, famines, earthquakes, etc.—which are recorded in vivid detail by such works as the *Hōjōki*, written in 1212.[87] Whether such calamities were actually more prevalent then or whether people simply became more attuned to them, it is difficult to say. It is nonetheless clear that people regarded such events as signs of the times and they embraced the concept of *mappō* to explain them. *Mappō* was likewise thought responsible for the social disorders that became more and more frequent as the Heian period wore on. These problems derived from

A BRIEF HISTORY OF PURE LAND BUDDHISM IN EARLY JAPAN

the disruption and gradual disintegration of the economic system based on estates (*shōen*) and from the emergence of the samurai or *bushi* class as the dominant force in the countryside. These occurrences slowly eroded the wealth and authority of Kyoto's aristocracy and spawned recurrent warfare over political control. Perhaps the first volley of Japan's *bushi* interlopers came in the tenth century when the provincial chieftain Taira no Masakado (d. 940), claiming descendance from Emperor Kammu (737–806) and therefore title to the throne, usurped eight provinces in northeastern Japan. This rebellion was eventually squelched, but it set a precedent for agitation by samurai which was repeated with increasing frequency over the Heian period. One particularly inauspicious incident, the *Zenkunen no Ran* which the warrior Abe no Yoritoki (d. 1057) initiated, began in 1050, just as Kyoto aristocrats braced themselves for the dawn of the *mappō* period.[88] *Bushi* insurgency, which escalated anxieties in Kyoto and spread a sense of *mappō* throughout the countryside, culminated in the ascendancy of the Taira family during the twelfth century and the subsequent rise of the Kamakura Bakufu headed by the Minamoto family.

As *mappō* fueled the dissemination of the Pure Land teachings, most schools of Buddhism absorbed its concepts under the influence of these developments. Throughout most of the Heian period, the Tendai school dominated Japan's Pure Land movement, but around the turn of the twelfth century the Nara schools reemerged as a center of Pure Land activity, primarily through the efforts of Yōkan (1033–1111) and Chinkai (1092–1152). Except for the fact that Yōkan spent his career outside of the Tendai tradition, his life resembles in many ways that of Genshin. Yōkan grew up in Kyoto as a member of a literati family, and in 1043 he became a disciple of Jinkan (1001–1050) at the Zenrinji, an aristocratic temple in Kyoto which had ties with the Tōji there and with the Tōdaiji in Nara. As a novitiate of great potential, Yōkan was sent to the Tōdaiji to receive instruction in Hossō and Sanron doctrine. He also became exposed to Pure Land concepts, partly through his teacher in Kyoto and partly through the Tōdaiji where Chikō's teachings were preserved. Around 1050 he began the practice of chanting the nembutsu ten thousand times daily. In 1057 Yōkan was chosen for a Buddhist debate at the Byōdōin temple, and seven years later he was honored with a similar invitation to the Hōjōji. This kind of prominence, however, did not suit Yōkan, and soon thereafter he withdrew to Mt. Kōmyō in Yamashiro province to live in isolation and presumably to pursue Pure Land practices. In 1072 Yōkan ended his ten year seclusion and returned to the Zenrinji temple in Kyoto, where he sought to carry on his religious activities. In time, he was again cited for his religious excellence with invitations to prestigious lectures and appointments to ecclesiastical titles. These he regularly declined. Around 1100, however, Yōkan was nominated to become one of the three heads (*bettō*) at the Tōdaiji, and in this case he accepted the office, serving in that capacity for a short two years. Ultimately, he chose to resign this position also, and he returned to the Zenrinji where he spent the rest of his years. His activities there included participation in a small and unpretentious nembutsu society and in 1104 the composition of his major Pure Land work, the *Ōjōjūin* (T. 2683).[89]

Chronologically, Yōkan lived almost exactly between Genshin and Hōnen. By the same token, his Pure Land ideas stand about halfway between their teachings. His concept of the nembutsu is in substance similar to Genshin's, but his heavy emphasis on the practice of nembutsu chanting anticipates Hōnen's doctrine of the exclusive nembutsu. Yōkan's *Ōjōjūin* advances the nembutsu as the supreme practice for people seeking salvation. In his words,

> Based on it, the practitioner does away with all other desires and all other practices, and seeks after and undertakes only the practice of the nembutsu. Among those who have a distracted mind, out of a thousand, there is not one reborn in the Pure Land, but among those who practice [the nembutsu] exclusively, out of ten thousand, there is not one who is lost.[90]

Never before had such uncompromising devotion to the nembutsu been expressed in a Japanese Pure Land work. Yōkan's use of such expressions as "practice exclusively" (*senju*) indisputably preludes Hōnen's formulation of the exclusive nembutsu. Yōkan's concept of the nembutsu, however, differs in certain ways from Hōnen's. Yōkan interprets it as a religious act which engages body, word, and mind— body in that the tongue is employed, word in that Amida's name is uttered, and mind in that thoughts are aroused. More importantly, the nembutsu must be intoned with singleness of mind (*isshin*) or complete mind (*shishin*) for it to be efficacious. This kind of definition is what distinguishes Yōkan's nembutsu from Hōnen's and places it in the same class as Genshin's—that is, one in which the mind is focused with exclusiveness of concentration (*sennen*). Though the verbalization of the nembutsu is taken for granted by Yōkan, it alone is not sufficient to fulfill the soteriological act. Only the infusion of a concentrated mind can do that.[91]

To arrive at his interpretation, Yōkan relies heavily on the writings of major Pure Land thinkers in China and on the *Ōjōyōshū* as well. In his preface to the *Ōjōjūin* Yōkan acknowledges the impact that Tao-ch'o's and Huai-kan's works had on him, but more significant than these is the "Sanzengi" section of Shan-tao's *Kanmuryōjubutsukyōsho*. Genshin, who also draws on Shan-tao's writings, does not quote this section of the commentary at all. Perhaps the most important passage from it cited by Yōkan is:

> The master Shan-tao states, "Among religious practices there are two types. One is the single-minded concentration on the name of Amida. This we call the correct act for establishing oneself (*shōjōgō*), in accordance with Amida's vow. Thus, if a person depends on worship, chanting of scripture, etc., we call these auxiliary acts (*jogō*). Outside of these two practices, all other kinds of good works we call miscellaneous practices (*zōgyō*)."[92]

This passage is the basis for Yōkan's allegiance to the nembutsu. His selection of it preempted in certain ways Hōnen's later use of it in his teachings. In this respect, Yōkan represents a link between Genshin and Hōnen in the development of Pure Land thought in Japan.[93]

After Yōkan revived Pure Land interests in the Nara schools, activities there continued during the next generation under the leadership of Chinkai. Like Yōkan, Chinkai was a Kyoto aristocrat who received his training in Sanron, Kegon, and Hossō doctrine at the Tōdaiji temple in Nara. He spent much of his career at the Tōdaiji and later moved to the Daigoji, where he cultivated interests in esoteric Buddhism also. Chinkai's major contribution to the history of Pure Land Buddhism is a work entitled the *Ketsujō ōjōshū* (T. 2684).[94] This essay, which in a certain sense is a logical extension of Yōkan's thought, focuses on the question indicated in the title—how a person establishes himmself so that he may be assured of rebirth in the Pure Land. Chinkai proposes three bases for this: 1) the Buddhist scriptures (*kyōmon*) which present the teachings of rebirth, 2) reason (*dōri*) which naturally leads one to desire rebirth as it is described in the scriptures, and 3) faith (*shinjin*) which dispels doubt and firmly fixes one in the assurances of rebirth.[95] The greater portion of this work is devoted to this third topic, the different ways that faith is established. Here, Chinkai emphasizes the nembutsu, just as Yōkan does, but he goes beyond Yōkan when he describes it as the most correct method among the correct (*shōchū no shō*) for achieving rebirth in the Pure Land. Nonetheless, he does not go as far as Hōnen in that Chinkai considers it the primary act (*shōgō*) but not necessarily the primary cause (*shōin*) of achieving rebirth.[96] To this extent, Chinkai, like Yōkan, bridged the gap between earlier Pure Land thought and the new interpretations that were to come with Hōnen.

While Buddhist schools, Tendai and otherwise, proceeded to enlarge upon Pure Land doctrine, nembutsu activities also continued to spread, especially with the force of *hijiri* behind them. During the twelfth century, the secluded district of Ōhara, to the north of Kyoto, became a stronghold for popular nembutsu practices, and it was there that the monk Ryōnin (1072–1132) emerged as an important figure in the nembutsu movement. A contemporary account of

A BRIEF HISTORY OF PURE LAND BUDDHISM IN EARLY JAPAN

him found in the *Goshūi ōjōden* describes little more than his seclusion at Ōhara to devote himself to Pure Land practices and his deathbed scene.[97] In addition, it is known that until 1103 Ryōnin was attached to a *fudan nembutsu* chapel at Mt. Hiei as a *dōsō*, or nembutsu attendant, and after that he withdrew to Ōhara to concentrate on nembutsu activities. This pattern, followed by numerous other Pure Land monks, foreshadowed the life of Shinran, who also began as a *dōsō* at Mt. Hiei. Ryōnin is traditionally depicted as a nembutsu teacher among the common people. A Kamakura biography of him contained in the *Kokon chomonjū* portrays him as such,[98] but there is little contemporary evidence to corroborate or disprove such a description. Overall, it would be safe to characterize Ryōnin as a Pure Land priest living in estrangement from Mt. Hiei and dedicated to the practice and the propagation of the nembutsu.[99] This style of life became more and more prevalent towards the end of the Heian period, and it did much to bring the Pure Land teachings alive outside of the large religious establishments.

Traditionally, Ryōnin is credited with the formation of the *yūzū* nembutsu movement in Japan. The philosophy behind this movement can be summed up in the following verses attributed to him:

> A single person is one with all people,
> And all people are one with a single person.
> A single religious act is one with all religious acts,
> And all religious acts are one with a single religious act.
> This we call rebirth in the Pure Land
>   based on the power of others.
> The single nembutsu of a person living in
>   any of the ten worlds,
> Is a nembutsu extending to one and all (*yūzū*).
> After hundreds and thousands and millions of repetitions,
> Merit [for us all] will be consummate and complete.[100]

This formulation of the verses is contained in a Tokugawa treatise written by the systematizer of *yūzū nembutsu* thought, Yūkan (1649–

1716). Ryōnin himself left no works, and so it is doubtful that the verses as they stand were actually composed by him. Nonetheless, they may express the spirit behind his thinking, since the term *yūzū nembutsu* and the idea that "Merit becomes extensive because the act of a single person is for all people" (*i ichinin gyō, i shunin ko, kudoku kōdai*), is linked to him as early as the Kamakura period in the *Kokon chomonjū*.[101] This type of thinking was not unique to Ryōnin but characterized other nembutsu monks of his time also. Standing behind such beliefs is the Tendai concept of original enlightenment (*hongaku shisō*) extending to all sentient beings.[102] With this philosophy of interrelatedness as a backdrop, Ryōnin and other nembutsu monks attempted to universalize the impact of the nembutsu as they spread it among Japan's population.

Over the twelfth century, as nembutsu practices penetrated a broader segment of society, the notion of what is required for rebirth in the Pure Land gradually began to change. During the tenth and eleventh centuries, the nembutsu rose gradually in importance but there remained lingering suspicions that it alone was not sufficient for rebirth. Yoshishige no Yasutane's *Nihon ōjō gokuraku ki* of 985 betrays such an attitude in that all the figures described therein, who achieve rebirth in the Pure Land, are not only adherents of Pure Land practices but also virtuous and upright persons. In the *Zoku honchō ōjōden*, the *Shūi ōjōden*, and the *Goshūi ōjōden*, all written in the early twelfth century, a new breed of Pure Land follower appears— one who has committed numerous wrongdoings but still achieves rebirth because of his conversion to the Pure Land teachings. Perhaps the most notable example of this is Fujiwara no Tadamune, whose biography is found in the *Goshūi ōjōden*. Throughout his life he practiced no good whatsoever, and even into old age he was consumed with wicked ideas and evil talk. Physically he always appeared drunk and mentally he appeared crazed. But on his deathbed, through the good services of a Buddhist monk, he repented of his wrongdoings and with singleness of mind he repeated the nembutsu. This last act reversed the course of his life and led him to rebirth in the

A BRIEF HISTORY OF PURE LAND BUDDHISM IN EARLY JAPAN

Pure Land.[103] Such stories reflected a new sense of the efficacy of Pure Land teachings emergent in the twelfth century, and they signaled the impending arrival of Hōnen's, Shinran's, and Ippen's more radical interpretations of the nembutsu.[104]

Among the traditional schools of Buddhism in Japan, the Shingon was relatively late absorbing the full impact of the Pure Land movement. During the eleventh century, a few Pure Land *hijiri* began to inhabit the vicinity of Mt. Kōya, the seat of Shingon practice, and over the course of the twelfth century they slowly increased in number. Biographies of such figures are now found in the *Kōyasan ōjōden* compiled around the beginning of the Kamakura period.[105] Most of these *hijiri*, however, were attracted to Mt. Kōya because it offered a secluded environment in which to pursue Pure Land practices, not because it was already a center of Pure Land activity. In addition to these hermits, there were a few regular Shingon monks—for example, Mukū (d. 921) and Jinkaku (955–1043)—who studied Pure Land teachings and followed Pure Land practices.[106] Nonetheless, the number of monks associated with both Pure Land and Shingon was insignificant enough to say that Shingon did not have a major Pure Land tradition before the twelfth century.

For all intents and purposes, Pure Land studies in the Shingon school began only during the life of Kakuban (1095–1145), the first Shingon monk to compose a work dealing with Pure Land doctrines. His *Gorin kuji myōhimitsushaku* (T. 2514) attempts to show the essential unity between Pure Land teachings and esoteric Buddhism. The Tendai monk Kakuun undertook a similar task more than a century earlier in his *Nembutsu hōgo*, but he employed the esoteric teachings of Tendai rather than those of Shingon. The central theme of Kakuban's work can be summarized by a quotation from its opening paragraph:

> In exoteric teachings there is, besides Śākyamuni, the Buddha Amida, but in the esoteric corpus, Dainichi, who is equivalent to Amida, is the master of the Pure Land. It should be realized that the Pure Lands of the ten directions are all transforma-

tion lands of a single Buddha and that all the Tathāgatas are Dainichi. Both Vairocana (i.e., Dainichi) and Amida are of the same substance, even though their names differ. And both Pure Land and [Dainichi's] Land of Secret Splendors (*mitsugon*) are the same place, despite their difference in names. Through the mysterious powers and protective forces gained in the *pratyavekṣaṇa-jñāna* sphere of knowledge, there appears over the substance of Dainichi the characteristics of Amida.[107]

The conceptual underpinnings for this identification of Amida and Dainichi is the Shingon doctrine of *sokushin jōbutsu* according to which Dainichi Buddha is embodied in all facets of reality. Within this comprehensive system of thought, the nembutsu becomes a mantra associated with Amida and his Pure Land, but is ultimately expressive of the esoteric macrocosm.[108] In this way Kakuban infused Pure Land themes with Shingon meaning.

Kakuban's life was by no means devoted to Pure Land Buddhism alone. His interests were broad and his impact on the history of the Shingon tradition was profound. Kakuban came from the province of Hizen in northern Kyushu, the son of a local tax official. He received his early religious training at the Ninnaji, a prominent Shingon temple in Kyoto, and in 1114 moved to Mt. Kōya to continue his studies. While there, Kakuban's associations were not so much with powerful and influential priests of the temple but rather with less politically inclined masters, such as Myōjaku (d. 1124), and with the Pure Land *hijiri* attached to the mountain. After seven years of intensive study there, he returned to Kyoto where he received additional initiations at several important temples. During this period, Kakuban's fame as an adept of various esoteric lineages rose, and he came to the attention of the retired Emperor Toba (1103–1156). With Emperor Toba's encouragement and support, Kakuban returned to Mt. Kōya with the intention of revitalizing it as a center of religious excellence. In 1132 he established the Daidenbōin and also a personal hermitage for nembutsu practice, the Mitsugon'in, both endowed with imperial lands. Kakuban's precipitous rise to prominence, heightened by

A BRIEF HISTORY OF PURE LAND BUDDHISM IN EARLY JAPAN

imperial recognition, aroused the jealousy and disfavor of the established clique in control at Mt. Kōya. During the following eight years, as Kakuban attempted to expand his influence in hopes of ascending to the position of head priest at Mt. Kōya, dissatisfaction flared into retaliation. In 1140, he along with seven hundred supporters were driven from the mountain and eventually took refuge at Negoro in the province of Kii. There, in subsequent generations, the Shingi branch of the Shingon school arose, claiming Kakuban as its founder. Though Pure Land–Shingon syncretism highlighted Kakuban's doctrinal activities, it is doubtful that Pure Land teachings were an issue in the power struggle. Nonetheless, to the extent that Pure Land *hijiri* at Mt. Kōya were sympathetic to Kakuban's side, the group that established itself at Negoro probably included a significant number of Pure Land adherents, thereby giving the Shingi branch of Shingon a certain Pure Land flavor.[109] Just as esoteric teachings, the flower of Shingon, had overwhelmed the Tendai school in the ninth century, so Pure Land teachings, the forte of Tendai, rooted themselves in the Shingon school in Kakuban's time.

By the end of the twelfth century, the religious climate in Japan was ripe for the appearance of Hōnen, Shinran and Ippen. Pure Land teachings and practices pervaded the country in multifarious forms, both within and outside the Buddhist establishment. The political events surrounding the rise of the Kamakura Bakufu intensified the sense of *mappō* among the people and at the same time paved the way for a variety of new Buddhist initiatives. The nembutsu, which had evolved from a meditational aid as found in Chikō's teachings, emerged as the quintessential practice uniting all Pure Land believers. It was therefore poised for the interpretations that Hōnen, Shinran, and Ippen would apply to it.

Hōnen divested the nembutsu of its meditational aspects and made it a purely invocational practice based on Amida's vow to save all living beings who called his name. At the same time, he discontinued other religious practices and advanced the nembutsu as the exclusive practice for salvation. Shinran, for his part, denied people's capacity to save themselves, even with the nembutsu, since both salvation and the nembutsu originate with Amida. Shinran emphasized instead the importance of faith which the nembutsu awakens in people, and their complete reliance on Amida for rebirth in the Pure Land. Ippen, by contrast, idealized not faith but the miraculous character of the nembutsu itself. He believed that Amida's name, when spoken, constitutes a timeless union between the Buddha and the believer and between the Pure Land and this world, whether or not people are aware of it. Ippen thus dedicated his life to wandering throughout Japan as a *hijiri* priest urging people to intone the nembutsu or to accept a simple nembutsu amulet (*fusan*), even if they had no Pure Land convictions.

The combined impact of Hōnen's, Shinran's, and Ippen's teachings was to create new directions for Pure Land doctrine and new modes of belief and practice for people in any situation or condition—whether wealthy or impoverished, learned or illiterate, virtuous or despicable. Their teachings thus mark them as pioneers of the so-called new Buddhism of the Kamakura period. Nonetheless, one must recognize—without denying the creativity and vision of these three—that what they said was not totally new. Rather, it emerged out of their interaction with the religious traditions they inherited. To this extent, Hōnen, Shinran, and Ippen represent the unfolding of Pure Land thought as much as the transformation of it. Just as Pure Land Buddhism would have been quite different without their teachings, so their teachings would have been quite different without those that came before them.

A BRIEF HISTORY OF PURE LAND BUDDHISM IN EARLY JAPAN

ABBREVIATIONS

BDJ *Bukkyō daijiten.* By Mochizuki Shinkō. 10 vols. Tokyo: Sekaiseiten kankōkyōkai, 1970.

DNBZ *Dai Nihon Bukkyō zensho.* 126 vols. Ed. Bussho kankōkai. Tokyo: Bussho kankōkai, 1912–22.

ESZ *Eshin sōzu zenshū.* 5 vols. Ed. Hieizan senshūin Eizangakuin. Kyoto: Shibunkaku, 1971.

JZ   *Jōdoshū zensho.* 20 vols. Ed. Jōdoshū shūten kankōkai. Tokyo: Jōdoshū shūten kankōkai, 1911–14.

NKBT *Nihon koten bungaku taikei.* 100 vols. Tokyo: Iwanami shoten, 1957–69.

SHSZ *Shōwa shinshū Hōnen shōnin zenshū.* Ed. Ishii Kyōdō. Kyoto: Heirakuji shoten, 1974.

T   *Taishō shinshū daizōkyō.* 85 vols. Eds. Takskusu Junjirō and Watanabe Kaikyoku. Tokyo: Taishō Issaikyō kankōkai, 1924–32.

NOTES

1. Inoue Mitsusada, *Shintei Nihon Jōdokyō seiritsushi no kenkyū* (Tokyo: Yamakawa shuppansha, 1975), 41 (hereafter cited as *Seiritsushi*.). I would like to express my indebtedness to Inoue's study which was a major influence in writing this article. Concerning Shōtoku's commentary, also see Ishida Mitsuyuki, *Jōdokyō kyōrishi* (Kyoto: Heirakuji shoten, 1969), 97–98 (hereafter cited as *Kyōrishi*); and Fujishima Tōru, "Nara jidai ni okeru Mida shinkō," *Ōtani daigaku kenkyū nempō* 16 (1963): 3 (hereafter cited as "Mida shinkō"). For original references see *Yuimakyō gisho* (T. 2186), 28a, ll. 25–26, and 27a, ll. 24, 27.

2. Ishida Mitsuyuki, *Kyōrishi*, 96–97; Inoue, *Seiritsushi*, 14. Inoue points out a resemblance between this quotation and one associated with Maitreya (Miroku) dated 525 at Lung-men, which uses the expression "...be reborn in heaven" (*shōten*).

3. Inoue, *Seiritsushi*, 10.

4. Tokiwa Daijō and Mochizuki Shinkō have been major proponents of this position. Others, such as Tsuji Zennosuke, identify Tenjukoku as Maitreya's Land. See Inoue, *Seiritsushi*, 14, n. 3. Ōno Tatsunosuke believes that Tenjukoku refers to an idealized view of India. See his *Shinkō: Nihon Bukkyō shisōshi* (Tokyo: Yoshikawa kōbunkan, 1975), 54, and 64. Hereafter cited as *Shisōshi*. Inoue argues that it probably refers to Pure Land but that the land of Amida, Maitreya, and Śākyamuni were not clearly distinguished in the minds of Buddhists at that period. Seiritsushi, 2–13.

5. Fujishima, "Mida shinkō," 3; Inoue, *Seiritsushi*, 41–42. For original references, see *Nihon shoki*, NKBT, vol. 68, 234–35 and 318–19.

6. Inoue places Pure Land Buddhism's beginnings in Japan during this period. See his *Seiritsushi*, 3–5.

7. Adapted from Inoue, *Seiritsushi*, 44. Original compilations taken from Ishida Mosaku, *Shakyō yori mitaru Naracho Bukkyō no kenkyu* (Tokyo: Tōyō bunko, 1966), 165–66.

8. Adapted from Inoue, *Seiritsushi*, 44–46. Original compilations taken from Ishida Mosaku, *Shakyō yori mitaru Naracho Bukkyō no kenkyū*, 160–64.

9. Inoue, *Seiritsushi*, 46–47.

10. Adapted from ibid., 8–9.

11. Ibid., 9.

12. Ibid., 20.

13. Hori Ichirō, *Jōdai Nihon Bukkyō bunkashi*, vol. 1 (Tokyo: Daitō shuppansha, 1941), 228–229. Reference taken from Inoue, *Seiritsushi*, 25, and 27 n. 2.

14. Inoue, *Seiritushi*, 21.

15. Ibid., 49–50, 59, and 75.

16. Fujishima, "Mida shinkō," 5–6. For original references, see *Hannya*

shingyō jutsugi, T. 2202, vol. 57, 3bc; Nihon ryōiki, NKBT, vol. 70, 193–201.

17. Fujishima, "Mida shinkō," 6; Tōiki dentō mokuroku, T. 2183, vol. 55, 1156b, 1. 24.

18. Chikō's Muryōjukyō ronshaku, as quoted in Ryōchu's Ōjōron chūki, JZ vol. 1, 310. See also Ishida Mitsuyuki, Kyōrishi, 105–106, and Inoue, Seiritsushi, 54.

19. Chikō's Ronshaku as quoted in Ryōchu's Ōjōron chūki, 313–14. See also Ishida Mitsuyuki, Kyōrishi, 106, and Inoue, Seiritsushi, 54.

20. Ishida Mitsuyuki, Kyōrishi, 104–107.

21. For a reproduction of the Chikō Mandala, see Mochizuki Shinkō, BDJ vol. 8, plate 1105.

22. Fujishima, "Mida shinkō," 10. For the original reference, see Nihon ōjō gokuraku ki, DNBZ, vol. 107, 7.

23. Fujishima, "Mida shinkō," 10–11. For the original reference, see the Kannen Amidabutsu sōkai zammai kudoku hōmon, T. 1959, vol. 47, 25a, ll. 11–12.

24. Fujishima, "Mida shinkō," 7.

25. Inoue, Seiritsushi, 50–55. Ishida Mitsuyuki, Kyōrishi, 105–106, and Fujishima, "Mida shinkō," 8, also hold this same view. Chia-ts'ai, (ca. 627–49) was a Chinese monk of the T'ang period, who resided at the Hung-fa ssu in Ch'ang-an and adhered to Pure Land practices. He wrote the three fascicle Jōdoron (T. 1963). Little else is know about him.

26. Fujishima, "Mida shinkō," 6. For original references, see the Shoshū shōshoroku, DNBZ, vol. 1, 120–21.

27. Ishida Mitsuyuki, Kyōrishi, 105.

28. Fujishima, "Mida shinkō," 4. For the original reference, see the Nihon ryōiki, NKBT vol. 70, 176–77.

29. Ōhashi Shunnō, Yugyō hijiri: Shomin no Bukkyō shiwa (Tokyo:

Daizō shuppansha, 1971), 20-23. See also Ōno, *Shisōshi*, 119.

30. Inoue, *Seiritsushi*, 85-86. See the *Makashikan*, T. 1911, vol. 46, 12ff.

31. Inoue, *Seiritsushi*, 86-87.

32. *Gokurakuj ōdo kubon ōjōgi*, JZ vol. 15, 1-36. On Ryōgen see Fugen Kōju, "*Ōjōyōshū* no seiritsu haikei," *Shinshūgaku* 38 (January, 1978): 19ff. Hereafter cited as "Seiritsu haikei."

33. *Kubon ōjōgi*, JZ vol. 15, 1-9.

34. Ibid., 1-2. See also Fugen, "Seiritsu haikei," 20-21.

35. Fugen, "Seiritsu haikei," 21-22; Ishida Mitsuyuki, *Kyōrishi*, 119-20.

36. The forty-eight vows are found in the *chūbonge* section of the *Kubon ōjōgi*, JZ vol. 15, 15-22.

37. *Kubon ōjōgi*, JZ vol. 15, 18.

38. Fugen, "Seiritsu haikei," 24-25.

39. Inoue, *Seiritsushi*, 140-45.

40. Taya Raishun, "Heianchō no Jōdokyō," *Ōtani gakuhō* 39, no. 2 (November 1959): 77-78.

41. Senkan's *Jūgan hosshinki* is published in the *Eizan Jōdokyō koten sōsho*, Part II (Kyoto: Ryūkoku daigaku ichjōbunka kenkyūkai, 1950). The text is also available in Satō Tetsuei, *Eizan Jōdokyō no kenkyū: Shiryōhen* (Kyoto: Hyakkaen, 1979), 159-220.

42. Fugen, "Seiritsu haikei," 27-30.

43. Zen'yu's *Amida shinjūgi* is published in the *Eizan Jōdokyō koten sōsho*, Part III, (Kyoto: Ryūkoku daigaku ichjōbunka kenkyūkai, 1951). The text is also available in Satō Tetsuei, *Eizan Jōdokyō no kenkyū: Shiryōhen* (Kyoto: Hyakkaen, 1979), 221-258.

44. *Ryōkan Muryōjukyo shūyō*, T. 1747, vol. 37, 129a, ll. 5-19. This passage is said to be quoted from the *Miroku hotsumongyō*. I have

not been able to identify it with any passages in either the *Miroku bosatsu shomon hongangyō* (T. 349) or the *Miroku bosatsu shomon'e* (T. 310.42), the only works I found with similar titles.

45. Fugen, "Seiritsu haikei," 34–38.

46. The three earliest *Ōjōden* are *Nihon ōjō gokuraku ki* written in 985–86 by Yoshishige no Yasutane (931?–1002), the *Zoku honchō ōjōden*, written around 1101 by Ōe Masafusa (1041–1111), and the *Shūi ōjōden*, written about 1111 by Miyoshi Tameyasu (1049–1139). A biography of Ryōgen first appears in the *Goshūi ōjōden*, compiled in 1132 also by Miyoshi Tameyasu. See DNBZ, vol. 107 for all four works.

47. Tokunō Mitsumaro, "Ryōgen to Genshin no shūkyō shakai teki tachiba," *Indogaku Bukkyōgaku kenkyū* 11, no. 2 (March 1963): 291–92.

48. Murayama Shūichi, *Nihon Bukkyōshi: Kodaihen*, ed. Ienaga Saburō (Kyoto: Hōzōkan, 1975), 242–44.

49. Inoue, *Seiritsushi*, 160–61.

50. Hori Ichirō, *Kōya* (Tokyo: Yoshikawa kōbunkan, 1963), 30–34, 36–37, 51–55, 65–66.

51. Inoue, *Seiritsushi*, 217–20. Hori, *Kōya*, 104–105. Inoue has relied on Hashikawa Tadashi's *Sōgō Nihon Bukkyōshi* (1932) for many of his ideas on the *hijiri* movement.

52. Inoue, *Seiritsushi*, 237–38; Hori, *Kōya*, 121.

53. Ōhashi, *Yugyō hijiri*, 55.

54. Inoue, *Seiritsushi*, 100–101. See also Ienaga Saburō, *Nihon bunkashi* (Tokyo: Iwanami shoten, 1968), 80–81.

55. Inoue, *Seiritsushi*, 94–96.

56. Shimada Tadaomi, *Denshi kashū*, in *Gunsho ruijū* (Tokyo: Keizai zasshisha, 1905), vol. 6, 828. Also see Inoue, *Seiritsushi*, 91.

57. Inoue, *Seiritsushi*, 91. *Jōdoji nembutsu engi* is found in DNBZ, vol. 117, 339.

58. Itō Shintetsu, *Heian Jōdokyō shinkōshi no kenkyū* (Kyoto: Heirakuji shoten, 1974), 270–73, 277–78; Inoue, *Seiritsushi,* 91–92, 148–50.

59. *Nihon ōjō gokuraku ki,* DNBZ, vol. 107, 1.

60. Itō, *Heian Jōdokyō shinkōshi no kenkyū,* 140–142.

61. *Nihon ōjō gokuraku ki,* DNBZ, vol., 1. See also Shigematsu Akihisa, *Nihon Jōdokyō seiritsu katei no kenkyū* (Kyoto: Heirakuji shoten, 1964), 125. For details on the other *Ōjōden* see note 46 above.

62. Mochizuki, BDJ, vol. 1, 276a, 326bc.

63. Inoue, *Seiritsushi,* 148–49. Ishida Mizumaro, *Gokuraku jōdo e no sasoi: Ōjōyōshū no baai* (Tokyo: Hyōronsha, 1976), 32–38. Hereafter cited as *Jōdo e no sasoi*. The chief primary sources that describe the activities of the *Nijūgozammaie* are the *Yokawa Shuryōgon'in nijūgo zammai shiki* (T. 2723) compiled by Genshin and the *Yokawa Shuryōgon'in nijūgo zammai kishō* (T. 2724) recorded by Yoshishige no Yasutane.

64. Ishida Mizumaro, *Jōdo e no sasoi,* 19–30. The earliest existing biographies of Genshin are found in the *Honchō Hokke genki* and the *Zoku honchō ōjōden,* both written within a century of his death.

65. *Ōjōyōshū,* T. 2682, vol. 84, 33a.

66. Ishida Mizumaro, *Genshin,* Nihon shisō taikei, vol. 6 (Tokyo: Iwanami shoten, 1970), 442–43.

67. *Ōjōyōshū,* T. 2682, vol. 84, 56b, ll. 3–5. Also see Ishida Mitsuyuki, *Kyōrishi,* 130–31.

68. Ishida Mizumaro, *Genshin,* 443–445; *Ōjōyōshū,* T. 2682, vol. 84, 47c–57b.

69. Inoue, *Seiritsushi,* 132–35, 139.

70. Inaba Shūken, "*Ōjōyōshū* to *Ōjōjūin* no nembutsu," *Indogaku Bukkyōgaku kenkyū* 3, no. 1 (September, 1954): 103–104.

71. Ishida Mizumaro, *Jōdo e no sasoi,* 42–45.

A BRIEF HISTORY OF PURE LAND BUDDHISM IN EARLY JAPAN

72. Ishida Mizumaro, *Genshin,* 468–49, 479–88.

73. Ibid., 496–97; Sasaki Motoki, "Edo jidai ni okeru *Ōjōyōshū* no kaihan" *Ōtani gakuhō* 44, no. 4 (March 1965): 73–74.

74. *Ōjōyōshū ryōken,* SHSZ 14. Also see Tsuboi Shun'ei, "Hōnen Jōdokyō ni okeru ikkō senju no keisei ni tsuite: *Ōjōyōshūshaku* to *Muryōjukyōshaku* o chūshin to shite," in *Tōyō bunka ronshū,* ed. Fukui Hakushi shōju kinen ronbunshū kankōkai (Tokyo: Waseda daigaku shuppanbu, 1969), 669–70.

75. *Ōjōyōshū,* T. 2682, vol. 84, 33a.

76. *Kanjin ryakuyōshū,* ESZ vol. 1, 273.

77. Taira Ryōshō, "Eshin sōzu no *Kanjin ryakuyōshū* ni tsuite," in *Tōyō bunka ronshū,* 603–605.

78. *Kanjin ryakuyōshū,* ESZ vol. 1, 276.

79. Ibid., 278.

80. Mochizuki, BDJ vol. 1, 956; Ishida Mizumaro, *Jōdo e no sasoi,* 52–60.

81. Sakamoto Shōzō, *Nihon no rekishi,* vol. 6, *Sekkan jidai* (Tokyo: Shōgakkan, 1974), 275–59.

82. *Eiga monogatari,* NKBT vol. 76, 326–27.

83. Mochizuki, BDJ vol. 1, 407.

84. Kakuun's works on Pure Land include *Nembutsu hōgō, Kanjin nembutsu,* and *Ichijitsu bodaige,* all contained in DNBZ, vol. 24.

85. *Nembutsu hōgō,* DNBZ, vol. 24, 306. See also Ōno, *Shisōshi,* 225–27.

86. *Nihon ryōiki,* NKBT vol. 70, 302–305.

87. Kamo no Chōmei, *Hōjōki,* NKBT vol. 30, 24–26, 29 34.

88. Sakamoto Shōzō, *Nihon no rekishi,* vol. 6, *Sekkan jidai,* 162-73, 368–76.

89. Inoue, *Seiritsushi*, 385-88. Mochizuki, BDJ vol. 1, 251–52.

90. *Ōjōjūin*, T. 2683, vol. 84, 97c, ll. 4–7.

91. Inaba, "*Ōjōyōshū* to *Ōjōjūin* no nembutsu," 104–07.

92. *Ōjōjūin*, T. 2683, vol. 84, 100c, ll. 25–28. Yōkan's quotation is apparently a paraphrase of Shan-tao's *Kanmuryōjubutsukyōsho*, T. 1753, vol. 37, 272b, ll. 6–10.

93. Akiyama Yasuo, "Nanto Jōdokyō to Zendō kyōgaku," in *Jōdokyō shisō to bunka*, ed. Etani Ryūkai sensei koki kinenkai (Kyoto: Bukkyō daigaku, 1972), 26–30; Inoue, *Seiritsushi*, 416–21.

94. Mochizuki, BDJ vol. 4, 3624–25.

95. Akiyama, "Nanto Jōdokyō to Zendō kyōgaku," 430–32.

96. Inoue, *Seiritsushi*, 423–24.

97. *Goshūi ōjōden*, DNBZ, vol. 107, 118.

98. *Kokon chomonjū*, in *Shintei zōho Kokuski taikei*, vol. 19 (Tokyo: Yoshikawa kōbunkan, 1930), 39–40.

99. Inoue, *Seiritsushi*, 205-208.

100. *Yūzū nembutsu shingeshō*, DNBZ, vol. 64, 16.

101. *Kokon chomonjū*, 39–40; Ōno, *Shisōshi*, 242.

102. Inoue, *Seiritsushi*, 207-208.

103. *Goshūi ōjōden*, DNBZ, vol. 107, 100–101.

104. Inoue, *Seiritsushi*, 251–53.

105. *Kōyasan ōjōden*, DNBZ, vol. 107, 169–182.

106. Inoue, *Seiritsushi*, 341–45.

107. *Gorin kuiji myōhimitsushaku*, T. 2514, vol. 79, 11a, ll. 24–28.

108. Inoue, *Seiritsushi*, 351–52; Ōyama Kōjun, "Kōgyō Daishi no Jōdokyō: *Kōyōshū* ni tsuite," in *Jōdokyō no shisō to bunka*, 556–58.

109. Inoue, *Seiritsushi*, 347–51.

Hōnen and *The Tale of the Heike*

Maya M. Hara

The sound of the Gion Shōja [Jetavana Garden] bells echoes the impermanence of all things; the color of the sāla flowers reveals the truth that the prosperous must decline. The proud do not endure, they are like a dream on a spring night; the mighty fall at last, they are as dust before the wind.[1]

Heike monogatari (*The Tale of the Heike,* hereafter the *Heike*) is an epic tale tracing the events surrounding the Genpei war, 1153 to 1199. The popular images presented in the *Heike* portray a world in decline. The idea of the latter age of the Dharma (*mappō*) appeared to be a source of distress and worry for all (although those affected and influenced by this thought were, for the most part, courtiers, warriors, and those who lived in the capital and its vicinities). The common notion that chaos and violence were prevalent can be seen through the works of contemporary figures such as the Buddhist recluse Kamo no Chōmei (1155?–1216), author of *Hōjōki* (*An Account of My Hermitage*).[2] In *Hōjōki,* Chōmei records several disastrous occurrences such as the great fire in 1177, which left a third of the capital in ashes, a tornado, a failed attempt to relocate the capital, and a great famine. These disasters led Chōmei to the conclusion that "all human enterprises are pointless."[3]

In his dissertation, "The Birth of an Epic: A Textual Study of the *Heike Monogatari,*" Kenneth D. Butler points out:

> As a social document, the *Heike monogatari* defines and illustrates the prevailing currents of thought of the late Heian (794–1185) and early Kamakura (1185–1333) periods, notably those of *mappō, unmei,* and *mujō.* In addition it presents a

HŌNEN AND THE TALE OF THE HEIKE

clear and concise picture of the compulsive appeal to the Japanese of this period of the principles of Jōdo (Pure Land) Buddhism, first clearly enunciated by the Buddhist saint Hōnen (1133–1212) in the opening years of the thirteenth century.[4]

Here, Butler points out that this *gunki mono* (war tale) illustrates the current social and religious climate. The popular image is that the concern of the arrival of *mappō* and the notion of impermanence (*mujō*) pervaded the minds of the people and permeated the literature of the period. As Butler indicates, there existed a "compulsive appeal ... of the principles of Jōdo Buddhism" in the *Heike*.[5] Although Pure Land thought is not the only form of Buddhism that appears in the *Heike*, it appears to be the prevailing one. In the *Heike*, we can see a shift from a courtly, this-worldly-oriented Buddhism to one which gave hope of birth in the Pure Land to everyone from all walks of life. Moreover, the appearance of the Pure Land master Hōnen in a poignant scene signifies the rising popularity of the Pure Land teachings in the *Heike* and in this period. Thus, in this paper, I will examine Hōnen's appearance in various extant versions of the *Heike* and show how Hōnen's Pure Land teachings of vocal (*shōmyō*) nembutsu influenced this epic tale (focusing specifically on the standard Kakuichi text).

TEXTUAL VARIANTS OF THE *HEIKE*

Although Hōnen appears in several versions of the *Heike*, he does not necessarily appear in all of them. Thus I would first like to introduce the variant texts of the *Heike*. The most well-known and complete text is known as the Kakuichi text,[6] primarily used in this paper. In 1371, an old *biwa hōshi* (lute priest) named Kakuichi is said to have recited a completely oral version of the *Heike*, which was taken from earlier texts and perhaps from earlier oral forms of the *Heike*. Butler indicates:

167

> ... in terms of understanding the oral qualities of Kakuichi's text, the most important point to realize is that although Kakuichi followed the written versions as they had come down to him, in his actual performance of short *Heike* tales in his capacity as a *biwa hōshi* singer, and in his dictation of the long version of the *Heike monogatari*, he utilized the techniques and language of oral composition.[7]

Here, Butler points out that the Kakuichi text was highly influenced by an oral tradition of the *Heike* as well as the existence of earlier texts, which were both read and recited. He lists them as follows:

READ TEXTS	RECITED TEXTS
1. *Shibu kassenjō daisanban tōjō*	Hiramatsuke
2. *Genpei tōjōroku*	Yashiro
3. *Nanto ihon*	Chikuhakuen
4. *Nagato*	Kamakura
5. *Enkyō*	Kakuichi
6. *Genpei jōsuiki*	

For the purposes of this paper, I refer to only the most recognized variants: these are the *Shibu kassenjō daisanban tōjō* (hereafter, *Shibu*) text, *Genpei tōjōroku*, *Genpei jōsuiki*, and the Kakuichi text. As mentioned above, Hōnen does not appear in a few versions of the *Heike*, most significantly in the Shibu text, which is often thought of as the oldest extant *Heike* text. Japanese scholars refer to an "original" *Heike monogatari*, which no longer exists. However, Butler indicates that the Shibu text is believed to have most closely resembled the original text in form and content.[8] Butler also reveals that the Shibu text "lacks the lyrical quality of the Kakuichi [text], and seems to verge on being an exposition of Buddhist sutras, rather than a fictional narrative."[9] This may be because it was written in "an almost pure Chinese form of *kanbun* writing"—its most distinguishing feature.[10] The authorship of this original text is attributed to a man named Yukinaga. Section 226 of *Tsurezuregusa* (c. 1330), written by

Yoshida Kenkō (1281–1350), indicates that Yukinaga was the author of the original *Heike*:

> In Retired Emperor Go-Toba's time [r. 1183–98, in. 1198–1221], the Former Shinano Official Yukinaga won praise for his learning. But when commanded to participate in a discussion of *yuefu* poetry, he forgot two of the virtues in the "Dance of the Seven Virtues," and consequently acquired the nickname "Young Gentleman of the Five Virtues." Sick at heart, he abandoned scholarship and took the tonsure.
>
> Archbishop Jien [the Enryakuji abbot] made a point of summoning and looking after anyone, even a servant, who could boast of an accomplishment; thus, he granted this Shinano Novice an allowance. Yukinaga composed *The Tale of the Heike* and taught it to a blind man, Shōbutsu, so that the man might narrative it. His descriptions of things having to do with the Enryakuji were especially good. He wrote with a detailed knowledge of Kurō Hōgan [Minamoto] Yoshitsune's activities, but did not say much about Gama no Kanja Noriyori,[11] possibly for lack of information. When it came to warriors, he had Yukinaga write what he learned. People say that our present-day *biwa hōshi* imitate Shōbutsu's natural voice.[12]

According to this entry, Yukinaga taught the tale to Shōbutsu. However, Butler explains that this may have been an oversight on Kenkō's part to assume that the original *Heike* was a recited text. Since "there are no pure *kanbun* versions of the *Heike* that were written and used as recited texts" and since the Shibu text is written in classical Chinese (*kanbun*), it seems unlikely that the Shibu text was originally recited as Kenkō's entry suggests.[13] Nevertheless, many continue to accept Kenkō's entry as being at least partially true, thus the original *Heike* is often attributed to Yukinaga. Moreover, if we accept the extant Shibu text as closely resembling the original as Butler argues, then it seems possible that Yukinaga may have written the Shibu text or a manuscript similar to the Shibu text.

The usual explanation for the absence of Hōnen in the so-called original text is that such an incident did not take place.[14] However, another explanation for Hōnen's absence may be due to the fact that Yukinaga was patronized by the Tendai abbot Jien, who publicly opposed Hōnen and his movement.[15] Butler also discusses Jien's influence over Yukinaga's writing. At the end of scroll one of the Shibu text, there is a lengthy digression, which appears in this text alone "concerning the function of Enryakuji as the spiritual protector of the Japanese court."[16] Butler explains that although this idea was not unique to Jien, it reflected his overall philosophical thought and "was strongly advocated by him as part of his general plan to seize political control for the Kujō family."[17]

However, if we look at other developmental theories of *Heike* texts such as that of Yamashita Hiroki, we see that the Shibu text is not necessarily always thought of as the original *Heike*. Yamashita examined the chronological connection of the various texts and came up with the following schema:[18]

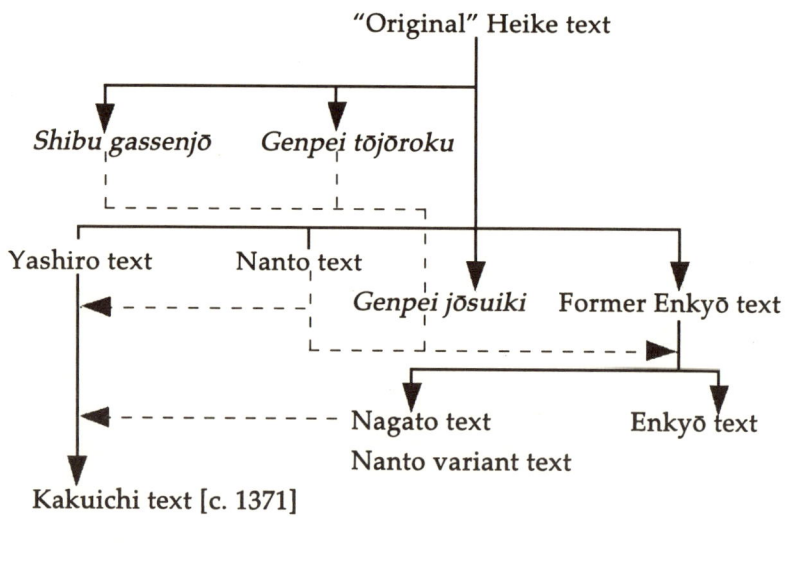

Here, we see that both the Shibu text and *Genpei tōjōroku* were influenced by an "original" *Heike* no longer extant and that both texts were part of the early developmental stage. Yamashita indicates that the "original," the Shibu text and *Genpei tōjōroku* influenced *Genpei jōsuiki* in the third stage, which eventually (along with several other variants) influenced the Kakuichi text. According to this schema, Hōnen may have appeared in the "original" since he appears in *Genpei tōjōroku*, which Yamashita says was directly influenced by the "original" text, as well as in *Genpei jōsuiki*, which he shows was influenced by both the Shibu text and *Genpei tōjōroku*.

Watanabe Sadamaro argues that although Shigehira's story of meeting Hōnen appears in these other extant texts, the story does not appear in early Hōnen biographies such as *Chion'in kōshiki*,[19] *Genkū shōnin shi nikki*[20] and *Honchō soshi denki ekotoba*.[21] However, the compilers of these early biographies may not have known this story or may not have wanted to associate Hōnen with Shigehira, whom they may have considered an evil man for burning great Buddhist temples. Whereas, later biographers may have been more sympathetic to Shigehira's fate, since enough time had passed from the incidents and the decline of the *Heike*.

A Statement of Precepts

In the Kakuichi text, Hōnen appears in "A Statement of Precepts," section five of chapter ten. This section has been translated by Helen C. McCullough as follows:

Shigehira's request to become a priest is denied—"In that case," Shigehira said when he was told, "might I see a holy man who has been my teacher for many years? I would like to talk to him about the next life."
"What is his name?"
"He is the man known as Hōnenbō of Kurodani."
Sanehira assented. "I see no objection."
Overjoyed, the Middle Captain sent for the monk. "I must

have been taken prisoner because I was destined to meet you again," he said in tears. "What ought I to do about the life to come? In the days when I was a man of some importance, I let myself be distracted by official duties and fettered by public affairs, too proud and arrogant to worry about my fate in the next world. And it was even worse after our luck ended and the disorders broke out: battling here and contending there, I was perpetually hampered by the evil desire to destroy others and save myself, perpetually unable to achieve purity of heart. In particular, there is the matter of the burning of the southern capital [Nara]. Under orders from the court and the military, and because I could not refuse to serve the Emperor or to comply with the demands of the times, I went to Nara to end the monks' violence. The destruction of the temples was quite unanticipated—quite beyond anyone's power to prevent—but I was Commander-in-Chief at the time; and that, I suppose, is why all the blame fell on me. I have come to realize that these present dreadful humiliations must all be regarded as punishments.

"Now I would like to shave my head, receive the precepts, and devote myself heart and soul to religious pursuits, but a man in my situation is not free to do as he pleases. Alas! Because today or tomorrow may bring my end, I fear I can perform no pious acts that would suffice to erase a single one of my sins. When I review my life, I understand that my evil deeds are higher than Mount Sumeru, that my good ones amount to less than a speck of dust. Beyond that question, I am doomed to the Three Evil Paths if I die in this state. Please, Your Holiness, be compassionate and merciful. If there is a way to save such a sinner, tell me of it."

The holy man remained silent for a time, choked with tears. By and by, he began to speak. "It is sorrow beyond sorrow that you should face the prospect of returning to the Three Evil Paths after having enjoyed the rare good fortune of being born a man. But the Buddhas of the Three Worlds must surely feel happiness because you have now abandoned wicked thoughts and embraced good ones, desirous of rejecting the impure world and achieving rebirth in the Pure Land. There are various ways of escaping from the world of illusion, but in these unclean tumultuous latter days of the Law, the best one is to recite the name of Amida Buddha. The goal, the Pure Land, has been divided into nine grades, and the necessary pious acts have been compressed into six syllables, which even the most slow-witted person can chant. You must not depreciate yourself because you think you have committed grave sins: even those who are guilty of the Ten Evils and the Five Deadly Sins can attain rebirth if they repent. Nor must you lose hope because you think you have performed few meritorious acts: Amida will come to meet anyone who has it in his heart to intone the sacred name one time or ten times. It is explained, 'He who intones the sacred name with all his heart will enter the Western Paradise.' It is taught, 'To intone Amida's name is to repent sins constantly.' Demons cannot approach the person who trusts in the words, 'Amida's name is a sharp sword.' It is written that a man's sins will all vanish if he recites, 'A single Buddha-invocation washes away all sins.'

"I have tried to summarize the essential elements of the Pure Land faith: these quotations may be considered its basic teachings. But belief is the key to rebirth. You must believe with all your heart: never, never entertain a doubt. If you believe these teachings without reservation, and if you meditate on Amida Buddha in your heart and keep his name on your lips, always and everywhere, whether you are walking, standing, sitting, or lying down, there can be no doubt that at the hour of death you will leave this cruel world for the Pure Land from which there is no return."

This instructive discourse delighted the Middle Captain. "I would like to receive the commandments now. May I do so without becoming a monk?"

"It is quite common for a layman to receive them." The holy man touched a razor to Shigehira's forehead, made shaving motions, and administered the Ten Commandments.

> Shigehira received the precepts with tears of joy streaming down his face, and Hōnen also wept as he spoke, moved by deep compassion and sympathy.
> Shigehira told Tomotoki to fetch a certain inkstone, one he had deposited with a samurai whose house he had frequented for poetry and music sessions. Then he presented it to the holy man as a pious offering. "Please do not give this away," he said, weeping. "Keep it where you can see it always, and whenever you remember, 'That object belonged to Shigehira once,' think of it as though it were myself and recite the sacred name. I would be truly grateful if you could chant an occasional scroll of holy writ on my behalf when you have the time." Unable to reply, Hōnen put the inkstone in his bosom and went home in tears, wringing the sleeves of his black robe.[22]

In this scene, the Kakuichi text indicates that Shigehira makes a request to Toi no Jirō Sanehira to see Hōnen. Shigehira is then allowed to see Hōnen, who elucidates the Pure Land teachings to Shigehira as well as to the audience of this tale. Hōnen is not only a character in this scene but is the transmitter of Pure Land thought. Hōnen also appears in several other *Heike* texts, which present a similar plot though in each the scene varies slightly.[23]

Genpei tōjōroku, the earliest extant *Heike* text in which Hōnen appears emphasizes the single practice of nembutsu (*nembutsu no ichigyō*) and perhaps remains most true to Hōnen's original doctrine. The doctrinal points discussed in *Genpei jōsuiki* closely resemble the Kakuichi text. However, in this text, Shigehira is under the care of a man identified as Kurō Yoshitsune, who is none other than Minamoto Yoritomo's younger brother, Minamoto Yoshitsune.

Another interesting point is the difference in the parting gift or alm that is given to Hōnen. In the Kakuichi text, Shigehira is shown giving Hōnen an inkstone, which was said to have been a gift from a Sung Emperor to Kiyomori named Matsukage (Pine Shadow).[24] However, the other texts as well as the Hōnen biographies, *Kukanden*[25] and *Shijūhakkanden*,[26] identify the gift as a *sōshibako* (hand-box).

Although these differences occur, for the most part, the major plot in the various *Heike* texts remains the same. Also, most of the doctrinal points which Hōnen teaches to Shigehira are similar. Here, I would like to discuss each of the doctrinal points in the Kakuichi text as indicated by Watanabe Sadamaro.[27]

First, there is an emphasis on *mappō* and on the recitation of Amida Buddha's name as the best practice. In the Kakuichi text, Hōnen is shown saying: "There are various ways of escaping from the world of illusion, but in these unclean, tumultuous latter days of the Law, the best one is to recite the name of Amida Buddha."[28] Next, he emphasizes "easy practice" (*igyō*). "The necessary pious acts have been compressed into six syllables [Namu Amida Butsu], which even the most slow-witted person can chant."[29] Third, he says that even the most evil persons "who are guilty of the Ten Evils[30] and the Five Deadly Sins[31] can attain rebirth."[32] Therefore, even the most sinful person, in this case, Shigehira, who was held responsible for setting ablaze Tōdaiji and Kōfukuji, could be saved and be reborn into Amida's Pure Land.

Fourth, Hōnen states that Amida will save anyone who intones his name once or ten times (*ichinen jūnen*), meaning that Amida does not question the quantity vocalized. Although some may question this point regarding Hōnen's doctrine, the problem of "once-calling" (*ichinen*) versus "many-calling" (*tanen*) continues to create controversy over what Hōnen "really" meant. Historically, we know that the problem existed early on as Hōnen's group split into different branches emphasizing one view or the other.[33]

Next, we find Hōnen quoting a few passages from Shan-tao's *Ōjōraisan* and *Hanjūsan*. From *Ōjōraisan,* he quotes, "He who intones the sacred name with all his heart will enter the Western Paradise." From *Hanjūsan,* he cites, "To intone Amida's name is to repent sins constantly." "Amida's name is a sharp sword." "A single Buddha-invocation washes away all sins." Lastly, he says belief is the key to rebirth and emphasizes the importance of practice to dispel disbelief. These key points which were brought into the *Heike* are essential points of Hōnen's teachings.³⁴

In this sermon to Shigehira, Hōnen states: "I have tried to summarize the essential elements of the Pure Land faith. These quotations may be considered its basic teachings."³⁵ Here, we clearly see that Hōnen was not attempting to claim these teachings as his own, much less take credit for them. Instead, he cites passages from Shan-tao's commentary, and acknowledges and reiterates the Pure Land teachings of the past. Moreover, it appears by distinguishing Shan-tao's teachings as part of the Pure Land faith, he attempts to prove the precedence for a Pure Land school (Jōdo Shū), which had not yet existed as a separate school. By acknowledging that these passages were Pure Land teachings of the past and by distinguishing that these teachings were from a "Pure Land tradition," Hōnen's character in the *Heike* is shown legitimizing Hōnen's actual Pure Land movement.

Here, we see within the *Heike* as well as historically, Hōnen's importance was that he pointed to the past to create and legitimate a new tradition. Thus Hōnen's uniqueness was not so much what he taught but what he did with those teachings. Although the content of his teaching was important, it was what Hōnen did with those teachings within the context of his time which proved to be truly significant and revolutionary.

In *The Making of a Saint: The Life, Times and Sanctification of Neophytos the Recluse,* Catio Galatariotou discusses the dynamics and process of sanctification. She cites Pierre Bourdieu in his use of "symbolic capital." "Symbolism addresses emotions and thoughts by a process of associations whose topology of operation also encompasses the individual and collective consciousness."³⁶ Here, I believe Hōnen's teachings acted as symbolic capital by resonating with the collective consciousness which was affected by *mappō* in the late Heian to early Kamakura periods.

The section on "Taking the Precepts" portrays a powerful scene in which Shigehira and Hōnen meet. Although Shigehira says that Hōnen was his spiritual master of several years, it is in this scene that Shigehira realizes spiritual awakening for the first time. Hōnen is shown not only as a Buddhist teacher with deep faith and belief but as a compassionate bodhisattva-like priest who saves even one who had committed the most evil crime. In this scene, Hōnen, like a bodhisattva, is not judgmental but full of compassion and wisdom. His words are touching and effective. *Genpei tōjōroku* and *Genpei jōsuiki*, and other early *Heike* variants also portray Hōnen comforting Shigehira with similar words. Hōnen biographies, on the other hand, completely omit or gloss over this scene. For example, *Hōnen shōnin gyōjō ezu*, an elaborate picture scroll biography in forty-eight scrolls (also known as *Shijūhakkanden*)[37] describes the meeting as follows:

> On the twenty eight of the twelfth month in the fourth year of Jishō (1180), when Lieutenant-General Shigehira of the Taira clan, who held the junior third grade of the Court rank, made an attack upon the southern capital, in accordance with his father's [Kiyomori] command, the famous Tōdaiji Temple with all its magnificent buildings was reduced to ashes. But after this at the battle of Ichinotani, he was taken prisoner on the seventh day of the second month of the first year of Genryaku (1184), and carried away to the capital, where he was marched through the streets in a triumphal procession and subjected to various indignities. Being anxious to ask some questions in regard to the future life, he was allowed to invite Hōnen to come and see him, when Hōnen made him promise to keep the commandments of the Buddhas, and explained to him in detail the doctrine of the *Nembutsu*. Shigehira, overjoyed at these instructions, said to him, "Surely my being taken alive was for the sole purpose of meeting you." Apparently as an outward expression of his gratitude for Hōnen's giving him the commandments, he took out a hand-box (*sōshibako*) he commonly used for holding his notebooks and handed it to Hōnen, with the words, "It may be of small use to you, but I wish you would put it somewhere you can easily see it, so that you may be occasionally reminded of me, and when you

are, that you would put a prayer to the Buddha for me." Hōnen, deeply impressed, gladly accepted it.[38]

The similarity of this scene to the scene in the Kakuichi text is striking. Nonetheless, here, Hōnen's words are reduced to an abbreviated explanation of the nembutsu doctrine. Rather than showing Hōnen actually saying the words, the biography merely described the action that took place. The actual conversation may have been deleted because Shunjō, the compiler of this biography, may have wanted to emphasize the importance of Hōnen rather than contextualizing him within a longer Pure Land tradition. However, those involved in producing the *Heike* were attempting not only to legitimize Hōnen, but also to contextualize him and the Pure Land teachings within the socio-religious climate in which they lived. Earlier Hōnen biographies, such as *Chion-in kōshiki*,[39] *Genkū shōnin shi nikki*,[40] and *Honchō soshi denki ekotoba*,[41] may not have wanted to include Shigehira's name within their story of Hōnen because they were produced shortly after Hōnen's death, when Shigehira may have been strongly associated with the bitter memory of the destruction of great temples, Tōdaiji and Kōfukuji. However, as time passed Shigehira's character was redeemed, allowing for more sympathy towards this tragic figure; thus showing that in his last days, Shigehira was able to receive spiritual solace through Hōnen. Even later Hōnen biographers may not have necessarily wanted to emphasize Hōnen's meeting with Shigehira, but since the popular *heikyoku*[42] began to include Hōnen in its story, Hōnen biographies may have not been able to ignore this scene completely.

In the end, however, we cannot know if this event ever took place, and although we cannot accept all the events in the *Heike* on face value, the *Heike*, perhaps, presents a realistic portrayal of this monk named Hōnen-bō, who lived in a complex time as one world tragically fell into ashes, while another seemed to have triumphantly rose from them.

Even with the rise of the Minamoto after 1185, we see that all was not stable. Petitions were sent to court against Hōnen's movement,[43] and Hōnen himself was exiled in 1207. His exile was not merely a matter of heresy; underlying it was a deep-seated political instability and uncertainty, which Hōnen's movement seemed to threaten. Therefore, the production of literary and oral creations such as the *Heike* texts and Hōnen biographies must be examined within their social, political, religious and historical background.

HŌNEN AND PURE LAND INFLUENCES IN THE HEIKE

The influence and impact of Hōnen's Pure Land teaching on the *Heike* was tremendous.[44] Although Pure Land thought existed in Japan early on, and even in the earlier part of the Heian period, we find figures such as Fujiwara Michinaga (966–1027) showing devotion to Amida, Hōnen transformed Pure Land practices. Moreover, he changed the way people thought about the Pure Land; he changed it from a "self-power" (*jiriki*) oriented faith based on virtue to one oriented towards the practice of calling Amida's name (*shōmyō nembutsu*) and relying on Amida's saving power (*tariki*).[45] This transformation can be seen throughout the *Heike*. Further, the numerous appearances of Pure Land thought in the *Heike* are indicative of the influence of Hōnen's Pure Land teachings.

The first example that appears in the Kakuichi text is in chapter one, section six on Giō, one of Kiyomori's favorite performers. In this section, Giō falls out of Kiyomori's favor because Kiyomori comes to favor another performer named Hotoke. In her sadness, Giō decides to become a nun with her mother and sister, and pray for rebirth in the Pure Land. The three women move to a humble thatched hermitage in the mountain. One night, a visitor comes. Fearing that it is a malevolent spirit, the mother says:

> If he is a merciless creature bent on our destruction, we must rely firmly on the Original Vow of Amida, in whom we have always placed our trust; we must maintain a constant stream of invocations. Since the heavenly host comes to meet believ-

ers, led by the sound of their voices, it will assuredly take us to the Pure Land. We must simply be careful not to falter in our invocations.[46]

The visitor turns out to be none other than Hotoke, who asks to join them. The narrator at the end of the section reads:

Secluded in a single dwelling, the four women offered flowers and incense before the sacred images morning and evening; and their prayers never flagged. I have heard that all of those nuns achieved their goal of rebirth in the Pure Land, each in her term.[47]

Three important doctrinal points are made in this section. First, the emphasis on relying on and firmly believing in the Original Vow of Amida, in other words, relying on "Other-power" (*tariki*), which Hōnen emphasized in his teaching. Hōnen also taught that "self-power" (*jiriki*) was futile in the age of *mappō*. Second is the stress upon rebirth in the Pure Land. According to Hōnen, Pure Land teachings assure the believers that they will be reborn in Amida's Paradise if they call his name. Finally, there is an emphasis in maintaining a constant stream of invocations. As mentioned above, the issue of "once-calling" and "many-calling" has not been resolved, yet Hōnen's own behavior and attitude towards practice seems to encourage "many-calling."

Even Jishinbō Son'e, a late Heian period scholar monk who read the *Lotus Sutra*, was said to have "kept Amida's name on his lips and concentrated wholeheartedly on the Buddha's compassionate vow to escort the faithful to the Western Paradise."[48] Here, too, we see the emphasis on "many-calling." However, again, as in life, the Hōnen that appears in the *Heike* does not seem to make a distinction, although "many-calling" seems to have been the preferred practice.

Another example can be found in chapter ten, section twelve: "The Suicide of Koremori." Koremori reflected on his life, "What is the matter with me? Am I still bound by worldly attachments?"[49] Although he chanted, intoning Amida's name, he thought of his former life. In the end, however, the *Heike* says:

> To Koremori it seemed a supremely favorable opportunity for rebirth in the Pure Land. He put away distracting thoughts immediately, intoned Amida's name a hundred times in a loud voice, and entered the sea with "Hail" on his lips. The Hyōe Novice and Ishidōmaru followed him into the waves, chanting, "Hail, Amida Buddha!"[50]

Finally, perhaps the most tragic and climactic scene in the *Heike* is "The Drowning of the Former Emperor" in chapter eleven, section nine. In this scene at the end of the Dan-no-ura battle, the Taira attempt to escape in their boats with the young Emperor Antoku, who was a child of eight years. The nun of the Second Rank (Kiyomori's principle wife and grandmother of the Emperor) held the child. "Where are you taking me, Grandmother?" he asked. Holding back her tears, she turned to him,

> "Don't you understand? You became an Emperor because you obeyed the Ten Good Precepts in your last life, but now an evil karma holds you fast in its toils. Your good fortune has come to an end. Turn to the east and say good-bye to the Grand Shrine of Ise, then turn to the west and repeat the sacred name of Amida Buddha, so that he and his host may come and escort you to the Pure Land. This country is a land of sorrow; I am taking you to a happy realm called Paradise."[51]

Here, we again see the emphasis on calling Amida's name as well as the idea that this act would guarantee them rebirth in the Pure Land.

Although the fateful meeting between Hōnen and Shigehira may not have historically taken place, we can see that Hōnen's teachings had left its mark in the *Heike*. As the light dims on the stage of *The Tale of the Heike*, we can still hear voices calling Amida's name in the distance. In an age of decline, Hōnen had provided an answer.

CONCLUSION

Although Hōnen's Pure Land school is often described as part of the "new Kamakura" Buddhism, Hōnen himself was very much a product of the late Heian world in the capital city of Kyoto—the world of *Heike monogatari*. Much of Hōnen's actions and thoughts seem to reflect the sadness of the ephemerality and impermanence of this world in the age of *mappō*. And Hōnen's Pure Land teachings and doctrine responded to the fear and chaos and human tragedies of those living in the age of decline.

As already mentioned, Hōnen looked to the teachings of the Pure Land, and specifically advocated the exclusive practice of calling Amida Buddha's name (*senju nembutsu*) as the most effective practice for the latter age of the Dharma. Moreover, he was the first to doctrinally legitimate a "Pure Land school."[52] In this role as an outstanding Buddhist teacher and the attributed establisher of the Pure Land school, not only did he move many to join him, he inspired and incited the popular mind which imaged him as a bodhisattva-like figure.[53] At the same time, this was a period when the *heikyoku* became increasingly popular. As we have seen, Hōnen himself appears in several *Heike* texts. Furthermore, Pure Land thought was infused throughout these texts, which has led some to believe that several of the *Heike* texts were probably didactic pieces that advocated and propagated Hōnen's teachings.[54]

At the end of the *Heike,* as the last of the once great Taira clan dies off, there seems to be hope for only one thing. As many of her family members had done before her, the Imperial Lady Kenshumon'in (Taira Kiyomori's daughter) uttered these last words before her passing, "'Hail, Amitābha Tathāgata, Teaching Lord of the Western Paradise! Please admit me to the Pure Land ....' After her chanting voice had gradually weakened, a purple cloud trailed in the west, a marvelous fragrance permeated the chamber, and the sound of music was heard in the heavens."[55]

NOTES

1. Helen C. McCullough, *The Tale of the Heike* (Stanford: Stanford University Press, 1988), 21.

2. For the translation of *An Account of My Hermitage*, see Helen C. McCullough, *Classical Japanese Prose: An Anthology* (Stanford: Stanford University press, 1990), 379–392.

3. Ibid., 382.

4. Kenneth Dean Butler, "The Birth of an Epic: A Textual Study of the *Heike Monogatari*" (Ph.D. dissertation, Harvard University, 1964), 2. Although this study as well as other articles by Butler used for this paper are now quite dated, they are still the most extensive and relevant study of the *Heike* in English.

5. Here, Butler is referring specifically to the Kakuichi text which is considered to be the standard version of the *Heike*.

6. There are six manuscripts bearing Kakuichi's name (Hiroshi Kitagawa and Bruce T. Tsuchida, trans., *The Tale of the Heike: Heike Monogatari* [Tokyo: University of Tokyo Press, 1975], xxxi). Here, I refer to the Kakuichi text (Ryūkoku Daigaku version) that was translated by Helen C. McCullough under the title, *The Tale of the Heike*.

7. Kenneth D. Butler, "The *Heike Monogatari* and Theories of Oral Epic Literature," *The Seikei University Bulletin of the Faculty of Letters* 2 (1966): 37–54.

8. Butler, "The Textual Evolution of the *Heike Monogatari*," *Harvard Journal of Asiatic Studies* 26 (1966): 5–51.

9. Ibid.

10. Ibid.

11. Minamoto Noriyori (d. 1193), one of Yoshitomo's sons.

12. McCullough, *The Tale of the Heike*, 7.

13. Butler, "Textual Evolution," 17. Butler points to several mistakes that Kenkō makes in his entry such as the error of Yukinaga's birth

place and the error in assuming that it was recited. As Butler points out, the Shibu text was a product of a traditional literate society (p. 23). These mistakes on Kenkō's part indicate that he did not know these facts firsthand.

14. Watanabe Sadamaro, *Heike monogatari no shisō* (Kyoto: Hōzōkan, 1988), 242.

15. Although many accept the theory that Yukinaga was the author of the original *Heike,* Fukui Kōjun presents an interesting argument in his article "Heike monogatari no bukkyōshiteki seikaku: Yukinaga gensaku setsu o utagau" in his collection of articles *Fukui Kōjun chosakushū*, vol. 6,*Nihon chūsei shisō kenkyū* (Kyoto: Hōzōkan, 1988), 107–132. In this article, Fukui questions the theory of Yukinaga as the author of the original *Heike,* based on the Pure Land influences attributed to Hōnen in the Kakuichi text. He points to the chapter on Giō and the chapter on Taira Shigehira accepting the precepts from Hōnen as specific examples. However, he fails to mention the Shibu text, which is believed to be the original *Heike* written by Yukinaga.

Nonetheless, Fukui makes an extremely elucidating point that Yukinaga and Hōnen's closest disciple, Hōrenbō Shinkū were both the sons of a man identified as the former Lesser Controller of the Left Yukitaka (cf. Butler's "Textual Evolution", 20; Harper H. Coates and Ryūgaku Ishizuka, *Hōnen the Buddhist Saint: His Life and Teaching* [An introduction and translation of *Hōnen shōnin gyōjō ezu* compiled by Shunjō] [Kyoto: Chion'in, 1925], 539, 552 and 695). Because of this relationship, Fukui conjectures that Shinkū may have had some role in the later formation of the *Heike,* in which Hōnen's religious ideas figure prominently. Further, Fukui rightfully notes that Yukinaga's connection to Jien made it difficult to include any messages that may have been seen as "pro-Hōnen."

16. Butler, "The Birth of an Epic", 38.

17. Ibid.

18. Hiroki Yamashita, *Genpei tōjōroku to kenkyū* (Nagoya: Mikan Kokubun Shiryō Kankōkai, 1963), 267.

19. *Chion'in kōshiki* is not a complete biography. According to Allan Andrews it was read at Hōnen's memorial services in the early years after his death.

20. *Genkū shōnin shi nikki* is regarded as one of the oldest complete biographies of Hōnen. It is a short piece written in *kanbun*, the date and author are unknown, see Maya M. Hara, "A Study and Translation of *Genkū Shōnin Shi Nikki*" (M.A. thesis, Graduate Theological Union/Institute of Buddhist Studies, 1995).

21. *Honchō soshi denki ekotoba* (*Den hō-e*) is a picture scroll biography in four volumes. It was said to have been edited by Tankū, a disciple of Hōnen in 1237. According to Coates and Ishizuka, the original manuscripts (picture scrolls) are still preserved at Zendōji temple in Chikugo. "The author, though a disciple of Hōnen, is probably not the one who bore a name having the same sound, but written with a different Chinese character" (*Hōnen the Buddhist Saint*, 81).

22. McCullough, *The Tale of the Heike*, 333–335.

23. This may have been due to the oral nature of these variant texts.

24. McCullough, *The Tale of the Heike*, 335.

25. This biography in nine volumes was compiled by Shunjō and completed in 1311.

26. This long picture scroll biography was compiled and completed by Shunjō in 1323, although it appears to have been a collaborative effort copied in the hand of several people. This biography was translated by Coates and Ishizuka under the title *Hōnen the Buddhist Saint*. Both this and the shorter Kukanden reflect the ideas of the Chinzei branch which emphasized "many-calling."

27. Watanabe, *Heike monogatari no shisō*, 246.

28. McCullough, 335.

29. Ibid.

30. *Jūaku* (the ten evils) consist of killing, stealing, committing adultery, lying, using immoral language, slandering, equivocating, coveting, anger, and false views.

31. *Gogyakuzai* (Skt. *pañcāvici-karmāni*) the five deadly sins consist of killing one's father, killing one's mother, killing a saint (*arhat*), injuring the body of a Buddha, and causing disunity in the commu-

nity of monks.

32. McCullough, 335.

33. We can also see this in Hōnen biographies that are produced by the different Pure Land branches. Often Hōnen is portrayed in a manner that legitimizes one practice over the other. Although it seems that Hōnen himself practiced vocal nembutsu quite profusely (several biographies agree that he chanted up to 70,000 nembutsu a day), this does not necessarily mean that he expected everyone to do the same.

34. Watanabe cites earlier examples such as Genshin's *Ōjōyōshū* to indicate that the idea of belief (*shinjin*) was not necessarily Hōnen's own idea (*Heike monogatari no shisō*, 249). However, Hōnen does not claim these as his ideas in this scene from the *Heike* as well as in life. Instead he points to a longer Pure Land tradition and claims the validity of its teachings in the age of *mappō*.

35. McCullough, 335.

36. Catio Galatariotou, *The Making of a Saint: The Life, Times and Sanctification of Neophytos the Recluse* (Cambridge: Cambridge University Press, 1991), 4.
37. Translated into English by Coates and Ishizuka as *Hōnen the Buddhist Saint* (1925).

38. Coates and Ishizuka, *Hōnen the Buddhist Saint,* 538–539.

39. *Chion'in kōshiki* is not a complete biography rather it is a piece, which Allan Andrews says, was read at Hōnen's memorial services in the early years after his death.

40. *Genkū shōnin shi nikki* is regarded as one of the oldest complete biographies of Hōnen. It is a short piece written in *kanbun,* the date and author are unknown, see Hara, "A Study and Translation of *Genkū Shōnin Shi Nikki.*"

41. *Honchō soshi denki ekotoba (Den hō-e)* is a picture scroll biography in four volumes. It was said to have been edited by Tankū, a disciple of Hōnen in 1237. According to Coates and Ishizuka, the original manuscripts (picture scrolls) are still preserved at Zendōji temple in Chikugo. "The author, though a disciple of Hōnen, is probably not

the one who bore a name having the same sound, but written with a different Chinese character" (*Hōnen the Buddhist Saint,* 81).

42. *Heikyoku* refers to the sung version of the text of the *Heike monogatari* or similar kinds of delivery. See Earl Miner, Hiroko Odagiri and Robert E. Morrell, *The Princeton Companion to Classical Japanese Literature* (Princeton: Princeton University Press, 1985), 277.

43. See Robert E. Morrel, *Early Kamakura Buddhism: A Minority Report* (Berkeley, Calif.: Asian Humanities Press, 1987), 75.

44. Several articles have been published in Japanese by Fukui Kōjun, Watanabe Sadamaro and Yamashita Hiroaki, among others, on Hōnen's doctrine in *Heike monogatari.* In "Bukkyō to bungaku: Hōnen gi o meguru ronsō kara (Buddhism and Literature: Revisiting the Discussion of Hōnen's Doctrine)," in *Heike monogatari kenkyū josetsu* (Tokyo: Meiji shoin, 1972), Yamashita explains that the issue of the influence of Hōnen's Pure Land teachings in the *Heike* has been an on-going debate for many years. In this article, he discusses the nature and history of the debate as well as those who were involved. Among those involved was Fukui, who also wrote an article explaining the ongoing discussion, entitled "Heike monogatari to Hōnen gi (*The Tale of the Heike* and Hōnen's Doctrine)," in *Fukui Kōjun chosakushū,* vol.6, 221–244.

45. Watanabe, *Heike monogatari no shisō,* 241.

46. McCullough, *The Tale of the Heike,* 36.

47. Ibid., 37.

48. Ibid., 213.

49. Ibid., 349.

50. Ibid., 350.

51. Ibid., 378.

52. Hōnen's doctrinal tract, *Senchaku hongan nembutsu shū,* for the first time, explained the precedence for a Pure Land school by tracing back to the Chinese Pure Land teachers such as Shan-tao.

53. Several Hōnen biographies and *setsuwa* collections such as *Kokonchomonjū* and *Shijūhyaku innen shū* explain that Hōnen was a reincarnation of Amida and/or the bodhisattva Mahāsthāmaprāpta (Seishi).

54. Fukui, "Heike monogatari no bukkyōshiteki kōsai," *Fukui Kōjun chosakushū,* vol. 6, 146.

In her introduction to *Ōkagami,* Helen McCullough discusses how *setsuwa* were used to proselytize among the masses. She indicates that "such stories were useful for the Heian preachers who delivered sermons to aristocratic congregations or to groups made up of mixed social classes, and who, like their European counterparts, made active efforts to entertain and move their audiences." McCullough also suggests that these stories were in circulation, both orally and in compilations from early in the Heian period (*Ōkagami [The Great Mirror]: Fujiwara Michinaga [966–1027] and His Times : A Study and Translation* (Princeton: Princeton University Press, 1980), 11–12.

Butler also extensively discusses the oral nature of short stories in *"The Heike Monogatari* and Theories of Oral Epic Literature", 42–43.

55. McCullough, *The Tale of the Heike,* 438.

Pure Land Belief and Popular Practice: The *Odori Nembutsu* of Ippen Shōnin

James H. FOARD

In discussing Shinran's understanding of the Pure Land believer's destiny, Alfred Bloom showed that Shinran recovered the Pure Land "altruism" of T'an-luan which had been lost by the intervening tradition.

> For both T'an-luan and Shinran, the conception implicit in the Vow makes it clear that there could be no desire for one's own salvation which was not immediately and indissolubly connected to the desire for the salvation of all men.[1]

In his later study of Shinran's life, Prof. Bloom again stressed this doctrinally driven altruism as the motivation for Shinran's proselytizing explicitly to the common people, especially his adoption of certain literary genres.[2] This theme in Prof. Bloom's work suggests that popular Pure Land propagation was not the same for all Pure Land Buddhists, but was motivated and shaped by distinct Pure Land theoretical stances.

In the following pages, I would like to demonstrate this point by showing the complex relationships between a particular Pure Land theoretical position on the one hand and its mode of popular propagation on the other. The case we will examine is that of the *odori nembutsu* (nembutsu dance) of Ippen (1239–1289), the founder of the Jishū. In particular, I wish to show that this dance was far more than a strategy for propagation, but was as well a practice suited for a distinct Pure Land theoretical position.

For a study of popular Pure Land practices, Ippen seems especially appropriate, because he explored the entire religious world of his time so relentlessly. Hōnen, Shinran, and Ippen all "selected" the nembutsu as their exclusive practice. For Hōnen and Shinran, this led to a quest to purify their religion of extraneous elements. For Ippen, however, it led to a quest to incorporate much of medieval religion into the Pure Land belief system. His was a life of enormously eventful travel through virtually every area of Japanese population and to nearly all the great religious centers of his day. Indeed, Ippen was the most widely traveled medieval Japanese we know of, religious or otherwise, and has recently been proclaimed by an ethnographer of Japanese tourism to be the "patriarch of Japanese travel."[3]

Ippen embraced many of the popular religious beliefs and practices he encountered on his travels, including those of Shinto shrines. He was most influenced by the *bessho hijiri*, the guilds of *hijiri* or holy men chartered by the great Buddhist temples to proselytize, distribute amulets, and collect funds. Ippen was something of a free-lance *hijiri* whose Pure Land beliefs gave new meanings to *hijiri* life and practices, meanings that cut across particular temple loyalties. By "free-lance," I mean that he did many of the things that *bessho hijiri* did, but that he legitimated them by the miracles that happened to him rather than those that happened at a particular temple. Eventually, Ippen's biography served to draw many of these *bessho hijiri* into the group he founded, the Jishū, which had its own *dōjō* as well, and which then emerged as the largest itinerant order in medieval Japan.

Through an examination of the *odori nembutsu*, I wish to suggest how Ippen used the popular religious practices of his day. First, I will describe the *odori nembutsu* as it is presented principally in the *Ippen Hijiri E*, an illustrated biography of Ippen composed in 1299, or ten years after Ippen's death. I will then briefly summarize the consensus of scholarship on these passages and offer my own judgments. What I hope to show is that, while Ippen was a bricoleur of sorts, there was method to his bricolage.[4] Specifically, he was

PURE LAND BELIEF AND POPULAR PRACTICE

employing popular practices not just to promulgate Pure Land Buddhism to the common people; he was also bringing popular, largely *hijiri* practices to Pure Land Buddhism in order to solve endemic Pure Land problems.

THE *ODORI NEMBUTSU* IN JISHŪ TEXTS

The *Ippen Hijiri E* (IV, 5)[5] records that Ippen's first nembutsu dance, involving both clergy and laity, was held in 1279 at the home of a samurai in Odagiri village in Shinano. The *Hijiri E* cites three authorities to justify this dance. The first is a passage on constant practice from an unknown text that "the *hijiri* [Ippen] always carried," attributed to Kōya Shōnin, a tenth century *hijiri*. The *Hijiri E* claims that Kōya began the nembutsu dance, although none of the earlier sources about Kōya make this claim, and even the passage quoted in the *Hijiri E* makes no clear reference to dancing. The second authority is a passage from the *Muryōjukyō* (although a convention in many sutras) in which those hearing the Buddha's words worship and dance with joy. The third authority given is a passage from Shan-tao's *Ōjō Raisan Ge*, which does mention dancing for joy.

In the account given in the *Ippen Ekotobaden* (II, 1), another biographical scroll, the dance begins spontaneously as Ippen is chanting the nembutsu together with a man who has come to him for guidance. Although the *Hijiri E* gives no such account, we can detect the spontaneity of the event in its illustration of it. Ippen stands on the veranda of a house, beating on a bowl. In the courtyard, fifteen people, in both clerical and lay dress, are dancing without apparent design, while seven people are shown watching in an attitude of prayer. The faces of the dancers show great joy: one with eyes closed and a blissful smile, another uplifted in prayer, still another contorted by passionate chanting.

Shōkai, the author of the *Hijiri E*, explains the dance this way:

191

The joy of the practitioner's faithful heart is manifested in the form of the dance. The compassion of Amida is revealed in the echo of the bell. Beings awaken from the sleep of a long night and those who are confused are caused to make salvific connections (*kechien*). Therefore, like children with hobby horses, we dance here and there, and in the fashion of widows [singing] with their fulling blocks, we join voices in chanting the nembutsu.

The passage concludes with a poetry exchange with a critic of the dance:

Later, when Ippen was [in Ōmi province], a man named Jōgō [from Enryakuji] came to see what Ippen was like. He declared that dancing while chanting the nembutsu was scandalous. To this, Ippen responded in verse:

If one wants to leap, leap,
If one wants to dance, dance—
Like a spring colt on the road,
The dharma-path is known
To one who knows.

Jōgō, too, responded in verse:

If you mounted and tamed
Your heart's colt,
Surely it would not
Dance and leap like this.

Ippen again responded:

But leap
And dance like this—
The heart's colt

PURE LAND BELIEF AND POPULAR PRACTICE

Joyful to hear
The teaching of Amida.

Afterwards, this person converted and became a nembutsu practitioner at a place called Onodera in Settsu.

The next passage in the *Hijiri E* (V, 1) also tells of the dance. In that same year, a disbelieving sister of a provincial warrior dreamed that many small Buddhas were walking around her house praising Ippen. After a yin-yang master declared the dream felicitous, she sponsored a service for three days and three nights, during which several hundred people danced. Although they broke a plank in her veranda, she did not repair it, but kept it as a memorial of the event.

There are six other nembutsu dances mentioned in the *Hijiri E*. Each of these but one is shown in the paintings as held on a raised stage before an audience. (The exception has simply a roof.) All are performed exclusively by the Jishū, in a serious demeanor and in an apparently practiced order.

INTERPRETING THE *ODORI NEMBUTSU*

A number of scholars have commented on these texts, including Gorai Shigeru, Hori Ichirō, Imai Masaharu, and especially Ōhashi Shunnō.[6] A scholarly consensus has emerged concerning the precedents for this dance and Ippen's transformation of it. Ōhashi begins by discussing the significance of dance in the *Nihongi* and *Kojiki*, and moves quickly to evidence that dancing placated the spirits of the dead in ancient Japan. Since the nembutsu, too, was used for this purpose by *hijiri*, such as Kōya, whom the *Hijiri E* mentions, the nembutsu and dance were connected, or so it is thought, in the *hijiri*'s efforts to dispatch the malevolent spirits of the dead in the late Heian Period. Ippen, it is further claimed, transformed this traditional nembutsu dance by making it an expression of religious ecstacy (the

English word is used by both Ōhashi and Imai). Imai makes the interesting point that this association of the nembutsu with ecstasy is in direct contrast to Shinran's denial of such feelings in the *Tannishō*.[7]

In this scholarly consensus there are two points that bear on the issues at hand: 1) that there was probably some association of the nembutsu dance with placating the dead by Ippen's time, although Ippen's is the first clear record, but 2) that Ippen redefined the dance as an ecstatic expression of one's salvation through Amida's Name. While I accept the historical outline and certainly the obvious indications of ecstacy in the first nembutsu dance, just repeating the *Hijiri E's* explanation that the dance was an expression of ecstasy seems naive and simplistic in light of the rest of Ippen's religious career. First of all, after the initial dance described in the passage above, no *odori nembutsu* appears in any biography of Ippen as the product of spontaneous ecstasy. On the contrary, they all are presented as orderly, well-planned performances on a stage for the benefit of an audience. Secondly, the idea that the nembutsu, danced or otherwise, is an expression of joy, or requires any emotion at all, is fundamentally opposed to the most explicit expressions of Ippen's views of the Name, which make it clear that the nembutsu is neither expressive nor instrumental. Finally, the expression-of-ecstasy interpretation does not explain why a dance to placate the dead would have been chosen to do this.

What we need is an understanding of Ippen's use of the dance that meets these objections while still accounting for the articulations of ecstasy that, in fact, appear in the passage quoted above. In seeking such an understanding, Catherine Bell's recent work on ritual seems particularly helpful.[8] One of her first and most fundamental arguments is that ritual belongs in the realm of action, in conjunction with other actions, and is neither an expression of thought nor reducible to ideas or, we might add, emotion. Rather, she claims, ritual deploys strategies for distinguishing some actions from others, and indeed, generates the contexts in which these strategies can succeed.

In light of Bell's work, we can see that the nembutsu dance was used by Ippen to generate a context within which the nembutsu could be distinguished from all other actions, and further, that the means of generating this context was the *rhetoric* of joy or ecstasy in the dance, regardless of how real or unreal that ecstasy was in any performance. In other words, the joyful dance was not just a way of performing nembutsu but was a rhetorical move, a way of distinguishing that performance as a special kind of action.

Notice in the exchange of verses quoted above that, while the surface point concerns whether one should still one's heart or go ahead and dance, this is very much an argument about whether one is beginning on the path of the Dharma or has completed it. To put it in Pure Land terms, Jōgō and Ippen differ, not over whether one should be happy at the moment of rebirth (and how could they differ on this?), but over whether the nembutsu is something to be practiced over a lifetime to attain future rebirth or rebirth is to be attained immediately through the nembutsu.

Through the claim of unstoppable joy, Ippen uses the dance to connect the nembutsu with immediate rebirth. This same point is made in the explanatory passage given by the *Hijiri E's* author, Shōkai, which was quoted above. Nevertheless, we should remember that, however the *odori nembutsu* began, we are in these texts reading justifications for carefully staged performances. Mindful that rituals do indeed perform people,[9] the dance—accompanied as it was by the claim of joy in rebirth—would engender any ecstasy rather than the other way around, and would therefore generate the context that would distinguish the nembutsu as an action. Ecstasy, whether experienced or claimed, should be considered a rhetorical strategy that permitted the dance to indicate what kind of action the nembutsu was.

Well, then, what sort of action was it? Simply stated, in the context of the joyous dance, the nembutsu was designated an action that was indistinguishable from its effects. There is a deliberate circularity here: with the nembutsu comes rebirth, with rebirth comes joyous dancing, with joyous dancing comes the nembutsu and so on. In the *odori nembutsu*, then, nembutsu and rebirth arise together outside of the flow of normal cause and effect, as one and the same event. As I have suggested elsewhere, Ippen's view of the nembutsu denied that uttering Amida's Name either caused rebirth or expressed faith. Rather, Amida's attainment of Buddhahood and the *ōjō* of all beings were the same event, an event that was both ten kalpas ago and the moment of each nembutsu, and which is contained in the six-character Name. The Name simply actualized this primordial, timeless rebirth.[10]

When viewed this way, Ippen's adoption of the nembutsu dance seems not so much a matter of giving an old rite new meanings, but one of rather using its recognized association with death and rebirth to articulate something about the nembutsu, as performed both in this life and at death. By dancing, the Jishū was chanting the nembutsu and attaining *ōjō* at the same time; the moment of nembutsu was the moment of rebirth in both this life and the next.

Such an approach also permits us to understand the purposes the dance would have had for an audience. In the paintings of later *odori nembutsu* performances, considerable attention is given the audiences, in part to show their great variety in the communal spaces of medieval society, such as roads, temples, and beaches. In these audiences, we find people who are listening and (more importantly) not listening. In one (VII, 1), a woman is running away covering her ears, and in a text such as this, the representation of such impiety can only be purposeful. In the most dramatic example of listening, a Dragon-King (*ryūō*) rises from the sea to hear the nembutsu dance, and in the process inundates the stage (VIII, 2). The suggestion here is that, since salvation comes through the Name itself, rather than through any faith or life of practice, the distinction of those who are reborn and those who are not is simply a matter of listening and not listening. The role of the audience for the dance, then, parallels that of the recipients of the *fuda*, the paper talismans upon which the Name was printed and which Ippen distributed by the tens of thousands. These talismans, too, were effective in and of themselves, and, as with the audience for the dance, the only choice for recipients was to take it or leave it. Both the dance and the *fuda*, then, embodied the timeless Name in the world.

CONCLUSION

This examination of Ippen's use of the *odori nembutsu* suggests two conclusions about his use of popular practices generally. First, Ippen used these practices in response to universal Pure Land problems. The issues resolved by the nembutsu dance, namely the relationship between the nembutsu and rebirth and the corollary problem of the status of the practitioner in this life, were issues for Pure Land Buddhists everywhere, because they were inherent in the mythology of the *Larger Sutra* and in the creedal distinction between *jiriki* and *tariki*. Ippen's use of popular practices, therefore, does not indicate that Ippen was merely a popularizer, and, by implication, more distant from the cosmopolitan, scriptural tradition than Hōnen and Shinran.[11] While he did promulgate Pure Land Buddhism more directly to a vastly wider populace than either of those two, he also brought the potentials of popular Buddhist practice to bear on general Pure Land problems. He did so with the nembutsu dance, with his *fuda* distribution, and in many other areas of his religious life. In Ippen's religion, the route between scriptural Buddhism and popular piety was a two-way street.

The second general conclusion involves what Ippen got from these popular practices that applied so well to Pure Land problems. The case of the *odori nembutsu* suggests that popular practices and even magic provided him with a discourse to express the immediate presence of the Pure Land that he found in Amida's Name. Nowhere is this tendency more obvious than in the use of sacred places—Zenkōji, Kumano, Shitennōji, Mt. Kōya, and many more—as sites for encountering Amida Buddha directly.

We must remember, however, that the distinction of the Pure Land tradition and popular practices is ours, not Ippen's. As the *odori nembutsu* shows us, in Ippen's view both were elements in a homogenous religious world. Within this world, all the miracles, divinations, gods, and Buddhas were, to use Ippen's own metaphor, "waves on the ocean of Amida's original vow."

The significance of these conclusions is enhanced by the popularity and later influence of the *odori nembutsu*. A stone memorial in Miyagi prefecture, for example, through which Ippen passed shortly after the events described above, commemorates a nembutsu dance performed in 1300, or 21 years after Ippen's first dance. Within ten years of Ippen's death, the dance had become so popular around the capital that two contemporary texts singled it out for scorn.[12] Its influence can be traced in the history of Japanese performing arts, with the term reversed as *nembutsu odori*, and contemporary folklore demonstrates its wide distribution in Japanese folk religion.[13] The most famous episode in the later history of the dance is the story of Izumo no Okuni, the legendary founder of Kabuki dance. At the capital's Kitano Shrine in 1603, she performed the *nembutsu odori* together with other dances to great acclaim, after which she was imitated widely. Okuni was a prostitute, dancer, and perhaps a medium, but the descriptions of her dance suggest that she aimed at entertaining spectacle. She even wore a cross and men's clothing.[14]

This in no way suggests that Ippen's meanings for the dance were shared by Okuni. Rather, the Pure Land legacy was that of making a dance so ubiquitous that a major performance tradition in early modern—and indeed modern—Japan could grow from it in the newly emerging urban pleasure quarters of the Tokugawa period. For our purposes, we should note that this ubiquitousness was not happenstance, but resulted from a distinctly Pure Land claim of an immediate salvation open to all people, both in life and at the moment of death, in the practice of the dance. Extending the initial suggestion of Prof. Bloom, then, the investigation of how particular Pure Land positions resulted in particular modes of popular propagation and practice may prove to be an important subject not only for Pure Land studies, but also for understanding how Pure Land Buddhism, out of its own religious vision, made distinct contributions to Japanese popular culture.

NOTES

1. Alfred Bloom, *Shinran's Gospel of Pure Grace*, Association for Asian Studies Monographs and Papers, no. 20 (Tucson: University of Arizona Press, 1965), 82.

2. Alfred Bloom, *The Life of Shinran Shonin: The Journey to Self-Acceptance*, rev. ed., Institute of Buddhist Studies Monograph Series, no. 1 (Berkeley: Institute of Buddhist Studies, 1994), 27-28.

3. Kanzaki Noritake, *Kankō minzokugaku e no tabi* (Tokyo: Kawade shobō, 1990), 182.

4. "Bricoleur" is a metaphor from Claude Levi-Strauss, *The Savage Mind* (Chicago: University of Chicago Press, 1966), 16–36.

5. The Roman numeral indicates the scroll; the Arabic, the section of that scroll.

6. Gorai Shigeru, "Ippen to Kōya, Kumano oyobi odori nembutsu," in *Ippen Hijiri E, Nihon emakimono zensho*, no. 10 (Tokyo: Kadokawa shoten, 1960), 16–37; Hori Ichirō, *Wagakuni minkan shinkōshi no kenkyū* (Tokyo: Sōgensha, 1953–55), 2: 350–1; Imai Masaharu, *Jishū seiritsushi no kenkyū* (Tokyo: Yoshikawa kōbunkan, 1981), 98–112; Ōhashi Shunnō, *Odori nembutsu* (Tokyo: Daizō shuppan, 1974).

7. Imai, 109.

8. Catherine Bell, *Ritual Theory, Ritual Practice* (Oxford: Oxford University Press, 1992).

9. A phrase borrowed from David L. Hall and Roger T. Ames, *Thinking through Confucius* (Albany, N.Y.: State University of New York Press, 1987), 274.

10. James H. Foard, "Prefiguration and Narrative in Medieval Hagiography: The *Ippen Hijiri E*," in *Flowing Traces: Buddhism in the Literary and Visual Arts of Japan*, James H. Sanford, William R. LaFleur, and Masatoshi Nagatomi, eds. (Princeton, N.J.: Princeton University Press, 1992), 89.

11. A suggestion found in, among others, Joseph M. Kitagawa, *Religion in Japanese History* (New York: Columbia University Press, 1966), 117.

12. Ōhashi, 124–131. For the memorial stone, see Ōhashi Toshio (Shunnō), *Ippen: sono kōdō to shisō* (Tokyo: Hyōronsha, 1971), 91–2.

13. Bukkyō daigaku minkan numbutsu shinkō no kenkyūkai, ed., *Minkan nembutsu shinkō no kenkyū: shiryōhen* (Tokyo: Ryūbunkan, 1966), 287–366.

14. Cecelia Segawa Seigle, *Yoshiwara: The Glittering World of the Japanese Courtesan* (Honolulu: University of Hawaii Press, 1993), 16–17; Benito Ortolani, *The Japanese Theatre: From Shamanistic Ritual to Contemporary Pluralism*, rev. ed. (Princeton, N.J.: Princeton University Press, 1990), 174–5.

Ordination Ceremony of the Honganji Priests in Premodern Japanese Society

Eisho NASU

The Jōdo Shinshū community which emerged during the early Kamakura period (1192–1333) was created upon the unique institutional vision of its founder Shinran (1173–1262).[1] Shinran defined himself as "neither a monk, nor one in worldly life (*hisō hizoku*),"[2] and encouraged his followers to live in a community of fellow followers (*dōbō*) or fellow practitioners (*dōgyō*)[3] united in mutual respect, rather than a hierarchical order based on the master-disciple relationship.[4] As the Jōdo Shinshū community grew after Shinran's death, however, professional priestly groups developed within the community to maintain its order under the tight scrutiny of the religious and political establishments in premodern Japanese society.[5]

Among the various groups of Jōdo Shinshū followers, the Honganji tradition, which was established upon Shinran's mausoleum by his descendants,[6] developed an ingenious system for the ordination of its priests. The ordination ceremony outwardly relied upon aristocratic authority to protect its social status among the established Buddhist institutions.[7] Internally, it appealed to the sentiment of founder worship to maintain its institutional cohesion. The Honganji tradition did not create a hierarchical order based on the master-disciple relationship, which had been strongly rejected by Shinran. Instead, it adopted a patrilineal hereditary system which was administrated under the authority of Shinran's descendants and which reflected the structure of premodern Japanese society.[8]

In this paper, I will examine the institutional meaning of the ordination system of the Honganji tradition, a system which provided the basis for the creation of one of the largest Buddhist denominations in premodern Japanese society. First I will review the ordination system of candidates for the position of the head priest of Honganji (*hossu*) during the late Kamakura through Muromachi and Sengoku (Civil War) periods (ca. thirteenth–sixteenth century C.E.). During this period, the Honganji tradition of Jōdo Shinshū established its institutional foundation. Then I will examine the formation of the ordination ceremony of Honganji priests, which evolved from the Honganji *hossu's* ordination system. Lastly I will discuss the transformation of the priestly ordination system of Honganji during the end of the Edo period (1603–1886).

ORDINATION CEREMONY OF THE CANDIDATE FOR HONGANJI *HOSSU*

The candidate for *hossu*, the head priest of Honganji, was traditionally ordained through the *tokudo*[9] ceremony at the Shōren'in temple of the Tendai school.[10] The Shōren'in was a *monzeki* temple[11] which was closely associated with the imperial house and influential aristocratic families.[12] An ordinand of a Tendai temple usually went to the Enryakuji *kaidan* (precept dais) on Mount Hiei to perform the ceremony for the confirmation of precepts (*jukai*) to start his career as an official priest (*kansō*) of the Tendai school. However, the candidate for the Honganji *hossu* declared his renunciation from the Tendai order (*tonsei*) after the *tokudo* ceremony in order to be eligible to advance in the lineage of Shinran as Honganji *hossu*.[13]

Through his connection to the high aristocratic families of the *monzeki*, the candidate for *hossu* demonstrated that his social status was as high as the administrators of the other Buddhist institutions.[14] In fact, although Honganji *hossu* were not officially affiliated with any of the traditional Buddhist orders, they were eligible to receive the rank of official priest through their connections with influential aristocratic families.[15]

The ordination of the candidate for *hossu* at the Shōren'in of the Tendai school did not offend the followers of Shinran. At the Shōren'in, the candidate symbolically followed Shinran's path. Shinran himself was believed to have been ordained at the Shōren'in at the age of nine.[16] By declaring renunciation from the Tendai school, the candidate identified himself with his great ancestor Shinran who had become independent from the rank of the Tendai priest. He also upheld Shinran's position of *hisō hizoku* by refusing to receive the *jukai* ceremony on Mount Hiei.[17]

Ordination at the Shōren'in was continued until the time of Kennyo (1543–1592), who succeeded Shōnyo (1516–1554) in 1554. Shōnyo, the tenth *hossu* of Honganji, was seriously ill at the time and was not able to arrange the proper ordination at Shōren'in for his son Kennyo, who was 11 years old. Therefore, Shōnyo himself ordained Kennyo at Honganji to be the eleventh *hossu*.[18] This was an emergency situation, and a messenger was sent to Shōren'in to confirm his ordination. Shōnyo passed away the day after the ordination of Kennyo. In 1559, while Kennyo was *hossu*, the authority of the Shōren'in *monzeki* became superfluous for the ordination of candidates because Honganji itself became a *monzeki* temple.[19] Since that time the ordination of the candidate for *hossu* has been handled directly under the authority of the current *hossu* who is also the head priest of the *monzeki* temple.[20]

FORMATION OF THE ORDINATION CEREMONY FOR HONGANJI PRIESTS

Before the era of the eleventh *hossu* Kennyo (1543–1592), there are no records describing the details of the ordination ceremony, except a few documents which simply mention that for priests it was traditionally officiated by the Honganji *hossu*.[21] According to Honganji's temple records, the ordination ceremony for Honganji priests was systematized during the era of Kennyo and Junnyo (1577–

1630). The essentials of the ordination ceremony developed during this period were as follows:[22]

1. Candidates for priest were, as a rule, ordained by the *hossu* at the Goeidō (Founder's Hall) of Honganji.
2. Each ordinand was given the initiation rite of *okamisori* (or *okōzori*), a symbolic shaving of the head, by the *hossu* to confirm his ordination.
3. The *tokudo* ceremony of Honganji did not include a *jukai* ceremony.

Although the details of the ceremony were minutely differentiated according to the hereditary family ranks of the ordinands, these three fundamental elements in the ordination ceremony of Honganji priests were the same as the *hossu's* ordination.[23]

The ordination of Honganji priests was also designed to appeal to the sentiment of founder worship. The ceremony was performed in the Founder's Hall in front of the statue of Shinran, which was traditionally revered as the living body of Shinran himself. According to a legend, the lacquered statue contains the relics of Shinran.[24] The ritual of *okamisori* was, in principle, to be performed during the night at the hour of the dog (*inu no toki*, about seven p.m.), since according to popular legend the initial ordination of Shinran was done at that particular time.[25]

This ordination ceremony without *jukai* clearly reflected Shinran's unique vision of the Jōdo Shinshū community. By refusing to accept the precepts mandated within the state-supported Buddhist institutions, priests of Shinran's tradition positively demonstrated that they were proud to be *mukai myōji no biku* (priests in name only who keep no precepts) in the Last Dharma Age (*mappō*) as Shinran did.[26]

The ordination ceremony of the Honganji tradition was, however, not merely a naive confirmation ceremony in memory of a revered founder. It also reflected the authoritarian institutional structure which placed the *hossu*, who was also an aristocratic *monzeki*, at the top of its hierarchical order of priests.²⁷ Through the ritual of *okamisori* the Honganji priests pledged loyalty to Shinran's family. Institutionally, they became part of the hierarchical priestly order in which the rank of a priest was determined according to how close he was to the lineage of Shinran's family (See Appendix, Origin of the Affiliate Temples and Disciples [*Matsuji migara ondeshi no kojitsu*] and Meaning of Ordination and Tonsure [*Tokudo teitō no shui*]).²⁸

TRANSFORMATION OF THE ORDINATION CEREMONY DURING THE EDO PERIOD

The hierarchical order within the Honganji tradition became obvious in the ordination ceremony after the era of Junnyo. Especially between the eras of Ryōnyo (1612–1662) and Monnyo (1744–1799), the ceremony for ordinands from higher ranking families gradually became similar to the ordination ceremonies of other Buddhist schools in order to differentiate them from ordinary priests.

The ordination ceremony for Honganji priests, originally simply called *okamisori* (or *okōzori*), was officially split into two levels according to the rank of the priestly order (See Appendix, Meaning of Ordination and Tonsure [*Tokudo teitō no shui*]).²⁹ The ordination ceremony for those from high-class priestly families was called *tokudo*; for those from ordinary priestly families, the ceremony was called *okamisori* (or *okōzori*).³⁰ The *hossu* who officiates the ceremony was officially titled *kaishi* (precept master). During the ceremony ordinands received *sankie* (the Three Refuges) from the *hossu* who acted as *kaishi*. They also recited the verses pledging to renounce secular life.³¹ By the end of the Edo period, the *tokudo* ceremony for high-class priestly families at Honganji had become almost identical to that of the other Buddhist schools.³²

The reason for the gradual assimilation to the conventional style of *tokudo* ceremony is not clear. However, it is highly questionable that the doctrinal validity of this ordination ceremony developed during the Edo period.[33] In this ceremony, which took place at the Founder's Hall, the *hossu* was a *kaishi* who held the highest rank among the official priests. At the same time he was considered to be a proxy for Shinran. Shinran, however, was a *mukai myōji no biku* who did not want to be anyone's master.[34]

The doctrinally controversial elements in the ordination ceremony, however, were maintained without any justifications after the fall of the Tokugawa shogunate in 1868. Honganji reformed its priestly ordination system into one unified *tokudo* ceremony in 1886 by abolishing its two-tier system based on the rank of the temples. No one, however, raised any question about the obviously contradictory role of *hossu* at the ordination ceremony until 1932, when Itō Giken, a renowned Shinshū scholar, published his critical study on Honganji's ordination system, *Honganji-ha doshiki kō*.[35]

CONCLUSION

The emergence of Jōdo Shinshū in the early Kamakura period (ca. thirteenth century) in Japan and the emergence of Protestantism in sixteenth century Europe are analogous in their reformative spirit.[36] Shinran's teaching is based solely on "the absolute incapacity of men to save themselves and the necessity for faith alone,"[37] and emphasizes immediate salvation and a direct relation to Amida Buddha in faith alone. Shinran's radical message of reformation was aimed at the collapsed hierarchical authoritarian system of monastic Buddhism. In premodern Japanese society, however, Jōdo Shinshū developed a hierarchical order based on the patrilineal hereditary system.[38]

Within the Honganji tradition two contradictory institutional visions collided: one, Shinran's radical reformational ideal represented by his three essential institutional visions, *hisō hizoku*, *dōbō dōgyō*, and *mukai myōji*; the other, the authoritarian social structure of premodern Japanese society. The two-sided character of the ordination system for Honganji priests developed under these contradictory institutional demands during the premodern era.

While going through the initiation, every ordained priest was required to turn a blind eye to this obvious contradictory situation.[39] An increased aristocratic presence at Honganji developed especially after it became a *monzeki* temple, introducing doctrinally questionable customs into the ordination ceremony.[40] Shinran's reformational vision, though not entirely lost, was obfuscated by the patrilineal hereditary institutional system in premodern Japanese society.[41] Jōdo Shinshū's institutional affinity to the premodern social system is well seen in the fact that Honganji maintained the title of *kaishi* in the priestly ordination system at least until the early Shōwa era, more than several decades after the abolishment of the *monzeki* system.

APPENDIX[42]

Origin of the Affiliate Temples and Disciples [of Jōdo Shinshū]
(*Matsuji migara ondeshi no kojitsu*)

According to the temple regulations of Honganji, the general headquarters of Jōdo Shinshū, all affiliated members of this temple are equally called *deshi* (disciple) or *monto* (followers of the [teaching-]gate) regardless of whether they are priests or laypersons.

The reason is as follows. The founding master [Shinran], at the age of seventy (the first year of Kangen [1243], the year of *mizunoto-u* [junior water-rabbit]), carved a statue of his own figure. He gave the statue to his daughter Iyanyo[43] as his proxy, together with his letter of transfer of ownership. After the founding master passed away, according to his will the statue was enshrined in the Goeidō (Founder's Hall) in the head temple as the authentic figure of the founder of our school, and was venerated as the head priest of Honganji.

The succeeding *monshu* (abbots) [of Jōdo Shinshū], who are all blood descendants of the founder, inherit the letter of transfer of ownership as the mark of the true successor of Honganji. The statue is venerated as the title holder of *jūjishiki* (the office of resident priest). Therefore, the position of the succeeding master is called *rusushiki* (the office of caretaker) or *bettōshiki* (the office of head administrator). Or his position may also be called *Honganji jūjishiki* (the office of resident priest of Honganji), since he inherits the disciples and followers of the founding master, and he has command over them as the proxy of the founding master.

For this reason, from the elders to the ordinary priests and laypersons, all are equally called the followers of one tradition of the Honganji without discrimination and regardless of their social status. At the time of the priests' *tokudo* (ordination), all ordinands receive *teitō* (tonsure) from the succeeding abbot, in front of the figure of the founding master, in order to become disciples of the abbot.

ORDINATION CEREMONY OF THE HONGANJI PRIESTS

Meaning of Ordination and Tonsure [of Jōdo Shinshū]
(*Tokudo teitō no shui*)

Tokudo is a common term for the ordination of priests in which the ordinands receive tonsure and confirm their priestly positions. However, according to the temple regulations, a difference exists in the use of the term. For the [ordinands of] *inge* (assistants of *monzeki*) temples such as Kōshōji, Hontokuji etc., and down to the ranks of *naijin* ([seated in] the inner sanctum) and *yoma* ([seated in] the annex room), the ordination is called *tokudo*. Beneath these ranks, from *sannoma* ([seated in] the third room[44]), *hien* ([seated under] the high rafter), *shochūgo* (attendees of the meal offerings[45]), *kunigesakan* ([allowed blue silk] surplice in native province), down to *heisō* (ordinary priests) and *zokuke* (laypersons), it is called *teitō*.

The *tokudo* of [ordinands of] *inge*, *naijin*, and *yoma*, except Kōshōji, Hontokuji, Kenshōji and other *renshi* (close relatives of the abbot of Honganji) temples, held at Honganji are amendable and can be officiated at the ordinand's temple upon his request to the head temple, if he is living in the provinces far away from [the head temple], or if he is not able to provide enough funds to have his ordination [at the head temple] even though he lives in the provinces close [to the head temple]. This is called *jitokudo* (self-ordination), since the ordinands receive tonsure at their own temples. *Jitokudo* has never been performed at the temples closely related to the head temple.

As for [the ordinands] of the *sannoma* rank down to ordinary priests, if they live in the provinces far away from [the head temple], and are not able to provide enough funds to have their ordination [at the head temple], they are able to receive tonsure at their own temples upon their requests to the head temple. This is called *jiteitō* (self-tonsure).

For this reason, from the elders to ordinary priests and laypersons, all are followers of one tradition of Honganji and disciples of the venerable founding master [Shinran]. The succeeding *monshu* has command over all of them as the proxy of the founding master. Therefore he is called *zenjishiki* (good knowledgeable teacher) of the followers. All followers [of Jōdo Shinshū] venerate the *monshu* of the head temple as their master.

NOTES

1. The early Jōdo Shinshū communities, or Shinran's followers, organized themselves by a network of *dōjō*, or meeting places, operated collectively by the members. "The centerpiece of worship in the Shinshū *dōjō* was usually a large inscription of Amida's name (*myōgō honzon*) hung over a simple altar. This kind of religious object was an innovation of Shinran's. . . . Shinran's creation of the Amida inscription supplied the ordinary believer with a simple and accessible object of reverence for use in worship, thereby freeing religious objects from the artistic domain controlled by aristocratic society. The actual content of *dōjō* worship varied from place to place, but was dominated by nembutsu chanting. In addition, simple sermons, the recitation of scriptures, and singing of hymns such as Shinran's *wasan* also became common features." (James Dobbins, *Jōdo Shinshū, Shin Buddhism in Medieval Japan* [Bloomington: Indiana University Press, 1989], 66.) See also Akamatsu Toshihide and Kasahara Kazuo, *Shinshūshi gaisetsu* (Kyoto: Heirakuji shoten, 1963), 74–112.

2. In the "postscript," of the *Kyōgyōshinshō*, Shinran stated, "Reflecting within myself, I see that in the various teachings of the Path of Sages, practice and enlightenment died out long ago, and that the true essence of the Pure Land way is the path to realization now vital and flourishing. Monks of Śākyamuni's tradition in the various temples, however, lack clear insight into the teaching and are ignorant of the distinction between true and provisional; and scholars of the Confucian academies in the capital are confused about practices and wholly unable to differentiate right and wrong paths. Thus, scholar-monks of Kōfukuji presented a petition to the retired emperor [Gotoba-in (1180–1239), personal name Takanari] in the first part of the second month, 1207. The emperor and his ministers, acting against the Dharma and violating human rectitude, became enraged and embittered. As a result, Master Genkū—the eminent founder who had enabled the true essence of the Pure Land way to spread vigorously [in Japan]—and a number of his followers, without receiving any deliberation of their [alleged] crimes, were summarily sentenced to death or were dispossessed of their monkhood, given [secular] names, and consigned to distant banishment. I was among the latter. Hence, I am now *neither a monk nor one in worldly life*. For this reason, I have taken the term Toku ["stubble-haired"] as my name. Master Genkū and his disciples, being banished to the provinces in different directions, passed a period of five years [in exile]." Emphasis added. (Yoshifumi Ueda, general editor, *The True Teaching,*

ORDINATION CEREMONY OF THE HONGANJI PRIESTS

Practice and Realization of the Pure Land Way, A Translation of Shinran's Kyōgyōshinshō, vol. 4, Shin Buddhism Translation Series [Kyoto: Honganji International Center, 1990], 613–614). This statement was Shinran's declaration of independence from the established Buddhist institutions. It was also his sharp critique of the state-supported Buddhist institutions which systematically suppressed the *nembutsu* communities created around the master Hōnen (1133–1212) and his disciples.

3. Dr. Bloom provides a concise explanation of Shinran's usage of this term. "The term used by Shinran to refer to his associates was *ondobo* (fellow followers) or *ondogyo* (fellow practicers of the faith). These words reflect Shinran's democratic ideal of human relations flowing from the meaning of Amida's Vows. These were not terms invented by Shinran, but were earlier employed in Zendo's writing as well as the Tendai *Makashikan* of China. . . . Rennyo Shonin wrote in his letters that Shinran declared he had no disciples, referring to his followers as *ondobo* or *ondogyo*, and this is why members of Shinshu call each other *dobo* or *dogyo*. It was erroneous in Shinshu to call a person *deshi* (disciple) because such term implied inferior status." (Alfred Bloom, *Strategies for Modern Living, A Commentary with the Text of the Tannisho* [Berkeley, California: Numata Center for Buddhist Translation and Research], 73.) See also *Tannishō*, Chapter 16. Translation is available in Bloom, 18–19. For Rennyo's saying in his *Gojō ofumi* (Letters in five fascicle) I-1, see Minor Rogers and Ann Rogers, *Rennyo, the Second Founder of Shin Buddhism* (Berkeley, California: Asian Humanity Press, 1991), 142–144.

4. Shinran's institutional ideal is clearly expressed in his saying recorded in the Tannishō, Chapter 6, in which he says, "It is absurd for those who practice the Nembutsu exclusively to quarrel among themselves, saying, 'These people are my disciples,' or 'These people are somebody else's disciples.' *I, Shinran, have not even a single disciple.* If I could bring people to say the Nembutsu, then I could call them 'my disciples.' But it would be preposterous to call somebody 'my disciple' when he says the Nembutsu solely through the working of Amida's compassion. If karmic conditions bring us together, we will come together. If karmic conditions separate us, we will part. Yet some say that if a person turns away from his teacher and follows another teacher, then even though he continues to say the Nembutsu, he will not be born in the Pure Land. This, too, is ridiculous. Are they saying that they can take back the true faith which was given by Amida as if it were their own? They should not speak

this way. When we are in accord with the principle of Naturalness and Spontaneity, we will feel grateful for the compassion of Amida Buddha and the compassion of our teachers." Emphasis added. (Yuien-bo, *Tannisho: Notes Lamenting the Differences*, Chapter 6, in Bloom, 6–7.)

5. The early Jōdo Shinshū community, which was a private association operated by the member supported *dōjō* system, gradually adopted the traditional temple system of a public institution supporting political and economic establishments. See James Dobbins, *Jōdo Shinshū*, 69. "Formal temples first came into existence in the Shinshū more than fifty years after Shinran's death. . . . The most prominent temples to appear were the Honganji, the Senjuji, the Bukkōji, the Kinshokuji, and the temples associated with the Sanmonto communities along the Hokuriku seaboard. Of these the Senjuji grew out of a congregation in the Kantō region at a place known as Takada, which had been a Shinshū stronghold even during Shinran's lifetime. Its pattern of development, from informal chapel into temple, became a common occurrence in later Shinshū history, but during this period only a few congregations actually made the transition from *dōjō* to formal temple. The Bukkōji, by contrast, was established as a temple from its inception. It rose to fame rapidly as hundreds of *dōjō* in the surrounding regions came under its religious influence. The Honganji, on the other hand, was unique in its transformation to temple status. It began as a memorial chapel at Shinran's grave site, a natural pilgrimage spot for Shinshū believers, and emerged in temple form under the initiative and leadership of Kakunyo." (Dobbins, 79.) Kakunyo (1270–1351) was a great-grandson of Shinran.

6. Shinran's mausoleum in Kyoto was privately owned by Shinran's descendants and supported by Shinran's followers who were mainly in the Kantō region. Kakushin'ni (1224–1283), Shinran's daughter, maintained the mausoleum. She called herself *ohaka no gosata* (supervisor of the grave site). Her son Kakue (?–1307), who succeeded the position, described his role as *gorusu* (a caretaker). Kakunyo, Kakue's son, was appointed to this position by the followers in the Kantō region over his younger half brother Yuizen (b. 1266) in 1310. Kakunyo also began using the name Honganji. Kakunyo called this position "*rusushiki*" (office of caretaker). "What Kakunyo actually intended by this word is spelled out in his letter of bequest dated 1339. 11. 28, in which he equated it with the 'office of head' (*bettōshiki*), an expression commonly used for the head administrator

of a major Buddhist temple. With this change in terminology Kakunyo sought to concentrate Honganji authority in the hands of the so-called caretaker, thereby undercutting the influence that the Kantō congregations derived from his grandmother's original will. His ability to do so was greatly enhanced by a judgment handed down in 1334 by the Shōren'in, a Tendai temple which exercised legal jurisdiction over the land on which the Honganji was situated. The judgment upheld Kakunyo's right to deny the Honganji caretakership to his oldest son, Zonkaku, even though the Kantō congregations favored him. This decision in effect guaranteed control of the Honganji to its titular caretaker and foreshadowed its independence form the Kantō community." (Dobbins, 84–85.)

7. In 1333, Prince Morinaga (1308–1335) recognized Honganji and its affiliate temple Kuonji as the prayer-offering site (*gokitōjo*) to secure Kakunyo's right to administrate these temples. This was the earliest record in which the name Honganji appeared in official documents. See Honganji Shiryō Kenkyūjo, *Honganjishi*, vol. 1 (Kyoto: Jōdo Shinshū Honganjiha, 1961), 183 and 205–206.

8. The Honganji established by Kakunyo "evolved a unique system of temple leadership whereby the head priest inherited his religious authority by birthright rather than by ascent through priestly ranks, as occurred in other Buddhist temples. This pattern of hereditary leadership subsequently became a common characteristic of temples in the Shinshū, distinguishing it from other schools of Buddhism." (Dobbins, 86)

9. The term literally means "attaining emancipation from the cycles of birth-and-death," or simply "to go-beyond." For the individual, *tokudo* is a ceremony to declare his/her renunciation of secular attachments. Institutionally, this ceremony symbolizes initiation into the religious order, or admittance as a professional member of a Buddhist community.

10. The Shōren'in was one of the most influential temples in the Tendai school, and it was one of the three *monzeki* temples associated with Enryakuji on Mount Hiei. These *monzeki* temples were administrated either by members of the imperial family or the regent family. The other two are the Myōhōin and the Sanzen'in. The Shōren'in "claimed absentee proprietorship rights to the land on which the Honganji stood. Based on this relationship the Shōren'in frequently litigated in behalf of the Honganji before civil and religious authorities."

(Dobbins, 100.)

11. The *monzeki* temple was founded or administrated by an ordained ex-emperor, prince, or princess. The title of *monzeki* was first given to Ninnaji when former emperor Uda (867–931) was ordained at the temple in 899 and started his residency in 904. Later the title was also given to temples administrated by ordained nobles. The *monzeki* system was abolished in 1871 after the Meiji Restoration. See Honganji Shiryō Kenkyūjo, *Honganjishi*, vol. 3 (Kyoto: Jōdo Shinshū Honganjiha, 1969), 148.

12. According to the records of Honganji, until the era of the eleventh *hossu* Kennyo (1543–1592), all candidates for *hossu* were ordained at the Shōren'in, except Kakunyo who was ordained at the Ichijōin, an affiliated temple of the Kōbukuji of the Hossō school. See Tatsuguchi Akio, "Shinshū Honganji kyōdan no tokudoshiki," *Shūgakuin ronshū* 54 (1983): 19; Matsuo Kenji, *Kamakura shinbukkyō no seiritsu, nyūmon girei to soshi shinwa* (Tokyo: Yoshikawa kōbunkan, 1988), 225; *Honganjishi*, vol. 1, 165 and 436.

13. *Tonsei*, literally "retreating from the world," meant retiring from the order of official priest in order to live in seclusion and practice Buddhism individually. It was a very common practice among the medieval Japanese Buddhist priests. Although the candidates for Honganji *hossu* were ordained in the temple associated with the Tendai school, they were not under the direct supervision of the Tendai order because they left the order (*tonsei*) after they took tonsure at the Shōren'in. See Matsuo, 180–181 and 224–227; *Honganjishi*, vol. 1, 436.

14. Kakunyo became a *risshi* (superintendent, a precept master), which was the third grade of priestly officer below *sōzu* (bishop) and *sōjō* (archbishop), at the time of his ordination. He obtained this position by becoming a *yūshi* (an adopted son) of Fujiwara Kanenaka when he was ordained. He eventually became the *hōin-gon daisōzu* (the Dharma-seal great bishop of the lower rank). The succeeding *hossu* of Honganji were all appointed to this rank. They received this title by becoming *yūshi* of the Hino family, a very influential branch of the Fujiwara family during the Muromachi period. The tenth *hossu* Shōnyo was appointed to *gon-sōjō* (archbishop of the lower rank) in 1549. And finally, the Honganji *hossu* became *daisōjō* (great archbishop), which was the highest rank of priestly officers, beginning with Kennyo who was appointed to the position in 1585. See Dobbins,

100; *Honganjishi*, vol. 1, 444–445 and 548; Kashiwahara Yūsen, *Bukkyō to buraku sabetsu* (Osaka: Buraku kaihō kenkyūsho, 1988), 32.

15. See Dobbins, 100; Kashiwahara, 31–34.

16. According to Honganji records, such as Kakunyo's *Godenshō*, Shinran was ordained by Jien (1155–1225), a brother of Regent Kujō Kanezane (1149–1207) in 1181. See Tatsuguchi, 19. For a popular account of Shinran's ordination, see Nakai Gendō, *Shinran and His Religion of Pure Faith* (Kyoto: The Shinshu Research Institute, 1937), 9–13.

17. The *tokudo* ceremony usually includes the ceremonies of taking the Three Refuges (*sankie*) and accepting the five precepts (*gokai*) for lay people (*ubasoku* and *ubai*), or the ten precepts (*jikkai*) for novices (*shami* and *shamini*). The three refuges are Buddha, Dharma [Buddha's teaching], and Samgha [community of Buddha]. According to the *Shibun-ritsu* (*Ssu fen lü*), which most commonly observed at the priestly ordination among the Buddhist community in the East Asia, the five precepts are to abstain from (1) taking life, (2) taking what is not given, (3) sexual misconduct, (4) lying, (5) drinking liquor. The ten precepts are, in addition to the five precepts, to abstain from (6) eating after noon, (7) watching dancing, singing, and shows, (8) adorning oneself with garland, perfumes, and ointments, (9) using a high bed, and (10) receiving gold and silver. Since the time of the founder, Saichō, however, the Japanese Tendai tradition adopted the bodhisattva precepts for the confirmation of precepts (*jukai*). There are, however, two kinds of the ten precepts used in the Japanese Tendai tradition. The ten precepts of the *Bonmō-kyō* (Brahma-net Sūtra, [Taisho, vol. 24, No. 1484]), which was an official source text of the Japanese Tendai's bodhisattva precepts, called *jūjūkai* (ten major precepts), are to abstain from (1) taking life, (2) taking what is not given, (3) sexual misconduct, (4) lying, (5) selling liquor, (6) telling others of errors by the four groups (lay and monastic bodhisattvas, monks and nuns), (7) praising oneself and defaming others, (8) begrudging others either property or the teaching, (9) becoming angry, and (10) slandering the Three Jewels. Another version of the ten precepts, called *jūzenkai*, are to abstain from (1) taking life, (2) taking what is not given, (3) sexual misconduct, (4) lying speech, (5) malicious speech, (6) harsh speech, (7) indistinct prattling, (8) covetousness, (9) ill will, (10) wrong views. (Edward Conze, translation, *The Perfection of Wisdom in Eight Thousand Lines* [Bolinas, California: Four Seasons Foundation, 1973]: 200.) And "all

these three sets of precepts have been used to initiate Tendai novices in the past." (Paul Groner, *Saichō: the Establishment of the Japanese Tendai School* [Berkeley, California: Berkeley Buddhist Study Series 7, 1984], 118–119.) According to Tatsuguchi Akio, the ordination of the candidate for Honganji *hossu* at the Shōren'in probably did not even include any of these confirmation of the precepts for the layperson or novice. Ordinary ordinands at the Shōren'in were, perhaps, required to take another confirmation ceremony of these precepts before their *jukai* ceremony for Buddhist monks or nuns. The candidate might have left the Shōren'in before this ceremony. See Tatsuguchi, 30.

18. Matsuo, 226; Tatsuguchi, 21–22.

19. *Honganjishi*, vol. 1, 436–448.

20. However, a formal relation continued between Honganji and Shōren'in with regard to the ordination of the candidate of *hossu* continued. A record dated 1795 noted that the *hōmyō* (ordained name) of the candidate of *hossu* was to be confirmed by letter from Shōren'in after the ceremony at Honganji. *Honganjishi*, vol. 1, 436–448; Matsuo, 226.

21. See Itō Giken, *Honganjiha doshiki kō* (Yamaguchi: Takeshita gakuryō shuppanbu, 1932), 33–36; Tatsuguchi, 19; Matsuo, 226–227.

22. See Matsuo, 226–228.

23. This ordination system enforced the hierarchical order of Honganji priests. However the administrator did not believe that it was against the founder's ideal because it was a legitimate secular social custom of succession of authority in premodern Japanese society. Kashiwahara, 51–53; Dobbins, 81–98 and 148–156. It should also be noted that this system created a class of priests who were not eligible to receive *okamisori* from the *hossu* because they represented communities which were segregated under the Tokugawa shōgunate. See Kashiwahara, 53–55.

24. Another legend says that they were hidden inside of the image. See Dobbins, 196 n. 23.

25. Genchi, "Shukke teihatsu no koto," *Kōshinroku*, vol. 5, in *Shinshū zensho, Zatsubu*, vol. 41 (Kyoto: Zōkyō shoin, 1913), 203–205. The

Kōshinroku is a collection of notes on various issues pertaining to Honganji's history, customs and rituals compiled by the Honganji priest Genchi (1734–1794).

26. A verse in the *Gutoku's Hymn of Lament and Reflection* (*Gutoku hitanjukkai*), goes as follows:

Although monks are so in name only and keep no precepts,
Now in this defiled world of the last dharma-age
They are the equals of Śāriputra and Maudgalyāyana,
And we are urged to pay homage to and revere them.

Shinran, *Hymns of the Dharma-Ages, A Translation of Shinran's Shōzōmatsu wasan*, Shin Buddhism Translation Series (Kyoto: Honganji International Center, 1993), 73.

27. The institutional structure of Honganji was based on the patrilineal hereditary system which was adopted by Kakunyo when he established Honganji. It developed into the family council of Shinran's descendants (*ikkeshū*) during the era of Rennyo (1415–1499), which resulted in the creation of a hierarchical order called the *hon-matsu* (branching) system in the priestly community of Honganji. The authority of the hereditary head priest of Honganji and its family council was further reinforced by the grant of *monzeki* status in 1559. Members of the family council were also appointed to the rank of priestly officer. See Chiba Jōryū, *Shinshū kyōdan no soshiki to seido* (Kyoto: Dōbōsha, 1978), 176–191; Michael Solomon, "Kinship and the Transmission of Religious Charisma: The Case of Honganji," *The Journal of Asian Studies* 33 (1974): 403–413.

28. See also Honganji Shiryō Kenkyūjo, *Honganjishi*, vol. 2 (Kyoto: Jōdo Shinshū Honganjiha, 1968), 234–239 and 453–454; Kashiwahara, 51–53.

29. See Itō, 148 and 243–245; Kashiwahara, 52–53; *Honganjishi*, vol. 2, 175–248.

30. Itō, 243–245.

31. The verse goes as follows,

I have been transmigrating in the three realms
[of desire, form, and non-form],

> And I have not been able to overcome (sever) the affections [to my family].
> Now I emancipate myself from the affection [to my family] to enter into the realm of eternity,
> In order to express my true gratitude [to them].

This verse is commonly used in the *tokudo* ceremony of other Buddhist schools. See Itō, 239; Genchi, "Shukke teihatsu no koto," in *Shinshū zensho*, Zatsubu, vol. 41, 203–205.

32. Itō, 226–243.

33. Ibid., 227 and 261.

34. And Shinran still lamented that:

> I am such that I do not know right and wrong
> And cannot distinguish false and true;
> I lack even small love and small compassion,
> And yet, for fame and profit, enjoy teaching others.

Shinran, *Hymns of the Dharma-Ages*, 83. According to Kakunyo's *Kudenshō*, Chapter 1, Shinran pledged to his master Hōnen not to be a teacher (*ninshi*) or precept master (*kaishi*).

35. Itō Giken, *Honganjiha doshiki kō* (Yamaguchi: Takeshita gakuryō shuppanbu, 1932).

36. "What the Reformation did was in principle, with the usual reservations and mortgage to the past, break through the whole mediated system of salvation and declare salvation potentially available to any man no matter what his station of calling might be." Robert Bellah, "Religious Evolution," *Beyond Belief, Essays on Religion in a Posttraditional World* (New York: Harper and Row, 1970), 36.

37. Bellah, "The Religious Situation in the Far East," in *Beyond Belief*, 112.

38. The Honganji followers organized under the family council of Shinran's descendants developed into the most well organized and the mightiest religio-political power during the age of the Civil War (1477–1573). Michael Solomon, "Dilemma of Religious Power, Honganji and Hosokawa Masamoto," *Momumenta Nipponica* 33

(1978): 51–65.

39. The famous formula often applied to solve this contradiction was one of Rennyo's sayings,: "Observe the sovereign's law (ōbō) loyally, store Other-power faith deep in your hearts, and respect the public moral code (jingi) sincerely." Rennyo, Ofumi II-6, in Rogers, and Rogers, Rennyo, 180.

40. Chiba, 337–346.

41. Honganji's ministry was institutionally assimilated with the established Buddhist orders in premodern Japanese society, although, in a verse in the *Gutoku's Hymn of Lament and Reflection* (*Gutoku hitanjukkai*), Shinran lamented:

> The sorrow of this evil world of the last dharma-age
> Is that Buddhists of the southern capital and
>   the northern peak
> Call servants "palanquin-carrier monks" and
>   "serving dharma-teachers"
> To show deference to the high-ranking priests.
>   (Shinran, *Hymns of the Dharma-Ages*, 73.)

One might think that Shinshū scholars in the premodern period would have noted these contradictions and decried them. Instead, Shinshū scholars' traditional lack of concern with ritual and institution contributed to the creation of a doctrinally questionable ordination ceremony. Even today, as far as I know, Itō's proposal to establish a priestly ordination system that is in accordance with the founder Shinran's institutional vision has never been seriously discussed by modern Shinshū scholars. See Itō, 1–2, and 261–263. For the institutional democratization of Honganji during the Meiji period, see Chiba, 337–346. For the reform movements in the modern period and their problems, see Kashiwahara, 59–73.

42. Translations of "Matsuji migara onndeshi no kojitsu" and "Tokudo teitō no shui" are based on the texts collcted in the third volume of the *Honganji tsūki*. The *Honanji tsūki* is a collection of the historical official documents of Honganji compiled by a certain officer of the temple during the early nineteenth century. The third volume is a collection of Honganji's official replies to the Edo bakufu's interrogations on various issues. The original text of the *Honganji tsūki* is available in Chiba, 452–453.

43. Iyanyo (Iya onna) was not Shinran's daughter but his servant. The letter of transfer of ownership was misidentified, perhaps during the Edo period. These letters were discovered at Honganji in 1917. See Akamatsu Toshihide, *Shinran* (Tokyo: Yoshikawa kōbunkan, 1961), 328–345; Dobbins, 39.

44. *Sannoma* is the room adjacent to the annex room. See Numa Hōryō and Kozuka Yoshikuni, eds., *Shinshū koji seigo jiten*, (Kyoto: Hōzōkan, 1983), 564–565.

45. Priests of this rank were allowed to attend the meal offerings served three times (beginning [*sho*], middle [*chū*] and end [*go*]) with other higher ranking officers during the official week-long services held at Honganji. See Numa and Kozuka, 772–774.

Glorious Gathas: Americanization and Japanization in Honganji Hymns

George J. TANABE, JR.

When I returned home in 1977 to begin my teaching career at the University of Hawaii, I knew next to nothing about the state of Buddhism in the islands. I was extremely fortunate, however, in that my colleague and *sempai* Alfred Bloom was not only a scholar of Japanese Buddhism but an active member of the Honpa Honganji Mission and a frequent participant in the activities of other Buddhist organizations as well. Al knew a great deal about Buddhism in Hawaii, and, true to his profession as a scholar, could not only describe the situation in detail but also provide a critical view about what needed to be done if Buddhism were to survive in Hawaii. With understanding and respect for the Japanese context of local Buddhism, Al knew that it had to develop beyond the boundaries of that cultural sphere, at least enough so that young Americans, including those of Japanese ancestry, could understand and accept the religion, rather than leave the temples, as many did and still do, where the sermons were often delivered in a foreign language and the rituals made no sense. In endless ways, Al has devoted enormous time and energy to the cause of making Buddhism understandable not only in the classroom but in the community as well, and his devotion to Buddhist education is reminiscent of a great predecessor, Ernest Shinkaku Hunt.

In our own time when there is a shortage of local ministers, all of whom must still go to Japan to be ordained, it is good to remember that Hunt and his wife Dorothy were ordained here in Hawaii. Bishop Emyō Imamura performed the investiture ceremony for the Hunts on August 11, 1924 at the Honolulu Betsuin.[1] Ernest Hunt took on the priestly name of Shinkaku, and, with Dorothy, worked for the promotion of Buddhism through lectures, sermons, publications, the development of the Sunday School system, and—here I make this the subject of this paper—the writing of gathas or hymns in English.

The story of Ernest and Dorothy Hunt deserves to be told someday in full detail, for theirs is a tale of remarkable foresight and achievement. Active in the Honpa Honganji Mission and later in the Sōtō Mission, they worked through mainstream Japanese Buddhist institutions here in Hawaii and pursued a vision of an international Buddhism that would spread not only in these islands but to the rest of the world through the medium of the English language. It is a vision that is still shared by the Buddhist community in Hawaii, although the scope of expectations has shifted from the global spread of Buddhism to the local survival of the faith. As language is a crucial element in this Westernization process, and ritual language is the least likely to change, or at least will be the last to change, it is not surprising therefore to hear chanting in Japanese and Sino-Japanese that few people understand. The singing of hymns by the congregation, however, is a product of Christian influence, even in Japan, and since its inception in the early 1920s, the English gatha thrives to this day. As in many areas, the Honpa Honganji Mission has been the leader in the development and promotion of the English hymn, and for that story we return to the Hunts and the publication of the *Vade Mecum* in 1924, the year of their ordination.

Vade Mecum is a Latin term meaning, literally, "go with me." It refers to any kind of manual or handbook that is carried as a constant companion providing on the spot instruction and guidance in subjects ranging from art to science. As the first English gatha book, the *Vade Mecum* was written and edited by the Hunts and A. Raymond Zorn with the intent of providing nonsectarian hymns and teachings that any English-speaking Buddhist could use regardless of institutional affiliation. Under the auspices of the Honpa Honganji, it was published by the International Buddhist Institute of Hawaii, the organization founded by the Hunts to promote their ideal of an international Buddhism. Befitting this ideal, much of the music for the lyrics was written by R. R. Bode, organist of St. Andrews Cathedral and later the director of the first Honganji choir. The *Vade Mecum* had an international and ecumenical flavor promoting a broad understanding of Buddhism that was relatively free of sectarian limitations. A short statement in the title page made this unequivocally clear:

> It is the fervent desire of the authors of this little volume that the heresy of separateness now prevailing among Buddhists of Honolulu may soon be abolished. They have endeavoured therefore to keep to the fundamental and ethical teaching hoping that all English-speaking Buddhists, whatever their affiliation, may be able to use it.[2]

For the fifteen years between 1924 and 1939, the *Vade Mecum* was the primary if not the only handbook for English hymns and services. By 1932 it had gone through five editions, and was even circulated in mimeographed form. Theravada Buddhism, which commanded the academic attention of European and American scholars in the early part of this century, was the basis for the "fundamental and ethical teaching" of the *Vade Mecum*, and its imprint could also be seen in the use of Pali terms for parts of the worship services. "Sato Sampagno" was the title given to the English chant led by the Bhikkhu with responses from the congregation that affirmed their commitment to the pursuit of truth and morality. The "Vandana" homage and "Ti-sarana" pledge were chanted, as they still are today, in Pali and English. The "Atthangiko Maggo" was a recitation of the Eightfold Path, while "Mettabhavana" was a dedication to send out thoughts of compassion to all living beings. The services made no reference to Amida, the Pure Land, or the Nembutsu, but concentrated instead on Shakyamuni as the Buddha, moral action, Nirvana, the true self, and the Law. The liturgical section ended with ten pages of excerpts from the Theravada classic, the *Dhammapada*.

The *Vade Mecum* had 114 gathas, all which had lyrics but no musical notation. Most of them were without titles. The themes of the songs were mostly the same "fundamental and ethical teachings" of a generalized Buddhism, but there are four hymns about Shinran (Nos. 11–14), several of which mention Amida. No. 14 tells of Shinran losing his parents and becoming a priest who gave up the pursuit of rank and wealth:

> Instead, he studied Shakya's Law
> And found Amida's name.
> Descending from the Holy Mount
> To cities he now came.
>
> He taught the truth that all must trust
> Amida in their hearts;
> And give up every selfish thought
> Thus knowledge he imparts.
>
> This Shinran called the other power,
> Tariki realized.
> While Ojo is a shewing forth,
> Re-birth in Paradise.

This hymn was later given the Japanese title "Hōon-kō" and has been retained in every hymnal including the one in current use (*Praises of the Buddha*, 1990). While these Shinran hymns, which were written by Dorothy and Shinkaku Hunt, display a sectarian orientation that underlies the "heresy of separateness now prevailing among Buddhists of Honolulu," the other 110 gathas do teach the tenets and values of a general, pansectarian Buddhism.

By 1939 the *Vade Mecum* was still being used widely, but could not meet a new demand that had arisen by that time. Nishu Utsuki, chairman of the committee to compile a new hymnal, acknowledged the great role that the *Vade Mecum* played in the propagation of Buddhism in English, but recognized that there was a need for Japanese hymns in addition to English ones.[3] The line of development of

Buddhism in Hawaii did not always go from Japanese to English, as one might expect from a more simple model of cultural adaptation, and here we see that the Americanization of Buddhist worship services required Japanese hymns to follow in the pioneering footsteps of the English-only *Vade Mecum*. As a uniquely American form of worship, congregational singing had established itself in Honganji (and other) temples in Hawaii, and its very success meant that Japanese speaking worshippers had to have their own repertoire or be left out of the singing. Unlike the English hymns, the Japanese ones did not all have to be composed in Hawaii since congregational singing had already begun to be adopted in Japan by Buddhist groups in the Meiji period.[4] Honganji ministers coming to serve in Hawaii in the early part of the century brought *sanka* (songs of praise) with them and even composed a few locally, such as "Hasu no Hana," which was written by Kiyoko Imamura, wife of Emyō Imamura.[5] To fill the need for Japanese hymns, Utsuki's committee drew from this ready supply of compositions and compiled them into a new hymnal called *Standard Buddhist Gathas and Services: Japanese and English* (hereafter referred to as *Standard Gathas*), which was published in 1939.

Based in Kyoto, the committee for the new hymnal organized the Japanese hymns into three sections for worship services, young people, and children; and made a fourth section of English gathas. The fifth and final section contained liturgies for a variety of worship services. Of the 57 English gathas, 51 were from the *Vade Mecum*, all of which were set to music and published under a new numbering system, though the old *Vade Mecum* numbers were cross-listed in the table of contents. Though it was replaced by *Standard Gathas*, the *Vade Mecum* still exerted a very strong influence through its many hymns that were reborn as "standard Buddhist gathas" bearing the approval of the Honganji headquarters in Japan. Thus affirmed and maintained in words and music, the Hunts' ideal of a nonsectarian, general Buddhism was still at the forefront in the late 1930s, at least in song. Even though the new hymnal was compiled at the Honganji headquarters in Japan, and included the songs about Shinran (and added more Shinshū sectarian hymns in Japanese), most of the English hymns dealt with general topics of morality, karma, peace, truth, discipleship, and devotion in ways in which most Buddhists (and even, in some cases, non-Buddhists) could agree with. The "Vandana," "Ti-sarana," "Atthangiko Maggo," "Mettabhavana," and the *Dhammapada* readings were all retained, thus preserving the Theravadin flavor congenial to the Hunts.

An important theme focused on the personal and intimate relationship one is to have with the Buddha. "Buddha, Lord, in Thine Embrace" (No. 514) written by A. R. Zorn starts off with "Buddha, Lord, in Thine Embrace/ We our children dear would place,/ In the dawn of life to be/ Consecrated, Lord, to Thee." F. Blanning-Pooley's "Homage to Buddha" (No. 521) speaks of praise, duty, and thanks that are due to the Buddha who loves and protects us. Dorothy Hunt in "Buddhist Children" (No. 524) describes the tender and loving relationship between children and the Buddha. In another one of her compositions, "Lord Buddha Speaks to Me" (No. 549), Dorothy Hunt imagines the Buddha speaking direct words of comfort in times of loneliness and trouble. Savior, lord, and friend, the Buddha is a person, almost moreso than a deity, with whom Buddhists can have a close and personal relationship. All of these hymns have survived the test of time and have been retained in every manual, including the one in current use.

At times the Buddha was portrayed as a military commander, and one's relationship was explicitly martial:

> Have you heard the sound of footsteps
> As of soldiers marching on?
> Have you seen their banners waving?
> Have you heard their battle song?
> Have you watch'd their blazing torches,
> Lighting up their columns long?
> ("Buddha's Soldiers," No. 516, by Dorothy Hunt)

Dorothy Hunt also wrote, "Arise, arise, all Buddhist soldiers true,/

And take your stand upon the rock of Truth!" ("Arise, Arise," No. 517), as well as "Who are these brave youths and maidens, / Bearing torches in their hands? / These are Buddha's noble soldiers / From the far-off Eastern lands" ("Light From the East," No. 518). All three have been dropped from the current hymnal; the 1962 edition eliminated the last two but kept "Buddha's Soldiers." The military imagery, of course, is well attested to in Protestant triumphalism, and it was this association with Christianity that led to the elimination of these compositions from the hymnals.[6]

Loyalty and piety are prominent themes in the hymns, and are directed toward "the Buddha." But who is the Buddha? In most of the songs, it is clearly Shakyamuni, not Amida, and the geographical settings are more often India than Japan. Amida figures in some of the hymns, "Namu Amida Butsu" (No. 525), for instance, but its theme of comfort in times of distress is exactly that of the hymns praising the personal relationship one can have with Shakyamuni. In "O Amitabha, Wondrous Thought" written by the well-known writer and scholar of Buddhism, Paul Carus, Amida is just that: a wondrous thought. Carus sings the praises of wisdom, the law of causation, transforming bad to good, truth that conquers doubt, the imminence of eternity, and the glories of realms transcendent. It may be that Jōdo Shinshū followers might recognize this Wondrous Thought as their Amida, but it would seem remote; and indeed the current hymnal has discarded this composition. Little is said in *Standard Gathas* about rebirth in the Pure Land or faith in Amida's vow, and the lyrics use a diction that is more familiar to general Buddhism rather than the religion of Shinran. While the grip of the *Vade Mecum* was loosened a bit, it still had a firm hold in *Standard Gathas*.

In 1949, the first edition of *Praises of the Buddha* was published by the Hawaii Federation of the Young Buddhist Associations, but this work did not represent a major departure from the past since the same Japanese and English hymns from *Standard Gathas* were published with the numbering system left unchanged. The only difference is that a new piece, "Y.B.A. Song" (No. 700), was added, and the Japanese gathas were romanized for the sake of English speaking worshippers. The relationship between Americanization and Japanization took another twist here: Americanization in the form of congregational singing required hymns in Japanese as well as English (in *Standard Gathas*), and further Americanization demanded that the Japanese hymns be romanized without, however, having to be translated (in *Praises of the Buddha*). The Japanese texts of the services were also eliminated, and in this sense the 1949 hymnal represents a greater degreee of Americanization with all traces of Japanese orthography no longer to be seen. Despite these changes, however, it is essentially a reprint of *Standard Gathas* and, as such, is accurately described as "basically a revision of *Vade Mecum* and included Japanese gathas."[7] Without any new material being added, the hymnal retained the understanding that "the Buddha" was still primarily Shakyamuni:

> The PRAISE OF THE BUDDHAS has played an important part in the lives of the people since the dawn of Buddhism. Millions of HIS followers have come to know HIM through the singing of familiar gathas, classical and modern as well.[8]

A second edition of *Praises of the Buddha* was issued in 1956, but this version also did not make major changes. The extended reach of the *Vade Mecum* through the *Standard Gathas* and the first two editions of *Praises of the Buddha* is really quite remarkable, and its musical and liturgical view of Buddhism, which, despite its Theravadin flavor and added Shinshū colors, was cast as being nonsectarian in nature, prevailed with only minor changes for 38 years from 1924 to 1962, when the first major revision was made. Even then its influence was further reduced but was far from eliminated.

Published in commemoration of Shinran's 700th memorial anniversary, the 1962 third edition made substantial deletions and additions that resulted in what is "more than a mere revision—the name is the same, but it is a new book."[9] Led by Rev. Yoshiaki Fujitani, the committee worked for a whole year correcting past errors, setting

GLORIOUS GATHAS

old lyrics to new music, translating Japanese hymns into English, and considering new compositions. Despite the increased use of English in temple life, the editorial committee reduced the overall number of English hymns to a total of 49 compositions, down from 57 in the *Standard Gathas* of 1939.

Dorothy Hunt and A. R. Zorn suffered the most number of cuts: Hunt had seventeen compositions in the *Standard Gathas* and was reduced to nine in 1962, while A. R. Zorn went from fifteen to ten. In addition to two of her Buddhist soldier songs, Hunt's arrangements of the ancient chants "The Nembutsu" (No. 504) and "The Buddha is My Refuge" (No. 546) did not make it into the new hymnal. Also eliminated were her "Go Forth, O Valiant Soul" (No. 542), which sang of the determined effort one must make to pursue the truth and find peace; "Holy Day of Wesak" (No. 507), Wesak being the Theravadin commemoration of the birth of the Buddha; and "Lord Buddha Found the Truth" (No. 531) with its refrain of "Rejoice! Rejoice! Rejoice! Rejoice!/ The temple bells shall ring/ Rejoice! Rejoice! Rejoice! Rejoice!/ Be glad and sing." Zorn's "Right Aspiration" (No. 539), "Right Mindedness" (No. 537), and "Nirvana's Bliss" (No. 553) all speak of traditional tenets like peace, Nirvana, the truth, the Eightfold Path, and Lord Buddha. Despite these and other cuts, Dorothy Hunt and A. R. Zorn still remained writers with more compositions than anyone else in the 1962 hymnal.

Two other hymns that were left out can be looked at with some interest in terms of Shinshū ideas and values. "Mortal and Immortal" (No. 550) does praise Amitabha, but it is somewhat heavy on the sorrows and woes of life, just as "Nirvana's Endless Day" (No. 547) contrasts Nirvana with earthly strife, hatred, suffering, pain, misery, chains that bind, and a weary soul. While modern Shinshū doctrine emphasizes the primacy of Amida's power to grant a salvation that cannot be won by one's self-power, the law of karma and the importance of self-effort is often cited to refute the efficacy of prayer. The *Jodo Shinshu Handbook for Laymen* clearly exhorts believers to "fully understand the law of karma and disavow all prayers of supplication, witchcraft and fortune-telling as being superstitions."[10] Prayer is a thorny issue in Shinshū dogmatics, and can either be affirmed or denied,[11] depending upon what is meant by prayer and whether the law of karma, which requires human effort, is understood to be abrogated by Amida's grace or not, but the usual rejection of prayer as found in the *Handbook* is reflected in "Nirvana's Endless Day" as well:

> And must we pray that we may find,
> The strength to break the chains that bind?
> By each one must the race be run
> And not by prayer is freedom won.

Whether Dorothy Hunt's rejection of prayer was informed by Shinshū doctrine or early Buddhist agnosticism is not clear, but the hymn, in either case, is no longer part of the active corpus.

Nine new hymns were added in the 1962 edition, most of which were children's songs. "Buddha Loves You" (No. 82), written by Kimi Hisatsune with music by Jane Imamura and rearrangement by Osamu Shimizu, a noted Japanese musician,[12] replays the theme of a loving Buddha who cares not only for children but for birds, cats, puppies, and fish. "Long Ago in India" (No. 83), "It's Raining" (No. 84), and "Happy Wesak Day" (No. 87, which is not to be confused with the deleted "Holy Day of Wesak") all focus on Shakyamuni, who is presumably the Buddha referred to as "our Lord above" in "Sunbeams" (No. 85). "Children in Japan" (No. 88) is interesting for being one of the few, if not the only hymn, that clearly places Hawaii as its setting:

> Do you know that children in Japan
>   go to Sunday School and learn of Buddha's love?
> But when I listen closely, I cannot understand,
>   for words we utter here are not the words they say.

As in "Sunbeams" the Christian sounding term "Lord" ("o ma i ri shi ma sho means let us thank our Lord") appears in the second verse, and the third and final verse sings of "Namu Amida Butsu Namu Amida." This hymn presents an interesting theological challenge, should anyone wish to think of it as such, of making a clear determination of divine identity: are "Buddha," "Lord," and "Amida" one and the same? Or are they different? "Remember" (No. 89) is unambiguous by mentioning only "Namu Amida Butsu." "Farewell" (No. 90) uses both "Buddha" and "Namu Amida Butsu," and here too, because of the clear relationship that is indicated between the two, there is little doubt that the Buddha is Amida. Also added to the hymnal were new essays on the biography of Shinran, the history of the Honganji, and the teachings of Jōdo Shinshū, and these clearly direct attention to Jōdo Shinshū in a way that previous hymnals did not. It is this prose section that makes this edition a "new book," for the hymns themselves, even with the deletions and additions, do not add a major redirection of attention from general Buddhism to Shin Buddhism. Of the 49 English gathas, 35 were still from the old *Vade Mecum*.

If the 1920s, when the *Vade Mecum* was compiled, represent the first (and rather long lasting) flowering of the glorious gatha in English, the decades after the publication of the third edition in 1962 surely can be called the second blossoming. Throughout the '60s, '70s and '80s the Honpa Honganji sponsored a series of gatha writing contests that yielded a rich crop of new hymns. In his informative account of the history of Buddhist music in Hawaii, Rev. Yoshiaki Fujitani highlights the significant achievements of Mieko Takamiya ("At Our Altar," "With These Hands" and "Flowers at Amida's Altar"), Shigeaki Fujitani ("Diamond Faith"), Geraldine Hamai ("Quest of Life"), Cecilio Lindo ("Becoming Free"), and Shigeko Miyashiro ("Walk On As You Are"). A variety of people wrote music for these songs: Osamu Shimizu; Toshiro Mayuzumi, world renowned composer of the "Nirvana Symphony"; Penelope Lawhn; Yvonne Takishita; and Allen Trubitt, professor of music at the University of Hawaii.[13] In 1979 a music committee was formed, and its first chairperson was Rev. Yasuaki Hayashi, who thereby oversaw the compilation of the fourth and still current edition of *Praises of the Buddha*.

Published in 1990, the fourth edition represents a quantum leap in the number of English gathas. There are 76 English hymns, about 35 of which had not appeared in English in previous hymnals. As in the past, some hymns were dropped, but a total of 28 *Vade Mecum* pieces still endured as old favorites that have withstood the passage of time and the scrutiny of several editorial committees. For the 1990 edition, the music committee explicitly adopted a more sectarian approach: "gathas or verses, which did not seem to reflect Jodo Shinshu teachings, were deleted from this edition."[14] With the deletion of "Buddha's Soldiers," Dorothy Hunt's compositions dropped from nine in 1962 to eight, while Zorn's works went from ten to eight. Both of them still retained the distinction of having more compositions than anyone else, Kimi Hisatsune and Yumi Hojo sharing third place with six hymns each.

Of the 76 English hymns, 15 are translations from the Japanese. Consistent with the sectarian interests of the music committee, eight of these translations deal with Amida, Shinran, or Jōdo Shinshū. While this certainly displays a more clearly sectarian consciousness, the described relationship that one has with Amida is the same as that with Shakyamuni or the Buddha. This relationship is intimate and reassuring since Amida is said to be like a caring parent or friend. In this context of a loving relationship, the ambiguity of identity noted previously does not really matter, for Shakyamuni, the Buddha, and Amida, be they different or identical, all love in the same way. Amida sings in our hearts ("Amida Is Such"), and when we, "children of the Buddha, Amida-sama," are sad "we will always have the Buddha's helping hand to hold" ("Amida's Children II"). In Sunday school, children "listen to the story of Amida's love" ("Happy Sunday Morning"), while adults as well as children can relate to the following lyrics of "Hotokesama II":

> To my dear Amida, "Hotokesama":
> When I call your name,

GLORIOUS GATHAS

> I think of mother dear;
> Just as in her arms,
> I'd like to be
> Held by you so tenderly,
> "Hotokesama."

The Japanese original, "Hotokesama I," is one of the great favorites of Honganji congregations, and nowhere does the word "Amida" appear in it. The word hoto*kesama* in Japanese is every bit as ambiguous as "the Buddha" in English, but the music committee equated the two in its translation. Here it can be seen again that the exact identity of the deity is not as important as is the relationship of loving reassurance. Despite the fact that "Mihotoke ni Idakarete" is translated with the title "In Amida's Embrace," it is the Japanese version that is sung frequently at funerals, and here again the original does not use the word "Amida." Even though there is reference to the "western shore" of Amida in verse one, the "Mihotoke" in the hymn probably remains in most worshipper's minds as "Mihotoke" or "the Buddha" (should they be doing simultaneous translation without reference to "In Amida's Embrace"), both of which are ambiguous but comforting at a time of sorrow. The figure of the loving Amida as parent-friend-teacher-deity can also be seen in several of the new hymns composed in English (e.g., "At Our Altar," "Diamond Faith," and "Welcome").

The theme of personal, spiritual freedom that results when one finds one's true self recurs several times in the new compositions. The chorus line of Cecilio Lindo's "Becoming Free" sings of this clearly:

> Yes, let go let go, your ego great
> And become your true self.
> Yes, let go your ego great
>   then freedom will be yours.

"Quest of Life" by Geraldine Hamai speaks of seeking and finding peace in our hearts and minds, joy in our home and land, and life in Amida's Pure Land. Even when "there are dark clouds hov'ring" and there is "no place to rest your heart," Shigeko Miyashiro's "Walk On As You Are" counsels that we keep walking down "this road with Buddha's love, ... this road which Shinran trod," and it will become "this road of boundless freedom." The ideal of the true self rooted in peace was an important theme in earlier hymns, and can be seen, for instance, in "Nirvana's Bliss," which, as we noted earlier, rejected prayer, but also affirmed a "true self" that is free of the desires born of the ego. Dropped from the 1962 edition, "Nirvana's Bliss" was restored in the 1990 hymnal.

The changes in the development of the glorious gatha from 1924 to 1990 cannot be characterized by any simple scheme of cultural adaptation that might be called Americanization. Or, to put this complexity in other terms, Americanization entails Japanization. No one would argue that the Japanese-American community in Hawaii has been Americanized in profound ways, increasingly so with the passing of each generation. And yet the history of the English gatha, like the history of Japanese Buddhism in Hawaii in general, shows that in the prewar period there was a much stronger sense and promotion of an internationalized form of Buddhism. With the support of Bishop Emyō Imamura, Ernest Shinkaku Hunt's International Buddhist Institute and the Young Men's Buddhist Association (YMBA) sponsored the Pan-Pacific YMBA Conference in Honolulu in the summer of 1930. About 170 delegates from the mainland, Hawaii, Canada, China, Japan, Korea, Thailand, India and Burma discussed two pressing issues: how to propagate Buddhism to young people everywhere in the world, and how to eliminate sectarian divisions. The conference passed a resolution naming Hawaii as the "nucleus from which nonsectarian Buddhism, adapted to Western countries, may be spread to Pacific countries."[15] That was in 1930, and never again would Buddhists in Hawaii focus so much energy and interest in developing a Buddhism that was international in nature. In certain ways, Buddhism became more Japanese thereafter despite changes that made it more

American in other ways.

Consider, for instance, the percentage of English gathas in relationship to Japanese hymns as they appeared in the major hymnals from 1924 to 1990, that is, from the *Vade Mecum* to the fourth edition of *Praises of the Buddha:*

1924 *Vade Mecum*	114 of 114 hymns, or 100%
1939 *Standard Gathas*	57 of 125 hymns, or 46%
1962 *Praises of the Buddha*	49 of 102 hymns, or 48%
1990 *Praises of the Buddha*	76 of 145 hymns, or 52%

Since 15 of the 76 hymns in the 1990 edition were translations of Japanese hymns, it can be argued that while the language of these hymns was Americanized, the content was not. Surely no one would suggest that the translation of Kawabata Yasunari's novels into English, for instance, represents the Americanization of Japanese fiction, but it can be suggested that such translations represent the Japanization of literature for English readers. Translation makes available Japanese ideas and values, and thus represents an aspect of the Japanization of the corpus of hymns. If we reduce the number of so-called English hymns by the 15 translations, which, by this reasoning we would consider to be in essence (though not in language) Japanese hymns, then we have 61 English gathas, or 42% of the total. Except for the slight increase in 1962, the percentage of English hymns relative to Japanese ones has thus declined over the years.

The case for an increasing Japanization can also be made apart from statistics by recalling what has already been pointed out, namely, that the hymns have taken on, at least on the linguistic surface, a greater Jōdo Shinshū sectarian focus. Even though the general Buddhism of the *Vade Mecum* persisted with surprising tenacity, the hymns increasingly sang of Amida, Shinran, and Shinshū. But here the tables can be turned again: just because Japanese hymns both in the original and in translation have gained strength in numbers, and original English hymns shifted attention from Shakyamuni to Amida,

India to Japan, and general Buddhism to Shinshū, does this mean that the *conceptual content* has undergone a similar change? Is there really a significant difference between the Buddhism of the *Vade Mecum* and the Jōdo Shinshū of the hymns? Though reduced in number, the *Vade Mecum* hymns still represent 37% percent of the 76 English gathas in the current hymnal, or 46% if the translations from the Japanese are disregarded. Worshippers do not make a distinction between the gathas of general Buddhism and the Shinshū hymns; both exist comfortably side by side. Could a case be made, therefore, that despite the seeming Japanization of the hymns, the international ideal of Ernest and Dorothy Hunt is alive and well, at least in song?

The implications of these possibilities are clear. If Japanization has taken place, then Shinshū teachings and values have been strengthened. If Americanization or internationalization has taken place, or, more accurately, has remained in place such that Shinshū teachings and values cannot be distinguished from the Buddhism of the *Vade Mecum*, then Shinshū sectarianism has not advanced, at least not in the musical world of the glorious gatha. I would suggest that the latter is the case: despite the Shinshū dressing of the newer hymns, they are still similar to the Shinran hymns of the Hunts themselves; that is, Shinran and Shinshū teach a Buddhism in which the Buddha, be he Shakyamuni or Amida, loves and comforts us as we travel the path leading to right instead of wrong action, personal freedom rooted in the true self instead of ego desires, and spiritual peace born of love for and by the Buddha, be he Shakyamuni or Amida. In the glorious gatha, the religion of the *Vade Mecum* still reigns.

NOTES

1. Louise H. Hunter, *Buddhism in Hawaii: Its Impact on a Yankee Community* (Honolulu: University of Hawaii Press, 1971), 152.

2. Dorothy Hunt, A. Raymond Zorn, and Kaundinya Shinkaku, *The Vade Mecum*, fifth edition (Honolulu: International Buddhist Institute of Hawaii, 1932).

3. Nishu Utsuki in "Introduction" to Publication Bureau of Buddhist Books, ed., *Standard Buddhist Gathas and Services: Japanese and English* (Kyoto: Honpa Hongwanji, 1939).

4. George B. Sansom, *The Western World and Japan* (New York: Alfred A. Knopf, 1968), 484.

5. Yoshiaki Fujitani, "History of Buddhist Music in Hawaii" (unpublished paper, 1994), 5.

6. Interview with Mrs. Toku Umehara, August 19, 1997.

7. Music Steering Committee, *Praises of the Buddha*, fourth edition (revised) (Honolulu: Honpa Hongwanji Mission of Hawaii, 1990), ii.

8. The Hawaii Federation of Young Buddhist Associations, *Praises of the Buddha* (Honolulu: The Hawaii Federation of Young Buddhist Associations, 1949), 4. The capitalized emphasis of certain words is in the original text.

9. *Praises of the Buddha*, third edition (Honolulu: Honpa Hongwanji Mission of Hawaii, 1962), i.

10. Hongwanji International Center, *Jodo Shinshu Handbook for Laymen*, second edition (Kyoto: Hongwanji International Center, 1983), 69.

11. The affirmation and denial of prayer in Jōdo Shinshū is discussed in detail in the chapter on practical benefits (*genze riyaku*) in Mikogami Eryū, *Shinshūgaku no konpn mondai* (Kyoto: Nagata bunshōdō, 1970), 287–328.

12. Fujitani, "A History of Buddhist Music in Hawaii," 7.

13. Ibid., 7–8.

14. *Praises of the Buddha*, fourth edition, i.

15. Hunter, *Buddhism in Hawaii*, 166.

PART THREE

Constructive Engagement of the Teachings and Practice

The Visions of Vaidehī: Transformative Symbolism in a Visualization Practice

Richard K. PAYNE

Visualization[1] is one of the most important kinds of meditation practice, being taught in one form or another in almost all Buddhist lineages.[2] While in some lineages it may be peripheral or preliminary, visualization practice is central to the Amitābha and Amitāyus cults[3] within Buddhism.[4] Although the *Larger* and *Smaller Sukhāvatīvyūha Sutras* are rich in visual imagery, it is the *Visualization Sutra*[5] which is most explicit in providing instruction for a visualization practice.

VISUALIZATION PRACTICE IN THE *VISUALIZATION SUTRA*

As it currently exists, the *Visualization Sutra* is clearly a compilation of three different elements:[6] the first is the story of King Bimbisāra and Queen Vaidehī's imprisonment by their son, Prince Ajātaśatru. The second is a sequence of thirteen stages for constructing a mental visual image of the Buddha Amitāyus, his attendant bodhisattvas and his land, Sukhāvatī—the Land of Utmost Bliss. The third section is a discussion of the nine grades of birth in Sukhāvatī, and includes an additional three ways of "keeping the Buddha in mind" (Skt. *buddhānusmṛti*). In contrast to the first thirteen, which employ mental imagery, the final three culminate in teaching recitative practice (Jpn. *shōmyō nembutsu*).

While the visualization practice at present includes thirteen stages, the thirteenth is distinctly different from the first twelve. The weight of scholarly opinion is that the first twelve form a coherent visualization practice and that this twelve-part visualization was one of the older pieces from which this sutra was compiled. The compiler appears to have added the thirteenth as a transition to the discussion of the nine grades of birth.[7]

The twelve-part visualization practice is a sequence of increasingly complex images which build upon one another until the practitioner has a clear mental image of Sukhāvatī, the Buddha Amitāyus and his attendant bodhisattvas. Since this visualization practice is taught to Queen Vaidehī by Śākyamuni Buddha, it will be referred to here as "The Visions of Vaidehī." It appears that the visualization as given in the text has been corrupted during the process of compilation.[8] Based on the suggestions of the Ryukoku University Translation Center, minor modifications have been made in the following summary of the visualization practice, so as to create a version which may more accurately represent the earlier practice. The sequence is as follows:

1. First, the practitioner is to develop a mental image of the sun "which, as it is about to set, looks like a drum suspended in the sky. After seeing the sun in this way, whether their eyes are closed or opened, they should make the image remain clear and distinct."[9]

2. Having stabilized this mental image, the practitioner is directed to "perceive the western quarter as being completely filled with water, and see the water clean and pure," after which this water becomes "brilliant and transparent" ice, which in turn becomes *vaiḍūrya*, i.e., lapis lazuli[10]; the support of the *vaiḍūrya* ground is eight "bannered pillars," made of adamant and seven kinds of jewels; the light from these are as bright as "a thousand *koṭis*[11] of suns, and it is impossible to see them all in detail"; the surface of the ground is criss-crossed by golden cords and covered with

THE VISIONS OF VAIDEHĪ

jewels, the light from which forms a "radiant pedestal" on which are ten million jeweled pavilions with flower banners and musical instruments; pure breezes arise from the light-rays and play upon the musical instruments which give forth the sounds "suffering, emptiness, impermanence, and non-self."

3. The third part of the visualization practice is strengthening the vision of the ground so that it can be seen "so clearly and distinctly that it is beyond verbal description."

4. The fourth part of the visualization practice concerns the trees of Sukhāvatī: each tree is eight *yojanas*[12] high, the flowers and leaves are jeweled, emitting different colors; seven layers of pearl nets cover the trees, and between each layer are five hundred *koṭis* of flower palaces equal to the royal palace of Brahmā inhabited by heavenly children wearing jeweled ornaments; the leaves and fruit of these rows of trees are orderly and jeweled, emitting a light which forms banners, flags and canopies; within the canopies are illuminated "all the works of the buddhas of the three-thousand-great-thousand worlds . . . and the buddha lands of the ten quarters also appear therein."

5. The next portion of the visualization is the waters of Sukhāvatī: there is a central lake whose waters are "made of seven kinds of soft and yielding jewels" and having the eight excellent qualities; from the wish-fulfilling gem flow fourteen streams with gold streambeds covered by multicolored sands; sixty *koṭis* of jeweled lotuses grow in the lakes, and the flowing waters proclaim the teachings of "suffering, emptiness, impermanence, non-self, and the *pāramitās*"; golden rays of light issue from the wish-fulfilling gem and become songbirds whose song extols mindfulness of the Buddha, Dharma and Sangha.

243

6. Next comes the visualization of jeweled pavilions: "five hundred *koṭis* of storied-pavilions" in every part of Sukhāvatī are filled with countless heavenly beings playing music; music instruments hanging in the sky proclaim mindfulness of the Buddha, Dharma and Sangha.

With this the visualization of Sukhāvatī *per se* is complete. The next portion of the visualization is of the Buddha Amitāyus and his attendants.[13]

7. The practitioner is to visualize a huge jeweled lotus blossom, with eighty-four thousand large petals. Each petal is covered with thousands of wish-fulfilling gems and each gem emits thousands of light rays. From the calyx of this jeweled lotus blossom four jeweled banners rise up "of their own accord; each jeweled banner is as large as a billion *koṭis* of Sumeru mountains." Above the banners are jeweled curtains, each jewel giving off eighty-four thousand light rays and each light ray shines with "eighty-four thousand different shades of gold." These lights shine over the entirety of the land where "it freely transforms itself and performs the works of the buddhas."

8. Having created a visualization of the lotus throne, the practitioner is to next visualize the Buddha Amitāyus seated upon the throne. The body of the Buddha Amitāyus is a reddish-yellow golden color surrounded by a purple aura.[14] Holding the entirety of the vision of Sukhāvati—jeweled ground, jeweled lakes, jeweled trees, jeweled curtains and nets, lotus throne and Amitāyus—in place, the practitioner adds two identical lotus thrones, one each to the left and right of Amitāyus. Seated upon the left lotus throne is the figure of the Bodhisattva Avalokiteśvara and upon the right is the Bodhisattva Mahāsthāmaprāpta. The bodies of these three figures emanate rays of light which illumine all of the

THE VISIONS OF VAIDEHĪ

trees in Sukhāvatī. Under each tree appear another three lotus thrones with figures of Amitāyus, Avalokiteśvara and Mahāsthāmaprāpta seated upon them.

9. In the next phase of the visualization the practitioner is to focus attention on the body of the Buddha Amitāyus. His body is immense in size and there is a tuft of white hair between his eyebrows. An immense circle of light spreads out from his body and in this light there are countless "miraculously created buddhas" each of whom "is attended by a great assembly of countless miraculously created bodhisattvas." There are eighty-four thousand primary features, each of which has eighty-four thousand secondary features, and each of the secondary features sends out eighty-four thousand rays of light. The sutra asserts that one can mentally envision more than can be described. Seeing "these things is to see all the buddhas of the ten quarters." Further, by envisioning the Buddha Amitāyus, "you see at once the countless buddhas of the ten quarters. Because you are able to see the countless buddhas, these buddhas, appearing in front of you, predict your future attainment."[15]

10. Having formed an image of the body of the Buddha Amitāyus, the practitioner then forms an equally complex, though not identical, image of the body of the Bodhisattva Avalokiteśvara.

11. This is in turn followed by visualizing the body of the Bodhisattva Mahāsthāmaprāpta, again equally complex but not identical with the body of the Buddha Amitāyus.

12. The practitioner is then to form an image of him/herself being born in Sukhāvatī. At first one is inside of a lotus blossom, then the lotus blossom opens so that one sees the

sky filled with buddhas and bodhisattvas, and hears the waters, birds and buddhas all proclaiming the Dharma.

With this the visualization practice is complete. The practitioner has created a mental image of Sukhāvatī, the Buddha Amitāyus and his attendant bodhisattvas, Avalokiteśvara and Mahāsthāmaprāpta, and visualized him/herself as being born in Sukhāvatī.

PSYCHOLOGICAL INTERPRETATION OF THE VISIONS OF VAIDEHĪ

In 1943 Carl Jung gave a lecture to the Schweizerische Gesellschaft der Freunde ostasiatischer Kultur entitled in its English translation "The Psychology of Eastern Meditation"[16] which was a discussion of the *Visualization Sutra*. (This lecture has itself been commented on by Ryukyo Fujimoto,[17] and more recently by Harold Coward.[18]) Since the lecture is a brief treatment of the Visions of Vaidehī, the following attempts to develop in more detail an interpretation from the perspective of analytical psychology. It is important to note, however, that the following is definitely not to be understood as intending to be "the interpretation." Interpretations derive from the theoretical perspective of the interpreter and are perhaps only convincing to the extent that the reader holds the same theoretical perspective. However, interpretations developed from a perspective unfamiliar to the reader may provide insights which might otherwise be overlooked.

Several aspects of the Visions of Vaidehī carry symbolic significance. First, there is the mandalic character of Sukhāvati as visualized. Second, the Buddha Amitāyus acts as a symbol of the *self*.[19] Third, the wish-fulfilling gem appears analogous to the philosophers' stone of alchemical tradition, another symbol of the *self*. Finally, there is the numeric significance of the Buddha and bodhisattvas as three in relation to the practitioner who plays the role of the "invisible fourth."

THE VISIONS OF VAIDEHĪ

1. The Mandalic Character of Sukhāvatī

Jung's lecture focuses on the mandalic quality of Sukhāvatī. Although not the classic "four-gated palace" mandala, Sukhāvatī seems to have been thought of as centering on the three lotus thrones growing out of the waters of a lake. While the specifics of the visualization are the subject of some debate,[20] psychologically the most important point is the structured, symmetrical character of the vision.

Jung has written extensively on the psychological significance of mandalic images. In his Terry Lectures he has said:

> The experience formulated by the modern mandala is typical of people who cannot project the divine image any longer. Owing to the withdrawal and introjection of the image they are in danger of inflation and dissociation of the personality. The round or square enclosures built round the centre therefore have the purpose of protective walls or of a *vas hermeticum*, to prevent an outburst or a disintegration. Thus the mandala denotes and assists exclusive concentration on the centre, the self. This is anything but egocentricity. On the contrary, it is a much needed self-control for the purpose of avoiding inflation and dissociation.[21]

In other words, the mandala serves an important protective function in the process of withdrawing the projection of the image of the divine from some outer object and recognizing that the divine image arises from one's own psyche. The withdrawal of projections is one of the key issues for Jung's theory of psychology. To the extent that one projects one's own psychic material out onto objects in the world, an entirely natural process, one is less than whole. The withdrawal of projections serves the process of moving to a more conscious condition, as formerly unconscious contents are reintegrated at a conscious level. As projections are withdrawn and reintegrated into oneself, one regains one's own wholeness. As Jung states following the above, it is "the complete man"[22] which is to be found at the center of modern mandalic structures. In Buddhist terms this might be expressed as the mandala providing the practitioner with the possibility of experiencing his/her own already enlightened consciousness.

Jung analyzes the withdrawal of projection into five stages. In the first, the projection is entirely identified with some object. In the example he employs, the voice heard by a Nigerian soldier is experienced by the soldier as coming from a tree. At the second stage, there is a distinction between the object and a spiritual presence inhabiting the object. In the example at hand, between the tree and a tree spirit, from whom the voice heard originates. At the third stage, a moral evaluation is made as to whether the spirit is good or evil. At the fourth stage, the experience is devalued as illusory. In other words, no spirit, either good or evil, exists as the source of the voice heard. At the fifth stage, the psychic reality of the voice is recognized. Although there is no spirit, there is a voice heard and that voice has its origins in the individual's psyche: "The fifth level is of the opinion that something did happen after all: even though the psychic content was not the tree, nor a spirit in the tree, nor indeed any spirit at all, it was nevertheless a phenomenon thrusting up from the unconscious, the existence of which cannot be denied if one is minded to grant the psyche any kind of reality."[23]

Thus, the mandalic enclosure of the Visions would seem to have arisen from the author of this visualization's own inability to go on projecting the image of the divine onto an outer object. Examining the religious milieu in which the Visions were created sheds additional light on this aspect of the mandalic quality of the visualization.

Stephan Beyer has suggested that the Visions of Vaidehī arose as part of "a wave of visionary theism sweeping over the whole of northern India, influencing Hindu contemplatives as well as the *yoga* masters of Kashmir."[24] He compares Buddhist visualization practices with the *bhakti* of the *Bhagavadgītā,* pointing out, however, that *bhakti* "is not the rather vague emotional dependence and devotionalism denoted by the term in current usage, but rather a specific contemplative activity, the iconographic visualization of the god—precisely the meditative technique that forms the episodic core of the Buddhist vision quest."[25]

While Jung's conception of the process by which projections are withdrawn is presented as a progressive movement on the part of an individual, it may be more useful to see the five stages as five different modalities by which an individual can be related to his/her projections.[26] The visualization practices which arose as part of the "wave of visionary theism" would seem to correlate to a shift from the third modality, perhaps embodied in the sacramental practices of Brahmanic religious culture, to the fifth modality. Rather than accessing the gods conceived as actually existing external entities by means of votive rituals, one now accesses them through one's own mental imagery.

Such a movement would mean that practitioners "cannot project the divine image any longer," opening them to the dangers of "inflation and dissociation." The psychic role of the mandala as protecting against these dangers is discussed by Michael Fordham, who says that "there is an acknowledged defensive content of the symbol which Jung alludes to when he reminds us of the magic circle which cannot be penetrated and cannot be broken from within. In calling this defensive, I do not wish to allude to ego defences but to an absolute protection of the symbol at the centre of the figure which combines and transcends opposites."[27] In the Visions of Vaidehī, Amitāyus is the symbol at the center of the mandalic Pure Land. As a symbol which "combines and transcends opposites," Amitāyus is both contained and protected by the mandalic Pure Land. This allows the practitioner to safely take the step to the fifth modality, avoiding the dangers of inflation and dissociation despite engaging in a visualization practice which withdraws the projection of the divine from an external to a psychic reality.

2. Amitāyus as a Symbol of the *Self*

Another aspect of the visualization is that Amitāyus, seated at the center of the mandalic Land of Utmost Bliss, serves as an image of the practitioner's *self*. The protection of the mandalic Pure Land makes possible the establishment of a relation between the ego and the image of the divine, i.e., the image of the *self*, the "whole man." Descriptions of the *self* appear to be more metaphors than definitions. For example, concerning the effects of withdrawing projections, Jung writes: ". . . the centre of gravity of the total personality shifts its position. It is then no longer in the ego, which is merely the centre of consciousness, but in the hypothetical point between consciousness and the unconscious. This new centre might be called the self."[28]

Edward Edinger has pointed out the heuristic quality of the concept of the *self*. The *self* is usually defined as the "totality of the psyche," however,

> If we speak rationally, we must inevitably make a distinction between ego and Self which contradicts our definition of Self. The fact is, the conception of the Self is a paradox. It is simultaneously the center and the circumference of the circle of totality. Considering ego and Self as two separate entities is merely a necessary rational device for discussing these things.[29]

In Edinger's formulation it is the establishment of a strong relation between the ego and the *self* which is the goal of personal development:

> . . . psychological development is characterized by two processes occurring simultaneously, namely, progressive ego-Self separation and also increasing emergence of the ego-Self axis into consciousness. If this is a correct representation of the facts, it means that ego-Self separation and growing consciousness of the ego as dependent on the Self are actually two aspects of a single emergent process continuous from birth to death.[30]

According to Michael Fordham, "any symbol that carries the

experience of or which is postulated as having a greater totality than man himself can be a symbol of the self."[31] However, it would seem that religious figures such as Amitāyus and Christ can function as particularly potent symbols of the *self*. Writing in reference to the Christian tradition, Jung emphasizes that "the spontaneous symbols of the self, or of wholeness, cannot in practice be distinguished from a God-image."[32] Further, regarding the renewing quality such images can have, Jung says that

> the "renewal" . . . of the mind is not meant as an actual alteration of consciousness, but rather as the restoration of an original condition, an apocatastasis. This is in exact agreement with the empirical findings of psychology, that there is an ever-present archetype of wholeness which may easily disappear from the purview of consciousness or may never be perceived at all until a consciousness illuminated by conversion recognizes it in the figure of Christ.[33]

The figure of Amitāyus carries a similar valence. Amitāyus is the Buddha of Infinite Life and is often, especially in East Asia, identified with Amitābha, the Buddha of Infinite Light.[34] Clearly these qualities of infinite life and infinite light suggest an archetypal, symbolic quality.

Above we quoted Jung describing the *self* as a midpoint between consciousness, centred on the ego, and the unconscious. There is a suggestive similarity here with the Buddhist three-body theory. Amitāyus is considered to be a *sambhogakāya*, the "reward-body . . . the body of a buddha received as a result of his meritorious practices."[35] This is in contrast to the *nirmāṇakāya*, "a body of a buddha manifested to correspond to the different needs and capacities of living beings."[36] The most familiar *nirmāṇakāya* is the historical figure of Śākyamuni Buddha. The third body is the *dharmakāya*, the "Dharma-body . . . the body of ultimate reality."[37] As an analogy with the individual psychic structure, the symbolic associations are that the ego corresponds with the specific, historically manifest Buddha, the *nirmāṇakāya*. The unconscious corresponds with the body of ultimate reality, the *dharmakāya*, as the fundamental ground from which individual ego-awareness arises. The reward body, in this case Amitāyus, standing midway between the ego / *nirmāṇakāya* and the unconscious / *dharmakāya*, corresponds to the *self*.

Jung's description of the renewing power of symbols of the *self* as "the restoration of an original wholeness" itself corresponds to the notion of originary awakening, the idea that all sentient beings already have awakened, pure consciousness as their fundamental actuality.[38] The reasons we fail to live in the awareness of this are incidental to originary awakening, what Herbert Guenther has referred to as "adventitious obscurations." Meditation practices, such as visualization, recitation and ritual, have the ability to clear away these adventitious obscurations, just as polishing a mirror reveals its originary reflectivity.[39] Thus, it is not "an actual alteration of consciousness, but rather . . . the restoration of an original condition, an apocatastasis."

3. The Wish-Fulfilling Gem and the Philosophers' Stone

In the reconstructed visualization the wish-fulfilling gem (*cintāmaṇi*) lies at the center of the lake from which arises the lotus throne upon which Amitāyus sits. The water of the lake flows out from the wish-fulfilling gem and is said to have eight excellent qualities: "the water is clear, cold, sweet, light, abundant, moderate, quenches pains like thirst and makes sense organs sound."[40] The wish-fulfilling gem is a very common symbol in Buddhist imagery. It is considered to be the king of jewels and is often linked to "water or mythical beings in water, such as *nāgas* or *makara*."[41]

Jung clearly identifies the philosophers' stone (lapis philosophorum) as one of the most important alchemical symbols. In many alchemical texts, the stone itself is the goal of the work. Jung interprets the stone as a symbol of the *self*. He gives the following description of the powers of the stone in the course of discussing its connection with immortality, i.e., infinite life:

> The lapis is the panacea, the universal medicine, the alexipharmic, the tincture that transmutes base metals into gold and gravel into precious stones. It brings riches, power, and health; it cures melancholy and, as the *vivus lapis philosophicus*, is a symbol of the savior, the Anthropos, and immortality. Its incorruptibility is also shown in the ancient idea that the body of a saint becomes stone.[42]

Jung then goes on to assert the relation between the stone and the *self:* "Psychological research has shown that the historical or ethnological symbols are identical with those spontaneously produced by the unconscious, and that the lapis represents the idea of a transcendent totality which coincides with what analytical psychology calls the self."[43] Edward F. Edinger has pointed out that the stone is also linked to the symbolic value of the number four. The first organizing principle of the *prima materia* of primal chaos is the four elements. "In order to produce the Philosophers' Stone, the four elements must then be reunited in the unity of a quintessence."[44]

That the wish-fulfilling gem is a symbol of the *self* comparable to the philosophers' stone is made evident by examining its place in the visualization of the Land of Utmost Bliss of Amitāyus. It is at the center of the land as visualized, at the base of the vertical axis which rises up from it in the form of the lotus blossom throne upon which Amitāyus is seated. Additionally, the waters of the lake flow out from it, with fourteen streams radiating out from the lake. It is as if the wish-fulfilling gem is the origin of the entire visualized land. Everything flows out and rises up from it.

The relation between the wish-fulfilling gem and Amitāyus also shows why it is that there is no incongruity about there being two symbols of the *self* embedded in the same visualization. The two are two different representations of the *self.* The wish-fulfilling gem would be the hard, condensed center, the foundation stone for the lotus blossom throne and Amitāyus. In contrast, Amitāyus represents the self as fully conscious. Above we cited Edinger regarding the paradoxical character of the conception of the *self*. It is both center and totality of the psyche. The wish-fulfilling gem would seem, then, to symbolize the *self* as center, while Amitāyus as infinite symbolizes the *self* as totality.[45]

4. The Three and the Four

The numeric relation between Amitāyus, Avalokiteśvara and Mahāsthāmaprāpta as three and the practitioner joining them at the end of the visualization as the fourth is suggestive of the process of psychic development toward a condition of wholeness. Jung has discussed the relation between three and four frequently. However, he consistently suggests that three is only apparently stable, and is a stage toward the actual stability of four:

> Three can be regarded as a relative totality, since it usually represents either a spiritual totality that is a product of thought, like the Trinity, or else an instinctual, chthonic one, like the triadic nature of the gods of the underworld—the "lower triad." Psychologically, however, three—if the context indicates that it refers to the self—should be understood as a defective quaternity or as a stepping-stone towards it.[46]

In his analysis of the Christian doctrine of the Trinity Jung points out that the Christian emphasis on the spiritual, good and masculine character of the Trinity correlates with the rejection of the material, evil and feminine.[47] Further, one can see how each cluster of characteristics is homologized, so that spiritual, good and masculine are linked together, while material, evil and feminine are also linked to each other. In the case of the Trinity, according to Jung, completion is surreptitiously approached through the Assumption of the Blessed Virgin Mary, which provides a bodily, i.e., material, and a feminine fourth.[48] This still leaves evil, which leads to a different pattern in which evil is constituted as the Antichrist in opposition to Jesus, the Christ.

THE VISIONS OF VAIDEHĪ

As Buddhism does not have the same notion of good in polar opposition to evil, the symbolic structuring implies a different kind of fourth as the completion of the three. These three figures, Amitāyus, Avalokiteśvara and Mahāsthāmaprāpta, are "celestial" figures, and as such are not instantiated in the historical reality of the practitioner. Through the visualization, the practitioner's own mind and body become the means by which these figures are instantiated. In the words of the *Visualization Sutra*: "When you perceive a buddha in your mind, it is your mind that possesses the thirty-two prominent features and the eighty secondary attributes; your mind becomes a buddha; your mind is a buddha; and the wisdom of the buddhas— true, universal and ocean-like—arises from this mind. Therefore, you should single-mindedly fix your thoughts and clearly perceive the *Buddha, Tathāgata, Arhat, Samyaksambuddha*."[49]

As already discussed *supra*, Amitāyus is the Buddha of Infinite Life. One of his two attendant bodhisattvas is Avalokiteśvara, who is widely known and associated with the quality of compassion. It seems that originally his name may have been Avalokita-śvara, meaning something like "one who perceives the sounds of the world," usually interpreted as the sounds produced by sentient beings as they suffer in the round of rebirth. When Avalokita-śvara was introduced into northwest India, however, the widespread popularity there of Iśvara, meaning roughly "lord" or "one who is able," and used as an epithet of Śiva, Indra and Kṛṣṇa, led to a conflation of the two names: Avalokita-śvara becoming Avalokita-iśvara, i.e., Avalokiteśvara.[50]

Avalokiteśvara appears to have been the object of an autonomous cult, i.e., he was worshipped in his own right. This perhaps explains why he appears so frequently in the sutras as an independent figure. In contrast Mahāsthāmaprāpta is relatively little known and most commonly only appears as a member of this triad. He is said to represent wisdom.[51] The Ryukoku translators give a couple of quotes which highlight the power of this bodhisattva:

> In Buddhist texts this bodhisattva often is connected with earthquakes or the like, e.g., "When the bodhisattva takes a

step, it makes the three-thousand-great-thousand worlds and the palace of evil deity quake." . . . "He, with great transcendental powers, flies to the ten quarters. Whichever land he may fly to, it quakes six times and any evil beings disappear."[52]

Thus, we have infinite life, compassion and wisdom. As the fourth to these three, the practitioner enters into a unified quaternity, thereby making these same characteristics manifest in his own consciousness through the visualization of their perfected anthropomorphic representations. The abstractions become instantiated.

ON VISIONS AND VISUALIZATION

Stephan Beyer has proposed that visualization practices are "a search for the control—for the conscious return—of originally uncontrolled and given visionary revelation."[53] Paul Harrison, following a suggestion by Étienne Lamotte,[54] indicates that visualization practices were intended to

> provide practitioners with the means to translate themselves into the presence of this or that particular manifestation of the Buddha-principle for the purpose of hearing the Dharma, which they subsequently remember and propagate to others. This can be seen . . . as an indication of the means by which at least some Mahāyāna *sūtras* were composed, i.e., as the result of meditational inspiration.[55]

Thus, one can approach the texts which prescribe visualization practices, e.g., the *Visualization Sutra*, or which describe rich visual imagery, e.g., the *Larger* and *Smaller Sukhāvatī Sutras*, as being based ultimately on some individual's spontaneous visionary experience.[56] There is, therefore, some psychological basis, despite the doubtless extensive codification which the descriptions/prescriptions found in the sutras have undergone.[57] Michael Fordham has made a similar

THE VISIONS OF VAIDEHĪ

point regarding the *Hermetic Corpus*. Beginning with Hermes Trismegistos' vision of Poimandres, ongoing exposition of the vision is influenced by Platonism and other philosophic systems of the time. This "shows how much the form of visions must be determined by the state of conscious knowledge and the general view of the world current at any given time."[58]

The *Visualization Sutra* is not a personal psychological record *per se*.[59] Yet if we turn our attention to the story which provides the context for the teaching of the twelve-part visualization, we find a very dramatic tale indeed. John Huntington sees this as a record of an historical event[60] but discounts it as "only a foil for introducing the meditations."[61] Whether or not the event is historically factual, the narrative is psychologically significant. Clearly, Queen Vaidehī is in a state of crisis when she experiences the vision of "all the pure and exquisite lands of the buddhas of the ten quarters."[62]

Her son, Prince Ajātaśatru, has imprisoned his father, King Bimbisāra, with the intent of starving him to death. Through a subterfuge, the Queen is able to provide the King with food. Upon learning of this, Ajātaśatru becomes so angry that, snatching up a sword, he sets off to kill his mother. Two of his ministers intervene, pointing out that history records many instances of sons killing their own fathers in order to gain the throne, but "never have we heard of anyone who committed the outrageous crime of harming his mother."[63] This is a very dramatic moment, the ministers portrayed as gripping their own swords and backing away from the angry prince. Ajātaśatru then decides to imprison his mother as well. "Vaidehī, being thus imprisoned, was stricken with sorrow and grief."[64] She appeals to Śākyamuni Buddha who appears to her in her imprisonment. She begs him to "describe for me in detail a place where there are neither sorrows nor afflictions, and where I should be born."[65] Rather than describing, the Buddha sends out a light-ray from between his eyebrows, illuminating all the countless worlds of the ten directions. The light-ray returns to rest atop the Buddha's head, "becoming a golden pedestal resembling Mount Sumeru."[66]

Then the lands of the Buddhas of the ten directions appear in this golden pedestal. Stephan Beyer emphasizes the difference between this first episode as "an involuntary visionary revelation" and the subsequent instruction as to "how to visualize the Buddha Amitāyus and his Buddhafield" as a matter of conscious effort. [67]

CONCLUSION

Examining the Visions of Vaidehī from a psychological perspective, we find four symbolic elements which can be understood as playing significant roles in the transformative function of the visualization practice. The mandalic quality of the visualized Land of Utmost Bliss provides a container for the establishment of a relation between the ego and the *self*. This relation would involve the withdrawal of the projection of divinity onto an external figure and the realization of one's own already awakened consciousness, i.e., one's identity with and as a Buddha. Two symbols of the self provide the basis for the evocation of the ego-self relation—Amitāyus and the wish-fulfilling gem. The movement from three—Amitāyus, Avalokiteśvara and Mahāsthāmaprāpta—to four with the birth of the practitioner in the Land of Utmost Bliss indicates a movement to a more stable psychic structure.

The Visions as we know them now have been subject to codification by the lineage of practitioners who have handed this practice down through perhaps centuries before being compiled as part of the *Visualization Sutra*. However, it seems highly probable that the Visions were in fact based on some individual's visionary experience. The story of Queen Vaidehī suggests the condition of psychic turmoil out of which the Visions arose.

Visualization practices have been a vital part of Buddhist practice for centuries. The maintenance of these practices over such long periods suggests that they are effective in producing psychic transformation. This examination of the symbolic content of one

THE VISIONS OF VAIDEHĪ

visualization practice points toward a way of understanding how such practices are effective.

NOTES

1. As used here, "visualization" refers to that portion of the broader set of practices known as *buddhānusmṛti* using mental imagery as a means of "keeping the buddha in mind." The other major practice within *buddhānusmṛti* is, of course, recitative in character. I find the two approaches distinct enough to believe that recitative practice requires a separate study.

2. Paul Harrison notes that *buddhānusmṛti* practices have in large part been slighted in much of the Western literature on Buddhist meditation, being dismissed as "little more than a devotional preliminary, a relatively insignificant 'ground-clearing' practice." Paul Harrison, "Commemoration and Identification in *Buddānusmṛti*" in Janet Gyatso, ed., *In the Mirror of Memory: Reflections on Mindfulness and Remembrance in Indian and Tibetan Buddhism* (Albany, N.Y.: State University of New York Press, 1992), 216.

3. While it has become conventional in Anglophone Buddhist studies to refer to the entire history and development of the Amitabha and Amitāyus cults with the term "Pure Land," such usage is misleading. Although "the Pure Land" is widely accepted as a conventional translation for Sukhāvatī, i.e., the Pure Land of Amitabha and Amitāyus Buddhas, there are of course many other pure Buddha lands which have also been important in the history of Buddhism.

4. Visualization practice is also central to the Vajrayāna lineages, which suggests that the two forms, Pure Land and Vajrayāna, originate from the same religious milieu.

5. T. 365. Ch. *Kuan wu liang shou fo ching;* Jpn. *Kanmuryōju-kyō;* reconstructed Skt. *Amitāyurbuddhānusmṛtisūtra*. Many of the translations of this text render "kuan" as contemplation or as meditation. Although there is no generally agreed upon terminology in English, it seems to me that these two latter terms form more general categories than does the term visualization. The practice taught in the sutra

259

explicitly prescribes the creation of mental visual images.

6. John C. Huntington, "Rebirth in Amitābha's Sukhāvatī" in James Foard, Michael Solomon and Richard K. Payne, eds., *The Pure Land Tradition: History and Development*, Berkeley Buddhist Studies Series, no. 3 (Berkeley: Berkeley Buddhist Studies Series, 1996), 73.

7. See *The Sūtra of Contemplation on the Buddha of Immeasurable Life as Expounded by Śākyamuni Buddha*, translated and annotated by the Ryukoku University Translation Center (Kyoto: Ryukoku University, 1984), xvii–xxx (hereafter cited as Ryukoku translation); and Huntington, "Rebirth in Amitābha's Sukhāvatī," 76–80.

8. Cf. Ryukoku translation, 38, n. 1.

9. The process described here is virtually identical with the process of concentrating on the *kasiṇas* as described by Buddhaghosa in his *Vissudhimagga* (tr. Bhikkhu Ñāṇamoli, 2nd ed. [Colombo: A. Senage, 1964]): the practitioner first gazes at the *kasiṇa* with eyes open, then with eyes closed forms a mental image. When this mental image can be formed identically to the physical *kasiṇa*, "then the learning sign is said to have been produced." (p. 130) At this point it is no longer necessary for the practitioner to sit gazing at the *kasiṇa*. Buddhaghosa then goes on to describe the shift from the "learning sign" to the "counterpart sign." The counterpart sign "appears as if breaking out from the learning sign, and a hundred times, a thousand times more purified, like a looking-glass disk drawn from its case, like a mother-of-pearl dish well washed, like the moon's disk coming out from behind a cloud, like cranes against a thunder cloud." (Ibid.) The similarity of Buddhaghosa's description of the counterpart sign and the development of the visualization of Sukhāvatī as given by the *Visualization Sutra* seems to suggest not only a common "technology" of visualization, but also a common experiential consequence.

10. See Ryukoku translation, 28, n. 1 for a discussion of the confusion surrounding this term in the Chinese.

11. According to Monier-Williams, one *koṭi* is ten million. See Monier Monier-Williams, *A Sanskrit-English Dictionary*, (Oxford: Oxford University Press, 1899; reprinted photographically in Japan, Tokyo: Oxford University Press, Tokyo, 1982), s.v. "koṭi."

12. One *yojana* is about nine English miles. Ibid., s.v. "yojana."

THE VISIONS OF VAIDEHĪ

13. This pattern—land, Buddha, attendants—appears to be consistent in the Pure Land visualization literature. See for example, my discussion of the *Ching tu lun* attributed to Vasubandhu, "The Five Contemplative Gates of Vasubandhu's *Rebirth Treatise* as a Ritualized Visualization Practice," in *The Pure Land Tradition: History and Development*, 233–66.

14. Ryukoku translation, 36, n. 1.

15. Here we find a theme, having Buddhas appear before the practitioner, which links the *Visualization Sutra* with the *Pratyutpanna-Samādhi-Sūtra* (Paul Harrison, trans., *The Samādhi of Direct Enounter with the Buddhas of the Present*. Studia Philologica Buddhica Monograph Series, no. 5 (Tokyo: The International Institute for Buddhist Studies, 1990), 49–53. See also, Paul M. Harrison, "Buddhānusmṛti in the *Pratyutpanna-Buddha-Saṃmukhāvsthita-Samādhi-Sūtra*," *Journal of Indian Philosophy*, 6 (1978): 35–57; and Paul Harrison, "Commemoration and Identification in *Buddānusmṛti*," 215–38.

16. The lecture was published as "Zur Psychologie östlicher Meditation," *Symbolik des Geistes* (Zurich: Rascher, 1948). "The Psychology of Eastern Meditation," tr. R. F. C. Hull, in C. G. Jung, *Psychology of Religion: West and East*, Collected Works of C. G. Jung, vol. 11, Bollingen Series, no. 20 (Princeton: Princeton University Press, 1958), 558–75.

17. Ryukyo Fujimoto, "Critical Notes on Jung's 'On the Psychology of Eastern Meditation'" (1958), reprinted as Appendix 2 in Ryukyo Fujimoto, *An Outline of the Triple Sūtra of Shin Buddhism*, vol. 2: *The Sūtra of Meditation on the Eternal Buddha* (Kyoto: Hyyaka-en Press, 1960), 154–8.

18. Harold Coward, "Jung's Commentary on the *Amitāyur Dhyāna Sūtra*," in Daniel J. Meckel and Robert L. Moore, eds., *Self and Liberation: The Jung/Buddhism Dialogue* (New York: Paulist Press, 1992), 247–60. Coward's essay appears to derive almost entirely and uncritically from two of Fujimoto's essays: "Critical Notes" (*supra*, n. 9) and "A Note on Jung's Psychology" (1957), reprinted as Appendix 1 in Fujimoto, *An Outline of the Triple Sūtra*, 147–53. Fujimoto's second essay is an attempt to draw out the parallels between Jung's psychological concepts and those of Yogācāra, and does not deal with the *Visualization Sutra*. Giving no justification, Coward identifies the

Visualization Sutra as a Yogācāra text (p. 248), perhaps not realizing that Fujimoto's two essays are separate pieces. Coward then goes on to interpret the sutra as if it were a Yogācāra text, discussing concepts such as *bodhicitta* and *ālayavijñāna*, which either do not appear or do not play a significant role in the sutra (while there is, for example, passing reference to bodhicitta, this is an idea found throughout the Mahāyāna, and can hardly serve to establish the *Visualization Sutra* as a Yogācāra text). The relation between proto-Pure Land Buddhism in India and Yogācāra is both complicated and contentious, and still far from settled.

19. As a convention I will indicate the concept of *self* as used by Jung and others in italics. In this usage, the *self* is the totality of the psychic reality and is distinguished from the ego. At the same time the *self* is not the atman which is denied in Buddhist thought. This latter is, of course, the idea of a permanent, eternal, absolute, unchanging essence of either persons or things. Where the *self* is a psychological concept, the atman is a metaphysical concept.

20. Ryukoku translation, 38, n. 1, and 41, n. 4.

21. C.G. Jung, "Psychology and Religion," in *Psychology and Religion: West and East*, Bollingen Series, no. 20, Collected Works of C.G. Jung, vol. 11, tr. R.F.C. Hull. 2nd ed. (Princeton, N.J.: Princeton University Press, 1969), 95 (§156). Also published as, Carl Gustav Jung, Psychology and Religion (New Haven: Yale University Press, 1938), 105.

22. Ibid., 106.

23. C. G. Jung, "The Spirit Mercurius," in *Alchemical Studies*, Bollingen Series, no. 20, Collected Works of C. G. Jung, vol. 13, tr. R. F. C. Hull. (Princeton: Princeton University Press, 1967), 200–1 (§ 248). Note that the five stages are presented as a developmental process. The implicit value judgment, while relevant to the context of Jungian therapy, is inappropriate for the comparative study of religions *per se*. Clearly Jung's text is itself subject to further postcolonial analysis, but that is beyond the scope of this essay.

24. Stephan Beyer, "Notes on the Vision Quest in Early Mahāyāna," in Lewis Lancaster, ed., *Prajñāparamitā and Related Systems: Studies in Honour of Edward Conze*, Berkeley Buddhist Studies Series, no. 1 (Berkeley: Berkeley Buddhist Studies Series, 1977), 337.

THE VISIONS OF VAIDEHĪ

25. Ibid., 333.

26. This qualification of Jung's view of the process is called for in part because in the Indian religious milieu, although there was a small materialist and skeptic movement, it never had the kind of prominence it had in the nineteenth and twentieth century Euro-American culture. Hence, the idea that one necessarily progresses through the fourth stage as it is described by Jung becomes questionable.

27. Michael Fordham, "The self in Jung's works," in Michael Fordham *Explorations into the Self* (1985; reprint, London: Society of Analytical Psychology, Karnac Books, 1994), 17–8.

28. C.G. Jung, "Commentary on 'The Secret of the Golden Flower'," in *Alchemical Studies*, Bollingen Series, no. 20, Collected Works of C.G. Jung, vol. 13, tr. R.F.C. Hull. (Princeton, N.J.: Princeton University Press, 1967), 45 (ß67).

29. Edward F. Edinger, *Ego and Archetype: Individuation and the Religious Function of the Psyche* (1972; reprint, Boston: Shambhala Publications, 1992), 6.

30. Ibid.

31. Fordham, 18.

32. C. G. Jung, *Aion: Researches into the Phenomenology of the Self.* 2nd ed., tr. R.F.C. Hull. Bollingen Series, no. 20, Collected Works of C. G. Jung, vol. 9, part II (Princeton, N.J.: Princeton University Press, 1968), 40 (§ 73).

33. Ibid.

34. The introduction to the Ryukoku translation, for example, asserts "that these are different names for the same buddha." (p. xix.) What exactly this means, however, is unclear. If this claim is intended as an historical one concerning the Indian origins of the East Asian cult of Ami-t'o/Amida, in whom the two names are clearly conflated, this seems to me to still need to be established. Our knowledge of medieval Indian Buddhism is still comparatively incomplete. It would need to be demonstrated, if at all possible, that there was a single cult directed toward one Buddha who was consciously understood as having two names. The fact that the *Larger* and *Smaller Sukhāvatī Sutras* concern

themselves with Amitābha, while the *Visualization Sutra* is concerned with Amitāyus would seem to point to the contrary.

35. Hisao Inagaki, *A Dictionary of Japanese Buddhist Terms Based on References in Japanese Literature,* (Kyoto: Nagata bunshōdō, 1984), s.v. "Hōjin."

36. Ibid., s.v. "Ōjin."

37. Ibid., s.v. "Hosshin."

38. Cf. Ruben Habito, *Originary Enlightenment: Tendai Hogaku Doctrine and Japanese Buddhism*, Studia Philologica Buddhica, Occasional Paper Series 11 (Tokyo: International Institute of Buddhist Studies, 1996).

39. See Richard Payne, "Realizing Inherent Enlightenment: Ritual and Self-Transformation in Shingon Buddhism" in Michael B. Aune and Valerie DeMarinis, eds., *Religious and Social Ritual: Interdisciplinary Explorations* (Albany, N.Y.: State University of New York Press, 1996), 71–104

40. Ryukoku translation, 41, n. 4.

41. Ryukoku translation, 38, n. 2.

42. C. G. Jung, "The Visions of Zosimos," in *Alchemical Studies*. Bollingen Series, no. 20. Collected Works of C. G. Jung, vol. 13 (Princeton, N.J.: Princeton University Press, 1967), 101 (§ 133).

43. Ibid. (§ 134).

44. Edward F. Edinger, *Ego and Archetype: Individuation and the Religious Function of the Psyche* (1972, Boston: Shambhala Publications, 1992), 265. Cf. also, Edward F. Edinger, *Anatomy of the Psyche: Alchemical Symbolism in Psychotherapy* (La Salle, Illinois: Open Court, 1985), 227–230.

45. Jung's conception of the *self* changed over the many years of his writings. A comprehensive discussion of the resulting complexities is to be found in Michael Fordham's essay "The self in Jung's works" (see *supra*, note 27).

46. C. G. Jung, *Aion*, 224 (§ 351).

47. C. G. Jung. "Psychological Approach to the Trinity." C. G. Jung, *Psychology and Religion: West and East*. 2nd ed., tr. R. F. C. Hull. Bollingen Series, no. 20, Collected Works of C. G. Jung, vol. 11 (Princeton, N.J.: Princeton University Press, 1969), 132 (§ 197).

48. Ibid., 170-2 (§ 251-2).

49. Ryukoku translation, 51 (III.8).

50. Ryukoku translation, supplementary notes, no. 17 in page 131-3. For additional information, see also Heinrich Zimmer, "Der Name Avalokiteśvara." *Zeitschrift für Indologie und Iranistik*, vol. 1 (1922): 73-88.

51. Hisao Inagaki, *A Dictionary of Japanese Buddhist Terms*, s.v. "Daiseishi."

52. Ryukoku translation, supplementary notes, no. 19 in page 133.

53. Beyer, "Vision Quest," 332.

54. Étienne Lamotte, tr., *Traité de la grande vertu de sagesse de Nāgārjuna (Mahāprajñāparmitāśāstra)*, 5 vols. (Louvain: Peeters, 1944-80), IV. 1927, n. 2.

55. Paul Harrison, *The* Samādhi *of Direct Encounter*, xx.

56. The variety of visionary experiences and visualization practices is very great. As used here, visions are spontaneous and unscripted, while visualization practices are not spontaneous and are scripted. Active imagination, as developed in analytic psychology, is not spontaneous and is not scripted.

	spontaneous	scripted
visions	+	−
active imagination	−	−
visualization	−	+

57. Jung makes the same point in relation to the codification of the mandala—he draws a distinction between the mandalas of Buddhist

tradition and the mandalic drawings of his patients on the basis that the latter "express the individual attitude of the patient far more clearly than the Eastern pictures, which have been subjected to a collective and traditional configuration." (C.G. Jung, "Concerning Mandala Symbolism," in *The Archetypes and the Collective Unconscious*, Bollingen Series, no. 20, Collected Works of C.G. Jung, vol. 9. I, tr. R.F.C. Hull. 2nd ed. [Princeton, N.J.: Princeton University Press, 1968], 362 [§647]). The same distinction could well be drawn between visualization practices which "have been subjected to a collective and traditional configuration" and both spontaneous visions and active imagination.

58. Fordham, 19.

59. Compare for example the personal character of the material presented by Barbara Hannah in her *Encounters with the Soul: Active Imagination as Developed by C.G. Jung* (Santa Monica, Calif.: Sigo Press, 1981).

60. Huntington, "Rebirth in Amitābha's Sukhāvatī," 79.

61. Ibid., 47.

62. Ryukoku translation, 19 (I. 14).

63. Ibid. 11 (I. 8).

64. Ibid., 13 (I. 10).

65. Ibid., 17 (I. 13).

66. Ibid., 19 (I. 14).

67. Beyer, "Vision Quest," 331.

Existentializing and Radicalizing Shinran's Vision by Repositioning It at the Center of Mahayana Tradition

Gregory G. GIBBS

Shinran's vision of the Way of nembutsu, walking the path to enlightenment by saying Amida Buddha's Name, has been institutionalized at the expense of formalizing and taming it. The Myōkōnin ideal is one example of how Jōdo Shinshū Buddhism (the true essence of the Pure Land Way) has been reduced to a charming and harmless teaching which can be easily tolerated by the watchdogs of authority. Other authors have attempted to reduce Shinran's teaching to an unremarkable restatement of Mahayana Buddhist ideology. This approach is insensitive to the unique power of Shinran's realization and sharing of Shinjin, the encompassing heart and mind of true entrusting. The uniqueness of Shinran's teaching regarding liberation via the nembutsu is best appreciated by repositioning it centrally within the Larger Vehicle of Buddhist teaching (Mahayana). This requires a view of what Mahayana fundamentally is. In the first section below, I briefly outline what I find fundamental Buddhism to be.

Shinran recognized that Shinjin is the foundation of a new center of identity within the Vow Mind of the Buddha of Infinite Light and Endless Life (Amida/Amitābha/Amitāyus). The radical and existential nature of this view depends upon the realizability of Shinjin. However unique Shinran's discernment of the essence of the Pure Land Way may be, it lacks importance if the receipt of Shinjin is rare. If Shinjin were an advanced attainment available to only a few, then the Pure Land Way would fail to keep its promise of salvation for ordinary people. Conservative Shinshū-gaku (the sectarian study of Jōdo Shinshū as a separate field from Buddhist studies) has resulted in the mistaken notion that Shinjin is rare—the attitude that "those who say they have Shinjin don't have it, and those who know they have received it don't say so."

In the next section I discuss my resolution of the problem of Shinjin being made to appear to be a rare occurrence. The realization of Shinjin takes place in the briefest instant of time. It leaves traces in the memory and begins a long and slow process of transformation of the person. The immediate and irreversible transformation is the discovery of one's identity within the Vow Mind of Amida Buddha. Shinran's description of the realization of Shinjin is that one "hears the Vow." That is, one recognizes one's own voicing of "Namo Amida Butsu" or some cognate, the nembutsu, as the activity of Amida Buddha to liberate oneself and others. Such an instantaneous discernment of the true significance of voicing Amida Buddha's name is often experienced and usually remembered. Everyone who has had this moment of recognizing the nembutsu as the compassionate activity of Amida Buddha has established a new center of personal identity within that activity and is a person of Shinjin.

The instantaneity of the first and subsequent thought-moments of Shinjin means that one cannot plan and act from one's new and vast center of identity within the activity of Universal Liberation. Nonetheless, these moments of Shinjin, these experiences of discerning the nembutsu as the active presence of the depths of Wisdom-Compassion, are guideposts for future living. Thus the person of Shinjin has the self-confidence to act in the world in hopes of participating in the liberation of all beings. Subsequent single thought-moments of Shinjin will display again and again that our actions are inadequate and that our understanding is imperfect. Nonetheless, the benchmark, the touchstone of truth and genuineness provided by the moments of hearing the Liberating Activity *as* the nembutsu, gives hope and self-confidence which manifests itself in action in the world. This action in the world by persons who have experienced the instant of meeting the Buddha via his Name will include action for social change. As an example I will present a plea for human rights based on the one thought-moment of Shinjin. In essence, the person who encounters the Vow of Amida as "namanda" or some other form of nembutsu has left behind saying the nembutsu as a means to an end. The nembutsu is neither a means to attain enlightenment nor an expression of gratitude for the person of Shinjin. Viewed externally, it may have that significance, but for the person of Shinjin, nembutsu is the presence of the depths of Wisdom-Compassion in his or her life. Nembutsu has been stripped of any instrumentality, any attempt to use it as a means to an end. Once the parallel is suggested to a person of Shinjin, he or she will affirm and support the struggle for human rights, the commitment to remove instrumentality from relations between persons, the insistence that persons are ends in themselves and not means to be used for external objectives.

The affirmation of human rights as paralleling the freeing of the nembutsu from some instrumentality such as attaining enlightenment or expressing gratitude will close this essay. I will clarify my assertions in the following sections. I believe those who have encountered the Activity of Universal Liberation (*honganriki*) in and through the saying of Amida Buddha's Name, aloud or in silent reflection, will agree with me in substance. Those who take the nembutsu deeply to heart and still disagree will no doubt show me errors in this paper. I have no concern for orthodoxy in the eyes of conservative Shinshū gaku. The orthodoxy of the various Jōdo Shinshū institutions is answerable to the actual, living experience of Shinjin.

FUNDAMENTAL BUDDHISM

Various attempts have been made to say what all Buddhism must be. They all suffer from an excessive focus on doctrine. There is also a sectarian slant involved in most cases. All schools of living Buddhism cannot be classified under the medieval Four Truths or the scholastic Eightfold Path. Such categories cannot include all streams of Buddhist tradition and lead to a mechanical approach when an attempt at universal application is made.

A more dynamic scholastic group of categories is the Three Learnings—conduct, concentration and wisdom. This system has more flexibility leaving more room for interpretation, it does not become mechanical or procrustean when the attempt is made to apply it existentially, unlike the Eightfold Path. However, it was explicitly rejected by Hōnen, Shinran and Dōgen. Thus two-thirds of Japanese Buddhism would have been non-Buddhist for the past eight hundred years if the Three Learnings were taken as definitive of Buddhism.[1] The usual understanding of the Three Learnings, viz., that concentration conditions and leads to wisdom, was also rejected by the great Korean Sŏn visionary monk Chinul.

Another group of three categories which is similarly flexible but more inclusive than the Three Learnings is the standard of Teaching, Practice and Realization. These three categories are often understood as organizing the three sorts of components which any school of Buddhism must have. I believe that if we understand practice and realization more generally than is usually done, we can see these categories as applicable to and illuminative of the dynamic within all schools of Buddhism.[2] These three dimensions of Buddhist path-traveling can especially help in bringing to light the actual life of nembutsu as it was embodied and elaborated by Shinran Shōnin.

TEACHING, PRACTICE AND REALIZATION: DYNAMICS OF THE PATH

Teaching, Practice and Realization are the dynamic structure which can be seen in all Buddhist living. There is a teaching or set of teachings which are put into practice and taken to heart. This existentializing of the teaching leads to moments of realization. "Realization" is a term which has been used as a synonym for the highest transformation, enlightenment, or more often for one of a variety of progressive discernments such as a stage in the ten bodhisattva *bhumis*.[3] I am relying on the implication of the term in English—to realize that something is true. In the most general sense of realization, it always has three characteristics: (a) it happens in a discrete moment of experience from which it can be distinguished; (b) it has such emotive force that it cannot be ignored and therefore serves to motivate the person; and (c) it is a recognition of a truth which is determined upon subsequent investigation to be veridical.

For a Buddhist, realization is realization of the truth of the Buddhist teaching. Which aspect of the teaching is not the most important concern. To realize the truth of any aspect of Buddhist teaching in a thoroughgoing manner is to attain to awakening. To realize the deep meaning of any Buddhist teaching will involve recognizing the non-duality of all persons, places and things. In other words, if we recount the philosophical implication of what we have realized it will always involve non-duality. For the path of nembutsu the key matter is to realize that the verbal form, e.g., "Namo Amida Butsu"—I rely on the Awakened Source of Infinite Light and Endless Life—is the active presence of Amida Buddha. To be struck forcefully by this fact is to receive Shinjin, the encompassing mind of true entrusting. Thus, for the Pure Land Buddhist, the teaching which must be taken deeply to heart is the sacred story that Amida Buddha has embodied his Wisdom-Compassion in the calling of his Name which he has turned over to us.

Practice is, in its most general sense, taking the teaching to heart. This may involve strenuous endeavor as in the visualization procedures of Tendai or as in koan reflection in a context of Great Doubt as recommended by modern Rinzai Zen. Practice can also be the natural turning over of "Namo Amida Butsu" from time to time in one's heart and mind. No serious exertion is involved in this activity. Thus, in translating the popular title of Shinran's masterwork, D. T. Suzuki translated "Gyō"—usually rendered "practice"—as "living." We must take the teaching to heart and make it part of, and ideally central to, our daily living. This is "Gyō/practice" in its most general and crucial sense.

These three dimensions of the Buddha Way, often called the three pillars, display the dynamics of walking the path to enlightenment. Taking the teaching to heart, i.e., in a broad sense practicing it, leads to moments of realization. These moments in which we are struck forcefully by the truth of the teaching motivate us to continue studying it, taking it to heart, and practicing it. This is the essence of what Buddhism is. The attempt to identify some doctrinal essence of all schools of Buddhism has failed again and again. My own understanding of the minimal characteristic of a teaching which would be Buddhist is that it reveals the non-duality of all persons, places and events. That is, everything is mutually identical with everything else *just as it is*. This is a difficult concept. But it is the essence of discovering the center of one's identity in Amida Buddha's compassionate activity. Experientially it can simply be to hear "Namo Amida Butsu" as the Buddha calling his assurance to you through your own voice. A sophisticated understanding of the philosophical implications of this experience is not of the essence. Let me now turn to the matter of having a new center of one's identity established by the receipt of Shinjin.

SHINJIN: THE ENCOMPASSING HEART AND MIND OF TRUE ENTRUSTING

In speaking of the teaching component to the three pillars of Buddhist living (Teaching/Practice/Realization), I mentioned that non-duality is always implied. Non-duality involves non-substantiality, impermanence, and no soul. Non-substantiality means that where we discriminate objects there are really processes, specifically, there are complexes of forces. Mahayana, the Larger Vehicle of Buddhist teaching, insists that any complex of forces is ultimately mutually identical with all others. Without affirming non-substantiality, Buddhist philosophy would be an uninspiring pluralism. In relation to Shinjin, the encompassing heart and mind of true entrusting, it is the aspect of no soul which is crucial. The teaching that there is no soul is the logical result of applying the fundamental Buddhist teaching, the constancy of change, to ourselves. No soul means no soul-thing. Just as we find processes underlying things, we find processes underlying the self and not a permanent soul. Since our self is an activity, the activity of unifying subprocesses, it is not fixed and can be transformed. On the path of the nembutsu, our self is transformed by being taken into the Activity of Universal Liberation (*honganriki*).

At the beginning of the nineteenth century, the Jōdo Shinshū philosopher Doshin emphasized that it is the non-fixed character of our selves which allows the transformation which we call Shinjin.[4] In other words, the potential to awaken to enlightenment is predicated upon no soul; or, no soul is Buddha-nature. With the proviso that no soul is not the same thing as no self, my view is the same here, so far as the negative side of the teaching goes. I am also stressing a positive aspect of the transformation of the self. A new center of self is established in the one thought-moment of Shinjin. That new center is in the activity of Amida Buddha to liberate all beings. Amida's heart/mind encompasses our finite self and is the source of true entrusting to the path of saying the nembutsu. My emphasis on the establishment of a new center of identity is somewhat unique. Actually, two models of thought are necessary to illumine this aspect of receiving Shinjin. The first model of thought I have already been using. At the moment of Shinjin, the first time one is struck by the fact that one's voicing of the nembutsu *is* the compassionate activity of Amida, our true identity is centered in the ongoing project of Universal Liberation (*honganriki*). We discover a vast surrounding Self within which our finite self finds its true home and its deep meaning. Shinran compares this transformation of identity to a stream entering into an ocean and becoming of the same essence of that greater reality into which it is absorbed:

When ordinary men, sages, grave sinners, and abusers of the
Dharma are all converted, they are like various waters turned
into one in taste on entering the sea.[5]

Shinran's student Kyōshin is using this sort of model of transformation, a model which highlights universality, when he describes awakening to enlightenment in Amida Buddha's Pure Land:

The statement, "one will realize nirvana," means that when
the heart of the person of true and real Shinjin attains the
fulfilled Buddha Land at the end of his present life, he becomes
one with the light that is the heart of Tathagata, for his reality
is immeasurable life and his activity is inseparable from
immeasurable light.[6]

Besides this sort of model of the transformation of personal identity through the receipt of Shinjin, a model highlighting the aspect of universality, a second model is needed. In order to understand the establishment of a new center of identity we also need a more concrete or personal model. This more conventional model will be quite familiar to most readers—we go to Amida's Pure Land at death, awaken to thoroughgoing enlightenment, and then return to this world to liberate others. According to this model we are distinctive, individual Buddhas after our enlightenment. This second conceptual model, one highlighting individuality, can be seen in many writings by Shinran, but is especially accessible in his oral teachings, for example, in Chapter Six of the *Tannishō*:

If [one] simply abandons self-power and quickly attains
enlightenment in the Pure Land, he will be able to save all
beings with transcendent powers and compassionate means,
whatever karmic suffering they may be sinking into in the six
realms and the four modes of birth, beginning with those with
whom his life is deeply bound.[7]

These two ways of understanding our transformation of identity in receiving Shinjin balance one another and together carry Shinran's vision.

ACTING IN THE WORLD AFTER THE ONE THOUGHT-MOMENT OF SHINJIN

The Problem of Momentariness

The momentariness of the thought-moments of Shinjin, of both the initial moment and of subsequent renewed realizations, means that one cannot plan and act from a basis of Shinjin. Nonetheless, experiencing the active presence of Amida Buddha's Compassion (*honganriki*) as the voicing of his Name (nembutsu) provides a touchstone of truth and genuineness which nurtures hope and conviction in acting in the world.

The Problem of Claiming Shinjin

Another problem which Jōdo Shinshū tradition presents is that it is generally considered presumptuous to claim that one has experienced Shinjin, but unless one has received Shinjin, saying the nembutsu is considered to be of questionable value. I believe that remaining in the context of saying and hearing Amida's Name helps to unravel this problem and to demystify Shinjin.

It is true that there is no objective way of verifying that one has really encountered the Vow (*honganriki*) as one's hearing and saying of, for example, "Namo Amida Butsu." One does know, however, if one has had an experience of realization in the sense we have already discussed. One does know if one has been struck powerfully by the worthiness and reliability of the nembutsu. This sort of experience, not at all uncommon amongst Jōdo Shinshū Buddhists, would seem to fit the criteria of the one thought-moment of Shinjin.

My approach is to abandon talk of Shinjin which is not sensitive to the instantaneous nature of the Shinjin experience. I am one of thousands (millions?) of people alive today who are aware of having experienced the discernment of Amida Buddha's Activity in and through the nembutsu. This experience of the nembutsu as the Activity of Universal Liberation (*honganriki*) transforms one's identity irreversibly. Although one's deepest and truest self has been recognized as centered in the Activity of Universal Liberation, this discernment slips away from one. This is because of the momentariness of realization.

My insistence that this momentary recognition of the nembutsu as Amida Buddha's enacting of his promises is Shinjin will strike some conservative Jōdo Shinshū Buddhists as arrogant. But if the experience of Shinjin is something too exalted to be identified with this quite accessible experience, the whole idea of Jōdo Shinshū Buddhism being a path for common people is invalidated. The context of institutionalized Jōdo Shinshū, the turning of Shinran's teaching into a particular denomination of Buddhism, takes it to be impious if one claims to have had the experience of Shinjin. Applied to oneself this attitude is a false kind of humility. When applied to others, this is mean-spirited resentment: "I've studied Shinran's texts for years [to no avail], and here he/she claims to have experienced Shinjin."

The difficulty of its appearing vain to claim to have experienced Shinjin is resolved by remaining cognizant of the momentary nature of such experiences. Shinjin, the encompassing heart and mind of true entrusting, flashes into our lives like a strobe light which has been set to shine at irregular intervals. I know that my life has been illumined in the past by discovering my true identity in the "body of boundlessness."[8] But I cannot act out of that center. Reflection and acting upon my convictions requires time. In that interval my own prejudices and hidden agendas, in some cases hidden from my own consciousness, will intervene.

This does not mean that Shinjin is irrelevant to wholesome thinking and acting in the world. Although it must contend with numerous conditioning causes, the infusion of light which occurs in the single thought-moments of Shinjin begins a process of renewed living.

EXISTENTIALIZING AND RADICALIZING SHINRAN'S VISION

TWO TRANSFORMATIONS AND
THE NEED TO ACT

The instantaneous transformation in identity which comes with encountering Amida's active compassion, i.e. with Shinjin, does not involve a total change in the nature of the person who has the experience. Lazy priests and complacent scholars insist that since we are accepted *just as we are* by the Wisdom-Compassion of Amida our life continues to be driven by greed, hatred and self-delusion. This is the party line. It is not so much false as it is the case that the implications drawn from it are false. Firstly, it ignores that such moments of inspiration (realizations of Shinjin) give us strength, hope and conviction to act in the world. Secondly, the party line consistently ignores the second sort of transformation. It takes time, but gradually we come to turn away from selfishness and turn toward caring for others. I will quote passages from two separate letters by Shinran which emphasize this second sort of transformation, an ongoing transformation of character:

> There was a time for each of you when you knew nothing of Amida's Vow and did not say the Name of Amida Buddha, but now, guided by the compassionate means of Sakyamuni and Amida, you have begun to hear the Buddha's Vow. Formerly you were drunk with the wine of ignorance and had a taste only for the three poisons of greed, anger and folly, but since you have begun to hear the Buddha's Vow you have gradually awakened from the drunkenness of ignorance, gradually rejected the three poisons, and come to prefer at all times the medicine of Amida Buddha.[9]

Consider also the following from a letter to a disciple in Kantō:

> Signs of long years of saying the nembutsu and aspiring for birth can be seen in the change in the heart which had been bad and in the deep warmth for friends and fellow-practicers . . . .[10]

277

Both types of transformation of identity are important to the need to act in the world. One has the confidence and hopefulness needed as the result of those enlivening experiences of realization which irreversibly establish a new center of identity in the Activity of Universal Liberation (*honganriki*). Also, the slow but genuine process of gentling one's character nurtures a wholesome will to do good without self-righteousness or the need to vilify those who oppose one's objectives.

LESSONS LEARNED ON THE WAY: BEYOND INSTRUMENTALITY

The single thought-moments of hearing the nembutsu as the Vow provide a sense of spaciousness in one's life. It is as if a burden had been lifted off of you. If you remove a heavy backpack three-quarters of the way through a long hike, you feel invigorated. There is still a long way to go of course, but the removal of the weight has an effect of inspiring you beyond the degree to which the difficulty of the task has been lessened. Similarly, encountering Amida Buddha's Compassion as one's own utterance of his Name provides powerful inspiration to act in the world, including the realms of political and social action. Specific guidance as to how to act is usually considered to be outside the domain of the nembutsu path.

In truth, however, we can learn about how to act in the larger social context by paying close attention to our experience of saying and hearing "Namo Amida Butsu" (and cognates). A key aspect of discerning the worthiness and reliability of the nembutsu is that it becomes freed from any sort of instrumentality. Jōdo Shinshū tradition is quite clear on Shinran's freeing of the utterance of Amida's Name from instrumental usages such as purifying one's mind or petitioning the Buddha for help. Recognizing what the nembutsu is, viz. the active presence of the Buddha in one's life, we are no longer concerned to use it for purposes of purification or petition. We would also avoid using the nembutsu as a means to express gratitude. Of course, a feeling of gratitude often ensues in the moments just following the instant of Shinjin's realization. But to describe the situation as the utterance of the nembutsu being for the purpose of expressing gratitude is very problematic. Freeing the true speech act of uttering the nembutsu from all tendencies to use it as a means to some end is a crucial aspect of the realization of Shinjin.[11]

In an intriguing book on tea ceremony Rev. Dennis Hirota has highlighted the rejection of instrumentality as the crucial point of connection between Japanese cultural arts and Buddhist religiosity:

> For students familiar with Japanese Buddhist traditions, the phrase "*just* heat the water and prepare tea" resonates with key expressions in Buddhist teachings such as "just say the Name of Amida Buddha" (Hōnen, Shinran) and "just sit" in Zazen (Dōgen). "Just" here implies acts free of all instrumentality and worldly distraction.[12]

For myself this is also a point of contact with an affirmation of human rights. As I turn to my saying of "Namo Amida Butsu" I see its utter lack of instrumentality. The worthiness of the nembutsu leads me to treat it as an end in itself and not as a means to accomplish some end extrinsic to it.

HUMAN RIGHTS FROM THE PERSPECTIVE OF THE NEMBUTSU

As I reflect on my saying of Amida's Name and look at the world in which I am living, I am led to make the following statement:

As a Jōdo Shinshū Buddhist I affirm the intrinsic worthiness of all persons. My experience of the intrinsic value of the nembutsu has led me to reject any approach to the saying of Amida's Name which treats it as a means to an end. Having rejected instrumental approaches to the nembutsu such as utterance for purposes of petitioning the Buddha, purifying the mind, or expressing gratitude, I am moved to widen the scope of my reverence. The same intrinsic worthiness which I have discovered to pertain to the nembutsu also pertains to persons. All persons are either nembutsu utterers, future sayers of Amida's Name, or individuals who will awaken to enlightenment on some other path. None can be treated as expendable means to ends, political, religious or otherwise. I am also concerned with the welfare of animals and of plant life. In experience, however, it is persons who are clearly within this circle of reverence which the saying of Amida's Name generates in my life. As a Jōdo Shinshū Buddhist I will oppose denying any person life, liberty, dignity or the pursuit of happiness. Pursuing happiness as they understand it will one day lead all persons to the pursuit of enlightenment, the only true freedom and happiness.

CONCLUSION

I have claimed that Shinran's teaching can be existentialized and radicalized by repositioning it centrally within Mahayana tradition. To facilitate this process I have explained the essence of Mahayana Buddhism as the dynamic of Teaching, Practice and Realization. Admittedly there is no distinctively Buddhist doctrine which is affirmed by all schools of Buddhism. This dynamism—teaching is taken to heart, producing startling recognition of its truth; teaching is appealed to with renewed conviction and taken to heart with even greater commitment, leading to new moments of realization—is present in all streams of Buddhist tradition. Also, any genuinely Buddhist teaching will deny duality and affirm some sort of unity-within-difference which pertains to all persons, places and events just as they are.

The key event in walking the path of the nembutsu under the guidance of Shinran's teaching is the one thought-moment of Shinjin. Although it is best to treat "Shinjin" as an untranslated technical term,

EXISTENTIALIZING AND RADICALIZING SHINRAN'S VISION

I have used the phrase "the encompassing heart and mind of true entrusting" to convey what Shinjin is. I have suggested that two different models are necessary to understand the transformation of identity which occurs with the experience of Shinjin. One model consists in our being one with Infinite Light and Endless Life when we are born in Amida's Land in the next life. The other model involves picturing ourselves as individual awakened persons (Buddhas) who return to lead others to liberation after awakening in Amida's Land. As these ways of thinking and imagining model a fulfillment in the next life which is *decisively settled at the moment we experience Shinjin*, I have claimed that an expanded identity becomes a fact in this life although the full fruits of this accomplishment are not ours until the next life.

I have proposed focusing on the momentariness of the realization of Shinjin as a way of unraveling the problem of affirming that we have experienced Shinjin without seeming arrogant. I am also distinguishing two sorts of transformation which occur with the one thought-moment of being taken into the encompassing heart and mind of true entrusting. One transformation of personal identity is established immediately—the vast encompassing reality of Wisdom-Compassion is our true center of self from that moment onward. The second sort of personal transformation is the gradual turning toward kindness and concern for others, particularly a concern for fellow travelers of the nembutsu path.

I have shared my personal conviction that, as a Jōdo Shinshū Buddhist, I must affirm human rights. I have explained how leaving behind an instrumental approach to the nembutsu provides inspiration to deny that persons may be treated instrumentally, as means to accomplishing ends. Persons are intrinsically valuable, are ends in themselves.

Shinran's teaching, what is called Jōdo Shinshū Buddhism, is radicalized in rejecting any form of instrumentality. My rejection of the notion that the nembutsu can be taken as an expression of gratitude (viz. as a means to the end of showing our appreciation of

Amida's compassionate acting) will be seen as radical by some. In its rejection of an aspect of the party line it might be an example of how Shinran's teaching is radicalized by holding to the central dynamic of the Buddha Way. That is to say, it is because we realize the intrinsic worthiness of saying, e.g., "Namo Amida Butsu" that we reassess the teaching and take it to heart while rejecting the "expression of gratitude" ideology. This centering on the Buddhist dynamic of Teaching-Practice-Realization radicalizes and existentializes our appropriation of Shinran's teaching.

On the basis of existentializing Shinran's teaching I have affirmed that I have experienced the one thought-moment of Shinjin and have asserted that thousands, perhaps millions, of other persons in the Pure Land stream of Buddhist tradition have as well. This will be seen by some as a radical departure from the institutionalized humility of Jōdo Shinshū denominations' approved ways of thinking. If others take the nembutsu teaching to heart and say the Name of Amida Buddha they too will have (in fact, have had) the experience of the one thought-moment of Shinjin. I believe that it is the institutionalized and enforced humility of conservative Shinshū-gaku which has deluded many into undervaluing the realization to which they have already come.

The various Jōdo Shinshū institutions and their notions of orthodoxy are answerable to the living experience of Shinjin. My reflections here are also answerable to the living experience of Shinjin. I will look forward to having my notions corrected, or perhaps expanded upon, by others on the basis of their realizations of the intrinsic worthiness of "Namo Amida Butsu."

NOTES

1. For a more succinct presentation of this point see Greg Gibbs, "Buddhist Realization: Accept No Substitutes," cover story of *Butsumon* 8 (Spring 1991) [Publication of Buddhist Bookstore, Buddhist Churches of America.]

2. The translation committee of the Shinshu Translation Series has argued that the traditional structure of Teaching, Practice and Realization is more descriptive of Shinran's approach than the four aspect Teaching, Practice, Faith and Realization structure which is reflected in the popular designation for his masterwork. See the "Introduction" to *Passages on the Pure Land Way*, Shin Buddhism Translation Series, Yoshifumi Ueda, general editor (Kyoto: Hongwanji International Center, 1982), 9–26.

3. For a brief explanation of the ten stages of a Bodhisattva's deepening realization, see Garma C. C. Chang, *The Buddhist Teaching of Totality* (University Park, Pa.: Pennsylvania State University Press, 1974), 28–48.

4. For a brief summary of Dōshin's view that Buddha-nature is predicated upon the teaching of no self (sic) see "Outline of Jodo Shinshu" in *Shinshu Seiten* (San Francisco: Buddhist Churches of America, 1978), 436–437.

5. *Shinshu Seiten*, 152.

6. *Letters of Shinran*, Shin Buddhism Translation Series, Yoshihumi Ueda, general editor (Kyoto: Hongwanji International Center, 1978), 44.

7. Dennis Hirota, *Tannishō: A Primer*, with a forward by Tokunaga Michio (Kyoto: Ryukoku University, 1982).

8. My view is that with the first thought-moment of Shinjin a new identity is established in a vast and encompassing self. In this life, the person who has encountered the Name as the Vow is aware of residing within that vast new identity only in moments of Shinjin. In the next life our self *is* this vastness. The sutra teaches that in the Pure Land "all receive the body of naturalness (*jinen*) or of nonexistence, the body of boundlessness." quoted in *Passages on the Pure Land Way*, 36. For a further explanation of Shinjin as hearing the Name *as* the Vow please see Gregory Gibbs, "The Problematics of Realization as a Basis for Dialogue in Shinshū and Zen," *Pacific World*, n.s. 9 (1993): 11–23.

9. *Letters of Shinran*, 60.

10. Ibid., 58.

11. On the matter of the nembutsu as true language, see Dennis Hirota, "Shinran's View of Language: A Buddhist Hermeneutics of Faith," Parts 1, 2, in *The Eastern Buddhist*, n.s. 26, no. 1–2, (Spring, Autumn 1993): 50–93, 91–130. For an analysis of the nembutsu as a sacramental speech act, see Rev. Gregory Gibbs, "Vocal Nembutsu as a Sacramental Speech Act," *Wheel of Dharma* (July 1995) [Publication of Buddhist Churches of America.]

12. Dennis Hirota, *Wind in the Pines, Classic Writings of the Way of Tea as a Buddhist Path* (Freemont, Calif., Asian Humanities Press, 1995), 22.

The Essence of Shinran's Teaching: Understanding to Praxis

Shigeki J. SUGIYAMA

Merely to repeat past formulations is to abjure the theological task and to guarantee a theology that is anachronistic and thereby void of living meaning; for the task of theology is to express the message in contemporary form, in terms relevant and meaningful in its own time and place.[1]

—*Langdon Gilkey*—

I am neither a scholar nor a cleric. Nevertheless, while serving as an officer of the National Board of the Buddhist Churches of America (of the Jōdo Shinshū Honpa Hongwanji-ha) several years ago, I suggested that more instructional materials on *Jōdo Shinshū* written in English *by* Americans *for* Americans are needed if the teaching of Shinran Shonin is to be propagated successfully beyond, let alone sustained within, the confines of the diminishing Japanese American community. My concern was, and still is, that materials written with a traditional Japanese approach and a Japanese cultural context are inadequate for conveying Shinran's thoughts meaningfully to Americans, including Sanseis and Yonseis (third and fourth generation Japanese Americans).

Most of Shinran's significant works, including his *Kyōgyōshinshō*, his *Sanjō wasan*, collections of his letters and his commentaries (*"Notes"*) on the writings of others, have been translated and published in English. Nevertheless, much of the writing that explains Shinran's teaching merely reiterates a church doctrine that serves largely to perpetuate feudal tradition. While some of these writings give the appearance of addressing contemporary lay concerns, they simply regurgitate old ideas dressed in contemporary garb. That is, there is little reexamination or reinterpretation of Shinran's ideas to seek out meaning that is pertinent to our contemporary situation and to pragmatic as well as philosophical concerns. Thus, what is lacking from the materials available for study and use are ideas and guidance on how one might convey Shinran's teaching to others who know little or nothing of his teaching *in a way that is believable and meaningful,* particularly as it may affect us in our everyday lives *in this world at this time.*

The difficulty of finding new or different approaches to conveying Shinran's soteriological thoughts to parishioners may stem in part from an overly narrow and rigid depiction of the concept of Other-power (*tariki*) versus self-power (*jiriki*) that gives the impression that personal salvation can be achieved only by relying totally on a *god-like being* and doing absolutely nothing other than *reciting* the nembutsu, and that the faith-like *shinjin* is some *thing* to be grasped and held in order to be embraced by Amida, the *savior-being*. Moreover, this deification and reification results in obscuring what I believe to be the meaning of "Oneness," the ultimate ground for Shinran's soteriology.

This paper, then, is an attempt to consider *de novo* Shinran's teaching, thoughts and ideas as expressed in his *wasan*, letters and "notes" from the last years of his long life and to outline an approach that may explain Shinran's teaching in a way that it can be understood and more readily accepted on the basis of reason and understanding rather than on the basis of "blind faith" and tradition. Thus, this is not an attempt to justify Shinran's teaching on the basis of scripture or writings of other Pure Land masters, but an attempt to set forth what I believe is the essence of Shinran's thoughts by citing his own words. And while some philosophical issues of contemporary relevance may be implicated, they may be mentioned only in passing—to suggest areas that may be worthy of further consideration and study.

SHINRAN'S THOUGHTS ON "GOOD" AND "EVIL"

People embrace religion for numerous reasons. Those who turn to religion volitionally may be seeking solace or help in dealing with problems in their personal lives; spiritual guidance for ordering their lives; moral and ethical guidance; or all and more of these reasons.[2] And while the interests and needs of each individual differ, it is generally expected in America that churches and temples give guidance on right or moral conduct, what one *ought* to do, how one should behave to be a "good" person.[3] Thus, while it is expected that ministers, regardless of religious tradition, give pastoral-type care and guidance to their parishioners and Sangha members, there does not appear to be a similar expectation of temple *jūshoku* in Japan, whose principal function is often seen by the Japanese to be solely that of conducting funeral and memorial services for the dead. Even in America, it is not uncommon for seekers to be told that Jōdo Shinshū is a *chōmon no shukyō*, a religion in which one simply "listens to sermons."[4] It is thus somewhat disconcerting for an American seeker to read or hear quoted from the *Tannishō*, a text attributed to Yuiembō, a follower of Shinran Shonin:

> The Master [Shinran] said, "I know absolutely nothing about good and evil! If I were to know good so thoroughly that the Tathāgata would recognize it in His mind as good, then I could say I know good. Were I able to know evil so thoroughly that the Tathāgata would recognize it as evil, then I could say I know evil. We are ordinary men possessed of evil passions and our world is the burning house of transiency; hence, all things are entirely empty and nonsense and not true. The Nembutsu alone is true."[5]

This quotation might lead one to conclude that *if* Shinran himself could not distinguish between good and evil, how can *I* be expected to do so, let alone turn to Shinran for moral guidance. If we are indeed "evil" and corrupted, why is there a need to be concerned about being "good" or "evil" when all one needs to do is recite the nembutsu? Such ideas may give rise to antinomian tendencies such as those Shinran himself had to deal with among his followers in his own time.

In fact, Shinran's own writings show clearly that he knew well what constitutes evil. In his *Notes* on Seikaku's tract, *Essentials of Faith Alone (Yuishinshō)*,[6] Shinran explains that "those who break precepts" refers to those who receive the precepts for monks or laymen but break and abandon them, and those whose "evil karma is profound" refers to "evil people who have committed the *ten transgressions* or the *five grave offenses*."[7] Seikaku also cites the passages from the *Contemplation Sutra (Kanmuryōjukyō)* in which Śākyamuni Buddha describes to Ānanda and Queen Vaidehī "the lowest rank of the lowest grade of beings" as those "who commit such evil acts as the five grave offenses and the ten transgressions and are burdened with various kinds of evil."[8] Shinran notes that "this is the teaching which urges the person guilty of *five grave offenses and ten transgressions* and of engaging in defiled expositions of the dharma . . . [to say the Name.]" Shinran also adds that "thinking" and "voicing" (i.e., saying the Name) have the same meaning; no voicing exists separate from thinking, and no thinking separate from voicing.[9]

Shinran's use of the terms "five grave offenses and ten transgressions" (*gogyaku jūaku*) without explanation indicates that he knew well what constituted evil. That he did not define the terms also suggests that he expected his readers to know what those evils are. In the early tradition, the five grave offenses were: 1) killing one's mother; 2) killing one's father; 3) killing an arhat; 4) causing blood to flow from the body of a Buddha; 5) disrupting the harmony of the assembly of monks.[10] And the "ten transgressions" are: 1) killing (*sesshō*); 2) stealing (*chūtō*); 3) committing adultery (*jain*); 4) telling a lie (*mōgo*); 5) duplicity (*ryōzetsu*); 6) slandering (*akku*); 7) equivocation (*kigo*); 8) greed (*ton'yoku*); 9) wrath (*shin'ni*); and 10) perverted views (*jaken*).[11]

Of the "ten transgressions," the first seven describe wrongful actions that may be committed by individuals, whereas the last three relate more to one's feelings or state of mind. And in his writings, Shinran refers infrequently (if at all) to specific acts of evil, but more often cites "greed," "anger" and "ignorance" as the fundamental causes of our "evil" *being*—in keeping with the cause of suffering expounded by Śākyamuni Buddha.

In the light of the foregoing, Shinran explains in his *Notes on Once-calling and Many-calling (Ichinen-tanen mon'i)*[12] that "foolish being" (*bombu*) refers to "none other than ourselves ... [because] we are full of ignorance and blind passion. Our desires are countless, and anger, wrath, jealousy, and envy are overwhelming, arising without pause; to the very last moment of life they do not cease, or disappear, or exhaust themselves."[13] While we *bombu* tend to look to others to find evil, upon looking into his own heart and soul, Shinran reminded us that the cause of evil is to be found within ourselves. Shinran's advice here may remind us of the Walt Kelly cartoon in which Pogo remarks: "We have met the enemy and they is us!"

With respect to the "good," Shinran does not encourage *doing* good simply for the sake of "doing good." Thus, his writings do not tell us about doing particular kinds of good deeds or describe what might be good deeds. He in fact discourages even *thinking* about "doing good." That is, thinking about doing good deeds suggests calculation on our part to gain benefits and rewards simply for "doing good deeds," or to avoid punishment for past transgressions.

Passages from sutras which Shinran relied upon give us additional grounds for understanding "good" and "evil" from Shinran's perspective. In the *Contemplation Sutra*, which Shinran considered to offer only a provisional, "self-power" way to Pure Land enlightenment, the Buddha informs Queen Vaidehī that "Those who desire to be born in that land must perform the three meritorious acts. First they should attend dutifully to their parents, serve their elders and teachers faithfully, possess the mind of compassion and refrain from killing, and undertake the *ten virtuous acts (jūzengō).*"[14] In the Mahāyāna sutras, such as the *Daimyōdokyō* and the *Jūjūkyō*, the *ten virtuous acts* are incorporated into the second of the six paramitas (*śīla-pāramitā, jikai*) and consist of *being free of the ten transgressions,* that is, *not* killing, *not* stealing, *not* committing adultery, etc.[15]

And in the *Sutra on the Buddha of Infinite Life* (*Muryōjukyō,* commonly referred to as the *Larger Sutra*), which Shinran declared gives us the true Pure Land teaching, the Buddha tells Bodhisattva Maitreya of the "five evils" and "five great goods." Here, the first evil is given in part as—because the devas, humans and lesser beings are bent on doing evil—the strong subduing the weak, inflicting serious injuries, killing each other, and devouring their prey. Following His discussion of this evil, the Buddha pronounces that the "first great good" is controlling one's thoughts with single-mindedness, doing worthy deeds with proper demeanor, committing no evil, and performing only good. Neither "worthy deeds" nor "performing good" is spelled out for us. And the remaining four "goods" are given in the same words as that for the first good, except that the fifth great good adds: *mindfully recollecting, harmonizing words and deeds, acting with sincerity, uttering true words, and speaking from the heart.*[16] Again, the sutra gives guidance on how one should behave or comport ourselves with respect to others, but does not describe specific kinds of deeds that are deemed "good." Instead, we are simply counseled to *not* commit those acts described as evil. And, Shinran's awareness of the guidance given by Śākyamuni Buddha in the *Larger Sutra* is reflected in the tone and content of his guidance to his followers.

That we do not find more specific guidance on what constitutes "good" is understandable, even though we may think at times that life would be much easier if we were given guidance—that we could easily follow—on what we should do to be good. Practically speaking, it is not possible to prescribe what constitutes "good" in all situations at all times. Giving water to a thirsty person may be a kindness, but giving water to a drowning person is simply foolishness. On the other hand, some kinds of acts, as in the ten transgressions, are not acceptable under all, or perhaps most, circumstances. Thus, we find in our criminal and penal codes specific actions that are proscribed by law. Even these are subject to repeal as circumstances and conditions change. On the other hand, we do not find laws specifying what constitutes "good" or "good behavior." At best, we may find statements of general principle as to the "good things" that a law is expected to accomplish.

SHINRAN'S CASUISTIC GUIDANCE

Shinran's concern that we should *not* commit evil is reflected clearly in his letters to his followers, some of whom were apparently being misled into believing that they could commit evil and engage in vices because they would be saved by Amida's grace by simply reciting the nembutsu. Thus, in letter 16 compiled in the *Mattōshō*, we find—

> If a person, justifying himself by saying he is a foolish being, can do anything he wants, then is he also to steal or to murder? Even that person who has been inclined to steal will naturally undergo a change of heart if he comes to say the nembutsu aspiring for the Buddha Land. Yet people who show no such sign are being told that it is permissible to do wrong; this should never occur under any circumstances.
>
> Maddened beyond control by blind passions, we *do* things we should not and *say* things we should not and *think* things we should not. But if a person is *deceitful* in his relations with others, *doing what he should not do* and *saying what he should not* because he thinks it will not hinder his birth, then it is not an instance of being maddened by passion. Since he purposely does these things, they are simply misdeeds which should never have been done.... One must seek to cast off the evil of this world and to cease doing wretched deeds; this is what it means to reject the world and to live the nembutsu.[17]

These thoughts are reiterated in letter 19 in which Shinran wrote:

You must not do what should not be done, think what should not be thought, or say what should not be said, thinking that you can be born in the Buddha Land regardless of it. Human beings are such that, maddened by the *passions of greed*, we desire to possess; maddened by the *passions of anger*, we hate that which should not be hated, seeking to go against the law of cause and effect; led astray by the *passions of ignorance*, we do what should not even be thought. But the person who purposely thinks and does what he should not, saying that it is permissible because of the Buddha's wondrous Vow to save the foolish being, does not truly desire to reject the world, nor does he consciously feel that he himself is a being of karmic evil. Hence he has no aspiration for the nembutsu nor for the Buddha's Vow; thus, however diligently he engages in nembutsu with such an attitude, it is difficult for him to attain birth in the next life . . . .[18]

And at the end of this letter (which may be a composite of two letters) Shinran added:

I hear that you urge people who are drunk with the *wine of ignorance* to greater and greater drunkenness and allow people who have long preferred to dine on the *three poisons* more and more poison, telling them that they should enjoy it; how painful it is. There is such sorrow in being drunk on the wine of ignorance, yet they partake with pleasure of the three poisons and the poisons have not yet abated. They have not yet awakened from the drunkenness of ignorance.[19]

In letter 20, Shinran again invokes the metaphor of the three poisons in the following way:

. . . Formerly you were drunk with the wine of ignorance and had a taste only for the *three poisons of greed, anger and folly*, but since you have begun to hear the Buddha's Vow you have gradually awakened from the drunkenness of ignorance,

THE ESSENCE OF SHINRAN'S TEACHING

gradually rejected the three poisons, and come to prefer at all times the medicine of Amida Buddha.

In contrast, how lamentable that people who have not fully awakened from drunkenness are urged to more drunkenness and those still in the grips of poison encouraged to take yet more poison. It is indeed sorrowful to give way to impulses with the excuse that one is by nature possessed of blind passions—excusing acts that should not be committed, words that should not be said, and thoughts that should not be harbored—and to say that one may not follow one's desires in any way whatever. It is like offering more wine before the person has become sober or urging him to take even more poison before the poison has abated. "Here's some medicine, so drink all the poison you like"—words like this should never be said.[20]

With the foregoing as background, we can now revisit the quotation from the *Tannishō* cited above. Before quoting Shinran, the author suggested that Shinran's thoughts are the same as those of Shan-tao given in the *Sanzengi*: "Know that we are, in reality, ordinary men of sins and evils, subject to Birth-and-Death, having been ever sinking and ever transmigrating since immeasurable kalpas up to the present, and that we have no chance for liberation."[21] While the *Tannishō* may well reflect Shinran's thoughts, Shinran's own words seem to reflect his thoughts more precisely. In his *Notes on "Essentials of Faith Alone,"* Shinran explains Shan-tao's admonition, also in the *Sanzengi*, that "We should not express outwardly signs of wisdom, goodness, or diligence, while inwardly possessing that which is empty and transitory"[22] to mean that people who aspire for the Pure Land must not behave outwardly as though wise or good, nor act as though diligent because, as stated, what we have within us is empty and transitory—our minds contain blind passions (*bonnō*) and are "vain," "not real," "not sincere," "provisional," and "not true." And for this reason, the Tathāgata teaches that this world is called the defiled world of the corrupt dharma and all beings lack a true and sincere heart, mock teachers and elders, disrespect their parents, distrust their companions and favor only evil. It is therefore taught that everyone, both in secular and religious worlds, is possessed of "heart and tongue at odds" (what we say and what is in our hearts are at odds) and "Words and thoughts both insincere" (what is said and what is thought are not sincere.) People's thoughts are insincere and those who wish to be born in the Pure Land think only of deceiving and flattering. Even those who renounce this world (i.e., enter the priesthood) think only of fame and profit. Therefore, we should know that we are not good men, nor men of wisdom; that we have no diligence, but only indolence; that which we hold in our heart is empty, deceptive, vainglorious, and flattering; and that we do not have a heart that is "true and real."[23]

And we find in the last two verses of the *Shōzōmatsu Wasan (Hymns on the Last Age)*, Shinran's final *wasan*—

> While people ignorant even of the words "good" and "bad"
> Are all of true heart (*makoto no kokoro*),
> My acting as though I knew "good" and "bad"
> Is a manifestation of total falsity.
>
> I do not know right from wrong
> Nor am [I] able to distinguish from falsity;
> Though I lack even a morsel of mercy and compassion
> For name and fortune, I desire to be a teacher of others.[24]

Thus, Shinran's own words reflect more clearly his own thought. It is not that he actually did not know the difference between "good" and "evil" or "right" or "wrong." It was that he expressed agreement with Shan-tao's admonition that one should not display pretensions of "goodness" while at the same time indicating that those who are sincerely faithful are not and need not be concerned about "good" and "evil" (because their hearts and minds are pure). He also alluded to the unseemly pretentiousness of the clerics of Shinran's time.

While admonishing us not to engage in evil nor partake further of the three poisons of greed, anger and ignorance, and not telling us of what kinds of good deeds we ought to perform, Shinran does tell us to single-heartedly make our hearts turn about and overturn and discard the mind of self-power; that since those who are born in the true fulfilled land are taken without fail into the heart of the Buddha of unhindered light, they realize diamond-like s*hinjin*; that "to abandon the mind of self-power" means to abandon the convictions that one is good, to cease relying on the self, to stop reflecting knowingly on one's evil heart, and further to abandon the judging of people as good and bad. Moreover, when we entrust ourselves to the Tathāgata's Primal Vow, we, who are like "bits of tile and pebbles," are turned into gold and are grasped and never abandoned by the Tathāgata's light. This comes about through true *shinjin* when we are embraced by the supreme wisdom and compassion of the Buddha of unhindered light.[25]

We need next to consider what Shinran meant by turning our hearts and minds and realizing *shinjin*.

SHINRAN'S DEFINITION OF TERMS LEADS TO UNDERSTANDING

Shinran is meticulous in explaining his understanding of the meaning of words used by others and what he means when he uses certain terms. One senses that his reading of words written by others may not necessarily comport with what the original author may have intended. Nevertheless, there is a clear logic and ideological consistency in his interpretations. Thus, tracking Shinran's explanation of significant terms appears to be not only crucial to an understanding and appreciation of Shinran's *Jōdo Shinshū*, but is also a means of gaining such understanding.

In his *Notes on Once-calling and Many-calling*, Shinran notes that "true reality-suchness" (*ichijitsu shinnyo*) is the supreme great nirvana; nirvana is dharma-nature (*hosshō*); and dharma-nature is Tathāgata. Also, "treasure ocean" likens Buddha's guidance to all sentient beings to the all-embracing waters of the great ocean and Bodhisattva Dharmākara is the *form* manifested from the "treasure ocean of oneness" who became Amida Buddha (upon fulfillment of his Vows). Thus, Amida is the "Tathāgata of fulfilled body" who is called "Buddha of unhindered light filling the ten quarters," and who is also known as *Namu-fukashigikō-butsu* (namu-Buddha of inconceivable light) and is the "dharmakaya as compassionate means." "Compassionate means" refers to manifesting form, revealing a name, and making itself known to sentient beings, and refers to Amida Buddha. This Tathāgata is light. Light is wisdom; wisdom is the form of light. Wisdom is also formless; thus this Tathāgata is the Buddha of inconceivable light. This Tathāgata who fills the countless worlds in the ten quarters is called the "Buddha of boundless light." Moreover, Vasubandhu gave this Tathāgata the name, "Tathāgata of unhindered light filling the ten quarters."[26]

Discussing a gatha by Fa-chao[27] in *Notes on "Essentials of Faith Alone,"* Shinran explains that *the Tathāgata* is the Tathāgata of unhindered light; *the holy name* is *namu-amida-butsu*; *gō* (name) indicates the name of a Buddha after the attainment of Buddhahood and *myō* (name) indicates his name before attainment of Buddhahood. (Thus, *myōgo* refers to both Bodhisattva Dharmākara and Amida Buddha as one entity.) Moreover, the *Name of the Tathāgata* is the *Name of the Vow*.[28] The line "Throughout the worlds in the ten quarters it prevails" means that, since no one—whether wise or ignorant, good or evil—can attain supreme nirvana through his own self-cultivated wisdom, we are encouraged to enter the ocean of the *wisdom-Vow* of the Buddha of unhindered light because his *form* is the *light of wisdom*. This form comprehends the *wisdom* of all the Buddhas and that light is *none other than wisdom*. And, *Namu-amida-butsu* is the Name embodying *wisdom*.[29]

Again, Shinran explains that in the phrase "Land of bliss is the realm of nirvana" in Shan-tao's *Hymns of the Nembutsu Liturgy*, "the realm of nirvana" refers to the place where one overturns the delusion of ignorance and realizes the supreme enlightenment. And

THE ESSENCE OF SHINRAN'S TEACHING

although *Nirvana* has innumerable names it may be called: *extinction of passions; the uncreated; peaceful happiness; eternal bliss; true reality; dharmakāya; dharma-nature; suchness; oneness;* and *Buddha-nature.* "Buddha-nature" is none other than Tathāgata that pervades the countless worlds and fills the "hearts and minds" (*shin*) of the "ocean of all beings."[30]

Enlarging on these ideas, Shinran sets forth what amounts to the core of his soteriologic theory. He tells us that since it is with this "heart and mind" that sentient beings entrust themselves to the Vow of the *dharmakāya-as-compassion*—

> [T]his *shinjin* is none other than *Buddha-nature*. This Buddha-nature is *dharma-nature*. Dharma-nature is the *dharmakaya*. For this reason there are two kinds of dharmakaya in regard to the Buddha. The first is called *dharmakaya-as-suchness* and the second, *dharmakaya-as-compassion*. Dharmakaya-as-suchness has neither color nor form; thus, the mind cannot grasp it nor words describe it. From this *oneness* was manifested form, called *dharmakaya-of-compassion*. Taking this form, the Buddha proclaimed his name as Bhikṣu Dharmākara and established the forty-eight great Vows that surpass conceptual understanding. Among those Vows are the *primal Vow* of immeasurable light and the *universal Vow* of immeasurable life, and to the *form* manifesting these two Vows Bodhisattva Vasubandhu gave the title "Tathāgata of unhindered light filling the ten quarters" (*Jinjippō mugekō butsu*). This Tathāgata has fulfilled the Vows, which are the cause of his Buddhahood, and thus is called "Tathāgata of the fulfilled body." This is none other than Amida Tathāgata. "Fulfilled" means that the cause for enlightenment has been fulfilled. From the fulfilled body innumerable personified and accommodated bodies are manifested from the fulfilled body, radiating the unhindered *light of wisdom* throughout the countless worlds. Thus appearing in the form of light called "Tathāgata of unhindered light filling the ten quarters," it is without color and form, that is identical with the

dharmakaya-as-suchness, dispelling the darkness of ignorance and unobstructed by karmic evil. For this reason it is called "unhindered light." "Unhindered" means that it is not obstructed by the karmic evil and blind passions of beings. Know, therefore, *Amida Buddha* is *light,* and light is the form taken by *wisdom.*[31]

In the *Mattōshō,* Shinran gives more pointed explanations through his letters. In Letter 21, Shinran notes that when a person has entered completely into the Buddha Land of Peace, he immediately realizes the "supreme nirvana," the "supreme enlightenment." And though the terms differ, they both mean to realize the enlightenment of the Buddha "who is dharma-body."[32]

In Letter 9, Shinran makes it clear that the *Name* and the *Vow* are the same—

> I fail to understand why your question should arise, for although we speak of Vow and of Name, these are not two different things. There is no Name separate from the Vow; there is no Vow separate from the Name. Even to say this, however, is to impose one's own calculation. Once you simply realize that the Vow surpasses conceptual understanding and with singleness of heart realize that the Name surpasses conceptual understanding and pronounce it, why should you labor in your own calculation?
>
> It seems to me that with all your attempts to understand reasoning and learning you have fallen into confusion. It is completely in error. Once you have simply come to realize that Vow and Name surpass conceptual understanding, you should not calculate it in this way or that. There must be nothing of your calculation in the act that leads to birth. . . . You must simply entrust yourself to Tathāgata.[33]

And in Letter 14, a letter by Kyōshin on which Shinran wrote editorial notes and an answer to a query—

THE ESSENCE OF SHINRAN'S TEACHING

It is the greatest of errors to say that one must *not* say *mugekō butsu* (Buddha of unhindered light) in addition to *namu-amida-butsu*. *Kimyo* corresponds to *namu*. *Mugekō butsu* is light; it is wisdom. This wisdom is itself Amida Buddha. Since people do not know the form of Amida Buddha, Bodhisattva Vasubandhu . . . created this expression in order that we might know Amida's form with perfect certainty . . . .[34]

In summary, we may conclude that in considering the words and terms used by Shinran, a number of different terms may be used to invoke or refer to a single entity or idea, while at the same time a single word or term may mean different "things" depending on Shinran's intent, which may not be readily apparent. Nevertheless, we may distill from the foregoing the following essence:

- Nirvana is a *state of being* of "suchness" (*tathāta*) attained through supreme wisdom. The attainment of this state is manifested by Buddha, a Tathāgata.
- "Light" is a metaphor for wisdom. Amida Buddha, the Buddha of immeasurable, unhindered, infinite, inconceivable light, is thus an embodiment of supreme wisdom.
- Amida's compassion is manifested through the transference of His wisdom to all sentient beings.
- *Shinjin* is the Buddha-nature awakened in us through Amida's compassionate transfer of His wisdom into us.
- The Name (Namo-Amida-Butsu and its variants), the Vow (and its variants), and Amida Buddha (and its variants) represent the same conceptualization of Wisdom—the Buddha-Dharma.

SHINJIN AND PRAXIS

The concept of *shinjin* needs to be discussed here since it is considered doctrinally by the Hongwanji to denote "the central religious experience of Shin Buddhism" and to denote "the realization of Other-power in which human calculation is negated through the working of Amida Buddha."[35] The literal meaning of *shinjin* is given as man's "true, real and sincere heart and mind" (*makoto no kokoro*) with the character *shin* (which can be read *makoto*) having the meaning "true, real and sincere" and the character for *jin* (which can also be read *shin* or *kokoro*) having the meaning "heart and mind" or "heart-mind." It is explained further that "this *heart-mind* has basically two aspects: a non-dichotomous identity wherein the *heart and mind* of Amida and the *heart and mind* of man are one, and a dichotomous relationship wherein the two are mutually exclusive and in dynamic interaction." And used as a verb, the *shin* of *shinjin* means "to entrust oneself to the Buddha," an act which is made possible by the working of the true, real and sincere heart and mind of Amida Buddha.

The foregoing explanation of *shinjin* provides a succinct definition of what *shinjin* means doctrinally. Unfortunately, it relies on anomalous metaphorical imagery as well as what may be an overly simplistic rendering of *shin* or *kokoro* as "heart and mind."[36] With respect to the linguistic problem first, it is doubtful that "heart," "mind" or both together can adequately express what *shin/kokoro* represents. "Heart" may refer to the affective component of a person's personality and "mind" to the cognitive aspects. Yet, the two even if taken together seem somehow to be significantly less than the whole of *shin/kokoro*. *Kokoro* seems to represent the core and source of one's being, the essence of one's personality. Thus, "soul," the essence of human personality, as defined by John McNeill, might give a better sense of what *shin/kokoro* means.[37] (Kenkyusha's dictionary does give "soul" as one of the terms that may be equivalent to *kokoro*.)

The metaphorical anomaly is significantly more problematic. "Heart and mind" refers to a human characteristic. However, can, *ought*, human characteristics be attributed to Amida Buddha, the *dharmakaya-of-compassion*? Moreover, how can the wisdom and compassion of Amida be thought of as being vested in Amida's *kokoro* when Amida Buddha *is* but the personification of the supreme wisdom and compassion that is encountered and becomes one with us?

Thus, any attempt to define *shinjin* in terms of "heart and mind" will assuredly fall short of the mark. It is noted, however, that *shinjin* was generally rendered as "faith" before the advent of the Hongwanji Shin Buddhism translation series. However, with the publication of that series, the use of "faith" has been discouraged because the term "so strongly and variously colored by its usage in the Judaeo-Christian tradition, would only blur the precision [sic] of the meaning of the original."[38] This position is rested on Paul Tillich's words, perhaps taken out of context, that "There is hardly a word in the religious language . . . which is more subject to more misunderstandings, distortions and questionable definitions that the word 'faith'." Rejecting the use of a term because of its uncertain and varied meanings in other traditions seems exceedingly parochial—particularly when developing an understanding of the meaning and implications of *Faith* in the respective traditions is the very point of religious inquiry.

In contrast to the negativistic attribution to Tillich, the words of Wilfred Cantwell Smith in his text *Faith and Belief* strike a responsive chord. Smith notes that "The temptation to say what faith is, is strong. Faith can never be expressed in words, however: neither in aphorism nor in many volumes."[39] Nevertheless, Smith also observes that "Faith . . . is an essential human quality. One might argue that it is *the* essential human quality: that it is constitutive of man as human; that personality is constituted by our universal ability, or invitation, to live in terms of a transcendent dimension, and in response to it."[40] He also writes: "Faith is not belief in doctrine. It is not even belief in the truth as such, whatever it be. It is 'assent' to the truth as such, in the dynamic and personal sense of rallying to it with delight and engagement. It is the exclamation mark in saying not merely 'yes' but 'Yes!' to the truth when one sees it. It is the ability to see and to respond . . . . Faith is, among other things, an attitude; and for intellectuals, an attitude to truth."[41] Smith also describes an element of faith as an *engagement* with a transcendent reality. These thoughts of Smith may help us unravel the implications of the remainder of this polemic—while we continue to use *shinjin* and *faith* as they are used in the references cited.

Continuing, Shinran states in *Notes on Once-calling and Many-calling*, that the eighty-four thousand dharma-gates are all good practices of the *provisional* means of the Pure Land teaching and are known as the Essential or Provisional (temporary; not true and real) Gate. This gate consists of the meditative and non-meditative practices taught in the *Contemplation Sutra*. Meditative good refers to the three types of meritorious behavior and the nine grades of beings, all belonging to the Essential Gate, also called the Provisional Gate. Encouraging and guiding all sentient beings to enter through this Essential or Provisional Gate, the Buddha teaches and encourages them to enter "the great treasure ocean of true and real virtue—the Primal Vow, perfect and unhindered, which is the one vehicle." Thus, all good acts of *self-power* are called *provisional* ways.[42]

He also explains that in the phrase "truly knowing the Tathāgata's Primal Vow," "truly" (*shin*) refers to the diamond-like heart (*kongō shin*). "Know" means to know that Amida guides sentient beings who are filled with blind passions and karmic evil. Moreover, "know" is to behold, which means to call to mind and think on. "Know" thus means "to call to mind and realize." *Shō* ("Saying") means to utter the Name, while also meaning to weigh, to determine the measure of something. Thus, when a person says the Name ten times or but once, hearing it and being without even the slightest doubt, he will be born in the true fulfilled land.[43]

In *Notes on "Essentials of Faith Alone,"* Shinran explains that faith (*shin*) is the heart and mind (*kokoro*) without doubt; it is *shinjin*, which is true and real (*sunawachi kore shinjitsu no shinjin nari*). It is the heart and mind free of that which is empty and transitory. Empty means "vain"; transitory means "provisional." Empty means "not real" and "not sincere"; transitory means "not true." "Faith alone" is, having entrusted oneself to the Other-power of the Primal Vow, being free of "self-power" (thoughts). "Faith alone" also means that

THE ESSENCE OF SHINRAN'S TEACHING

nothing is placed equal with this *shinjin* of Other-power (*tariki no shinjin*), for it is the working of the universal Primal Vow (*honguzeigan*).[44]

In the same tract, Shinran explains that the *shinjin* of "oneness" becomes the diamond-like heart because of Amida's grasp. This is the threefold shinjin of the Primal Vow of birth through the nembutsu, not the three minds of the *Contemplation Sutra*.[45] Moreover, Vasubandhu declares that this true and real *shinjin* (*shinjitsu shinjin*) is none other than the aspiration to become a Buddha, the great thought of the enlightenment of the Pure Land, and "this aspiration for Buddhahood is none other than the wish to save all beings," the wish to carry all beings across the great ocean of birth-and-death, the aspiration to bring all beings to the attainment of supreme nirvana. It (*shinjin*) is the heart of great love and great compassion. This *shinjin* is Buddha-nature and Buddha-nature is Tathāgata.[46]

However, to lack the "three minds" (of the *Contemplation Sutra*) is to lack *shinjin* and is to lack the true and real threefold *shinjin* of the Primal Vow (of the *Larger Sutra*). To realize the three minds of the *Contemplation Sutra* and then the threefold *shinjin* of the *Larger Sutra* is to realize the one mind. When this one mind is lacking, one is not born in the real fulfilled land. The three minds of the *Contemplation Sutra* are parts of the mind of self-power of a person who pursues meditative and non-meditative practice. The deep mind and sincere mind, which are means, are intended to bring the two goods—meditative and non-meditative—into the aspiration for the threefold *shinjin* of the *Larger Sutra*.[47] Here, it is apparent that Shinran is reconciling his view that the practices of the *Contemplation Sutra* are merely provisional whereas the *Larger Sutra* gives us the true teaching. That is, the self-power practices of the *Contemplation Sutra*, while necessary, are of themselves insufficient for attaining or achieving the *shinjin* of Amida's grace, wisdom and compassion.

And in the *Shōzōmatsu Wasan*, Shinran gives us, in brief poetic and metaphoric lines given below, additional insights into his thoughts on true faith in terms of self-power, Other-power and *shinjin*.

Those of the Path of Sages all depend primarily on the mind of self-power. But when they enter completely into the Other-power, which is beyond comprehension, they realize that no reasoning is the true reasoning (*gi naki o gi to su*). (Verse 55)[48]

Those who believe in the efficacy of doing good and evil doubt the inconceivable Buddha-wisdom and stop in the castle of doubt or the womb-palace. Thus, they are separated from the three treasures. (Verse 62)

For doubting the Buddha's wisdom, one stops in the border land, the realm of sloth and complacency. The offense of doubting is so great that he is held there many years and kalpas. (Verse 63)

When one prefers to pronounce the nembutsu through self-power because one doubts the inconceivable Buddha-wisdom, he stops in the border land, the realm of sloth and complacency. (Verse 61)

Since the desire to pronounce the Name with true faith is transferred to us by Amida, it is not of our own efforts and is called non-transference. Thus reciting the nembutsu through self-power (*jiriki no shōmon*) is detested (*kirawa ruru*). (Self-power recitation of the nembutsu is unacceptable.) (Verse 39)

When the "waters of the good and evil hearts of foolish beings" (*Bombu zen'aku no shinsui*) flow into the ocean of Amida's Wisdom-Vow, they immediately turn into the heart of great compassion. (Verse 40)

The determination (desire) to become enlightened is a determination to save all beings—by leading them also to enlightenment. (Verse 20)

The desire to save all sentient beings is given (transferred) to us by Amida's Vow (*Chigan*) (which is wisdom). Those who attain faith (*shingyō*), this transference, realize the great *nirvana*. (Verse 21)

It is lamentable that these days in Japan, all whether cleric or lay, perform the rites and rituals of Buddhism, but worship the demons and deities of heaven and earth. (Verse 104)

In the end, Shinran's explication of his thoughts on *shinjin* in terms of "mind" (*shin*), "self-power" faith and "Other-power" faith bring us into the realm of everyday *being*, which we take up finally.

JINEN HŌNI

Interpreting a passage from the *Larger Sutra*,[49] Shinran explains that people who realize *shinjin* will realize the supreme nirvana "as such." "As such" means immediately; it also means "dharmicness" (*hōsoku*). In entrusting ourselves to the Tathāgata's Primal Vow and saying the Name once, necessarily, without seeking it, we are made to receive the supreme virtues and without knowing it, we acquire the great and vast benefit. This is "dharmicness" by which one will immediately realize the various facets of enlightenment naturally. "Dharmicness" (the way that things are in themselves) means not brought about in any way by the practicer's calculation. It indicates the nature of *jinen*. "Dharmicness" expresses the natural working (*jinen*) in the life of the person who realizes *shinjin* and says the Name once.[50]

The concept of *jinen* is elaborated more extensively in Shinran's *Notes*, in his letters, and in the *Shōzōmatsu Wasan*. In *Notes on "Essentials of Faith Alone,"* Shinran explains that *ji* means "of itself." "Of itself" is a synonym for *jinen*, which means "to be made to become so." "To be made to become so" means that without the practicer's calculating in any way whatsoever, all his past, present, and future evil karma is transformed into the highest good. To be transformed means that evil karma, without being nullified or eradicated, is made into the highest good, just as all waters, upon entering the great ocean, immediately become ocean water. We are made to acquire the Tathāgata's virtues through entrusting ourselves in his Vow-power. Since there is no contriving in any way to gain such virtues, it is called *jinen*. The person who has attained true and real *shinjin* is taken into and protected by this Vow which grasps him, never to abandon him; therefore, he realizes the diamond-like mind without any calculation on his part, and thus dwells in the stage of the truly settled. Because of this, constant mindfulness of the Primal Vow arises in him naturally (by *jinen*). Even with the arising of this *shinjin*, it is written that supreme *shinjin* is made to awaken in us through the compassionate guidance of Śākyamuni, the kind father, and Amida, the mother of loving care. This is the benefit of the working of *jinen*.[51]

In his *Notes on the Inscription on Sacred Scrolls (Songō shinzō meimon)*, quoting a passage from the *Larger Sutra* Shinran explains that in the line "Their attainment of non-retrogression coming about of itself," "of itself" (*ji*) means that the calculation of sentient beings is not involved at all; it being made to become so, one is brought to attainment of the stage of non-retrogression. "Of itself" expresses *jinen*. Thus "The person who entrusts himself to the Name embodying the Tathāgata's Primal Vow is brought to the stage of non-retrogression naturally, by *jinen*." "Non-retrogression" is the stage at which a person becomes settled as one who will necessarily attain Buddhahood.[52]

In the same *Notes* on the Scrolls, Shinran in quoting Shan-tao's words, explains that in the expression "One necessarily attains birth," "necessarily" means that one is brought to the attainment of birth in the Pure Land naturally, by *jinen*. *Jinen* means that one does not calculate in any way whatsoever.[53]

Finally, Shinran's thoughts with respect to the concept of *jinen* are summarized concisely in what is often called the *Jinenhōnishō* as incorporated as Letter 5 of the *Mattōshō* and inserted by Rennyo Shōnin in the Bunmei era edition of the *Shōzōmatsu Wasan* just ahead of the final two verses of that *wasan* quoted above.

THE ESSENCE OF SHINRAN'S TEACHING

The character "*gyaku*" means to attain when one is in the causal stage (Dharmakara) and "*toku*" to attain when one has entered the resultant stage (Amida Buddha). The character "*myō*" means the name in the causal stage, and "*gō*" the name in the resultant stage.[54]

As for *jinen*, "*ji*" means "of itself"—it is not through the practicer's calculation; one is made to become so. "*Nen*" means "one is made to become so"—it is not through the practicer's calculation; it is through the working of the Vow of Tathāgata. As for "*hōni*," it means "one is made to become so through the working of the Vow of Tathāgata." "*Hōni*" means that one is made to become so (*ni*) by the virtue of the dharma (*hō*), being the working of the Vow where there is no calculation on the part of the practicer. In short, there is no place at all for the practicer's calculation. We are taught, therefore, that in Other-power no self-working is true working.

Jinen means that from the very beginning one is made to become so. Amida's Vow is, from the very beginning, designed to have each person entrust himself in Namo-amida-butsu and be received in the Buddha Land; none of this is through the practicer's calculation. Thus there is no room for him to be concerned with being good or bad. This is the meaning of *jinen* as I have learned it.

This Vow is the Vow to make us all attain the supreme Buddhahood. The supreme Buddha is formless, and because of being formless is called *jinen*. When this Buddha is shown as being with form, it is not called the supreme nirvana (Buddha). In order to make us realize that the true Buddha is formless, it is expressly called Amida Buddha; so I have been taught. Amida Buddha is the medium through which we are made to realize *jinen*. After we have realized that this is the way it is, we should not be forever talking about *jinen*. If one always talks about *jinen*, then the truth that Other-power is no self-working will again become a problem of self-working. This is the mystery of the wisdom of the Buddhas. Gutoku

Shinran at 86."[55]

The *Jinenhōnisho* seems to me to encapsulate the essence of Shinran's teaching. It sets forth his idea that one is made to be *so, thus*, through the working of the Primal Vow (Wisdom) of Amida Buddha, by the Dharma (Truth) working upon us. This comes about absolutely without human calculation because it was meant to be from the very beginning long before our appearance in this world. Moreover, it means to me further that when one becomes one with Amida Buddha (the Buddha-Dharma) and drops off all the "baggage" a person has accumulated 'til then—that which causes one *not* to have "right view" but to have a perverted, jaundiced view of our living, human condition—we are able to conduct our lives with wisdom and compassion without consciously or unconsciously measuring the cost benefits of each step we take. *Shinjin*, within this context, is then that *state of being* we can attain when our *kokoro*, the core of our being, the essence of our personality, our *mortal* soul, is fused with the wisdom and compassion represented by the Name, Namo-amida-butsu (and its variants), the Primal Vow, the Buddha of Immeasurable Life and Infinite Light, Amida Buddha. Thus, as a matter of editorial convenience as well as a means of alerting readers to the uniqueness of Shinran's *shinjin* concept, it may be well to adopt the term "Shin faith" to represent *shinjin* in English.

CONCLUSION

Understanding Shinran's teaching is most difficult if one tries to find full support and justification for each of his ideas and conclusions in the writings of the seven masters to whom he expresses his obeisance and gratitude in his writings. This is because Shinran's perception and understanding are uniquely his. Certainly, he gained his insights from his mentor, Hōnen, and predecessor masters. However, his understanding and interpretation of the import of the Bodhisattva Dharmākara-Amida Buddha metaphors and attendant mythology arise from within his frame-of-reference, just as our frames-of-reference shape the understanding and appreciation of Shinran's words. What makes considering Shinran's teaching in the context of his predecessors' ideas even more difficult is that Shinran does not directly reject nor express disagreement with the words of the masters. Rather, and as it is well illustrated above, Shinran adopts the words of his predecessors, but assigns his own meanings to those words so that they will convey the meaning *he* wishes. The reason why Shinran used this technique is beyond the scope of this paper. Nevertheless, we may assume that he had to give at least the appearance of conforming with the conventional wisdom *of the time*, just as we today often feel compelled to conform to "political correctness" and institutional dogmatism.

And, it may be the necessity for conformance that results in an apparent contradiction in this guidance with respect to the concept of nembutsu as meaning "reciting the Name" with the Name expressed in various forms. On the one hand, Shinran's many references to reciting the Name suggests that he encourages the oral invocation of the Name. But in the *Shōzōmatsu wasan* as quoted above and in other writings, Shinran makes it clear that self-power recitation of the Name is unacceptable. Yet today, the recitation and chanting of the nembutsu is an essential part of Jōdo Shinshū liturgy.

With respect to what may be taken as a rather cynical view of the human condition taken and expressed by Shinran, that becomes readily understandable when it is considered in the light of what little is known of Shinran's own life experience and the sociopolitical conditions in Japan during his lifetime. He entered the priesthood on Mt. Hiei at the outset of the Gempei war that saw the ascendancy of the warrior class and the establishment of the military government in Kamakura. It was a time when internecine, intrafamilial warfare was accepted, if not *de rigueur*. Even the great temples of Nara and Kyoto joined in the warfare with armed might. And the commission of the ten transgressions, particularly hypocrisy, duplicity and greed, was rampant throughout Shinran's long lifetime.

However, the conditions that existed were not unique to Shinran's Japan. Similar, if not worse, conditions existed in medieval Europe. And can we say that conditions today in the whole world are much different or improved? The only differences we could point out would probably be in terms of scope, kinds and methods of dealing with problems (ranging from small group through tribalistic to national and international in scale) made intractable by intransigent stands on irrational and untenable positions and ideas held by the parties concerned.

Here in America, the idea of avoiding and resolving interpersonal and intergroup conflicts through the exercise of wisdom and compassion by all parties concerned has never taken hold. In fact, the current American ethos serves to strengthen attachment to ego and individual response to personal difficulties on the basis of self-centeredness, anger and illusory notions of self-righteousness. Urban gangs attempt to resolve interpersonal and intergroup conflicts through violent confrontation, whereas the more sophisticated approach of individuals and special interest groups of all stripes is to wage their battles in ever increasing numbers of accessible fora, including now international hard copy and electronic mass media and expanding cyberspace. And rather than seeking resolution of disputes through mutual exchange and bona fide consideration of opposing perceptions of reality, argumentation relying on rhetoric, hyperbole, manipulation of facts and false logic seems to be the standard.

Thus, gaining wider acceptance in America for Shinran's introspective approach to personal salvation—without enmeshing it in self-power gimmickry—would be difficult enough as it is, and more difficult to impossible unless Shinran's message is translated into terms that will help overcome the serious barriers to understanding and acceptance that now exist. Nevertheless, it should be clearly evident that Shinran's idea of *jinenhōni* and the underlying basis therefore would provide a way out of the downward spiral of American civilization.

NOTES

1. Langdon Gilkey, *Message and Existence: An Introduction to Christian Theology* (New York: Seabury Press, 1979), 17.

2. William A. Clebsch and Charles R. Jaekle identify four pastoral functions elicited from Christian church history: (1) healing (some impairment in one's spirit); (2) sustaining (a person who has overcome an adversity); (3) guiding (perplexed persons in making choices of action); and (4) reconciling (a broken relationship with one's God or others.) Howard Clinebell, *Basic Types of Pastoral Care and Counseling* (Nashville: Abingdon Press, 1984), 42. Please note that this reference is *not* given to suggest that Jōdo Shinshū ministry should conform to the Christian model. Rather, it is given only to suggest what people socialized in a Euro-American cultural milieu are conditioned to expect of any church or minister.

3. In a survey of the parents of children who attend Dharma Schools in a number of Jōdo Shinshū temples in California, a number of parents gave as their reason for sending their children to Dharma School, "To learn to be "good" Buddhists," or words to the same effect.

4. It is also noted that the first concern of lay leaders and members of BCA temples when a resident minister is to be absent for a period is often "Who will perform *makuragyō* (last rites) and conduct funerals in the minister's absence?"

5. *The Tanni Shō: Notes Lamenting Differences*, translated and annotated by the Ryukoku University Translation Center (Kyoto: Ryukoku University, 1962), 79–81. Hereafter cited as *Tannishō*.

6. *Notes on "Essentials of Faith Alone": A Translation of Shinran's Yuishinshō-mon'i*, Shin Buddhism Translation Series, Yoshifumi Ueda, general editor (Kyoto: Hongwanji International Center, 1979), 36 and 60. (Hereafter cited as *Faith Alone.*) In the referenced passage, Seikaku quotes a gatha by Tz'u-min (in Fa-chao's *Goehōjisan [Hymns of the Nembutsu Liturgy in Fivefold Harmony]*) which recounts Bodhisattva Dharmākara's (universal) vow that when beings hear his name and think on him, he would come and welcome each of them without discrimination between rich and poor, between inferior and highly gifted, not choosing between those who uphold the precepts nor rejecting those who break precepts and whose evil karma is profound.

7. Ibid, 39.

8. *The Sūtra of Contemplation on the Buddha of Immesurable Life as Expounded by Śākyamuni Buddha*, translated and annotated by the Ryukoku University Translation Center (Kyoto: Ryukoku University, 1984), 107. Hereafter cited as *Contemplation Sutra*.

9. *Faith Alone*, 51–52.

10. *Letters of Shinran: A Translation of Mattōshō*, Shin Buddhism Translation Series, Yoshifumi Ueda, general editor (Kyoto: Hongwanji International Center, 1978), 72. Hereafter cited as *Letters*.

11. *Contemplation Sutra*, 107; *Letters*, 85.

12. *Notes on Once-calling and Many-calling: A Translation of Shinran's Ichinen-tanen mon'i,* Shin Buddhism Translation Series, Yoshifumi Ueda, general editor (Kyoto: Hongwanji International Center, 1980). Hereafter cited as *Notes on Once-calling and Many-calling*.

13. Ibid, 48.

14. *Contemplation Sutra*, 23 and fn 1, 22.

15. Ibid, 124–125.

16. Hisao Inagaki, *The Three Pure Land Sutras* (Kyoto: Nagata bunshōdō, 1994), 291–301.

17. *Letters*, 51–52.

18. Ibid, 57–58.

19. Ibid, 59.

20. Ibid, 60–62.

21. *Tannishō*, 79. See also Dennis Hirota, *Tannishō: A Primer*, with a forward by Tokunaga Michio (Kyoto: Ryukoku University, 1982), 43.

22. *Faith Alone*, 66.

23. Ibid, 48–49.

24. *Shōzōmatsu Wasan*, translated and annotated by the Ryukoku University Translation Center (Kyoto: Ryukoku University, 1980), 119–120. Hereafter cited as *Shōzōmatsu Wasan*.

25. *Faith Alone*, 39–41. This paragraph is based on Shinran's explanation of the line "Solely making beings turn about and abundantly say the Name, I can make bits of rubble turn into gold" in Tz'u-min's gatha cited earlier.

26. *Notes on Once-calling and Many-calling*, 45–46.

27. *The holy Name of the Tathāgata is exceedingly distinct
   and clear;
Throughout the worlds in the ten quarters it prevails.
Only those who say the Name attain birth;
Avolokiteśvara and Mahāsthāmaprāpta come of themselves
   to welcome them.*
(*Faith Alone*, 30 and 59.)

28. *Faith Alone*, 30.

29. Ibid, 31.

30. Ibid, 42.

31. Ibid, 42–44. Author's emphases added.

32. *Letters*, 63.

33. Ibid, 37.

34. Ibid, 46.

35. See Glossary to *Faith Alone*, 103–104.

36. Kenkyusha's *New Japanese-English Dictionary* (1974 edition) gives four pages of definitions for *kokoro* and its variants. See Koh Masuda, editor in chief, *Kenkyusha's New Japanese-English Dictionary*, Fourth edition (Tokyo: Kenkyusha, 1974), 897–901, and 1542.

37. John T, McNeill, *A History of the Cure of Souls* (New York: Harper

& Brothers, 1951), vii. McNeill sets forth the following: "The soul is the essence of human personality. It is related to the body, but it is not a mere expression or function of the bodily life. It is capable of vast ranges of experience and susceptible to disorder and anguish." McNeill continues "[B]ut it is indestructible and endowed with possibilities of blessedness with and beyond the order of time." Buddhists might take exception to this latter point, while Professor Archie Smith, Jr. of the Pacific School of Religion observed to me in a personal note "This is precisely the premise rejected by modern, western Secularism."

38. *Faith Alone*, 104.

39. Wilfred Cantwell Smith, *Faith and Belief* (Princeton, N.J.: Princeton University Press, 1979), 133.

40. Ibid, 129.

41. Ibid, 168.

42. *Notes on Once-calling and Many-calling*, 45–46.

43. *Notes on Once-calling and Many-calling*, 49. The line at issue is, "Now, truly knowing Amida's Primal Vow and saying the Name," quoted from Shan-tao's *Hymns of Birth in the Pure Land*.

44. *Faith Alone*, 29.

45. *Faith Alone*, 45. This passage is given in the Honpa Hongwanji's *Jōdo Shinshū Seiten* as: *Kore wa 'Daikyō' no hongan no sanshinjin nari*, which I take to mean: "This is the *Larger Sutra's* threefold *shinjin* of the Primal Vow." See Jōdo Shinshū seiten hensan iinkai, ed., *Jōdo Shinshū seiten: Chūshakuban* (Kyoto: Jōdo Shinshū Hongwanjiha, 1988), 712.

46. *Faith Alone*, 45–46.

47. Ibid, 47–48.

48. *Shōzōmatsu Wasan*, 55. All the *wasan* that follow, with some editing and paraphrasing, are from the same reference, with the page numbers the same as the verse number.

49. "There are those who, having been able to hear the Buddha's Name, dance with joy and say it even once. Know that these people acquire the great benefit and, as such, are furnished with the supreme virtues." Quoted in *Notes on Once-calling and Many-calling*, 39.

50. Ibid, 40.

51. *Faith Alone*, 32.

52. *Notes on the Inscriptions on Sacred Scrolls: A Translation of Shinran's Songō shinzō meimon*, Shin Buddhism Translation Series, Yoshifumi Ueda, general editor (Kyoto: Hongwanji International Center, 1981), 35–36.

53. Ibid, 51.

54. *Shōzomatsu Wasan*, 115. These lines are not found in the *Mattōshō* version. However, a similar explanation is found in the *Ichinen tanen mon'i*, as cited above.

55. *Letters*, 29–30. Cf. *Shōzomatsu Wasan*, 115–118.

A Bibliographical Summary of Studies on *Myōkōnin*: Retrospect and Prospects

Zenshō ASAEDA

In the Jōdo Shinshū tradition, people with extraordinarily deep *shinjin* (faith-mind) are often called "*myōkōnin*" (wondrous excellent people). This terminology was first applied in the *Myōkōnin-den* (*Biographies of myōkōnin*) compiled during the Edo period (1603–1867). In this paper, I will examine the origin of the idea of *myōkōnin* and development of the scholarship on *myōkōnin* in order to discuss current issues in studies on *myōkōnin*. I will also examine the significance of the existence of *myōkōnin* in the Jōdo Shinshū tradition.

Since scholars have approached the study of *myōkōnin* from a variety of academic disciplines, such as religious studies, Buddhist studies, or Jōdo Shinshū studies, it is very difficult to present a comprehensive overview within a single framework. In this paper, therefore, I will focus my discussion on the bibliographical issues of the texts of the *Myōkōnin-den* and the scholarship of historical studies of *myōkōnin*.

DEVELOPMENT OF THE *MYŌKŌNIN-DEN*

The origin of the term *myōkōnin* is found in the *Kangyōsho Sanzengi* (Ch. *Kuan-ching-shu, San-shan-i*, Chapter on Non-meditative practice, *Commentary on the* Contemplation Sutra)[1] written by a Chinese Pure Land master, Shan-tao (Jp. Zendō, 613–681). Shan-tao uses a phrase "the wondrous excellent person (*myōkōnin*) among people" when he explains the meaning of the metaphor of a nembutsu

A BIBLIOGRAPHICAL SUMMARY OF STUDIES ON MYŌKŌNIN

practitioner as a pure white lotus (*fundarike*, Skt. *puṇḍarīka*). Shinran Shōnin (1173–1262), in the passage of the *Shōshinge* (Hymn of true Shinjin and nembutsu), makes reference to Shan-tao when he equates a person with deep *shinjin* to a pure white lotus:

> All foolish beings, whether good or evil,
> When they hear and entrust to Amida's universal Vow,
> Are praised by the Buddha as people of vast and excellent understanding;
> Such a person is called a *pure white lotus*.[2]

The origin of the idea of *myōkōnin* in Jōdo Shinshū is thus thought to stem from Shinran's reference to nembutsu followers as a pure white lotuses, and Master Shan-tao's interpretation of "the wondrous excellent person (*myōkōnin*) among people." As Kashiwahara Yūsen points out, it is agreed that, after the *Myōkōnin-den* was first compiled and written by Gōsei (1721–1794) in the first year of the Bunsei era (1818),[3] this term came to be used to identify people with extraordinarily deep *shinjin* among the Jōdo Shinshū followers.

Modern scholarship on the subject of *myōkōnin* either focuses on bibliographical studies on the *Myōkōnin-den*, particularly on the process of the development of the text, or on doctrinal issues, especially the development of *shinjin* by the devout followers of Jōdo Shinshū who are described as *myōkōnin*.[4] Regardless of which emphasis scholars choose, in order to discuss the existence of *myōkōnin*, they must rely on authentic historical sources. Doi Jun'ichi's study on the biographies of *myōkōnin* first paved the way to understanding the process of the compilation of the text of *Myōkōnin-den*.[5] Prior to Doi's study, Sasaki Rinshō had already discussed problems of the authors and editors of the *Myōkōnin-den*.[6] Tatsuguchi Myōsei continued the discussion further into the problems of editorship.[7] Based on the results of these bibliographical studies, Hayashi Chikō examined *myōkonin* from a doctrinal perspective.[8]

Doi's study introduced a theory explaining the development of the biographies of *myōkōnin* from an earlier manuscript called the

317

Shinmon Myōkōnin-den into the popular printed edition of the *Myōkōnin-den*. His study eventually made it possible to draw a genealogical chart of the various existing manuscripts and prints of the *Myōkōnin-den* from the one-volume edition to the two-volume edition. The bibliographical studies mentioned above have pointed out the key importance of Gōsei's move from the Meikakuji temple in Iga province to the Jōsenji temple in Iwami province. As shown in the following chart, this move allowed Gōsei to collect twenty-six additional stories, which expanded the *Myōkōnin-den* from one to two volumes.[9]

Gōsei's encounter with Yamato no Seikurō (1677–1750), when Gōsei was the head priest of Meikakuji in Iga province, provided him an opportunity to develop the one-volume edition called the *Shinmon Myōkōnin-den*. After he moved to Iwami province, he revised the text into the two-volume edition, which is the text we know as the *Myōkōnin-den*. Although I do not have space to discuss the details of bibliographical research, I have included a chart illustrating the genealogy of the existing manuscripts of the *Myōkōnin-den*.[10]

Scholarship on *myōkōnin* within the study of Jōdo Shinshū doctrine has extended the scope of its research into the time of Shinran Shōnin and subsequent development of the Jōdo Shinshū community.[11] Studies on Gōsei, the author and editor of the *Myōkōnin-den*, and a biography have been written.[12] A chronological list of Gōsei's works has appeared,[13] and there have been further studies on the successors in Gōsei's scholarly lineage,[14] Rizen of the Sekishū school,[15] as well as others.[16] A collection of major academic papers on studies of *myōkōnin* has also been published.[17]

PERSPECTIVES ON THE STUDIES ON *MYŌKŌNIN*

Scholarship on *myōkōnin* studies has developed based on bibliographical studies, partly as a response to Ienaga Saburō's study, a negative critique pointing out the lack of historical progressiveness

A BIBLIOGRAPHICAL SUMMARY OF STUDIES ON MYŌKŌNIN

**Hypothetical Chart of the Genealogy of the
Shinmon Myōkōnin-den and the Myōkōnin-den**

The stories of *myōkōnin* collected around
Iga province (text contains more than ten stories)
|
The *Shinmon Myōkōnin-den*
(One-volume edition)
(text contains ten stories)

┌─ Zuisenji text

├─ Shaku Shindō's copy ── Ryukoku University text

├─ Jōkenji text ───────── Kyoto University text
│ 常見寺
└─ Jōkenji text
   浄謙寺

The stories of *myōkōnin* collected around
Iwami province (text contains twenty-six stories)
|
Denmon Myōkōnin-den (hypothetical title)
(twenty-six-story edition)

Myōkōnin-den (original manuscript edited by Gōsei)
(text contains thirty-six stories)
(Two-volume edition)
|
Original manuscript of
Tsutchida Sairakuji text
|
Tsutchida Sairakuji text
|
Rizen's manuscript
(copied in Bunka 5 [1808])
|
Rizen's edition
|
Rizen's edition with Seigai's introduction
(published in 5th month of Bunsei 5 [1822])
|
Kokujō's original manuscript
(copied in the 8th month of Bunsei 5 [1822])
|
Kokujō's clean copy
(Suyama Bunko text)

in *myōkōnin* as social figures. Ienaga maintained that the *myōkōnin* reflects the Marxist view of religion as an opiate for the people.[18]

Ienaga's study is based primarily on the printed edition of the *Myōkōnin-den*. However, when scholars compared the printed edition with earlier manuscript editions of the *Myōkōnin-den*, they noticed editorial alterations in the printed edition of the text. In order to solve the problems of editorial alterations in the print edition, bibliographical studies of the *Myōkōnin-den* developed. Eventually, a genealogical chart of existing manuscripts of the *Myōkōnin*-den was produced to identify which editorial alterations had been added later.

On the other hand, studies focusing on the positive characteristics of the spirituality of *myōkōnin* have been published by Suzuki Daisetsu,[19] Yanagi Muneyoshi,[20] and Nakamura Hajime.[21] Robert Bellah discussed the significance of Jōdo Shinshū spirituality in Japanese history from the perspective of the influence of *myōkōnin* spirituality on the economic ethics of Ōmi merchants.[22] Also, the following remarks by Alfred Bloom indicate the significance of studying *myōkōnin*:

> The Myokonin have great religious significance because they reveal the inner side of religious experience and life. Institutional histories and doctrines mean little without the faith throbbing in the lifeblood of ordinary people who are the real dynamic and power of faith.
>
> Though some may raise question [sic] that singling out such persons makes their ordinariness extraordinary, there is no other way to highlight or focus the meaning of faith without representative examples of the power of that faith in someone's life. Consequently, all major religions and existential faiths have produced their saints and ideal personalities.[23]

Bloom maintains that the history of a religious institution and its doctrine means very little "without the faith throbbing in the lifeblood of ordinary people." Yanagi Muneyoshi even says that "if there were no *myōkōnin*, the teaching of Shinshū would be a lie."[24]

A BIBLIOGRAPHICAL SUMMARY OF STUDIES ON MYŌKŌNIN

Some scholars discuss *myōkōnin* as a form of Jōdo Shinshū spirituality that has existed since the time of Shinran Shōnin. Others think that *myōkōnin* first appeared when the *Myōkōnin-den* was compiled during the Edo period. And there are some who are willing to discuss the spirituality of *myōkōnin* in a broader context, in terms of their genuine religious experiences, beyond the boundary of Shinshū. However, we must be aware of the existence of positive and negative aspects of the spirituality of *myōkōnin* when we discuss the subject. We must also further develop the current bibliographical research on the historical material that comprises the foundation of the academic study of *myōkōnin*. Working from the basis of solid bibliographical studies, it will also be necessary to discuss doctrinal aspects of *myōkōnin* such as *genshō shōjōju* (the attainment of the stage of truly settled in this life).[25]

SCHOLARLY AND POPULAR WRITINGS ON *MYŌKŌNIN*

In this section, I will first indicate the present state of the studies on *myōkōnin* by detailing a list of studies of the modern *myōkōnin* Saichi, who has come to be well-known since his introduction by Suzuki Daisetsu to the modern academic world. I will then introduce books focusing on other *myōkōnin* and other related publications.

Asahara Saichi was born in the second month of Kaei 3 (1850). He died on January 17 in Shōwa 7 (1932) at the age of eighty-three. He began writing his spiritual poems in notebooks in about September of Taishō 2 (1913). At that time he was already sixty-four.

Among those who have studied Saichi are Teramoto Etatsu,[26] Fuji Shūsui,[27] and Suzuki Daisetsu.[28] A review of the history of scholarship on Asahara Saichi has been published,[29] and Satō Taira has published a biographical study of Saichi.[30] Saichi's poems have been published by Kusunoki Kyō,[31] and are also available in several books produced more recently.[32] Igarashi Daisaku examined his life from a doctrinal perspective,[33] and Takagi Setsuyū conducted a bibliographical study on Saichi's writings.³⁴ Moreover, Minakami Tsutomu's popular novel on Saichi has also been well received among general readers.³⁵ Among the many studies on Asahara Saichi, Kawakami Seikichi's work³⁶ is generally regarded as the best. In addition, recently I have introduced three newly discovered notebooks in which Saichi recorded his poems.³⁷

In recent years, the number of the scholars studying Saichi has increased. Comparative studies of other *myōkōnin* in the Jōdo Shinshū tradition have also begun to appear.³⁸ I will name several popularly known *myōkōnin* and a few publications about each. Among *myōkōnin* living during the Edo period, Yamato no Seikurō has been studied by Hanaoka Daigaku³⁹ and Leslie Kawamura.⁴⁰ Okaru has been studied by Ōzu Shōnen⁴¹ and Ishida Hōyū.⁴² Osono has been studied by Kuga Sunao.⁴³ Zentarō has been studied by Suga Shingi.⁴⁴ Among *myōkōnin* living during the Meiji period, there is a work on Ashikaga Genza by Yanagai Muneyosi,⁴⁵ and works on Monodane Kichibei by Inagaki Zuiken and Kusunoki Kyō.⁴⁶ Other noteworthy titles are *Ima terasareshi ware,*⁴⁷ *Shinja meguri,*⁴⁸ and *Myōkōnin no sekai.*⁴⁹ A study on Akao no Dōshū has also been published.⁵⁰ There are also noteworthy contributions from European Jōdo Shinshū, such as a work about Rev. Harry Peper⁵¹ and a book written by Rev. Jean Eracle.⁵²

CONCLUSION

The most representative modern scholarship on *myōkōnin* studies has been collected and published in the monograph *Myōkōnin-den kenkyū*.⁵³ However, in this paper, I have briefly introduced the origin of the idea of *myōkōnin* and the results of contemporary scholarship on *myōkōnin* studies.

Bibliographical studies have provided us a genealogical chart of various manuscripts and prints of the *Myōkōnin-den* that clarifies the process of the development of the text from the one-volume edition to the two-volume edition. I have also shown that these studies pinpoint problems concerning the meaning of editorial alterations discovered in the manuscripts and printed editions. How scholars evaluate the spirituality of *myōkōnin* depends on how they handle the historical sources on *myōkōnin,* i.e., whether they rely on the printed edition of the *Myōkōnin-den* or they also include the manuscript editions. Objective bibliographical studies have assisted scholars in evaluating these historical sources.

I then introduced major works studying *myōkōnin.* When the manuscripts of the *Myōkōnin-den* were edited and prepared for the print edition, there occurred a doctrinal controversy called *sangōwakuran* (confusion in the manner of faith and practice) within the Hongwanji-ha branch of Jōdo Shinshū. This controversy was not merely coincidental to the publication of the *Myōkōnin-den.*[54] Therefore, it is also necessary to examine the significance of the presence of *myōkōnin* from the broader perspective of early modern Japanese Buddhism during the Edo period. It is also necessary to research historical materials on *myōkōnin* further in order to examine the process of how they realized *anjin* (mind-at-rest). Though Yanagi Muneyosi has discussed the case of Genza in detail, we also need to search for more historical materials on many other *myōkōnin* so that we can discuss *anjin* more generally. Even in the case of a famous *myōkōnin* like Asahara Saichi, I was able to edit and introduce three new notebooks to academic study. Takagi Setsuyū's publication of the *Saichi dōgyō* also sheds new light on the subject by providing concrete evidence that Saichi met Rev. Shichiri Gōjun and was influenced by his spiritual guidance.

As I reexamine the history of scholarship on *myōkōnin* studies from these various perspectives, further bibliographical studies of historical materials seem to be necessary. In the future, I hope more historical materials will become available for examination by the many researchers on *myōkōnin.*

(Translated by Eisho Nasu)

NOTES

1. *Kangyōsho Sanzengi*, in *Shinshū shōgyō zensho*, vol. 1., Shinshū shōgyo zensho hensan iinkai, ed. (Kyoto: Ōyagi kōbundō), 558.

2. *The True Teaching, Practice and Realization of the Pure Land Way*, vol. 1, Shin Buddhism Translation Series (Kyoto: Hongwanji International Center, 1983), 162. See also, *Kyōgyōshnshō*, in *Jōdo Shinshū seiten: Gentenban*, Jōdo Shinshū seiten hensan iinkai, ed. (Kyoto: Jōdo Shinshū Hongwanjiha, 1985), 255.

3. Kashiwahara Yūsen, "Saikin ni okeru myōkōnin kenkyū no dōkō," in *Kinsei shomin bukkyō no kenkyū* (Kyoto: Hōzōkan, 1971), 145.

4. A few review articles on the history of the scholarship on the studies of *myōkōnin* are available in Japanese. See Asaeda Zenshō, "*Myōkōnin-den* kenkyūshi" in *Myōkōnin-den kiso kenkyū* (Kyoto: Nagata bunshōdō, 1982), 13–27, and "Myōkōnin kenkyū no mondaiten, in *Shinjitsu no shūkyō*, ed. Fukuhara Ryōgon (Kyoto: Nagata bunshodō, 1986), 469–476. See also Kashiwahara Yūsen, "Saikin ni okeru myōkōnin kenkyū no dōkō," in *Kinsei shomin bukkyō no kenkyū* 114–146; Kodama Shiki, "*Myōkōnin-den* shōkō," *Kinsei bukkyō* 6, no. 2 (1984): 12–27.

5. See, Doi Jun'ichi, *Myōkōnin-den no kenkyū* (Kyoto: Hyakkaen, 1981).

6. Sasaki Rinshō, "*Myōkōnin-den* to sono sakusha tachi," *Bukkyō bungaku kenkyū* 2 (1964), 283–317.

7. Tatsuguchi Myōsei, "Gōsei sen *Myōkōnin-den* hensan no hottan," *Bukkyōshi kenkyū*, 19–20 (1984): 135–146.

8. Hayashi Chikō, "Myōkōnin no kenkyū," *Indogaku bukkyōgaku kenkyū* 29, no. 2, (1981): 348–351.

9. See, chapter 2 of Asaeda Zenshō, *Myōkōnin-den kiso kenkyū*, 63–143.

10. Asaeda Zenshō, "Shinshiryō, Jōkenji shozō *Shinmon myōkōnin-den* no ichikōsatu," in *Kimura Takeo sensei kiju kinen: Nihon bukkyōshi no kenkyū*, Nihon bukkyōshi no kenkyūkai, ed. (Kyoto: Nagata bunshōdō, 1986), 703–725.

11. See, Asaeda Zenshō, *Myōkōnin-den no shūhen* (Kyoto: Nagata bunshōdō, 1984)

12. Miyawaki Eisei, *Sekishū Ichiki Jōsenji Jitsujo-in Gōsei, Hōshuku-in Rizen ryō wajō no kenkyū* (Ichiki, Shimane: Jōsenji, 1978).

13. Uehara Yasuo, "Jitsujō-in Gōsei no nenpu oyobi chosaku mokuroku," *Kinsei bukkyō*, 5, no. 2–3 (1982): 52–57.

14. Asaeda Zenshō, "*Yūhō nikki* kō," *Ryūkoku shidan* 99–100 (1992): 445–462; "Shinshutsu *Mizoguchi asobi, Hinui asobi, Yagami asobi* kō," *Ryūkoku shidan* 101–102 (1994): 19–29; and "Shinshutsu Nishida Zuisenji zō *Kōjōenbo* kō," in *Nakanishi Chikai sensei kanreki kinen ronbunshū: Shinran no bukkyō* (Kyoto: Nagata bunshōdō), 787–798.

15. Asaeda Zenshō, "Shinshutsu, Rizen-shi jitokusho kō," *Bukkyōshi kenkyū* 22–23 (1986): 32–38; and "Shinshutsu, Jimyōji Chikō-shi *Kange itokusho* kō," *Bukkyōshi kenkyū* 24 (1987): 28–33.

16. Asaeda Zenshō, "Esaki, Kyōsenji Daigon-shi kō," *Ryūkoku kyōgaku* 25 (1990), 71–82.

17. A monograph which gathered major academic papers on the *Myōkōnin-den* edited by Zenshō Asaeda and published as *Myōkōnin-den kenkyū* (Kyoto: Nagata bunshōdō, 1987). Followings are some of my papers published thereafter. Asaeda Zenshō, "*Myōkōnin-den* no seiritsu katei no kōsatsu," *Ryūkoku shidan* 88 (1986): 22–37; "Shahon *Myōkōnin-den* no seiritsu katei," *Indogaku bukkyōgaku kenkyū* 35, no. 1 (1986): 279–283; "Shinshiryō Zenjō ki *Mutsumaru myōjū no ki* kō: Zenjō *Shōdō nisshi* shoshū," in *Hino Akira sensei kanreki kinen ronshū: Rekishi to denshō* (Kyoto: Nagata bunshōdō, 1988), 979–1001; "Gōsei hen *Shōdō mōgyū* kenkyū josetsu," *Ryūkoku daigaku ronshū* 429 (1986): 60–74; "Shinshū no dendō ni kansuru ichikōsatsu: tokuni shōdō, hōdan, hōwa nitsuite," *Ryūkoku kyōgaku* 24 (1989): 16–24; and "Shinshiryō *Shōdōshi tebikae* kō," in *Chiba Jōryū hakase koki kinen ronshū: Nihon no shakai to bukkyō*, Nihon bukkyōshi no kenkyūkai, ed. (Kyoto: Nagata bunshōdō, 1981), 478–496.

18. Ienaga Saburō, *Chūsei bukkyō shisōshi no kenkyū* (Kyoto: Hōzōkan, 1966), 345.

19. Suzuki Daisetsu, *Myōkōnin* (Kyoto: Ōtani shuppansha, 1948).

20. Yanagi Muneyoshi, "Myōkōnin no nyūshin," *Daihōrin* 22, no. 4 (April 1955): 37–43.

21. Nakamura Hajime, *Nihon shūkyō no kindaisei* (Tokyo: Shunjūsha, 1964).

22. Robert N. Bellah, *Taokugawa Religion, the Cultural Roots of Modern Japan* (New York: Free Press, 1957), 117–122.

23. Alfred Bloom, "Introduction," in Asaeda Zenshō, *Myōkōnin-den no shūhen*, 1.

24. Yanagi Muneyoshi, and Kinugasa Issei, *Myōkōnin Inaba no Genza* (Kyoto: Hyakkaen, 1960), 193.

25. In this area of *myōkōnin* studies, see, Igarashi Myōhō, "Myōkōnin no honshitsuteki kaimei," *Indogaku bukkyōgaku kenkyū* 13, no. 2 (1965): 696–700.

26. Teramoto Etatsu, *Asahara Saichi-ō wo kataru*, (Tokyo: Chiyoda joshigakuen, 1952).

27. Fuji Shūsui, *Junjō no hitobito* (1947). This book was re-published under a new title, *Shinsen Myōkōnin retsuden* (Kyoto: Hōzōkan, 1984).

28. Suzuki Daisetsu, *Myōkōnin* (Kyoto: Hōzōkan, 1948).

29. Asaeda Zenshō, *Saichi-san* (Kyoto: Nagata bunshōdō, 1991).

30. Satō Taira, "Asahara Saichi nenpu," *Ōtani joshi daigaku kiyō* 20, no. 2 (1986): 30–49.

31. Kusunoki Kyō, *Teihon Myōkōnin Asahara Saichi no uta, zen* (Kyoto: Hōzōkan, 1988).

32. Minakami Tsutomu and Satō Taira, eds., *Myōkōnin*, in Daijōbutten vol. 28 (Tokyo: Chūōkōronsha, 1987); Asahara Saichi-ō kenshōkai, ed., *Goon ureshiya*, (Nima-gun, Shimane-ken: Asahara Saichi-ō kenshōkai, 1981); Myōkōnin Iwami no Saichi kenshōkai, *Zangi to kangi*, (Yunotsu-chō, Shimane-ken: Myōkōnin Iwami no Saichi kenshōkai, 1991).

A BIBLIOGRAPHICAL SUMMARY OF STUDIES ON MYŌKŌNIN

33. Igarashi Daisaku, "Rennyo Shōnin no shisō to myōkōnin no tanjō," *Rennyo kyōgaku kenkyū* 3, (1993): 121–137.

34. Takagi Setsuyū, *Saichi dōgyō* (Kyoto: Nagata bunshōdō, 1991).

35. Minakami Tsutomu, *Saichi* (Tokyo: Kōdansha, 1989).

36. Kawakami Seikichi, *Saichi san to sono uta* (Kyoto: Hyakkaen, 1957).

37. Asaeda Zenshō, "Shinshutsu *Saichi-dōgyō* nōto kō," *Ryūkoku daigaku ronshū*, 436 (1990): 126–159; "Shinshutsu *Saichi no uta* no ichikōsatsu," *Indogaku bukkyōgaku kenkyū* 43, no. 2 (1995): 586–594; and "Shishutsu Asahara Saichi dōgyō *Nōto kō*," *Ryūkoku daigaku ronshū* 445 (1995), 159–181.

38. Kashiwahara Yūsen, "Myōkōnin: Sono rekishi zō," in *Jōdo bukkyō no shisō*, vol. 13 (Tokyo: Kōdansha, 1992), 1–232.

39. Hanaoka Daigaku, *Myōkōnin Seikurō* (Kyoto: Hyakkaen, 1966), and *Myōkōnin no sekai* (Tokyo: Yayoi shobō, 1984). Hanaoka's work, *Myōkōnin Seikurō*, is reviewed by Asaeda Zenshō, "Hanaoka Daigaku no bungaku to shūkyō: Sono Shinshū teki shiten," *Indogaku Bukkyōgaku kenkyū* 42, no. 1 (1993): 193–199.

40. Leslie S. Kawamura, "The Myokonin, Yamato no Seikuro," in Asaeda Zenshō, ed., *Myōkōnin den kenkyū* (Kyoto: Nagata bunshōdō, 1987), 25–55.

41. Ōzu Shōnen, *Okaru dōgyō monogatari* (Kyoto: Hyakkaen, 1955).

42. Ishida Hōyū, *Myōkōnin Okaru no uta* (Kyoto: Nagata bunshōdō, 1991).

43. Kuga Sunao, *Myōkōnin Osono* (Kyoto: Hōzōkan, 1993).

44. Suga Shingi, *Myōkōnin Zentarō-ō* (Kyoto: Asoka shorin, 1959).

45. Yanagi Muneyoshi and Kinugasa Issei, eds., *Myōkōnin Inaba no Genza* (Kyoto: Hyakkaen, 1960).

46. Inagaki Zuiken, *Shinja Kichibei* (Kyoto: Hyakkaen, 1956); Kusunoki Kyō, ed., *Myōkōnin Monodane Kichibei goroku* (Kyoto:

Hōzōkan, 1991).

47. Asaeda Zenshō, *Ima terasareshi ware: Aki no myōkōnin Saitō Masaji shōden* (Kyoto: Nagata bunshōdō, 1985).

48. Uno Saizō, *Shinja meguri* (Kyoto: Ōyagi kōbundō, 1922).

49. Kusunoki Kyō and Kanemitsu Toshio, eds., *Myōkōnin no sekai* (Kyoto: Hōzōkan, 1991).

50. Iwami Mamoru, *Akao no Dōshū* (Kyoto: Nagata bunshōdō, 1956).

51. Kokusai Bukkyōbunka kyōkai kenkyūkai, ed., *Yōroppa no myōkōnin Harry Peper shi* (Kyoto: Nagata bunshōdō, 1989).

52. Jean Eracle, *Jūjika kara fundarikie e*, (Kyoto: Nagata bunshōdō, 1992).

53. See note 17.

54. Asaeda Zenshō, "Sangō wakuran," in *Jōdo Shinshū hōwa taikei* (Kyoto: Dōhōsha, 1988), 979–1001.

Healing Laughter:
A Shin Dharmology of Māra

Roger CORLESS

The academic study of Buddhism is allowed to be taken seriously in the West[1] only when Buddhism itself is not taken seriously. The approach is known as Buddhology, and it shares the etic and quasi-objective presuppositions that have become accepted as normative in academe. However, the reign of the Olympian, transhistorical scholar who is implicitly the most wise of humans is coming to an end. Western scholars of Buddhism are beginning to see that what is normative to academe may be un-Buddhist or anti-Buddhist, and are reflecting on how they might write emically and normatively, as Buddhists, without sacrificing the real insights that have been gained through etic observation. This approach does not yet have an agreed upon name, and I suggest that it be called *Dharmology*. This term is used (in the form "dharmalogically") by Alfred Bloom,[2] but he claims that it was invented by Taitetsu Unno.[3] The neologism Dharmology is preferable to the proposed term Buddhist Theology, since although there are "gods" (*devas*) in Buddhism, there is clearly no "God" (*theos*), in the Christian sense, whose *logos* could be studied.[4]

DHARMOLOGY

Buddhology not only regards Buddhism as Other, it preserves it in the amber of history[5] and does not recognize that Buddhism is a living and, therefore, changing and developing phenomenon.

Dharmology, on the other hand, allows Buddhism to be Buddhism, and to interact creatively with the academic topology of the West. It supports and extends the work of Dharma teachers such as the Dalai Lama, who transmit the traditional doctrine, and of reformers and innovators such as Kiyozawa Manshi.

Dharmology, I have argued, must have the following presuppositions, none of which are accepted by Buddhology:

- the Buddhas are omniscient (either actually or potentially), because they have developed (or manifested) the full freedom of body, speech and mind;
- the Buddha-dharma, in its essence, is true for all time-structures and world-systems, and its differences arise from upāyic adaptations to particular time-space continua;
- the trichiliocosm (*trisahasrāralokadhātavah*) is the universal stage within which rebirth and liberation take place;
- reality arises interdependently (*pratītyasamutpā*) so that propositions such as theism, atheism, realism and idealism are nonsensical.[6]

A specifically Shin Dharmology would have, in addition to the above, the following presuppositions:

- the story of Dharmākara Bodhisattva becoming Amitābha Tathāgata is not a fantasy but, in some sense or another, a true description of reality-as-it-is, or a true account of how reality came to be as-it-is;
- Other-power (*tariki*) and non-Practice (*higyō*) are privileged teachings, superior to teachings about self-power and gradual cultivation.

Within these parameters, this article will attempt to reflect on the nature of evil and the appropriate Shin response to it.

THE REALITY OF MĀRA

Biblical theologian Walter Wink has proposed a reinterpretation of evil in the New Testament in a way that is Dharmologically provocative.[7] The New Testament, in accord with the worldview of its time, recognized beings, having many names but assumable under the general designation Powers (*exousiai*), associated with human institutions. The spirit or angel of a church, a country, or so forth, was believed to reside in the heavens or sky. Because of a cosmology of "as above, so below," a disturbance, such as a war, on earth, was thought to be paralleled by a war in heaven between the Powers of the earthly warring nations, and vice versa. Earthly and heavenly events caused each other.

This *Weltanschauung* is no longer credible, since a cosmos of solar systems and galaxies does not have an "above" or a "below" in anything more than a metaphorical sense. Modern humans (or are we all postmodern now?) divide reality into physical and spiritual realms, and humans are themselves divided into how much credence they give to these realms. Wink suggests that there are three variations—the spiritualistic, the materialistic, and the theological worldviews. In the spiritualistic worldview, associated anciently with Gnosticism and currently popular in occult and so-called New Age systems, spirit is real and matter is illusory or, at best, irredeemably corrupt and therefore to be rejected. The materialistic worldview, favored by modern science, is the mirror image of the spiritualistic, denying reality to anything other than matter. The theological worldview sits on the fence, allowing the simultaneous existence of spiritual and material realms, but keeping them divided, so that theology and science can go about their tasks separately, without interfering with, or embarrassing, each other.[8]

The theological worldview, it seems to me, is also the Buddhological worldview. Buddhologists study Buddhism safely protected behind the walls of their discipline and do not have to answer to anyone about the truth-claims of their remarks. Dharma teachers are permitted to function as objects for Buddhological study but they are not accepted into the academic establishment unless they pretend to a willing suspension of disbelief in, or at any rate neutrality towards, Buddhist truth-claims. In Japan (where the universities are "western," in the Hodgsonian sense) there is a more or less formal split between scholars of Buddhism and practitioners of Buddhism, and an academic split between Departments of Buddhology (*Bukkyōgakubu*) and Departments of Dharmology (called, for example, in a Shin affiliated institution, *Shinshūgakubu*), paralleling the split between Departments of Religion and Divinity Schools at some American universities.

Wink proposes a fourth "integral" worldview which ". . . attempts to take seriously the spiritual insights of the ancient or biblical worldview by affirming a withinness or interiority in all things, but sees this inner spiritual reality as inextricably related to an outer concretion or physical manifestation."[9] Wink asserts that this interiority to things is the case, and that it ". . . is emerging from. . . the reflections of Carl Jung, Teilhard de Chardin, Morton Kelsey, Thomas Berry, Matthew Fox, process philosophy, and the new physics."[10] The origin of this interiority, however, remains unexplained—it is simply, for Wink, a given which is observable by those who will allow themselves to be sensitive to, for example, the spirit of place.[11]

Dharmologically, such an interiority is less mysterious—it is the sense of self which arises interdependently with the arising of a sufficiently sophisticated physical entity. Traditionally, this sense of self or "mere *ātman*" is taught only in regard to *sattvas*, but if it is legitimate to regard beings as psychosomatic committees or institutions, it does not seem unreasonable to regard committees or institutions as psychosomatic beings. As Wink points out, the "corporate spirit" certainly *acts* like a being. I therefore propose that we adopt Wink's Integral Worldview and, by the indicated slight tweaking, adapt it as the Dharmological Worldview. We would then have an acceptable twentieth-century way of taking Māra, and the Host of Māras, seriously.

Wink further says that the Powers have three characteristics: from a Christian perspective, they are good, they are fallen, and they can be redeemed.[12] Dharmologically, we can rewrite this for the Māras as: they are not inherently evil, they are trapped in *saṃsāra* and the *kleśas*, and they can be liberated. In a Shin Dharmology, we can add that the Māras, being embraced by the *Hongan*, have the nature of *bodhi*, and are already liberated, while simultaneously remaining trapped in the *kleśas*.

This Dharmology of Māra involves a subtle but important shift of focus from that of traditional Buddhism. Māra and the Māras are usually regarded as problems, malevolent obstacles to be defeated, and they are seldom the explicit objects of that compassion which, in theory, is extended by Buddhists to all sentient beings.[13] Śākyamuni sitting under the Bodhi Tree is victorious over Māra, and Māra slinks away, only to come back and make a nuisance of himself later. Since he is not healed (i.e., converted to a follower of the Buddha and a *Dharmapāla* or Protector of the Dharma) his status as a suffering *sattva* is not taken seriously. Evil, then, becomes an abstract principle, and there is no other possible attitude to it other than submission or victory. But, when a Māra is regarded as the interdependently arising interiority of a human institution, we can approach the institution with compassion and hope as well as caution and fear, and we can expect to find ways of transforming the evil. This Dharmology permits, in other words, a social activism which is more creative than mere violence intended to destroy a corrupt institution.

The evil and the hope must be simultaneously affirmed. The evil is obvious, and it is affirmed, Dharmologically, as beginningless because of the teaching of beginningless ignorance or unawareness (*anādyavidyā*). The hope is not so obvious, but it follows from the teaching that not only unawareness but awareness, or wisdom, is beginningless. This teaching is found mainly in Vajrayāna but it is consonant with a Shin Dharmology. Vajrayāna schools argue that if awareness were not beginningless there could be no escape from beginningless unawareness. Put another way, Pure Perspective, the Vajrayāna "no-practice" of living in the non-duality of *samsāra* and *nirvāna,* is impossible if wisdom is a created phenomenon. For Pure Perspective to be possible, Primordial Awareness must be a feature of reality-as-it-is, and Vajrayāna "no-practice" must be an awakening in time to this extra-temporal wakefulness.

Rebirth in the Pure Land can be understood as another way of expressing this awakening to Pure Perspective.[14] The Pure Land sutras describe the arising of the Pure Land as an event that took place within time, but it is not a time that is historically identifiable. Described as being many *kalpas* ago, it must have occurred, if it is plotted within our currently accepted worldview, long before the emergence of humans. Therefore, we are forced either to delete the story from our Dharmology or to reinterpret what is meant by "many *kalpas* ago." Shinran helps us here. In a surprisingly modern (postmodern?) demythologization of the sutra account, he tells us that the *Hongan* has been in effect for so long that the passions of beings have been transformed from the infinite past.

> Since the infinite past, the river waters of the sundry practices and disciplines performed by ordinary people and sages, and the ocean waters of the ignorance—infinite as the sands of the Ganges—of those who commit the five grave offenses, who slander the dharma, or who lack the seed of Buddhahood, have been transformed into the waters of the great treasure ocean of all the true and real virtues—countless as the sands of the Ganges—of the great wisdom-compassion of the Primal Vow.[15]

The *Hongan* is, for all practical purposes, the way reality is in itself. It does not seem illegitimate to identify Shinran's teaching of the infinite past time, or *illud tempus,* of the *Hongan*[16] with the Vajrayāna teaching of Primordial Pristine Awareness.

I would further suggest that we can see the story of Dharmākara as an *upāya* for *sattvas*. It is typical of Mahāyāna to read the life of Śākyamuni as *upāya*—to teach that the awakening to *bodhi* of the

HEALING LAUGHTER

nirmāṇakāya is the skillful play of the Dharmakāya. It is not that the nirmāṇakāya does not really attain *bodhi* (it is inappropriate to import, as has sometimes been done, a Gnostic Christology of Docetism into Mahāyāna Buddhalogy[17] or Vajrayāna *rnam thar*), it is more that the attainment of *bodhi* occurs at the level of *saṃvṛtti-satya*, while at the level of *paramārtha-satya* Śākyamuni has, as he claims in the *Lotus Sutra*, never not been enlightened. In the same way, then, we can say that Dharmākara's progress along the bodhisattva path is the skillful play of Amitābha Tathāgata. Further, it is taught in Vajrayāna that the life of Śākyamuni is a model for the attainment of *bodhi* by *sattvas* even though *bodhi* is primordial so that there is, ultimately, nothing to attain. We can adapt this Vajrayāna teaching to Shin by saying that although Dharmākara's progress is *upāya* this does not detract from its being used as a model for Shin practice of non-practice.

Finally, according to the established Shin principle of *ki-hō ittai*, the timelessness of the *Hongan* and the temporal *upāya* of the Nembutsu can be seen as co-inhering (i.e., each containing and being contained by the other) in the *bombu*.

With these presuppositions about a Shin Dharmology of Māra, we can suggest nonviolent ways of what Walter Wink calls "engaging the Powers."

ENGAGING THE MĀRAS

Wink makes much of the futility of meeting violence with violence. He relates this to the psychological structure of mirroring or violent mimesis, and warns us how easy it is to become what we hate.[18] Buddhists are familiar with this principle from the opening verse of the *Dhammapada* which clearly states that, due to the way in which karma is observed to operate, hate only leads to suffering, that is, to more hate, as the wheels of a cart follow the hooves of the draft animal.[19] However, Wink does not simplistically, and unrealistically, counsel a passive nonviolent response. His nonviolence is more proactive, recommending that we deal with the evil light-heartedly, maintaining a trust in a benevolent outcome. For instance, by reading the famous logion about turning the other cheek (Matthew 5:39) in the cultural context of the time (what Biblical scholars call the text's *Sitz im Leben*) he is able to see Jesus' advice to "resist not evil" not as resignation to the evil but as a way of frustrating the evil by creating mischievous confusion.[20] The point, he tells us, is made by the fact that the person is first struck on the *right* cheek and is advised to offer his *left* cheek for a second slap. A menial could be disciplined, or humiliated, by striking him with the back of the right hand, and, thus, on the right cheek. Using the fist or the flat of the right hand implied that one's opponent was one's equal—it was aggression, but it did not humiliate. Using the left hand was unthinkable, since it was ritually unclean. So, if the menial turned his left cheek towards his master, he was putting the master in the awkward position of either going through the undignified contortions of trying to hit the servant's left cheek with the back of his right hand, or forcing him to acknowledge that the servant was a human on equal terms with his master. In either case, evil would be thwarted nonviolently, by maneuvering it into a position where it made a fool of itself, in the confident expectation that good would prevail.

We can adapt Wink's suggestions to Dharmology by clearly seeing the transparency (*śūnyatā*) of the Māras' egos, and the co-inherence (*sōnyū*) of *kleśa* and *bodhi*.

If we fight evil with evil, not only does the evil, according to the fruiting of karma, come back to us, magnified, but we act as if the Māras were inherently evil. When we apply our insight (*vipaśyanā*) to their evil, we see it as conditioned, and realize that when the conditions change the evil will change and, eventually, vanish. We also see, from a Shin perspective, that the Māras are embraced by the *Hongan* in the same way that we are and, therefore, are powerless to harm us in any ultimate (*lokottara*) way although they may well do us conditioned, or intra-samsaric (*laukika*) harm. We can then show the same compassion for the Māras that Amida shows to them and to us, and which the Amida in us shows to the Māras in us.

Humor is, according to Buddhism, as powerful a weapon against the Māras as, according to Wink, it is against the Powers in the New Testament. Apart from the explicitly humorous story in *Saṃyutta-Nikāya* 11: 3: 2 about the anger-eating demon, a story which, told in a humorous way, teaches humor as an effective response to evil, there is the common teaching that Māra feeds on the *kleśas:* a bhikṣu is called, in the Chinese tradition, "One who causes Māra to tremble"[21] because, by his ascesis, he is threatening Māra's supply of lust, hate and confusion. Humor and light-heartedness, then, being the opposite of the *kleśas*, are cogent nonviolent responses to Māra.

It is important to notice that what is being counseled is not laughing *off* the evil, as if it were unimportant or did not really exist, but laughing *at* it so as to neutralize it. On the hither-shore (*saṃvṛtitas*), intra-saṃsāric (*laukika*), or unliberated being (*bombu*) level, evil is evil, and must be fully acknowledged and resisted—with force indeed, if all else fails. But at the further-shore (*paramārthitas*), extra-saṃsāric (*lokottara*), or Amida's vow (*hongan*) level, there is serene confidence (*shinjin*) in the ultimate benevolence of reality-as-it-is, and from this confidence, the healing laughter of the *myōkōnin* (those who have realized *shinjin*) can arise.

This healing laughter is, perhaps, what Shinran was experiencing when he said that ". . . without the practicer's calculating in any way whatsoever, all his past, present, and future evil karma is transformed into the highest good."[22] Why should we restrict this transformation to humans? Why not include Māra and his host? *Namu Amida Butsu!*

NOTES

1. Understanding "the west" ideologically, following Marshall Hodgson's interpretative definition, rather than geographically. See, for example, "The great Western Transmutation" in *Rethinking World*

ROGER CORLESS

History: Essays on Europe, Islam, and World History, Marshall G. S. Hodgson, ed., with an Introduction and a Conclusion by Edmund Burke, III (Cambridge: Cambridge University Press, 1993), 44–71.

2. *Shoshinge: The Heart of Shin Buddhism* (Honolulu: Buddhist Study Center Press, 1986), 20.

3. Alfred Bloom, personal communication, September 24, 1994. Bloom says that he changed the spelling from Unno's original suggestion of *Dharmology* to what he considered the more correct form *Dharmalogy*. I take the liberty of changing the spelling back to *Dharmology*, for it seems to me more natural, and is consistent with the form *Buddhology*. (The term *Buddhalogy* has been proposed by Paul Griffiths in *On Being a Buddha: The Classical Doctrine of Buddhahood* [Albany, N.Y.: State University of New York Press, 1994] to refer to emic accounts of the Buddha, apparently as a Buddhist equivalent of the term *Christology*.)

4. See my "Hermeneutics and Dharmology: Finding an American Buddhist Voice" in *Buddhist Theology: Critical Reflections by Contemporary Buddhist Scholars*, edited by Roger Jackson and John Makransky, Curzon Critical Studies in Buddhism, (London: Curzon Press, forthcoming).

5. This is true even for sociological studies of contemporary Buddhism. Since the Buddhological observer does not consciously participate in the evolution or modification of Buddhism, the Buddhism which is presented for analysis is implicitly historicized. We might call this subtle historicism, to distinguish it from the gross historicism of studying ancient texts without regard to the living lineage which gives them contemporary significance.

6. List slightly adapted from my "Hermeneutics and Dharmology."

7. Walter Wink, *Naming the Powers: The Language of Power in the New Testament* (Minneapolis, Minn.: Fortress Press, 1984); *Unmasking the Powers: The Invisible Forces that Determine Human Existence* (Minneapolis, Minn.: Fortress Press, 1986); and *Engaging the Powers: Discernment and Resistance in a World of Domination* (Minneapolis, Minn.: Fortress Press, 1992).

8. Wink, *Engaging the Powers*, 4–5.

9. Ibid., 5.

10. Ibid.

11. Wink instances, as places that have a "palpable evil," Nazi Germany in the late 1930s, South Africa during the period of apartheid, and the U.S.A. at the time of the assassination of President John F. Kennedy. Ibid., 8.

12. Ibid., 10. Wink at first says, with missionary fervor, that the Powers *must* be redeemed, but he almost immediately modifies this to the more theological statement that they *can* be redeemed.

13. There are exceptional cases, associated especially with Tibetan *siddhas*, where malevolent entities are invited to approach and are compassionately instructed in Dharma.

14. See my "Pure Land and Pure Perspective: A Tantric Hermeneutic of Sukhāvatī," *The Pure Land*, New Series 6 (1989): 205–217.

15. *The True Teaching, Practice and Realization of the Pure Land Way: A Translation of Shinran's Kyōgyōshinshō*, vol. 1, Shin Buddhism Translation Series, Yoshifumi Ueda, general editor (Kyoto: Hongwanji International Center, 1983), 150.

16. Shinran uses the characters *jū ku-on irai*, "from the very long-ago until now", which I interpret as *mukashi-mukashi* (once upon a time)—i.e., extra-temporal mythic time—what Eliade called *illud tempus*. Hoshino Gempō, Ishida Mitsuyuki, and Ienaga Saburō, eds., *Shinran*, Nihon shisō taikei, vol. 11 (Tokyo: Iwanami shoten, 1971), 295.

17. For the term Buddhalogy, see note 3.

18. Wink, *Engaging the Powers*, chapter 10, "On Not Becoming What We Hate."

19. manasā ce paduṭṭhena bhāsati vā karoti vā /
    tato naṃ dukkhamanveti cakkaṃ va vahato padaṃ //
               —Dhammapada 1:1b—

20. Wink, *Engaging the Powers*, 175–177.

21. Personal communication from a bhikṣu at the City of Ten Thousand Buddhas, Talmage, California. The bhikṣu did not offer a textual reference but spoke of the term as something commonly known in his tradition.

22. *Notes on "Esentials of Faith Alone": A Translation of Shinran's Yuishinshōmon'i*, Shin Buddhism Translation Series, Yoshifumi Ueda, general editor (Kyoto: Hongwanji International Center, 1979), 32.

An Abridged Curriculum Vitae
of
DR. ALFRED BLOOM

An Abridged Curriculum Vitae of
DR. ALFRED BLOOM

EDUCATION:

Eastern Baptist Theological Seminary, A.B., Th.B., 1947–51.

Andover Newton Theological School, B.D., S.T.M., 1951–53.

Harvard Divinity School, Ph.D., 1963.

Ph.D. Dissertation: "Shinran, His Life and Thought."

Fulbright Student Grantee, 1957–59 for study in Japan, Ryūkoku University.

ACADEMIC POSITIONS:

1994–   Professor Emeritus, Institute of Buddhist Studies.

1986–1994 Dean, Honganji Professor of Shin Buddhism, Institute of Buddhist Studies, Berkeley, CA.

1988–   Professor Emeritus, University of Hawaii.

1986–1988 In Residence at Institute of Buddhist Studies, Berkeley, CA.

1974–1986 Professor of Religion, Department of Religion, University of Hawaii at Manoa.

1970–1974 Associate Professor of Religion, Department of Religion, University of Hawaii at Manoa.

1961–1970 Associate Professor of Religion, University of Oregon.

1961   Lecture in History of Religion, Newton Junior College.

1959–1961 Proctor for Center for the Study of World Religions, Harvard Divinity School.

Teaching Fellow in History of Religion, Harvard Divinity School.

ORGANIZATIONS:

Kent Fellow, Society for Values in Higher in Higher Education, 1955–present

International Association of Shin Buddhist Studies, Vice President, present

LECTURESHIPS:

Spring and Fall 1996: Buddhist Study Center, Honolulu, Hawaii, "Lectures on *Kyōgyōshinshō*," and "Life and Thought of Rennyo Shōnin."

Spring 1993: Numata Visiting Professor, Center for the Study of World Religions, Harvard University, Divinity School.

Fall 1992: Ryukoku University, Kyoto Japan, "Shin Buddhism in Modern Culture."

PUBLICATIONS:

BOOKS

Shinran's Gospel of Pure Grace. Society for Asian Studies monograph series. Tucson, Arizona: University of Arizona Press, 1965. (Eighth Edition, 1991, Association of Asian Studies.)

The Life of Shinran Shonin: the Journey to Self-Acceptance. Leiden: E.J. Brill, 1968. (Reprint from *Numen* 15 [1968].)

"Far Eastern Religious Tradition." In *Religions and Man*, W. Richard Comstock, general editor, New York: Harper & Row, 1971. (*Religions and Man* is also published in three separate volumes. The article "Far Eastern Religious Traditions," concerning on Chinese and Japanese Religions, is included in *Indian and Far Eastern Religious Traditions*, coauthored with Robert D. Baird, New York: Harper and Row, 1972.)

Shinran wo meguru mōhitotsu no bunkaron. Kyoto: Nishi Honganji shuppanbu, 1978. Coauthored with Robert N. Bellah and Futaba Kenkō. (Published in Japanese. Dr. Bloom was in charge of the section "Shinran to Gendaibunka—sonzai no tameno tetsugaku." Republished in 1997 with English essay from Nagata Bunshōdō.)

Tannisho: A Resource for Modern Living. Honolulu, Hawaii: Buddhist Study Center, 1981.

Shinran to sono jōdokyō. Kyoto: Nagata bunshōdō, 1983. (Japanese translation of *Shinran's Gospel of Pure Grace* by Fujisawa Masanori, Hayashi Nobuyasu, and Nomura Nobuo. Originally published in *Shinshū kenkyūkai kiyō* [Journal of the Postgraduate Research Institute of Ryukoku University] 11 [1978], 12 [1979], and 13 [1980]. *Shinran's Gospel of Pure Grace* was also translated into Korean and published in 1985.)

Shoshinge: the Heart of Shin Buddhism. Honolulu, Hawaii: Buddhist Study Center Press, 1986.

Gendai shisō to Tannishō. Tokyo: Mainichi shinbunsha, 1987. (Japanese Translation of *Tannisho: A Resource for Modern Living* by Michio Tokunaga.)

Strategies for Modern Living, A Commentary with the Text of the Tannisho. Berkeley, California: Numata Center for Buddhist Translation and Research, 1992. (Republication of *Tannisho: A Resource for Modern Living* with an English translation of the *Tannishō* prepared by the Numata Center for Buddhist Translation and Research.)

The Life of Shinran Shonin: The Journey to Self-Acceptance. Institute of Buddhist Studies Monograph Series Number One. Berkeley, Calif.: Institute of Buddhist Studies, 1994. (Republication of *The Life of Shinran Shonin: the Journey to Self-Acceptance.* Leiden: E.J. Brill, 1968.)

Shinran wo meguru mōhitotsu no bunkaron. Futaba Kenkō, ed. Kyoto: Nagata Bunshōdō, 1997. (Republication of *Shinran wo meguru mōhitotsu no bunkaron.* Kyoto: Nishi Honganji shuppanbu, 1978, with English essay "Shinran and Modern Culture: A Philosophy for Existence," 1–97.)

TRANSLATIONS

Watanabe, Shōkō. *Japanese Buddhism: A Critical Appraisal.* Tokyo: Kokusai Bunka Shinkōkai, 1964 (First Edition), 1968 (Revised Edition).

Kaigo, Tokiomi. *Japanese Education: Its Past and Present.* Tokyo: Kokusai Bunka Shinkōkai, 1965.

Graphic Biography of Chigaku Tanaka: Accompanying Commentary. Tokyo: Kokuchūkai, 1965.

Forthcoming:

Translation of *Selected Essays of Soga Ryōjin* in collaboration with Bishop Hōsen Fukuhara, for the Gankai Association.

ARTICLES

"Human Rights in Israel's Thought: A Study of Old Testament Doctrine." *Interpretation* 8 (1954): 422–432.

"A Basis for the Comparison of Religions: Christianity and Buddhism." *Journal of Bible and Religion* 24 (1956): 269–274.

"Methodology in the Comparison of Religions." *Japan Christian Quarterly* 24 (1958): 137–139.

"Is the Nembutsu Magic?" *Japanese Religions* 1, no. 3 (1959): 31–35.

"Meditation on a Swimming Pool: Essey in Buddhist Philosophy." *The Young East* (Winter 1963).

"Shinran's Philosophy of Salvation." *Contemporary Religions in Japan* 5 (1964): 119–142.

"Shinran's Gospel of Pure Grace." *Journal of Bible and Religion* 32 (1964): 305–316. (Japanese translation published in *Chūgai Nippō* [Japanese newspaper of religion], July 1965.)

"Observations in the Study of Contemporary Nichirern Buddhism." *Contemporary Religions in Japan* 6 (1965): 58–74.

(Japanese translation published in *International Religious News*, July–August 1965.)

"The Historical Significance of Nichiren's Religion." *The Young East*, 14, no. 55 (1965): 2–6 and 28 (Japanese translation published in *Chūgai Nippō* [Japanese newspaper of religion], December 1965).

"Shinran and Nichiren: A Comparison." *Mahabodhi* (May–June 1966).

"The Sense of Sin and Guilt and the Last Age [Mappō] in Chinese and Japanese Buddhism." *Numen* 14 (1967): 144–149.

"A Modern Perspective on Buddhism." *World Buddhism* 15, no. 11 (1967): 305–307.

"Life of Shinran Shōnin: Journey to Self-Acceptance." *Numen* 15 (1968): 1–62. (Reprinted and published under the same title as a monograph from E. J. Brill in 1968).

"Buddhism, Nature and the Environment." *Eastern Buddhist*, n.s. 5, no. 1, (1972): 115–129.

"Biblical Faith as a Zen Koan." *Christian Century* 89 (1972): 774–775.

"Ancient Wisdom and Modern Man." *PHP* (*Peace Happiness Prosperity*) 4, no. 12 (December 1973): 6–12.

"Personal Reflections on the Teaching of Shinran." *The Young East* 1, no. 4 (1975): 10–16.

"The Humanism of the Lotus Sutra." *Dharma World* 3, no. 10 (1976): 18–20.

"Reflections on the Center for the Study of World Religions, Harvard Divinity School." *Studies in Religion/Sciences Religieuses* 6, no. 5 (1976–1977): 497–498.

"Contemporaly Meaning of Buddha's Birth." *The Young East* 2, no. 3 (1976): 15–20.

"Buddhist Guidelines in a Confused World." *The Young East* 3, no. 2 (1977): 5–10, 24.

"Japanese Religion and Interpretation." In *Cherry Blossom Festival Booklet* (Spring, 1977).

"Shinran's Vision of Absolute Compassion." *Eastern Buddhist*, n.s. 10 (1977): 111–123.

"Shinran to Gendaibunka—sonzai no tameno tetsugaku." Translated by Kuchiba Masuo and Takemura Naohiko. In Robert N. Bellah, Alfred Bloom, and Futaba Kenkō *Shinran wo meguru mōhitotsu no bunkaron*. Kyoto: Nishi Honganji shuppanbu, 1978, 79–160.

"Shinran's Way in Modern Society." *Eastern Buddhist*, n.s. 11 (1978): 85–97.

"Revolutionary Character of Pure Land Teaching." *The Young East* (Summer 1979).

"Shinran, A Man with Nothing to Hide." *Metta* (July 1980).

"Amida and Myself." *Gankai* (August 1980).

"Ethical Perspectives in Shinran's Teachings." *Gankai* (November 1980).

"What Does It Mean to be Human." *Gankai* (May 1981).

"Shinran's Vision and Mission." *Gankai* (November 1982).

"To There and Back." *Eastern Buddhist*, n.s. 16 (1983): 148–152.

"Sakyamuni and Amitabha: Which is the True Primordially Eternal Buddha?" In *Sekiguchi Shindai Festschrift*. (1984).

"Shinran." In *Kōdansha Encyclopedia of Japan*, vol. 7 (Tokyo; New York: Kōdansha, 1983): 122–123.

"Wasan." In *Kōdansha Encyclopedia of Japan*, vol. 8 (Tokyo: New York: Kōdansha, 1983): 231.

"Shinran's Praises on the Nembutsu of True Faith, The Reality of Faith in History." *Junshin Gakuhō* (December 1984).

"A Report on the Symposium on Shin Buddhism and Christianity, Textual and Contextual Translation, At Harvard University." *Metta*, 11, no. 7 (September, 1984). (Reprinted in *The Pure Land,* n.s. 2 [1985]: 3–8. Japanise translation was also published in *Amerika no shūkyō wo tazunete* [Shin Buddhism Meets American Religion], [Kyoto: Nishi Hongwanji naijibu, 1986.]: 30–36, with original English text.)

"Jōdo Shinshū: the Cosmic Connection." *The Pure Land,* n.s. 1 (1984): 36–61.

"Buddhism Shall not Die in the Hawaiian Islands." *English Mainichi* (July 11, 1985).

"Second Biennial Conference of the IASBS in Hawaii, Keynote Address, Reflections on the Theme: 'Shin Buddhist Studies Look Toward the 21st Century'." *The Pure Land,* n.s. 2 (1985): 16–20.

"A Report on the Symposium on Shin Buddhism and Christianity, Textual and Contextual Translation, At Harvard University." *The Pure Land,* n.s. 2 (1985): 3–8. (Reprint, *Metta,* 11–7 [September 1984].)

"The Light of the East Moves West: Shin Buddhism in the United States and Hawaii." *Spring Wind* (Winter 1985–1986)

"A Vision of Jōdo Shinshū: Fullfilling the Primal Vow in History." *The Pacific World,* n.s. 1 (1985): 5–6.

"Shinran's Praises on the Nembutsu of True Faith, The Reality of Faith in History, Part II." *Junshin Gakuhō* (December, 1985).

"Fulfilling the Primal Vow in America." *Wheel of Dharma* (December 1985 and January 1986).

"Spiritual Potentials for Quality Living." *The Pacific World,* n.s. 2 (1986): 42–48.

"Jōdo Shinshū to Kirisutokyō ni kansuru shinpojiumu, genten no honyaku to seishin bunka no dentatsu." In *Amerika no shūkyō wo tazunete* [Shin Buddhism Meets American Religion], (Kyoto: Nishi Hongwanji naijibu, 1986): 30–36. (Japanese translation of "A Report on the Symposium on 'Shin Buddhism and Christianity: Textual and Contextual Translation' at Harvard University." *Metta,* 11, no. 7 [September 1984]. Original English text was also reprinted in the same publication, pages 230–224. The page numbers run opposite to the normal English convention due to Japanese format and binding.)

"Shinran." In T*he Encyclopedia of Religion.* Edited by Mircia Eliade, 13. New York: Macmillan (1987): 278–280.

"Confucian and Buddhist Values in Modern Context." *The Pacific World*, n.s. 4 (1988): 60–68.

"Jishinkyoninshin: Shareing Our Faith with the World." *BCA Pamphlet* (1988).

"Introduction to Jōdo Shinshū." *The Pacific World*, n.s. 5 (1989): 33–39.

"The Unfolding of the Lotus: A Survey of Recent Developments in Shin Buddhism in the West." *Buddhist Christian Studies* 10 (1990): 157–164.

"A Spiritual Odyssey: My Encounter with Pure Land Buddhism." *Buddhist Christian Studies* 10 (1990): 173–175.

"Seeing Beneath the Surface: Shinran's View of Scripture." *The Pure Land*, n.s. 7 (1990): 11–16.

"Human Rights and the Buddhadharma." *Wheel of Dharma*, 18, no. 7 (July 1991).

"Shinran in the Context of Pure Land Tradition." *Japanese Religions* 17 (1992): 4–30.

"Shin Buddhism in Encounter with a Religiously Plural World." *The Pure Land*, n.s. 8–9 (1992): 17–31. (Japanese translation, by Higuchi Shoshin of Ōtani University, published in *Ōbun shinshū kenkyū*, 1 [1993].)

"The Tannisho as a Manifesto of Spiritual Liberation: A Shin Buddhist Perspective on Wholeness of Personhood." *Bauddha Dharmankur Sabha volume: Hundred Years of the Bauddha Dharmankur Sabha* (Bengal Buddhist Association) (1992).

"Problematics of Buddhist Christian Dialogue." *The Pacific World*, n.s. 8 (1992): 93–99.

"The Ultimacy of Jōdo Shinshū: Shinran's Response to Tendai." *The Pure Land*, n.s. 10–11 (1994): 28–55.

"A Buddhist Perspective on Dual Worship." *Buddhist Christian Studies* 14 (1994).

"Kokuchūkai e oiwai no kotoba." *Shinsekai,* 11 (1994).

"Hokkekyō: sono seishinteki na igi." *Nichiren shugi kenkyū* 17 (1994).

"Buddhist Awakening in a Post-Modern Age." *Hawaii Association of International Buddhists Newsletter* (Winter 1994–5): 3–4. (Reprented in *Goji: Hongwanji Newsletter* (February 1995): 47–42.)

"The Western Pure Land: Shin in America." *Tricycle* 4, no. 4 (Summer 1995).

"The Shinshū Approach to Peace." In *Jōdo Shinshū no Heiwagaku,* edited by Hiroshima Betsuin (Kyoto: Dōbōsha, 1995), 159–172.

"Keynote Speech: Shin Buddhism Advances on the Post-Modern Horizon." *The Pure Land,* n.s. 12 (December 1995): 15–37.

"Rennyo Shonin's 500th Anniversary." *Wheel of Dharma* 23, no. 2 (February 1996): 3.

"Perspectiva Sobre El Budismo Japones." *Gran Via* 1 (Universidad Moderna de Lisboa en Madrid, February 1996): 48–54.

"The Unique Potential of Shin Buddhism in Western Society." *Metta* 23, no. 3 (March 1996).

"Shinran and Modern Culture: A Philosophy for Existence." In *Shinran wo meguru mōhitotsu no bunkaron.* Futaba Kenkō, ed. (Kyoto: Nagata Bunshōdō, 1997), 1–97.

Forthcoming:

"Shin Buddhism Takes Root in America." In *The Faces of Buddhism in America,* edited by Charles Prebish and Kenneth K. Tanaka (University of California Press).

"The Legacy of Shinran." In *Encyclopedia of Spirituality,* ed. Paul Swanson (Crossroad Press)

"Rennyo's View of the Salvation of Women: Overcoming the Five

Obstacles and Three Subordinations." Essay submitted for Nishi Honganji Rennyo Project.

REVIEWS

Japanese Buddhism and Christianity: A Comparison of the Christian Doctrine of Salvation with that of Some Major Sects of Japanese Buddhism, by Tucker N. Callaway. In *Japan Christian Quarterly* 24 (April 1958): 176–178.

A Comparative Study of Buddhism and Christianity, by Fumio Masutani. In *Japan Christian Quarterly* 24 (April 1958): 178–180.

Zen and Shinto: A History of Japanese Philosophy. by Fujisawa Chikao. In *Harvard Divinity Bulletin* 25 (1960): 23.

Mudra: A Study of Symbolic Gestures in Japanese Buddhist Sculpture, by Ernst Dale Saunders. In *Harvard Divinity Bulletin* 25 (April–July 1960): 23–24.

History of Zen Buddhism, by Heinrich DuMoulin. In *Asian Student* (April 21, 1962).

East and West: A Study of Their Psychic and Cultural Characteristics, by Lewis Gulick. In *Journal for Asian Studies* 23-3 (1964): 460–461.

History of Japanese Religions: with Special Reference to the Social and Moral Life of the Nation, by M. Anesaki. In *Journal for Asian Studies* 23, no. 3 (1964): 476.

Buddhism in China, by Kenneth Chen. In *Asian Student* (March 20, 1965).

Source Book in Chinese Philosophy, by Wing Tsit Chan. In *Journal of Bible and Religion* 33 (1965): 180–182.

Ways in thinking of Eastern Peoples, by H. Nakamura. In *Asian Student* (May 22, 1965).

Scheliermacher on Christ and Religion, by R. R. Niebuhr. In *Western Humanities Reviews* (Summer 1965).

The Sutra of the Sixth Patriarch on the Pristine Orthodox Dharma, by Paul F. Fung and George D. Fung. In *Asian Student* (October 9, 1965).

Israel in Christian Religious Instruction, by Theodore Filthaut. In *Eugene Register-Guard* (December 12, 1965).

The Sociology of Religious Belonging, by Herve Carriere. In *Manila Chronicle* (Nobember 2, 1966).

Man in Estrangement, by Guyton Hammond. In *Manila Chronicle* (December 6, 1966).

Religion in Japanese History, by Joseph Kitagawa. In *Asian Student* (January 14, 1967).

Nichiren no shiso to kamakura bukkyo, by Tokoro Shigemoto. In *Journal of Asian Studies* 27, no. 1 (1967): 153–154.

Practice of Chinese Buddhism, by Holmes Welch. In *Asian Student* (December 23, 1967).

Nichiren to iu hito, by Tokoro Shigemoto. In *Journal of the American Academy of Religion* 26 (1968): 170–172.

Shinto no chikara (The Power of Shinto), by Ueda Kenji. In *Monumenta Nipponica* 23, no. 3–4 (1969): 505–506.

The Great Asian Religions, by Wing Tsit Chan, et al. In *Asian Student* (October 4, 1969).

Kindai nihon no shukyo to nashyonarizumu, by Tokoro Shigemoto. In *Journal for the Scientific Study of Religion* 7, no. 2 (1968): 316.

The Buddhist Revival in China, by Holmes Welch. In *Asian Student* (February 1969).

The Buddhist Philosophy of Assimilation, by Alicia Matsunaga. In *Asian Student* (Winter 1970).

Soka Gakkai, Builders of the Third Civilization, by James Dator. In *Journal for the Scientific Study of Religion* 9, no. 2 (1970): 175–176.

Japanese Religion, Unity and Diversity, by H. Byron Earhart. In *Journal for the Scientific Study of Religion* 9, no. 2 (1970): 176–177.

Motoori Norinaga, by Matsumoto Shigeru. In *Asian Student* (Spring 1971).

Religion and Society in Modern Japan, by Edward Norbeck. In *Journal of Asian Studies* 30 (1971): 679–681.

Happiness and Immortality, by P. J. Saher. In *Philosophy East and West* 21 (1971): 346–347.

The Buddhist Bible, by Dwight Goddard. In *Philosophy East and West* 21 (1971): 347–348.

Japan's New Buddhism, by Kiyoaki Murata. In *Journal for the Scientific Study of Religion* 10, no. 1 (1971): 55–56.

Japanese Religiosity, by Joseph Spae. In *Philosophy East and West* 22 (1972): 108–110.

Kukai: Major Works, by Yoshito Hakeda. In *Asian Student* (March 1972).

The Zen Master Hakuin: Selected Writings. by Philip B. Yampolsky. In *Asian Student* (April 1972).

The Recorded Sayings of Layman P'ang: A Ninth Century Zen Classic, by Ruth Fuller Sasaki, et al. trans. In *Review of Books and Religion* 1–10 (June 1972).

The Way of All the Earth, by John S. Dunne. In *Review of Books and Religion* 2, no. 1 (September 1972).

Early Buddhist Japan, by J. Edward Kidder. In *Asian Student* (November 1972).

Buddhism: A Historical Introduction to Buddhist Values and the Social and Political Forms They Have Assumed in Asia, by Peter A. Pardue. In *Philosophy East and West* 23 (1973): 407–409.

Buddhism in Hawaii: Its Impact on a Yankee Community Societies, by Louise Hunter. (1973).

Shinran: His Life and Thought, by Norihiko Kikumura. In *Asian Student* (Fall 1973).

Shinto Man, by Joseph Spae. In *Philosophy East and West* 23 (1973): 547–549.

Japanese Religion: A Survey by the Agency for Cultural Affairs, ed. by Ichiro Hori. In *Asian Student* (January, 1974.)

The Feast of Kingship: Accession Ceremonies in Ancient Japan, by Robert S. Ellwood. In *Journal of Asian Studies* 33, no. 3 (1974): 481–483.

Foundation of Japanese Buddhism, Volume I, *The Aristocratic Age,* by Daigan and Alicia Matsunaga. In *Monumenta Nipponica* 30, no. 3 (1975): 481–483.

Collected Writings on Shin Buddhism, and *The Kyogyoshinsho,* by Daisetz Teitaro Suzuki. In *Eastern Buddhist,* n.s. 8, no. 2 (1975): 163–169.

Zen Comments on the Mumonkan, by Zenkei Shibayama. In *Journal of Asian Studies* 35 (1975): 152–154.

The Road East: America's New Discovery of Eastern Wisdom, by Harrison Pope, Jr., and *Christianity Meets Buddhism,* by Heinrich Du Moulin. In *Review of Books and Religion,* 4–6 (February 1975): 15.

Miraculous Stories from the Japanese Buddhist Tradition, by Kyoko Motomochi. In *Asian Student* (Spring 1975).

Christianity: Japanese Way, by Carlo Caldarola. In *Journal of American Academy of Religion* 48 (1980): 622–623.

Timeless Spring: A Soto Zen Anthology, ed. by Thomas Cleary. In *Monumenta Nippoinca* 34, no. 1 (1981): 109–110.

Buddhist Faith and Sudden Enlightenment, by Sung Bae Park. In *Buddhist Christian Studies* 4 (1984): 145–148.

Tannisho: A Primer, trans. by Dennis Hirota. In *Journal of the American Academy of Religion* 52 (1984): 408–409.

Jōdo Shinshū: Shin Buddhism in Medieval Japan, by James Dobbins. In *Monumenta Nipponica* 44, no. 3 (1989): 380–383.

Shinran, An Introduction to His Thought, by Yoshifumi Ueda and Dennis Hirota. In *Wheel of Dharma* (August 1989).

Shinran, An Introduction to His Thought, by Yoshifumi Ueda and Dennis Hirota. In *Buddhist Christian Studies* 10 (1990): 294–296.

The summary of the Great Vehicle, trans. by John P. Keenan. In *The Pacific World,* n.s. 9 (1993): 150–151.

The Natural Way of Shin Buddhism, by Ruth Tabrah and Shoji Matsumoto. In *Wheel of Dharma* (October 1994).

A Glossary of Shin Buddhist Terms, by Hisao Inagaki. In *Metta* (August 1995).

The list of Dr. Alfred Bloom's publications is compiled by the editors based on the vitae provided by Dr. Alfred Bloom, and information gathered at the libraries of the Institute of Buddhist Studies, the Graduate Theological Union, and the University of California at Berkeley. We would also like to thank Rev. Senkei Kazuyoshi Sasaki and Rev. Akiyo Yokota who provided additional information. [Eisho Nasu]

Contributors

Zenshō Asaeda is a Professor of Japanese Buddhist History at Ryūkoku University, Kyoto. He is a specialist in Ancient Japanese Buddhist history and *myōkōnin* studies. His major publications are *Myōkōnin-den kiso kenkyū* (1982), *Nihonryōiki kenkyū* (1990), and *Zoku Myōkōnin-den kiso kenkyū* (1998).

Roger Corless is a Professor of Religion at Duke University. He has a B.D. from King's College, University of London, and a Ph.D. in Buddhist Studies from the University of Wisconsin-Madison. A specialist in Pure Land Buddhism, he has published four books and over fifty articles on Buddhism, Christian Spirituality, and Buddhist-Christian Studies.

James C. Dobbins is an Associate Professor at Oberlin College in Ohio. He has served as Chair of the Religion Department and Director of the East Asian Studies Program at Oberlin. His major publications are *Jōdo Shinshū: Shin Buddhism in Medieval Japan* (Indiana University Press, 1989) and *The Legacy of Kuroda Toshio* (*Japanese Journal of Religious Studies*, 1996).

James H. Foard received his Ph.D. from Stanford University and is a Professor in the Department of Religious Studies at Arizona State University. His previous publications include studies of medieval and early modern popular Buddhism in Japan and of the religious responses to the atomic bombing of Hiroshima.

James Fredericks is a Roman Catholic theologian who specializes in Buddhist-Christian dialogue. He teaches comparative theology at Loyola Marymount University in Los Angeles. He has published in

CONTRIBUTORS

The Eastern Buddhist, Theological Studies and *The Pure Land*. He has translated a series of articles by Masao Abe which have been published in *International Philosophical Quarterly*. He is currently working in Kyoto on a book exploring Christianity using Shinran's thought.

Gregory G. Gibbs is a resident minister at Los Angeles Hompa Hongwanji Buddhist Temple. He is a graduate of the Institute of Buddhist Studies (M.A. in Buddhist Studies and Master of Jōdo-Shinshū Studies) and an active member of the North American Branch of the International Association of Shin Buddhist Studies. His publications include, "Understanding Shinran and the Burden of the Traditional Dogmatics" (*The Eastern Buddhist*, Fall, 1997), and "Shinjin as a Transformation in Personal Identity" (*The Pure Land*, 1998).

Maya M. Hara graduated from the Institute of Buddhist Studies (M.A. in Buddhist Studies). Her study focused on the history of the development of Japanese Pure Land tradition [centered around Honen]. She published an article, "Genku shōnin shi nikki: A Study and Translation of an Early Hōnen Biography," in *Japanese Religions* (1997).

Paul O. Ingram is Professor of Religion at Pacific Lutheran University, Tacoma, Washington. He is the author of *Wrestling with the Ox: A Theology of Religious Experience* (Continuum Press, 1997). He is also the coeditor (with Sallie B. King) of a collection of essays in honor of Frederick J. Streng entitled *The Sound of Liberating Truth: Buddhist-Christian Dialogues in Honor of Frederick J. Streng* (forthcoming from Curzon Press). He currently serves as president of the Society for Buddhist-Christian Studies.

Eisho Nasu is Assistant Professor of Shin Buddhism at the Institute of Buddhist Studies. He received his Ph.D. from the Graduate Theological Union, focusing on Jie Daishi Ryōgen (912–985), the eighteenth abbot of the Japanese Tendai school. He has published articles on

CONTRIBUTORS

Jōdo Shinshū and Japanese religious studies in *Pacific World* and *The Pure Land*.

Richard K. Payne is Dean and Associate Professor of Japanese Buddhism and religion at the Institute of Buddhist Studies, and a member of the Core Doctoral Faculty of the Graduate Theological Union, teaching in Area VIII: Cultural and Historical Studies of Religions. He is author of *The Tantric Ritual of Japan* (1991), coeditor with James Foard and Michael Solomon of *The Pure Land Tradition: History and Development* (1996), and editor of *Re-Visioning "Kamakura" Buddhism* (1998). His work focuses on visualization and ritual in the Japanese esoteric Buddhist tradition.

Shigeki J. Sugiyama graduated from the Institute of Buddhist Studies in 1994 with a Master of Jōdo-Shinshū Studies degree. He retired from the United States Army in 1966 with the rank of lieutenant colonel. He completed his B.A. in political science at the University of California, Berkeley, in 1967 and entered the civil service until 1988, when he retired as a career senior executive in Washington, D.C. He was a founding member and president of the Ekoji Buddhist Temple at Springfield, Virginia, and served on the National Board of the Buddhist Churches of America, as vice president from 1983–88. He has published an article "Honganji in the Muromachi–Sengoku Period (*The Pacific World*, Fall 1994) and a number of essays in *The Wheel of Dharma*.

George J. Tanabe, Jr. is Professor of Religion at the University of Hawaii. He is the author of *Myoe the Dreamkeeper* (Harvard University Press), coeditor with Willa Jane Tanabe of *The Lotus Sutra in Japanese Culture* (University of Hawaii Press), co-author with Ian Reader of *Practically Religious: This Wordly Benefits and the Common Religion of Japan* (forthcoming from University of Hawaii Press), and editor of *Religions of Japan in Practice* (forthcoming from Princeton University Press).

CONTRIBUTORS

Kenneth K. Tanaka received his Ph.D. from Univ. of California, Berkeley and was appointed in 1991 as the Rev. Yoshitaka Tamai Professor at the Institute of Buddhist Studies. His recent writings have focused on contemporary Jōdo Shinshū doctrinal interpretation. His publications include *The Dawn of Chinese Pure Land Buddhist Doctrine* (State Univ. of New York Press), *Ocean: An Introduction to Jōdo Shinshū Buddhism in America* (WisdomOcean Publications), and as coeditor *The Faces of Buddhism in America* (The University of California Press). He is an active participant in the Buddhist Council of Northern California and interfaith activities.

Mark T. Unno is currently Assistant Professor of East Asian Religions, Department of Religion, Carleton College. He received his Ph.D. from Stanford University where he did his work on *Myōe Kōben and the Problem of the Vinaya in Early Kamakura Buddhism*. Author of over a dozen articles on topics ranging from Shin Buddhist thought to comparative religion and Japanese religion and culture, he has also published book and article translations and edited volumes on teaching in religious studies.

Taitetsu Unno is the Jill Ker Conway Professor of Religion at Smith College in Massachusetts. Among his recent works is *River of Fire, River of Water* (Doubleday, 1998), an introduction to the Pure Land tradition of Shin Buddhism.